THE BEST
ELIZABETHAN PLAYS

THE BEST
ELIZABETHAN PLAYS:

THE JEW OF MALTA, by Marlowe;
THE ALCHEMIST, by Jonson;
PHILASTER, by Beaumont and Fletcher;
THE TWO NOBLE KINSMEN,
    by Fletcher and Shakespeare;
THE DUCHESS OF MALFI, by Webster.

EDITED BY

WILLIAM ROSCOE THAYER

Play Anthology Reprint Series

BOOKS FOR LIBRARIES PRESS
FREEPORT, NEW YORK

First Published 1890
Reprinted 1970

STANDARD BOOK NUMBER:
8369-8207-X

LIBRARY OF CONGRESS CATALOG CARD NUMBER:
76-111114

PRINTED IN THE UNITED STATES OF AMERICA

CONTENTS.

	PAGE
PREFACE	3
BIBLIOGRAPHY	20
THE JEW OF MALTA	21
THE ALCHEMIST	113
PHILASTER	261
THE TWO NOBLE KINSMEN	363
THE DUCHESS OF MALFI	489

PREFACE.

MY object in this volume is to present specimens of the best work of the five Elizabethan dramatists who stand highest among Shakespeare's contemporaries. Collections of separate scenes and special editions of single plays have frequently been made, and they have their value; but it seemed to me that in binding together the masterpieces which follow, I should enable not only the general reader but also the college student to taste the quality of Shakespeare's rivals, and thereby to esteem the more adequately Shakespeare himself. Few persons possess the fifteen or twenty large volumes in which the Elizabethan drama is published, and fewer still have the time or the patience to plod through many tedious or dirty pages in order to come upon the treasures they contain. For, just as a traveller in an Oriental city is often obliged to turn his eyes from some mosque or graceful minaret to the ground beneath his feet so as to avoid ordure and garbage, so the reader of the Elizabethan plays has his attention often distracted, and his sense of decency shocked by the vulgarity of many passages in them. This coarseness was due in part to the habit of the time, when men spoke openly to each other and even to women on subjects about which we are, if not ignorant, at least reticent, and in part to the deliberate effort of the playwright to please the vulgarest persons in the audience. But as filth is always filth, though it be thrust upon us in a work of art, or come to us along with much that is noble under the sanction of a great name, and as each age has more than enough of its own obscenity to flounder free from, without falling back into the sty of a former generation, I have selected plays as little as possible tainted. Moreover, I have not scrupled to strike out phrases or lines where it seemed proper, being guided by decency and not by prudery; yet it will not be found that this purging interferes in the least in the understanding of the following dramas, — a sufficient evidence, if evidence be needed, of the unnecessariness of obscenity from the artistic as from the ethical standpoint.

In making my selection I had less difficulty than might have been expected. Of Marlowe's four chief works, *Tamburlaine* is too crude and tedious, in spite of several fine passages; *Doctor Faustus*, though admirable in outline, lacks interest in detail, and is, besides, permanently superseded by the mighty work of Goethe; finally, *Edward II*, though its scenes are knitted together more closely than those of its predecessors, and though its murder-scene is indeed masterly, yet as a whole lacks vivid characters. So I have chosen *The Jew of Malta*, which exhibits Marlowe's great qualities and their defects, and which will always be interesting from the comparisons to be made between Barabas and Shylock.

Among Ben Jonson's plays two have ranked, and deservedly ranked, foremost, — *Volpone* and *The Alchemist*. The former seems to me to be the superior, but its ineradicable coarseness precluded its publication in this volume; whereas *The Alchemist* is both an admirable example of Jonson's skill in applying the rules of classic composition to an English subject, and a fair representative of his satire and erudition. It is, furthermore, a mirror in which are reflected with wonderful accuracy, the social, scientific, religious, and philosophical quacks of the time of James the First.

Fifty-two plays are printed in the complete edition of the works of Beaumont and Fletcher, — many of them being wholly Fletcher's; but only three of those which I have read come within my scope. These are *The Maid's Tragedy*, *Valentinian*, and *Philaster:* the first two contain passages equal to the best their authors ever wrote, but they are besmirched with so much coarseness, and brutality is so hopelessly interwoven in their plots, that I was forced to reject them; *Philaster* shows Beaumont and Fletcher at their best, and is thoroughly characteristic of their genius.

The Two Noble Kinsmen, commonly attributed to Fletcher and Shakespeare, is surely one of the most beautiful plays of that period, and deserves from the public such admiration and popularity as it has long enjoyed from scholars. Its right to be published among Shakespeare's works is certainly equal to that of *Henry VIII*, and superior to that of some of the poorer plays which have few marks of his collaboration.

Webster left two masterpieces, — *The White Devil* and *The Duchess of Malfi;* both are great, but the latter excels, and is not only the most original and imaginative drama in this volume, but superior to every other Elizabethan tragedy except Shakespeare's best.

In some measure, therefore, the reader can form from these five plays — supplemented, of course, by acquaintance with Shakespeare — some idea of the methods and range of the amazing dramatic inspiration in the reign of Elizabeth and the first James, — unsurpassed in the history of literature, and equalled only once, in Greece. The dominant influence was that of the Renaissance, transmitted to

England by way of France, and modified by an intensely English patriotism, — the Renaissance, when classical learning revived, when great discoveries in geography opened new lands and peoples to the view of Europe; when a bolder commerce brought not only richer merchandise, but strange and fascinating lore, from the races of the Orient; when the sway of a single religion was broken, and throughout Christendom men ordered their lives by new beliefs; when science, assisted by experiment and criticism, began its conquest of nature; when the legends of chivalry, and the traditions of the crusades, and mediæval myths and superstitions, were still so fresh as to appeal to the imaginations while they no longer distorted the convictions of poets. It was the age when romance seemed real, and when the revelations of science seemed romantic. Curiosity, insatiable and enthusiastic, scrutinized all things. The divorce between passion and action, between the scholar and the man of affairs, had not yet been proclaimed: many-sided men were common, — philosophers were courtiers and diplomats; soldiers were poets. Intense individualism produced extreme types of character, prodigies of virtue or monsters of wickedness. Political conditions, the strife of noble with noble and of king with king, the dangers and excitements of foreign voyages, awakened qualities and passions which in quieter times lie dormant. It was as if mankind conspired to place the whole circle of its capacities on exhibition. To the great stimulus of the recovered appreciation of classical antiquity was added the impulsion of that modern spirit, which mysteriously and almost imperceptibly was remoulding society. And just as Bacon took all knowledge for his province, so the great poets of the age of Elizabeth took all human nature for theirs. Literary precedents and the conventional rules prescribed by writers of rhetorics and grammars did not hamper them. They were too busy endeavoring to portray the mighty pageant sweeping before them, to rummage old attics for the musty colors and warped palettes of by-gone painters.

Taking the implements at hand, — the tedious moralities and the loosely spun miracle plays, — they soon improved upon them, soon invented a drama-form not so rigid as to be cramped, nor so loose as to be redundant, but articulate like a highly developed organism, and as elastic as the various material furnished by nature required. And for their metre they adopted and perfected a line susceptible of almost infinite modulations, suited alike to the simplest narration, and to the highest outbursts of passion, and to the most delicate whisperings of fancy. In their hands, blank verse became the peer of the Homeric hexameter, and of Dante's *terza rima*, — a metre superior to that which any other modern language offers to its dramatic writers.

To Christopher Marlowe is due the honor of having first shown the capacity of this " mighty line." We know but little about his life. He was born at Canterbury, and christened there on Feb. 26, 1564, almost exactly two months before the date of Shakespeare's birth. He attended the King's School in his native place, and, in March, 1581, matriculated at Benet (now Corpus Christi) College, Cambridge, where he took a bachelor's degree two years later. In 1588 *Tamburlaine* was acted, and *The Tragical History of Doctor Faustus* appeared a little later. Then followed *The Jew of Malta* and *Edward II*. These, and *The Massacre of Paris, Dido* (in which he was assisted by Nash), some journeyman work on the three parts of *Henry VI*, and a fragmentary poem entitled *Hero and Leander*, —

comparable with Shakespeare's *Venus and Adonis*, — were all that he had time to do before he was killed in a quarrel over a courtesan, at Deptford, June 1, 1593. It is common, while deploring his early death, to speculate whether he might not, had he lived to maturity, have equalled Shakespeare himself; but such speculation seems to me to betray the uncritical temperament of those who indulge in it. We cannot reasonably doubt but that Marlowe, at forty, would have produced works far superior to any he has left: he had great powers, and they were surely ripening, but there is no indication that he could ever have excelled in two very important fields, where Shakespeare is supreme, — in humor and in fancy. Humor is inborn, and shows itself early, — yet there are not among Marlowe's creations any germs of such characters as Falstaff or Mercutio; fancy, again, is preeminently a young poet's gift, yet Marlowe's lack of it is almost as surprising as are the ease and confidence with which he steps upon the stage for the first time. There is no bashfulness, no imitation, but the air of one who feels sure of his powers. He was full of vitality, intoxicated at beholding the mighty forces which uphold and perpetuate the universe; and he seems to have believed that man, let him but cultivate his titanic possibilities, may master those forces, and cease to be their puppet. So his heroes are marvels of energy, devoting themselves to the acquisition of power which shall place them above the limitations of human nature: with Tamburlaine, it is desire of empire, — the whole world shall be his slave; with Faustus, it is desire of knowledge and pleasure, — the mysteries of fate shall be revealed to him, and all delights shall be concentrated in a cup for him to quaff; with Barabas, it is desire of gold, — he will have the means of exterminating all Malta to satisfy his vengeance. Even Edward II, who seems an exception, illustrates the power of weakness, — if I may use an apparent paradox. For the most part, therefore, the personages of Marlowe's dramas are types of amazing passions, rather than sharply defined individuals: he did not attain the supreme excellence of dramatic characterization in which the type lives in the individual, as, for example, in Shylock. Vigor and exuberance, — those are the qualities which distinguish Marlowe's thought; and in his rhythm we meet lines and passages, now informed by an imperial stateliness, now by a subtle unforgetable melody, to find parallels for which we must turn to Shakespeare himself.

Of very different mettle was Ben Jonson, the posthumous son of a clergyman, born at Westminster in 1574, and educated there at the famous school, then under Camden's direction. But the widow Jonson married a bricklayer, and young Ben was forced for a time to work at his step-father's trade. When he could endure this no longer, he ran away, joined a regiment in the Low Countries, and after a brief military service, turned up in London, where his first comedy, *Every Man in his Humour*, was produced in 1596. Then followed, in 1599, 1600, and 1601, *Every Man out of his Humour, Cynthia's Revels*, and *The Poetaster*, comedies in which he satirized the foibles of the day, — and as, among other affectations, he laughed at the new romantic fashion of writing plays, he was in turn ridiculed by Dekker and Marston in *Satiromastix*. Yet, while they laughed at him, no man was so great a favorite as he among that illustrious group of playwrights and poets which used to meet and carouse at the Mermaid; and although, in spite of his protests, the Elizabethan drama steadily progressed along romantic lines, no plays were more popular than his. In

1603 he wrote *Sejanus*, a tragedy; in 1605, *Volpone;* in 1609, *The Silent Woman;* in 1610, *The Alchemist;* in 1611, another tragedy, *Catiline*. *Eastward Ho*, in which he had Chapman and Marston for collaborators, proved too strong a satire on the Scottish people for the taste of the Scotch-born James I, and its authors were imprisoned, only to be restored to liberty and favor a little while afterward. In 1619 Jonson was appointed Poet Laureate, with the usual perquisite of £100, and a butt of canary from the royal cellars, every year. In his old age he published *The Sad Shepherd*, and, having outlived all his great companions, he died Aug. 16, 1637. In erudition, he was reputed the most learned poet of his time, and it is even asserted that no other English poet except Milton has had a wider and more various knowledge than he. His models in the drama were the classic playwrights of Rome and Athens. Condemning the romantic principles of his contemporaries, which led to excess and a luxuriant confusion, he insisted on a rigid observance of the three unities, of time, place, and subject. His own plays, constructed in obedience to the Aristotelian methods, are marvels of ingenuity. No other English plots are more homogeneous and skilful; in none is there so little superfluity, so few digressions. In scene after scene you behold the author compressing a spring, till its tension is ready for the final, sudden discharge; yet he does this so adroitly, that your interest is excited from moment to moment, lest that discharge burst upon you unawares. In this respect he is the true descendant of the classic dramatists, and the kinsman of the Frenchmen who, in the seventeenth century, created the French drama on classic models. Unlike Marlowe, who sketches his plot but vaguely, and wanders whithersoever his love of splendor points, Jonson has drawn every detail before sitting down to write. His material is the humors — or, as we should now say, the moods — of mankind, rather than their elemental passions; he produces his effects by cumulation and repetition, rather than by the swift, single, perfect strokes of a Shakespeare or a Webster. In *The Alchemist* this is well illustrated: he proposes to expose a popular imposture; to do this he introduces two varieties of the same species of quacks, and their female accomplice; and then he marshals before us, not one or two gulls, but a whole flock of them, — an epicure, a bragging young gentleman from the country, a sanctimonious Puritan, a simpleton of a clerk, a conceited tobacconist, — and we see how the same greed for unearned wealth affects each differently, yet drives all into a communion of dupery. So clever a weaving of various threads in one compact web has rarely been achieved; Jonson leaves no seams and no thrums in his work. He had not the highest imagination; but he had its best substitutes, — judgment, taste, sense of form, and culture.

As he is pre-eminently classic, so Beaumont and Fletcher are pre-eminently romantic. Most of the Elizabethan dramatists sprang from lowly families: not so Francis Beaumont, who came of noble stock. His father, Sir John Beaumont, was a Justice of the Common Pleas in Leicestershire, where Francis was born in 1586. At the age of eleven he was admitted a gentleman commoner at Broadgate-hall (now Pembroke) College, Oxford. Going to London, he read law in the Inner Temple, but soon was drawn towards the stage. He formed a literary partnership with John Fletcher, and had already become renowned, when he was cut off by death in 1615. Fletcher, whose father was Dean of Peterborough, and then Bishop of Worcester, was born at Rye, in Sussex, in December, 1579. We know little about him, except that he was educated at Benet College, Cambridge, went to London early, devoted himself to playwriting, died of the plague in 1625, and was buried at St. Saviour's, Southwark. An old tradition has it that Beaumont supplied judgment, and Fletcher fancy, to their joint productions. Owing to the early death of the former, it is easy to separate those plays which they wrote together from those which Fletcher wrote alone, and by this process the reader who is curious can determine more or less accurately which parts should be assigned to Beaumont, and which to Fletcher, in their united works. That eminent critics, despite this clue, should have hitherto failed to agree, seems to indicate that no ultimate certainty can be reached, and that therefore opinions which have only probability for their basis ought not to be too vehemently attacked or defended. Be the division what it may, the quality which prevails in their dramas is the quality of romance. Their best heroes are earlier Hernanis, bred in the ideals of Castilian honor; even their villains — and monstrous villains some of them are — utter very noble sentiments. You feel that such persons never existed, and yet you know the thoughts to be true, and you cannot resist the fascination, the glamour — if you will — of ideals borrowed from the age of chivalry. There is, in Beaumont and Fletcher, "a constant recognition of gentility," as Emerson has remarked; this, and their picturesque descriptions, their genuine sentiment, and their occasional flashes of imagination revealing intense passion, constitute their chief merits, and interfuse through their dramas the spirit of romance I have noted. To be delightfully unnatural is their privilege at their best; they approach the actual human nature of their time only on its most depraved side, and are abominably coarse at their worst.

The Two Noble Kinsmen has furnished critics with a multitude of pleasant difficulties. Even a novice, in reading the play for the first time, must detect the impression of two different minds upon it; and, since it was believed that those two were Shakespeare and Fletcher, every resource of criticism has been employed to determine the share of each. The tests applied have been intellectual and metrical: Has a given scene those imaginative qualities peculiar to Shakespeare? Has its versification his familiar style? The latter test is perhaps the more helpful; for Fletcher adopted, whether from preference or carelessness, a form of blank verse by which he can usually be recognized. More frequently than any of his contemporaries, he writes lines with a double ending. Again, Shakespeare employs "run-on lines"—those whose meaning does not stop at the end of a verse—much more freely than Fletcher. The construction of the play gives further hints. Besides the main story of the two Kinsmen, there is the subordinate story of the gaoler's daughter. Her mad-scenes, drawn without pathos or much skill, are evidently copied from Ophelia's. Indeed, the style of the prose passages, and the commonplaceness of the secondary characters, afford other clues as to their authorship. Nevertheless, it must not be inferred that all the inferior work is Fletcher's; one of the finest scenes in the play—the dialogue of Palamon and Arcite in prison—was almost certainly written by him. Concerning the date of its composition, we have only vague suggestions. It must have come between 1603 or 1604,—the latest date assigned to *Hamlet*, and 1613, when Shakespeare retired to Stratford. As Fletcher's talents began to be renowned only about 1607, and as he worked with Shakespeare on *Henry VIII* after that time, we may probably assign *The Two Noble Kinsmen* to the period between 1608 and 1612. It may well be, as Mr. Skeat suggests, that the play in its present form was revised by Fletcher, and even that parts of Shakespeare's share were altered by him after Shakespeare's death. As I have given in the notes the opinions of the critics most competent to decide the question of authorship, I need not pursue the matter here, and will only add that *The Two Noble Kinsmen* deserves to be known and admired because it is, first of all, a fine drama; that it happens to be a first-rate puzzle in literary criticism, is a minor reason for its republication.

Of John Webster's personal history we can learn nothing. A few entries in Henslowe's *Diary*, of payments made to Webster for theatrical properties, a few dates of the performances of his plays — and "the rest is silence." The first mention of him is in 1601, as the author of *The Guise, or the Massacre of France*, which may have been, as Dyce suggests, only a *rifacimento* of Marlowe's piece; together with Dekker, he wrote *Westward Ho* and *Northward Ho*, published in 1607; *The White Devil* was printed in 1612; *The Duchess of Malfi* in 1623 (but performed earlier); long afterwards, in 1654, *Appius and Virginia* issued from the press. On one title-page Webster is styled "merchant-tailor," and there are commendatory epigraphs by Middleton, Rowley, and Ford. All that we know of his character we glean from two or three short addresses to the reader, and from two dedications: these show him to have been conscious of his own powers, yet modest; not without a dignified contempt of the opinions of the majority of playgoers, who, he says, "resemble those ignorant asses, who, visiting stationers' shops, their use is not to inquire for good books, but new books." "To those who report I was a long time finishing this tragedy," he continues, in the preface to *The White Devil*, " I confess, I do not write with a goose quill winged with two feathers; and if they will needs make it my fault, I must answer them with that of Euripides to Alcestides, a tragic writer. Alcestides objecting that Euripides had only, in three days, composed three verses, whereas himself had written three hundred, 'Thou tellest truth,' quoth he, 'but here's the difference, — thine shall only be read for three days, whereas mine shall continue three ages.' Detraction is the sworn friend to ignorance: for mine own part, I have ever truly cherished my good opinion of other men's worthy labors; especially of that full and heightened style of Master Chapman; the labored and understanding works of Master Jonson; the no less worthy composures of the both worthily excellent Master Beaumont and Master Fletcher; and lastly (without wrong, last to be named), the right happy and copious industry of Master Shakespeare, Master Dekker, and Master Heywood; wishing what I write may be read by their light; protesting that, in the strength of mine own judgment, I know them so worthy, that though I rest silent in my own work, yet to most of theirs I dare (without flattery) fix that of Martial, *Non norunt haec monumenta mori*." Generous to his fellow-craftsmen, not fawning to the " groundlings " nor servile to his patrons, that is all that, from too scanty evidence, we can infer about Webster, the man; of the dramatist, we have at least two works which reveal his astonishing genius. As long as *The White Devil* and *The Duchess of Malfi* are read, so long will John Webster's title to rank among the four or five supreme tragic writers of the world be open to the scrutiny of all.

PREFACE.

It has been the fashion of some critics to speak of Webster as a strange and terrible genius, a sort of ogre who delighted in bloody scenes by day, and supped nightly with horrors; or as a fellow of morbid imagination, whose favorite haunts were church-yards and dark charnel-houses, who gloated over chronicles of crime, and had no other purpose in writing, save that of causing a vulgar shudder to ripple over the shoulders of his hearers. If these views were correct, we might dismiss him and his plays as summarily as we dismiss the latest melodrama with its sheet-iron thunder and promiscuous slaughters. But these views are not correct, and to understand such a play as *The Duchess of Malfi* we must recall the state of society throughout a large portion of Europe during the sixteenth century. Webster needed not to appeal to his imagination for materials so terrible; the history of almost any Italian city, in any decade of that century, could supply them. From the court of the Vatican down to that of a princeling in Perugia or Mantua, abominable vices, refined cruelty, atrocious crimes, were common: ties of kindred were no restraint upon the cravings of lust or of ambition; pledges sealed by oath, promises bound by honor, melted as the snow melts in April, for there was no sanctity in religion, no self-respect in men; selfishness, insatiate and unscrupulous, directed the policy of states and the actions of individuals. Personal courage, which gives to the bloody deeds of a less enlightened time some show of fairness, had withered; this was the age when treachery was reduced to a fine art, — when poison was sprinkled on a rose and smeared on the door-latch or the missal, — when the sword was exchanged for the dagger, which never struck in front, — when reputations could be done to death by Iago-insinuations as surely as the body by subtle, invisible poisons. The glorious seeds of the Renaissance had produced in Italy this upas-forest, covered with splendid but deadly blossoms. The current religion did not supply moral leaven adequate to so rapid an intellectual growth, and there was no sentiment of nationality to counteract the tendency towards individualism. What thoughtful man, be he a rationalist or a dogmatist, can behold such periods without amazement, and without realizing that the problem of human destiny is infinitely complex and unspeakably tragic? And John Webster sought, merely by presenting an episode typical of hundreds, — nay, of an epoch, — to show the actual terror and tragedy of life, that must be reckoned with by every one who would estimate its possibilities and its purpose.

Unlike Dante, his Duchess needed to be transported to hell by no vision: her very surroundings were hell, as they must have been to any pure and noble man or woman. In the contrast between her character and her conditions lies the real tragedy; the terrific ordeals which test but do not overcome her fortitude — scenes which only Webster could depict — are but accessory and external. It may be urged, indeed, that her sufferings were unwarranted, because she was innocent: to this it is sufficient to reply: "Such is the fact; if only the wicked suffered, there would be no problem of evil; neither art nor ethics can be true, if they garble facts." And because Webster recognized this spiritual truth, he is profoundly moral; and because he was able to embody it in the concrete, he is among the few supreme tragic poets of the world. In his play, as often happens in real life, the virtuous seem to be defeated, the wicked to be victorious, but the triumph and the defeat are only apparent: virtue remains uncontaminated, — there is its reward; sin remains unregenerate, — there is its punishment. "Merely to live," said Socrates, " is nothing; a good life is everything." And Webster, after painting with inexorable fidelity and supreme power the tragic career of his heroine, concludes, —

> " I have ever thought
> Nature doth nothing so great for great men
> As when she's pleased to make them lords of truth:
> Integrity of life is fame's best friend,
> Which nobly, beyond death, shall crown the end."

It is necessary to make this brief analysis in order to prepare readers for a right understanding of Webster; they will need no guide to show them his more patent merits. His detached thoughts, clear and compressed as diamonds; his revelations of a character in a line; his sombre sublimity; his naturalness amid almost preternatural circumstances, — these characteristics of his genius need no elucidation. He had not Shakespeare's skill in dramatic construction; nor Shakespeare's complete mastery of verse, but he had, within a narrower range, an imagination as penetrating and as vivifying as Shakespeare's, and a moral sense akin to that which expresses itself in *Macbeth* and in *Lear*.

From Marlowe to Webster is less than thirty years, less than an average lifetime; yet within that brief period the Elizabethan Drama blossomed and withered. After Webster's, there is no great name in the Drama. English Poetry, indeed, did not die, but its subsequent glories have been epic, lyric, and descriptive; it has become introspective and personal, and has left the more diffuse and less permanent art of fiction to incarnate in objective creations the passions and vicissitudes of human life.

A word should be added concerning the rule which I have followed in editing these five plays. I have made the notes as brief as possible, keeping in mind that this volume is to be read as literature, and not as a text-book to furnish puzzles in antiquarian difficulties nor in philological niceties. I have compared the explanations of the best editors, and adopted the best, supplementing them from my own researches where it seemed necessary. I have set the notes at the bottom of each page, rather than at the end of the book, so that the reader can see at a glance whether the information he seeks is there, or not: those who, like myself, have often wasted time by turning to the back of a volume only to find that the editor has passed over without comment the word they wished him to explain, will, I trust, approve of this arrangement.

BIBLIOGRAPHY.

For the benefit of those who wish to pursue their reading in the Elizabethan Drama, the following short bibliography is added: —

MARLOWE.   Edited by Dyce, "The Old Dramatists": new edit., 1887. Edited by Bullen, 1886.

JONSON.   Complete works edited by Gifford, 1816; new edit., 1860.

BEAUMONT AND FLETCHER.   Edited by Darley, "The Old Dramatists," new edit., 1883.

TWO NOBLE KINSMEN.   The edition by Littledale (*New Shakspere Society* publications, Series II, 7, 8, 15) is exhaustive. For students, Skeat's edition, 1875, is very convenient; Rolfe's, 1883, is also excellent. See also essays by Spalding, Hickson, Furnivall, Fleay, and Swinburne.

WEBSTER.   Edited by Dyce, "The Old Dramatists."   Also Swinburne's admirable essay, *Nineteenth Century, 1886*, Vol. XIX.

The chief works of all these dramatists are also republished in the recent "Mermaid Series." Charles Lamb's *Specimens of English Dramatic Poets*, and Leigh Hunt's *Selections from Beaumont and Fletcher*, are chosen with rare taste, and are as satisfactory as fragments can ever be. The chapters in Taine's *English Literature* referring to the Elizabethan Drama, may be consulted for a foreigner's opinion, although they seem to me to lack spiritual insight.

I.

THE JEW OF MALTA.

By Christopher Marlowe.

Probably written in 1589 or 1590: acted in 1591, with Alleyn as Barabas. Kean brought out an adaptation of the play at the Drury-Lane Theatre in 1818. The source of the story has not been discovered.

THE JEW OF MALTA.

DRAMATIS PERSONÆ.

FERNEZE, Governor of Malta.
LODOWICK, his Son.
SELIM CALYMATH, Son of the Grand Seignior.
MARTIN DEL BOSCO, Vice-Admiral of Spain.
MATHIAS, a Gentleman.
BARABAS, a wealthy Jew.
ITHAMORE, his Slave.
PILIA-BORSA, a Bully.
JACOMO, } Friars.
BARNARDINE, }
Two Merchants.
Three Jews.
Knights, Bassoes, Officers, Guard, Messengers, Slaves, and Carpenters.
KATHARINE, Mother of Mathias.
ABIGAIL, Daughter of Barabas.
BELLAMIRA, a Courtesan.
Abbess.
Two Nuns.
MACHIAVEL, Speaker of the Prologue.

SCENE: *Malta.*

THE PROLOGUE.

Enter MACHIAVEL.

Machiavel. Albeit the world thinks Machiavel[1] is dead,
Yet was his soul but flown beyond the Alps,
And now the Guise[2] is dead, is come from France,
To view this land, and frolic with his friends.

---

[1] Machiavelli, the Florentine statesman, died in 1527. His name was long a synonym for political perfidy and cold-blooded cruelty.
[2] The Duke of Guise, organizer of the Massacre of St. Bartholomew, in 1572, was assassinated in 1588.

To some perhaps my name is odious,
But such as love me guard me from their tongues;
And let them know that I am Machiavel,
And weigh not men, and therefore not men's words.
Admired I am of those that hate me most.
Though some speak openly against my books,   10
Yet they will read me, and thereby attain
To Peter's chair: and when they cast me off,
Are poisoned by my climbing followers.
I count religion but a childish toy,
And hold there is no sin but ignorance.
Birds of the air will tell of murders past!
I am ashamed to hear such fooleries.
Many will talk of title to a crown:
What right had Cæsar to the empery?
Might first made kings, and laws were then most sure   20
When like the Draco's they were writ in blood.
Hence comes it that a strong-built citadel
Commands much more than letters can import;
Which maxim had but Phalaris observed,
He had never bellowed, in a brazen bull,
Of great ones' envy. Of the poor petty wights
Let me be envied and not pitièd!
But whither am I bound? I come not, I,
To read a lecture here in Britain,
But to present the tragedy of a Jew,   30
Who smiles to see how full his bags are crammed,
Which money was not got without my means.
I crave but this — grace him as he deserves,
And let him not be entertained the worse
Because he favours me.   [*Exit.*

ACT I.

SCENE I. — BARABAS *discovered in his Counting-house, with Heaps of Gold before him.*

Bar. So that of thus much that return was made:
And of the third part of the Persian ships,
There was the venture summed and satisfied.
As for those Sabans, and the men of Uz,
That bought my Spanish oils and wines of Greece,
Here have I purst their paltry silverlings.[1]
Fie; what a trouble 'tis to count this trash.
Well fare the Arabians, who so richly pay
The things they traffic for with wedge of gold,
Whereof a man may easily in a day   10
Tell[2] that which may maintain him all his life.
The needy groom that never fingered groat,
Would make a miracle of thus much coin:
But he whose steel-barred coffers are crammed full,
And all his lifetime hath been tired,
Wearying his fingers' ends with telling it,
Would in his age be loth to labour so,
And for a pound to sweat himself to death.
Give me the merchants of the Indian mines,
That trade in metal of the purest mould;   20
The wealthy Moor, that in the eastern rocks
Without control can pick his riches up,
And in his house heap pearls like pebble-stones,
Receive them free, and sell them by the weight;
Bags of fiery opals, sapphires, and amethysts,

[1] Silver coins; cf. *Isaiah* vii, 23.   [2] Count.

Jacinths, hard topaz, grass-green emeralds,
Beauteous rubies, sparkling diamonds,
And seld-seen[1] costly stones of so great price,
As one of them indifferently rated,
And of a carat of this quantity,   30
May serve in peril of calamity
To ransom great kings from captivity.
This is the ware wherein consists my wealth;
And thus methinks should men of judgment frame
Their means of traffic from the vulgar trade,
And as their wealth increaseth, so inclose
Infinite riches in a little room.
But now how stands the wind?
Into what corner peers my halcyon's bill?[2]
Ha! to the east? yes: see, how stand the vanes?   40
East and by south: why then I hope my ships
I sent for Egypt and the bordering isles
Are gotten up by Nilus' winding banks:
Mine argosies from Alexandria,
Loaden with spice and silks, now under sail,
Are smoothly gliding down by Candy shore
To Malta, through our Mediterranean sea.
But who comes here?

Enter a Merchant.

How now?

Merch. Barabas, thy ships are safe,
Riding in Malta-road: and all the merchants   50

[1] Seldom seen.
[2] A stuffed kingfisher (the halcyon), suspended by a string, **was** supposed to show the direction of the wind. *Halcyon days* were *calm days*, the belief being that the weather was always calm when kingfishers were breeding. Cf. *King Lear*, ii, 2; Sir T. Browne, *Vulgar Errors*, lii, 10.

With other merchandise are safe arrived,
And have sent me to know whether yourself
Will come and custom[1] them.
    Bar. The ships are safe thou say'st, and richly fraught.
    Merch. They are.
    Bar. Why then go bid them come ashore,
And bring with them their bills of entry:
I hope our credit in the custom-house
Will serve as well as I were present there.
Go send 'em threescore camels, thirty mules,
And twenty waggons to bring up the ware.   60
But art thou master in a ship of mine,
And is thy credit not enough for that?
    Merch. The very custom barely comes to more
Than many merchants of the town are worth,
And therefore far exceeds my credit, sir.
    Bar. Go tell 'em the Jew of Malta sent thee, man:
Tush! who amongst 'em knows not Barabas?
    Merch. I go.
    Bar. So then, there's somewhat come.
Sirrah, which of my ships art thou master of?
    Merch. Of the *Speranza*, sir.
    Bar. And saw'st thou not   70
Mine argosy at Alexandria?
Thou could'st not come from Egypt, or by Caire,
But at the entry there into the sea,
Where Nilus pays his tribute to the main,
Thou needs must sail by Alexandria.
    Merch. I neither saw them, nor inquired of them:
But this we heard some of our seamen say,
They wondered how you durst with so much wealth

---

[1] Pay the duty on them.

Trust such a crazèd vessel, and so far.

Bar. Tush, they are wise! I know her and her strength. 8c
But go, go thou thy ways, discharge thy ship,
And bid my factor bring his loading in. [*Exit* Merch.
And yet I wonder at this argosy.

Enter a second Merchant.

2d Merch. Thine argosy from Alexandria,
Know, Barabas, doth ride in Malta-road,
Laden with riches, and exceeding store
Of Persian silks, of gold, and orient pearl.

Bar. How chance you came not with those other ships
That sailed by Egypt?

2d Merch. Sir, we saw 'em not.

Bar. Belike they coasted round by Candy shore 9c
About their oils, or other businesses.
But 'twas ill done of you to come so far
Without the aid or conduct of their ships.

2d Merch. Sir, we were wafted by a Spanish fleet,
That never left us till within a league,
That had the galleys of the Turk in chase.

Bar. O!— they were going up to Sicily:—
Well, go,
And bid the merchants and my men despatch
And come ashore, and see the fraught[1] discharged. 10c

2d Merch. I go. [*Exit.*

Bar. Thus trowls[2] our fortune in by land and sea,
And thus are we on every side enriched:
These are the blessings promised to the Jews,
And herein was old Abram's happiness:

---

[1] Freight.   [2] Rolls.

What more may heaven do for earthly man
Than thus to pour out plenty in their laps,
Ripping the bowels of the earth for them,
Making the seas their servants, and the winds
To drive their substance with successful blasts?   110
Who hateth me but for my happiness?
Or who is honoured now but for his wealth?
Rather had I a Jew be hated thus,
Than pitied in a Christian poverty:
For I can see no fruits in all their faith,
But malice, falsehood, and excessive pride,
Which methinks fits not their profession.
Haply some hapless man hath conscience,
And for his conscience lives in beggary.
They say we are a scattered nation: 120
I cannot tell, but we have scambled[1] up
More wealth by far than those that brag of faith.
There's Kirriah Jairim, the great Jew of Greece,
Obed in Bairseth,[2] Nones in Portugal,
Myself in Malta, some in Italy,
Many in France, and wealthy every one;
Ay, wealthier far than any Christian.
I must confess we come not to be kings;
That's not our fault: alas, our number's few,
And crowns come either by succession,   130
Or urged by force; and nothing violent
Oft have I heard tell, can be permanent.
Give us a peaceful rule, make Christians kings,
That thirst so much for principality.
I have no charge, nor many children,

[1] Collected, used for *scrambled*, as in *Henry V*, i, 1.
[2] Beyrout?

But one sole daughter, whom I hold as dear
As Agamemnon did his Iphigen:
And all I have is hers. But who comes here?

Enter three Jews.[1]

1st Jew. Tush, tell not me; 'twas done of policy.
2d Jew. Come, therefore, let us go to Barabas, 140
For he can counsel best in these affairs;
And here he comes.
Bar. Why, how now, countrymen!
Why flock you thus to me in multitudes?
What accident's betided to the Jews?
1st Jew. A fleet of warlike galleys, Barabas,
Are come from Turkey, and lie in our road:
And they this day sit in the council-house
To entertain them and their embassy.
Bar. Why, let 'em come, so they come not to war;
Or let 'em war, so we be conquerors— 150
Nay, let 'em combat, conquer, and kill all!
(*Aside*) So they spare me, my daughter, and my wealth.
1st Jew. Were it for confirmation of a league,
They would not come in warlike manner thus.
2d Jew. I fear their coming will afflict us all.
Bar. Fond[2] men! what dream you of their multitudes?
What need they treat of peace that are in league?
The Turks and those of Malta are in league.
Tut, tut, there is some other matter in't.
1st Jew. Why, Barabas, they come for peace or war. 160
Bar. Haply for neither, but to pass along
Towards Venice by the Adriatic Sea;

[1] Here the scene is shifted to a street, or to the Exchange.
[2] Foolish.

With whom they have attempted many times,
But never could effect their stratagem.
 3d Jew. And very wisely said. It may be so.
 2d Jew. But there's a meeting in the senate-house,
And all the Jews in Malta must be there.
 Bar. Hum; all the Jews in Malta must be there?
Ay, like enough, why then let every man
Provide him, and be there for fashion-sake.   170
If anything shall there concern our state,
Assure yourselves I'll look (*aside*) unto myself.
 1st Jew. I know you will. Well, brethren, let us go.
 2d Jew. Let's take our leaves. Farewell, good Barabas.
 Bar. Farewell, Zaareth; farewell, Temainte.
          [*Exeunt* Jews.
And, Barabas, now search this secret out;
Summon thy senses, call thy wits together:
These silly men mistake the matter clean.
Long to the Turk did Malta contribute;
Which tribute, all in policy I fear,   180
The Turks have let increase to such a sum
As all the wealth of Malta cannot pay;
And now by that advantage thinks belike
To seize upon the town: ay, that he seeks.
Howe'er the world go, I'll make sure for one,
And seek in time to intercept the worst,
Warily guarding that which I ha' got.
Ego mihimet sum semper proximus.[1]
Why, let 'em enter, let 'em take the town.   [*Exit.*

[1] Misquotation from Terence, *Andria*, iv, 1, 12, *Proximus sum egomet mihi.*

SCENE II. — *Inside the Council-house.*

Enter FERNEZE, *Governor of Malta,* Knights, *and* Officers;
    met by CALYMATH *and* Bassoes *of the Turk.*

   Fern. Now, Bassoes,[1] what demand you at our hands?
   1st Bas. Know, Knights of Malta, that we came from
       Rhodes,
From Cyprus, Candy, and those other Isles
That lie betwixt the Mediterranean seas.
   Fern. What's Cyprus, Candy, and those other Isles
To us, or Malta? What at our hands demand ye?
   Cal. The ten years' tribute that remains unpaid.
   Fern. Alas! my lord, the sum is over-great,
I hope your highness will consider us.
   Cal. I wish, grave governor, 'twere in my power   10
To favour you, but 'tis my father's cause,
Wherein I may not, nay, I dare not dally.
   Fern. Then give us leave, great Selim Calymath.
                   [*Consults apart with the* Knights.
   Cal. Stand all aside, and let the knights determine,
And send to keep our galleys under sail,
For happily[2] we shall not tarry here;
Now, governor, say, how are you resolved?
   Fern. Thus: since your hard conditions are such
That you will needs have ten years' tribute past,
We may have time to make collection   20
Amongst the inhabitants of Malta for't.
   1st Bas. That's more than is in our commission.
   Cal. What, Callipine! a little courtesy.
Let's know their time, perhaps it is not long;

---

[1] Pashas, formerly spelt *bashaws*.   [2] Haply.

And 'tis more kingly to obtain by peace
Than to enforce conditions by constraint.
What respite ask you, governor?
   Fern. But a month.
   Cal. We grant a month, but see you keep your promise.
Now launch our galleys back again to sea,
Where we'll attend the respite you have ta'en,   30
And for the money send our messenger.
Farewell, great governor and brave Knights of Malta.
   Fern. And all good fortune wait on Calymath!
                  [*Exeunt* CALYMATH *and* Bassoes.
Go one and call those Jews of Malta hither:
Were they not summoned to appear to-day?
   Off. They were, my lord, and here they come.

        Enter BARABAS *and three* Jews.

   1st Knight. Have you determined what to say to them?
   Fern. Yes; give me leave:—and, Hebrews, now come
      near.
From the Emperor of Turkey is arrived
Great Selim Calymath, his highness' son,   40
To levy of us ten years' tribute past;
Now then, here know that it concerneth us—
   Bar. Then, good my lord, to keep your quiet still,
Your lordship shall do well to let them have it.
   Fern. Soft, Barabas, there's more 'longs to't than so.
To what this ten years' tribute will amount,
That we have cast, but cannot compass it
By reason of the wars that robbed our store;
And therefore are we to request your aid.
   Bar. Alas, my lord, we are no soldiers: 50
And what's our aid against so great a prince?

1st Knight. Tut, Jew, we know thou art no soldier;
Thou art a merchant and a moneyed man,
And 'tis thy money, Barabas, we seek.
    Bar. How, my lord! my money?
    Fern. Thine and the rest.
For, to be short, amongst you't must be had.
    1st Jew. Alas, my lord, the most of us are poor.
    Fern. Then let the rich increase your portions.
    Bar. Are strangers with your tribute to be taxed?
    2d Knight. Have strangers leave with us to get their wealth?   60
Then let them with us contribute.
    Bar. How! equally?
    Fern. No, Jew, like infidels.
For through our sufferance of your hateful lives,
Who stand accursèd in the sight of Heaven,
These taxes and afflictions are befallen,
And therefore thus we are determinèd.
Read there the articles of our decrees.
    Officer (*reads*). "First, the tribute-money of the Turks shall all be levied amongst the Jews, and each of them to pay one half of his estate."   70
    Bar. How, half his estate? (*Aside*) I hope you mean not mine.
    Fern. Read on.
    Off. (*reading*). "Secondly, he that denies[1] to pay shall straight become a Christian."
    Bar. How! a Christian? (*Asid*) Hum, what's here to do?
    Off. (*reading*). "Lastly, he that denies this shall absolutely lose all he has."

[1] Refuses.

The three Jews. O my lord, we will give half. 80
Bar. O earth-mettled villains, and no Hebrews born!
And will you basely thus submit yourselves
To leave your goods to their arbitrament?
Fern. Why, Barabas, wilt thou be christenèd?
Bar. No, governor, I will be no convertite.[1]
Fern. Then pay thy half.
Bar. Why, know you what you did by this device?
Half of my substance is a city's wealth.
Governor, it was not got so easily;
Nor will I part so slightly therewithal. 90
Fern. Sir, half is the penalty of our decree,
Either pay that, or we will seize on all.
Bar. Corpo di Dio! stay! you shall have the half;
Let me be used but as my brethren are.
Fern. No, Jew, thou hast denied the articles,
And now it cannot be recalled.
           [*Exeunt* Officers, *on a sign from* FERNEZE.
Bar. Will you then steal my goods?
Is theft the ground of your religion?
Fern. No, Jew, we take particularly thine
To save the ruin of a multitude: 100
And better one want for the common good
Than many perish for a private man:
Yet, Barabas, we will not banish thee,
But here in Malta, where thou gott'st thy wealth,
Live still; and, if thou canst, get more.
Bar. Christians, what or how can I multiply?
Of naught is nothing made.
1st Knight. From naught at first thou cam'st to little wealth,

---

1 Convert; so used in *As You Like It* and *King John.*

From little unto more, from more to most:
If your first curse fall heavy on thy head, 110
And make thee poor and scorned of all the world,
'Tis not our fault, but thy inherent sin.

    Bar. What, bring you Scripture to confirm your wrongs?
Preach me not out of my possessions.
Some Jews are wicked, as all Christians are:
But say the tribe that I descended of
Were all in general cast away from sin,
Shall I be tried by their transgression?
The man that dealeth righteously shall live:
And which of you can charge me otherwise? 120

    Fern. Out, wretched Barabas!
Sham'st thou not thus to justify thyself,
As if we knew not thy profession?
If thou rely upon thy righteousness,
Be patient and thy riches will increase.
Excess of wealth is cause of covetousness:
And covetousness, O, 'tis a monstrous sin.

    Bar. Ay, but theft is worse: tush! take not from me then,
For that is theft! and if you rob me thus,
I must be forced to steal and compass[1] more. 130

    1st Knight. Grave governor, listen not to his exclaims.
Convert his mansion to a nunnery;
His house will harbour many holy nuns.

    Fern. It shall be so.

              Re-enter Officers.

              Now, officers, have you done?

    Off. Ay, my lord, we have seized upon the goods

---

[1] Cheat.

And wares of Barabas, which being valued,
Amount to more than all the wealth of Malta.
And of the other we have seizèd half.
  Fern. Then we'll take order for the residue.
  Bar. Well then, my lord, say, are you satisfied?   140
You have my goods, my money, and my wealth,
My ships, my store, and all that I enjoyed;
And, having all, you can request no more;
Unless your unrelenting flinty hearts
Suppress all pity in your stony breasts,
And now shall move you to bereave my life.
  Fern. No, Barabas, to stain our hands with blood
Is far from us and our profession.
  Bar. Why, I esteem the injury far less
To take the lives of miserable men   150
Than be the causers of their misery.
You have my wealth, the labour of my life,
The comfort of mine age, my children's hope,
And therefore ne'er distinguish of the wrong.
  Fern. Content thee, Barabas, thou hast naught but right.
  Bar. Your extreme right does me exceeding wrong:
But take it to you, i' the devil's name.
  Fern. Come, let us in, and gather of these goods
The money for this tribute of the Turk.
  1st Knight. 'Tis necessary that be looked unto: 160
For if we break our day, we break the league,
And that will prove but simple[1] policy.
          [*Exeunt all except* BARABAS *and the* Jews.
  Bar. Ay, policy! that's their profession,
And not simplicity, as they suggest.
The plagues of Egypt, and the curse of Heaven,

          [1] Foolish.

Earth's barrenness, and all men's hatred
Inflict upon them, thou great *Primus Motor!*
And here upon my knees, striking the earth,
I ban their souls to everlasting pains
And extreme tortures of the fiery deep, 170
That thus have dealt with me in my distress.
   1st Jew. O yet be patient, gentle Barabas.
   Bar. O silly brethren, born to see this day;
Why stand you thus unmoved with my laments?
Why weep you not to think upon my wrongs?
Why pine not I, and die in this distress?
   1st Jew. Why, Barabas, as hardly can we brook
The cruel handling of ourselves in this;
Thou seest they have taken half our goods.
   Bar. Why did you yield to their extortion? 180
You were a multitude, and I but one:
And of me only have they taken all.
   1st Jew. Yet, brother Barabas, remember Job.
   Bar. What tell you me of Job? I wot his wealth
Was written thus: he had seven thousand sheep,
Three thousand camels, and two hundred yoke
Of labouring oxen, and five hundred
She-asses: but for every one of those,
Had they been valued at indifferent rate,
I had at home, and in mine argosy, 190
And other ships that came from Egypt last,
As much as would have bought his beasts and him,
And yet have kept enough to live upon:
So that not he, but I may curse the day,
Thy fatal birth-day, forlorn Barabas;
And henceforth wish for an eternal night,
That clouds of darkness may inclose my flesh,

And hide these extreme sorrows from mine eyes:
For only I have toiled to inherit here
The months of vanity and loss of time,   200
And painful nights, have been appointed me.

  2d Jew. Good Barabas, be patient.

  Bar. Ay, I pray, leave me in my patience. You,
Were ne'er possessed of wealth, are pleased with want;
But give him liberty at least to mourn,
That in a field amidst his enemies
Doth see his soldiers slain, himself disarmed,
And knows no means of his recovery:
Ay, let me sorrow for this sudden chance;
'Tis in the trouble of my spirit I speak;   210
Great injuries are not so soon forgot.

  1st Jew. Come, let us leave him; in his ireful mood
Our words will but increase his ecstasy.[1]

  2d Jew. On, then; but trust me 'tis a misery
To see a man in such affliction. —
Farewell, Barabas!   [*Exeunt the three* Jews.[2]

  Bar. Ay, fare you well.
See the simplicity of these base slaves,
Who, for the villains have no wit themselves,
Think me to be a senseless lump of clay
That will with every water wash to dirt: 220
No, Barabas is born to better chance,
And framed of finer mould than common men,
That measure naught but by the present time.
A reaching thought will search his deepest wits,
And cast with cunning for the time to come:
For evils are apt to happen every day. —

---

[1] Violent emotion.
[2] Dyce suggests that the scene is now shifted to a street near Barabas' house.

Enter ABIGAIL.

But whither wends my beauteous Abigail?
O! what has made my lovely daughter sad?
What, woman! moan not for a little loss:
Thy father hath enough in store for thee.   230
   Abig. Not for myself, but agèd Barabas:
Father, for thee lamenteth Abigail:
But I will learn to leave these fruitless tears,
And, urged thereto with my afflictions,
With fierce exclaims run to the senate-house,
And in the senate reprehend them all,
And rend their hearts with tearing of my hair,
Till they reduce[1] the wrongs done to my father.
   Bar. No, Abigail, things past recovery
Are hardly cured with exclamations.   240
Be silent, daughter, sufferance breeds ease,
And time may yield us an occasion
Which on the sudden cannot serve the turn.
Besides, my girl, think me not all so fond
As negligently to forego so much
Without provision for thyself and me:
Ten thousand portagues,[2] besides great pearls,
Rich costly jewels, and stones infinite,
Fearing the worst of this before it fell,
I closely hid.
   Abig. Where, father?
   Bar. In my house, my girl.   250
   Abig. Then shall they ne'er be seen of Barabas:
For they have seized upon thy house and wares.

[1] Lessen, diminish. Dyce suggests *redress*.
[2] Portuguese gold coins.

Bar. But they will give me leave once more, I trow,
To go into my house.
   Abig. That may they not:
For there I left the governor placing nuns,
Displacing me; and of thy house they mean
To make a nunnery, where none but their own sect[1]
Must enter in; men generally barred.
   Bar. My gold! my gold! and all my wealth is gone!
You partial heavens, have I deserved this plague?   260
What, will you thus oppose me, luckless stars,
To make me desperate in my poverty?
And knowing me impatient in distress,
Think me so mad as I will hang myself,
That I may vanish o'er the earth in air,
And leave no memory that e'er I was?
No, I will live; nor loathe I this my life:
And, since you leave me in the ocean thus
To sink or swim, and put me to my shifts,
I'll rouse my senses and awake myself.   270
Daughter! I have it: thou perceiv'st the plight
Wherein these Christians have oppressèd me:
Be ruled by me, for in extremity
We ought to make bar of no policy.
   Abig. Father, whate'er it be to injure them
That have so manifestly wrongèd us,
What will not Abigail attempt?
   Bar. Why, so;
Then thus, thou told'st me they have turned my house
Into a nunnery, and some nuns are there?
   Abig. I did.
   Bar. Then, Abigail, there must my girl   280

[1] Sex.

Entreat the abbess to be entertained.

Abig. How, as a nun?

Bar. Ay, daughter, for religion
Hides many mischiefs from suspicion.

Abig. Ay, but, father, they will suspect me there.

Bar. Let 'em suspect; but be thou so precise
As they may think it done of holiness.
Entreat 'em fair, and give them friendly speech,
And seem to them as if thy sins were great,
Till thou hast gotten to be entertained.

Abig. Thus, father, shall I much dissemble.

Bar. Tush! 290
As good dissemble that thou never mean'st,
As first mean truth and then dissemble it, —
A counterfeit profession is better
Than unseen hypocrisy.[1]

Abig. Well, father, say that I be entertained,
What then shall follow?

Bar. This shall follow then;
There have I hid, close underneath the plank
That runs along the upper-chamber floor,
The gold and jewels which I kept for thee.
But here they come; be cunning, Abigail. 300

Abig. Then, father, go with me.

Bar. No, Abigail, in this
It is not necessary I be seen:
For I will seem offended with thee for't:
Be close, my girl, for this must fetch my gold. [*They retire.*

Enter Friar JACOMO, *Friar* BARNARDINE, Abbess, *and a* Nun.

F. Jac. Sisters, we now are almost at the new-made nunnery.

[1] This passage is corrupt.

Abb. The better; for we love not to be seen:
'Tis thirty winters long since some of us
Did stray so far amongst the multitude.
 F. Jac. But, madam, this house
And waters[1] of this new-made nunnery
Will much delight you.
 Abb. It may be so; but who comes here?
  [ABIGAIL *comes forward.*
 Abig. Grave abbess, and you, happy virgins' guide,
Pity the state of a distressèd maid.
 Abb. What art thou, daughter?
 Abig. The hopeless daughter of a hapless Jew,
The Jew of Malta, wretched Barabas;
Sometime the owner of a goodly house,
Which they have now turned to a nunnery.
 Abb. Well, daughter, say, what is thy suit with us?
 Abig. Fearing the afflictions which my father feels
Proceed from sin, or want of faith in us,
I'd pass away my life in penitence,
And be a novice in your nunnery,
To make atonement for my labouring soul.
 F. Jac. No doubt, brother, but this proceedeth of the spirit.
 F. Barn. Ay, and of a moving spirit too, brother; but come,
Let us entreat she may be entertained.
 Abb. Well, daughter, we admit you for a nun.
 Abig. First let me as a novice learn to frame
My solitary life to your strait laws,
And let me lodge where I was wont to lie,
I do not doubt, by your divine precepts

---

[1] Bullen suggests *cloisters.*

And mine own industry, but to profit much.
　　Bar. (*aside*). As much, I hope, as all I hid is worth.
　　Abb. Come, daughter, follow us.
　　Bar. (*coming forward*). Why, how now, Abigail,
What makest thou amongst these hateful Christians?
　　F. Jac. Hinder her not, thou man of little faith,
For she has mortified herself.
　　Bar. How! mortified?
　　F. Jac. And is admitted to the sisterhood.　　　　　340
　　Bar. Child of perdition, and thy father's shame!
What wilt thou do among these hateful fiends?
I charge thee on my blessing that thou leave
These devils, and their damnèd heresy.
　　Abig. Father, give me —[1]　　　[*She goes to him.*
　　Bar. Nay, back, Abigail.
(And think upon the jewels and the gold;
　　　　　　　　　　[*Aside to* ABIGAIL *in a whisper.*
The board is markèd thus that covers it.)
Away, accursèd from thy father's sight.
　　F. Jac. Barabas, although thou art in mischief,
And wilt not see thine own afflictions,　　　　　350
Yet let thy daughter be no longer blind.
　　Bar. Blind friar, I reck not thy persuasions,
(The board is markèd thus [2] that covers it.)
　　　　　　　　　　[*Aside to* ABIGAIL *in a whisper.*
For I had rather die than see her thus.
Wilt thou forsake me too in my distress,
Seducèd daughter? (*Aside in a whisper*) (Go forget not,)
Becomes it Jews to be so credulous?
(To-morrow early I'll be at the door.) [*Aside in a whisper.*

　　[1] Dyce suggests *forgive me.*
　　[2] The original edition has † inserted here, to indicate the sign Barabas was to make.

No, come not at me; if thou wilt be damned,
Forget me, see me not, and so be gone.   360
(Farewell, remember to-morrow morning.)
                                    [*Aside in a whisper.*
Out, out, thou wretch!
        [*Exeunt, on one side* BARABAS, *on the other side*
                Friars, Abbess, Nun, *and* ABIGAIL; *as they
                are going out,*

                Enter MATHIAS.

Math. Who's this? fair Abigail, the rich Jew's daughter,
Become a nun! her father's sudden fall
Has humbled her and brought her down to this:
Tut, she were fitter for a tale of love,
Than to be tirèd out with orisons.

                Enter LODOWICK.

Lod. Why, how now, Don Mathias! in a dump?
Math. Believe me, noble Lodowick, I have seen
The strangest sight, in my opinion,   370
That ever I beheld.
Lod. What was't, I prithee?
Math. A fair young maid, scarce fourteen years of age,
The sweetest flower in Cytherea's field,
Cropt from the pleasures of the fruitful earth,
And strangely metamorphosed nun.
Lod. But say, what was she?
Math. Why, the rich Jew's daughter.
Lod. What, Barabas, whose goods were lately seized?
Is she so fair?
Math. And matchless beautiful;
As, had you seen her, 'twould have moved your heart,

Though countermined with walls of brass, to love, 380
Or at the least to pity.

  Lod. And if she be so fair as you report,
'Twere time well spent to go and visit her:
How say you, shall we?

  Math. I must and will, sir; there's no remedy.

  Lod. And so will I too, or it shall go hard.
Farewell, Mathias.

  Math. Farewell, Lodowick.   [*Exeunt severally.*

ACT II.

SCENE I. — *Before* BARABAS'S *House, now a Nunnery.*

Enter BARABAS *with a light.*

  Bar. Thus, like the sad presaging raven that tolls
The sick man's passport in her hollow beak,
And in the shadow of the silent night
Doth shake contagion from her sable wings;
Vexed and tormented runs poor Barabas
With fatal curses towards these Christians.
The uncertain pleasures of swift-footed time
Have ta'en their flight, and left me in despair;
And of my former riches rests no more
But bare remembrance, like a soldier's scar,   10
That has no further comfort for his maim.
O thou, that with a fiery pillar led'st
The sons of Israel through the dismal shades,
Light Abraham's offspring; and direct the hand
Of Abigail this night; or let the day
Turn to eternal darkness after this!

No sleep can fasten on my watchful eyes,
Nor quiet enter my distempered thoughts,
Till I have answer of my Abigail.

Enter ABIGAIL *above.*

Abig. Now have I happily espied a time
To search the plank my father did appoint;
And here behold, unseen, where I have found
The gold, the pearls, and jewels, which he hid.

Bar. Now I remember those old women's words,
Who in my wealth[1] would tell me winter's tales,
And speak of spirits and ghosts that glide by night
About the place where treasure hath been hid:[2]
And now methinks that I am one of those:
For whilst I live, here lives my soul's sole hope,
And, when I die, here shall my spirit walk.

Abig. Now that my father's fortune were so good
As but to be about this happy place;
'Tis not so happy: yet when we parted last,
He said he would attend me in the morn.
Then, gentle sleep, where'er his body rests,
Give charge to Morpheus that he may dream
A golden dream, and of the sudden wake,
Come and receive the treasure I have found.

Bar. Bueno para todos mi ganado no era:
As good go on as sit so sadly thus.
But stay, what star shines yonder in the east?[3]
The loadstar of my life, if Abigail.
Who's there?

---

[1] Bullen suggests that this is a misprint for *youth*.   [2] Cf. *Hamlet*, i. 1
[3] Cf. *Romeo and Juliet*, ii, 2:

"But soft! what light through yonder window breaks!
It is the east, and Juliet is the sun!"

Abig. Who's that?
Bar. Peace, Abigail, 'tis I.
Abig. Then, father, here receive thy happiness.
Bar. Hast thou't?
Abig. Here, (*throws down the bags*) hast thou't?
There's more, and more, and more.
    Bar. O my girl,
My gold, my fortune, my felicity!
Strength to my soul, death to mine enemy!
Welcome the first beginner of my bliss!   50
O Abigail, Abigail, that I had thee here too!
Then my desires were fully satisfied:
But I will practise thy enlargement thence:
O girl! O gold![1] O beauty! O my bliss!   [*Hugs the bags.*
    Abig. Father, it draweth towards midnight now,
And 'bout this time the nuns begin to wake;
To shun suspicion, therefore, let us part.
    Bar. Farewell, my joy, and by my fingers take
A kiss from him that sends it from his soul.
                                [*Exit* ABIGAIL *above.*
Now Phœbus ope the eyelids of the day,[2]   60
And for the raven wake the morning lark,
That I may hover with her in the air;
Singing o'er these, as she does o'er her young,
Hermoso placer de los dineros.[3]   [*Exit.*

    Cf. Shylock's "My daughter! O my ducats! O my daughter!" *Merchant of Venice*, ii, 8.
    [2] Cf. *Job* xli, 18: "His eyes are like the eyelids of the morning;" and Milton, *Lycidas:* "Under the opening eyelids of the morn."
    [3] Spanish; "beautiful pleasure of money."

Scene II.— *The Senate-house.*

Enter Ferneze, Martin del Bosco, *and* Knights.

Fern. Now, captain, tell us whither thou art bound?
Whence is thy ship that anchors in our road?
And why thou cam'st ashore without our leave?
 Bosc. Governor of Malta, hither am I bound;
My ship, the *Flying Dragon*, is of Spain,
And so am I: Del Bosco is my name;
Vice-admiral unto the Catholic King.
 1st Knight. 'Tis true, my lord, therefore entreat[1] him
  well.
 Bosc. Our fraught is Grecians, Turks, and Afric Moors.
For late upon the coast of Corsica, 10
Because we vailed[2] not to the Turkish fleet,
Their creeping galleys had us in the chase:
But suddenly the wind began to rise,
And then we luffed and tacked, and fought at ease:
Some have we fired, and many have we sunk;
But one amongst the rest became our prize:
The captain's slain, the rest remain our slaves,
Of whom we would make sale in Malta here.
 Fern. Martin del Bosco, I have heard of thee;
Welcome to Malta, and to all of us; 20
But to admit a sale of these thy Turks
We may not, nay, we dare not give consent
By reason of a tributary league.
 1st Knight. Del Bosco, as thou lov'st and honour'st us,
Persuade our governor against the Turk;
This truce we have is but in hope of gold,

---

[1] Treat. [2] Lowered not our flags.

And with that sum he craves might we wage war.
　Bosc. Will Knights of Malta be in league with Turks,
And buy it basely too for sums of gold?
My lord, remember that, to Europe's shame, 30
The Christian Isle of Rhodes,[1] from whence you came,
Was lately lost, and you were stated [2] here
To be at deadly enmity with Turks.
　Fern. Captain, we know it, but our force is small.
　Bosc. What is the sum that Calymath requires?
　Fern. A hundred thousand crowns.
　Bosc. My lord and king hath title to this isle,
And he means quickly to expel you hence;
Therefore be ruled by me, and keep the gold:
I'll write unto his majesty for aid, 40
And not depart until I see you free.
　Fern. On this condition shall thy Turks be sold:
Go, officers, and set them straight in show.　　[*Exeunt* Off.
Bosco, thou shalt be Malta's general;
We and our warlike Knights will follow thee
Against these barb'rous misbelieving Turks.
　Bosc. So shall you imitate those you succeed:
For when their hideous force environed Rhodes,
Small though the number was that kept the town,
They fought it out and not a man survived 50
To bring the hapless news to Christendom.
　Fern. So will we fight it out; come, let's away:
Proud daring Calymath, instead of gold,
We'll send thee bullets wrapt in smoke and fire:[3]
Claim tribute where thou wilt, we are resolved,
Honour is bought with blood and not with gold.　　[*Exeunt.*

[1] Rhodes was wrested from the Knights of St. John by Solyman II, in 1522.　　[2] Established.　　[3] Cf. *King John*, i, 2.

SCENE III. — *The Market-place.*

Enter Officers *with* ITHAMORE *and other* Slaves.

1st Off. This is the market-place, here let 'em stand:
Fear not their sale, for they'll be quickly bought.
 2d Off. Every one's price is written on his back,
And so much must they yield or not be sold.
 1st Off. Here comes the Jew; had not his goods been seized,
He'd given us present money for them all.

Enter BARABAS.

Bar. In spite of these swine-eating Christians, —
Unchosen nation, never circumcised,
Such as (poor villains!) were ne'er thought upon
Till Titus and Vespasian conquered us, —   10
Am I become as wealthy as I was:
They hoped my daughter would ha' been a nun;
But she's at home, and I have bought a house
As great and fair as is the governor's;
And there in spite of Malta will I dwell,
Having Ferneze's hand, whose heart I'll have;
Ay, and his son's too, or it shall go hard.
I am not of the tribe of Levi, I,
That can so soon forget an injury.
We Jews can fawn like spaniels when we please: 20
And when we grin we bite, yet are our looks
As innocent and harmless as a lamb's.
I learned in Florence how to kiss my hand,
Heave up my shoulders when they call me dog,[1]

[1] Cf. this passage with Shylock's speeches with Antonio; *Merchant of Venice*, i, 3.

And duck as low as any barefoot friar;
Hoping to see them starve upon a stall,
Or else be gathered for in our synagogue,
That, when the offering-basin comes to me,
Even for charity I may spit into't.
Here comes Don Lodowick, the governor's son, 20
One that I love for his good father's sake.

Enter LODOWICK.

Lod. I hear the wealthy Jew walkèd this way:
I'll seek him out, and so insinuate,
That I may have a sight of Abigail;
For Don Mathias tells me she is fair.
Bar. (*aside*). Now will I show myself
To have more of the serpent than the dove;
That is — more knave than fool.
Lod. Yond' walks the Jew; now for fair Abigail.
Bar. (*aside*). Ay, ay, no doubt but she's at your command.
Lod. Barabas, thou know'st I am the governor's son. 41
Bar. I would you were his father, too, sir;
That's all the harm I wish you. (*Aside*) The slave looks
Like a hog's-cheek new singed.
Lod. Whither walk'st thou, Barabas?
Bar. No farther: 'tis a custom held with us,
That when we speak with Gentiles like to you,
We turn into the air to purge ourselves:
For unto us the promise doth belong.
Lod. Well, Barabas, canst help me to a diamond? 50
Bar. O, sir, your father had my diamonds.
Yet I have one left that will serve your turn: —
(*Aside*) I mean my daughter: but ere he shall have her
I'll sacrifice her on a pile of wood.

I ha' the poison of the city for him,[1]
And the white leprosy.
  Lod. What sparkle does it give without a foil?
  Bar. The diamond that I talk of ne'er was foiled:[2]—
(*Aside*) But when he touches it, it will be foiled:—
Lord Lodowick, it sparkles bright and fair.   60
  Lod. Is it square or pointed, pray let me know.
  Bar. Pointed it is, good sir—(*aside*) but not for you.
  Lod. I like it much the better.
  Bar. So do I too.
  Lod. How shows it by night?
  Bar. Outshines Cynthia's rays.
  Lod. And what's the price?
  Bar. (*aside*). Your life an if you have it. O my lord,
We will not jar about the price; come to my house
And I will give't your honour (*aside*) with a vengeance.
  Lod. No, Barabas, I will deserve it first.
  Bar. Good sir,   70
Your father has deserved it at my hands,
Who, of mere charity and Christian truth,
To bring me to religious purity,
And as it were in catechising sort,
To make me mindful of my mortal sins,
Against my will, and whether I would or no,
Seized all I had, and thrust me out o' doors,
And made my house a place for nuns most chaste.
  Lod. No doubt your soul shall reap the fruit of it.
  Bar. Ay, but, my lord, the harvest is far off.   80
And yet I know the prayers of those nuns
And holy friars, having money for their pains,
Are wondrous; (*aside*) and indeed do no man good:

[1] Dyce suggests that this is a misprint.   [2] Defiled.

And seeing they are not idle, but still doing,
'Tis likely they in time may reap some fruit,
I mean in fulness of perfection.
    Lod. Good Barabas, glance not at our holy nuns.
    Bar. No, but I do it through a burning zeal, —
(*Aside*) Hoping ere long to set the house afire ;
For though they do a while increase and multiply,   90
I'll have a saying[1] to that nunnery.—
As for the diamond, sir, I told you of,
Come home and there's no price shall make us part,
Even for your honourable father's sake. - –
(*Aside*) It shall go hard but I will see your death. —
But now I must be gone to buy a slave.
    Lod. And, Barabas, I'll bear thee company.
    Bar. Come then — here's the market-place.
What's the price of this slave ? Two hundred crowns !
Do the Turks weigh so much ?
    1st Off. Sir, that's his price.   100
    Bar. What, can he steal that you demand so much ?
Belike he has some new trick for a purse ;
And if he has, he is worth three hundred plates,[2]
So that, being bought, the town-seal might be got
To keep him for his lifetime from the gallows :
The sessions day is critical to thieves,
And few or none 'scape but by being purged.
    Lod. Rat'st thou this Moor but at two hundred plates ?
    1st Off. No more, my lord.
    Bar. Why should this Turk be dearer than that Moor ? 110
    1st Off. Because he is young and has more qualities.

---

[1] Cf. Barnes's *Divil's Charter*, 1607: "For I must have a saying to those bottels."
[2] Pieces of silver.

Bar. What, hast the philosopher's stone? an thou hast, break my head with it, I'll forgive thee.

Slave. No, sir; I can cut and shave.

Bar. Let me see, sirrah, are you not an old shaver?[1]

Slave. Alas, sir! I am a very youth.

Bar. A youth? I'll buy you, and marry you to Lady Vanity,[2] if you do well.

Slave. I will serve you, sir.   119

Bar. Some wicked trick or other. It may be, under colour of shaving, thou'lt cut my throat for my goods. Tell me, hast thou thy health well?

Slave. Ay, passing well.

Bar. So much the worse; I must have one that's sickly, an't be but for sparing victuals; 'tis not a stone of beef a day will maintain you in these chops; let me see one that's somewhat leaner.

1st Off. Here's a leaner, how like you him?

Bar. Where wast thou born?

Itha. In Thrace; brought up in Arabia.   130

Bar. So much the better, thou art for my turn.
An hundred crowns? I'll have him; there's the coin.
                                          [*Gives money.*

1st Off. Then mark him, sir, and take him hence.

Bar. (*aside*). Ay, mark him, you were best, for this is he
That by my help shall do much villainy.
My lord, farewell: Come, sirrah, you are mine.
As for the diamond, it shall be yours;
I pray, sir, be no stranger at my house,
All that I have shall be at your command.

---

[1] This term of contempt was originally applied to priests with shaven crown.

[2] An allegorical character in the old morality plays; cf. *I Henry IV*, ii, 4.

Enter MATHIAS *and his* Mother KATHERINE.

Math. What makes the Jew and Lodowick so private? 140
(*Aside*) I fear me 'tis about fair Abigail.
Bar. Yonder comes Don Mathias, let us stay;[1]

[*Exit* LODOWICK.

He loves my daughter, and she holds him dear:
But I have sworn to frustrate both their hopes,
And be revenged upon the governor.
Kath. This Moor is comeliest, is he not? speak, son.
Math. No, this is the better, mother; view this well.
Bar. Seem not to know me here before your mother,
Lest she mistrust the match that is in hand:
When you have brought her home, come to my house; 150
Think of me as thy father; son, farewell.
Math. But wherefore talked Don Lodowick with you?
Bar. Tush! man, we talked of diamonds, not of Abigail.
Kath. Tell me, Mathias, is not that the Jew?
Bar. As for the comment on the Maccabees,
I have it, sir, and 'tis at your command.
Math. Yes, madam, and my talk with him was but
About the borrowing of a book or two.
Kath. Converse not with him, he's cast off from heaven.
Thou hast thy crowns, fellow; come, let's away. 160
Math. Sirrah, Jew, remember the book.
Bar. Marry will I, sir.

[*Exeunt* MATHIAS *and his* Mother.

Off. Come, I have made reasonable market; let's away.

[*Exeunt* Officers *with* Slaves.

Bar. Now let me know thy name, and therewithal
Thy birth, condition, and profession.

[1] Break off our conversation.

SCENE III.]   THE JEW OF MALTA.   57

 Itha. Faith, sir, my birth is but mean : my name's
Ithamore, my profession what you please.
 Bar. Hast thou no trade? then listen to my words,
And I will teach thee that shall stick by thee :
First be thou void of these affections,   170
Compassion, love, vain hope, and heartless fear,
Be moved at nothing, see thou pity none,
But to thyself smile when the Christians moan.
 Itha. O brave ! master, I worship your nose[1] for this.
 Bar. As for myself, I walk abroad o' nights[2]
And kill sick people groaning under walls :
Sometimes I go about and poison wells ;
And now and then, to cherish Christian thieves,
I am content to lose some of my crowns,
That I may, walking in my gallery,   180
See 'em go pinioned along by my door.
Being young, I studied physic, and began
To practise first upon the Italian ;
There I enriched the priests with burials,
And always kept the sextons' arms in ure[3]
With digging graves and ringing dead men's knells :
And after that was I an engineer,
And in the wars 'twixt France and Germany,
Under pretence of helping Charles the Fifth,
Slew friend and enemy with my stratagems.   190
Then after that was I an usurer,
And with extorting, cozening, forfeiting,
And tricks belonging unto brokery,

---

 [1] Barabas was represented with a large false nose. So Rowley, in his *Search for Money* (1609), alludes to the " artificiall Jewe of Maltaes nose."
 [2] In *Titus Andronicus* (v, 1,) there is a similar catalogue of villanies.
 [3] Use.

I filled the jails with bankrupts in a year,
And with young orphans planted hospitals,
And every moon made some or other mad,
And now and then one hang himself for grief,
Pinning upon his breast a long great scroll
How I with interest tormented him.
But mark how I am blest for plaguing them;   200
I have as much coin as will buy the town.
But tell me now, how hast thou spent thy time?
   Itha. 'Faith, master,
In setting Christian villages on fire,
Chaining of eunuchs, binding galley-slaves.
One time I was an ostler in an inn,
And in the night-time secretly would I steal
To travellers' chambers, and there cut their throats:
Once at Jerusalem, where the pilgrims kneeled,
I strewèd powder on the marble stones,   210
And therewithal their knees would rankle so,
That I have laughed a-good[1] to see the cripples
Go limping home to Christendom on stilts.
   Bar. Why this is something: make account of me
As of thy fellow; we are villains both:
Both circumcisèd, we hate Christians both:
Be true and secret, thou shalt want no gold.
But stand aside, here comes Don Lodowick.

   Enter LODOWICK.[2]

   Lod. O Barbaras, well met;
Where is the diamond you told me of?   220

---

[1] Heartily.
[2] Dyce suggests that the scene is shifted to the outside of Barabas's house.

Bar. I have it for you, sir; please you walk in with me:
What ho, Abigail! open the door, I say.

Enter ABIGAIL *with letters.*

Abig. In good time, father; here are letters come
From Ormus, and the post stays here within.
 Bar. Give me the letters. — Daughter, do you hear,
Entertain Lodowick the governor's son
With all the courtesy you can afford;
(*Aside*) Use him as if he were a Philistine,
Dissemble, swear, protest, vow love to him,
He is not of the seed of Abraham. —   230
I am a little busy, sir, pray pardon me.
Abigail, bid him welcome for my sake.
 Abig. For your sake and his own he's welcome hither.
 Bar. (*aside*). Daughter, a word more; kiss him; speak him fair,
And like a cunning Jew so cast about,
That ye be both made sure[1] ere you come out.
 Abig. O father! Don Mathias is my love.
 Bar. (*aside*). I know it: yet I say, make love to him;
Do, it is requisite it should be so —
Nay, on my life, it is my factor's hand —   240
But go you in, I'll think upon the account.
   [*Exeunt* ABIGAIL *and* LODOWICK *into the house.*
The account is made, for Lodowick he dies,
My factor sends me word a merchant's fled
That owes me for a hundred tun of wine:
I weigh it thus much (*snapping his fingers*); I have wealth enough.
For now by this has he kissed Abigail;

---

[1] Betrothed.

And she vows love to him, and he to her.
As sure as Heaven rained manna for the Jews,
So sure shall he and Don Mathias die:
His father was my chiefest enemy. 250

Enter MATHIAS.

Whither goes Don Mathias? stay awhile.
   Math. Whither, but to my fair love Abigail?
   Bar. Thou know'st, and Heaven can witness this is true,
That I intend my daughter shall be thine.
   Math. Ay, Barabas, or else thou wrong'st me much.
   Bar. O, Heaven forbid I should have such a thought.
Pardon me though I weep: the governor's son
Will, whether I will or no, have Abigail:
He sends her letters, bracelets, jewels, rings.
   Math. Does she receive them? 260
   Bar. She? No, Mathias, no, but sends them **back**,
And when he comes, she locks herself up fast;
Yet through the keyhole will he talk to her,
While she runs to the window looking out,
When you should come and hale him from the door.
   Math. O treacherous Lodowick!
   Bar. Even now as I came home, he slipt me in,
And I am sure he is with Abigail.
   Math. I'll rouse him thence.
   Bar. Not for all Malta, therefore sheathe **your sword**; 270
If you love me, no quarrels in my house;
But steal you in, and seem to see him not;
I'll give him such a warning ere he goes
As he shall have small hopes of Abigail.
Away, for here they come.

Re-enter LODOWICK *and* ABIGAIL.

Math. What, hand in hand! I cannot suffer this.
Bar. Mathias, as thou lovest me, not a word.
Math. Well, let it pass, another time shall serve.
[*Exit into the house.*
Lod. Barabas, is not that the widow's son?
Bar. Ay, and take heed, for he hath sworn your death. 280
Lod. My death? what, is the base-born peasant mad?
Bar. No, no, but happily he stands in fear
Of that which you, I think, ne'er dream upon,
My daughter here, a paltry silly girl.
Lod. Why, loves she Don Mathias?
Bar. Doth she not with her smiling answer you?
Abig. (*aside*). He has my heart; I smile against my will.
Lod. Barabas, thou know'st I've loved thy daughter long.
Bar. And so has she done you, even from a child.
Lod. And now I can no longer hold my mind. 290
Bar. Nor I the affection that I bear to you.
Lod. This is thy diamond, tell me shall I have it?
Bar. Win it, and wear it, it is yet unsoiled.
O! but I know your lordship would disdain
To marry with the daughter of a Jew;
And yet I'll give her many a golden cross [1]
With Christian posies [2] round about the ring.
Lod. 'Tis not thy wealth, but her that I esteem.
Yet crave I thy consent.
Bar. And mine you have, yet let me talk to her.— 300
(*Aside*) This offspring of Cain, this Jebusite,[3]

[1] A coin with a cross stamped on one side, like the Portuguese *cruzado*.
[2] Mottoes.
[3] The Jebusites were one of the seven Canaanitish nations which, according to the writers of the *Old Testament*, were doomed to destruction.

That never tasted of the Passover,
Nor e'er shall see the land of Canaan,
Nor our Messias that is yet to come;
This gentle maggot, Lodowick, I mean,
Must be deluded: let him have thy hand,
But keep thy heart till Don Mathias comes.
   Abig. What, shall I be betrothed to Lodowick?
   Bar. It's no sin to deceive a Christian;
For they themselves hold it a principle,   310
Faith is not to be held with heretics;
But all are heretics that are not Jews;
This follows well, and therefore, daughter, fear not. —
I have entreated her, and she will grant.
   Lod. Then, gentle Abigail, plight thy faith to me.
   Abig. I cannot choose, seeing my father bids. —
(*Aside*) Nothing but death shall part my love and me.
   Lod. Now have I that for which my soul hath longed.
   Bar. (*aside*). So have not I, but yet I hope I shall.
   Abig. (*aside*). O wretched Abigail, what hast thou done?
   Lod. Why on the sudden is your colour changed?   321
   Abig. I know not, but farewell, I must be gone.
   Bar. Stay her, but let her not speak one word more.
   Lod. Mute o' the sudden? here's a sudden change.
   Bar. O, muse not at it, 'tis the Hebrews' guise,
That maidens new betrothed should weep awhile:
Trouble her not; sweet Lodowick, depart:
She is thy wife, and thou shalt be mine heir.
   Lod. O, is't the custom? then I am resolved:
But rather let the brightsome heavens be dim,   330
And nature's beauty choke with stifling clouds,
Than my fair Abigail should frown on me. —
There comes the villain, now I'll be revenged.

Re-enter MATHIAS.

Bar. Be quiet, Lodowick, it is enough
That I have made thee sure to Abigail.
　Lod. Well, let him go.　　　　　　　　[*Exit.*
　Bar. Well, but for me, as you went in at doors
You had been stabbed, but not a word on't now;
Here must no speeches pass, nor swords be drawn.
　Math. Suffer me, Barabas, but to follow him.　340
　Bar. No; so shall I, if any hurt be done,
Be made an accessory of your deeds;
Revenge it on him when you meet him next.
　Math. For this I'll have his heart.
　Bar. Do so; lo here I give thee Abigail.
　Math. What greater gift can poor Mathias have?
Shall Lodowick rob me of so fair a love?
My life is not so dear as Abigail.
　Bar. My heart misgives me, that, to cross your love,
He's with your mother; therefore after him.　350
　Math. What, is he gone unto my mother?
　Bar. Nay, if you will, stay till she comes herself.
　Math. I cannot stay; for if my mother come,
She'll die with grief.　　　　　　　　[*Exit.*
　Abig. I cannot take my leave of him for tears:
Father, why have you thus incensed them both?
　Bar. What's that to thee?
　Abig. I'll make 'em friends again.
　Bar. You'll make 'em friends!
Are there not Jews enow in Malta,　　　　360
But thou must doat upon a Christian?
　Abig. I will have Don Mathias, he is my love.
　Bar. Yes, you shall have him: go put her in.

Itha. Ay, I'll put her in. [*Puts* ABIGAIL *in.*
Bar. Now tell me, Ithamore, how lik'st thou this?
Itha. Faith, master, I think by this
You purchase both their lives; is it not so?
Bar. True; and it shall be cunningly performed.
Itha. O master, that I might have a hand in this.
Bar. Ay, so thou shalt, 'tis thou must do the deed: 370
Take this, and bear it to Mathias straight, [*Gives a letter.*
And tell him that it comes from Lodowick.
Itha. 'Tis poisoned, is it not?
Bar. No, no, and yet it might be done that way:
It is a challenge feigned from Lodowick.
Itha. Fear not; I will so set his heart afire,
That he shall verily think it comes from him.
Bar. I cannot choose but like thy readiness:
Yet be not rash, but do it cunningly.
Itha. As I behave myself in this, employ me hereafter. 380
Bar. Away then. [*Exit* ITHAMORE.
So, now will I go in to Lodowick,
And, like a cunning spirit, feign some lie.
Till I have set 'em both at enmity. [*Exit.*

ACT III.

SCENE I. — *Outside of* BELLAMIRA'S *House.*

Enter BELLAMIRA, *a Courtesan, on a balcony.*

Bell. Since this town was besieged, my gain grows cold;
And yet I know my beauty doth not fail.
From Venice merchants, and from Padua
Were wont to come rare-witted gentlemen,

Scholars I mean, learnèd and liberal;
And now, save Pilia-Borsa, comes there none,
And he is very seldom from my house;
And here he comes.

Enter PILIA-BORSA.

Pilia. Hold thee, wench, there's something for thee to spend. [*Shews a bag of silver.*

Bell. 'Tis silver. I disdain it.

Pilia. Ay, but the Jew has gold,
And I will have it, or, it shall go hard.

Bell. Tell me, how cam'st thou by this?

Pilia. 'Faith, walking the back-lanes, through the gardens, I chanced to cast mine eye up to the Jew's counting-house, where I saw some bags of money, and in the night I clambered up with my hooks, and, as I was taking my choice, I heard a rumbling in the house; so I took only this, and run my way: but here's the Jew's man.

Bell. Hide the bag.

Enter ITHAMORE.

Pilia. Look not towards him, let's away; zoons, what a looking thou keep'st; thou'lt betray's anon.

[*Exeunt* BELLAMIRA *and* PILIA-BORSA.

Itha. O the sweetest face that ever I beheld! I know she is a courtesan by her attire: now would I give a hundred of the Jew's crowns that I had such a concubine.
Well, I have delivered the challenge in such sort,
As meet they will, and fighting die; brave sport. [*Exit.*

SCENE II. — *A Street.*

Enter MATHIAS.

Math. This is the place ; now Abigail shall see
Whether Mathias holds her dear or no.

Enter LODOWICK.

What, dares the villain write in such base terms?
                                    [*Reading a letter.*
Lod. I did it ; and revenge it if thou dar'st. [*They fight.*

Enter BARABAS, *above, on a balcony.*

Bar. O ! bravely fought ; and yet they thrust not home.
Now, Lodovico ! now, Mathias ! So —— [*Both fall.*
So now they have showed themselves to be tall[1] fellows.
  [*Cries within.*] Part 'em, part 'em.
Bar. Ay, part 'em now they are dead. Farewell, farewell.   [*Exit.*

Enter FERNEZE, KATHERINE, *and* Attendants.

Fern. What sight[2] is this ! — my Lodowick slain ![3] 10
These arms of mine shall be thy sepulchre.
Kath. Who is this? my son Mathias slain !
Fern. O Lodowick ! had'st thou perished by the Turk,
Wretched Ferneze might have 'venged thy death.
Kath. Thy son slew mine, and I'll revenge his death.

---

[1] Brave.

[2] What a sight; the article was often omitted; cf. " What night is this," *Julius Cæsar*, i, 3.

[3] Here, and frequently in the play, *Lodowick* should be written and pronounced as in Italian, *Lodovico*. The error is probably due to the copyist who first transcribed the play for the press.

Fern. Look, Katherine, look!—thy son gave mine these
   wounds.
Kath. O leave to grieve me, I am grieved enough.
Fern. O! that my sighs could turn to lively breath;
And these my tears to blood, that he might live.
Kath. Who made them enemies? 20
Fern. I know not, and that grieves me most of all.
Kath. My son loved thine.
Fern. And so did Lodowick him.
Kath. Lend me that weapon that did kill my son,
And it shall murder me.
Fern. Nay, madam, stay; that weapon was my son's,
And on that rather should Ferneze die.
Kath. Hold, let's inquire the causers of their deaths,
That we may 'venge their blood upon their heads.
Fern. Then take them up, and let them be interred 30
Within one sacred monument of stone;
Upon which altar I will offer up
My daily sacrifice of sighs and tears,
And with my prayers pierce impartial[1] heavens,
Till they reveal the causers of our smarts,
Which forced their hands divide united hearts:
Come, Katherine, our losses equal are,
Then of true grief let us take equal share.
          [*Exeunt with the bodies.*

SCENE III.—*A Room in* BARABAS' *House.*

Enter ITHAMORE.

Itha. Why, was there ever seen such villainy,
So neatly plotted, and so well performed?
Both held in hand,[2] and flatly both beguiled?

[1] Unkind.   [2] Kept in expectancy.

Enter ABIGAIL.

Abig. Why, how now, Ithamore, why laugh'st thou so?
Itha. O mistress, ha! ha! ha!
Abig. Why, what ail'st thou?
Itha. O my master!
Abig. Ha!
Itha. O mistress! I have the bravest, gravest, secret, subtle, bottle-nosed knave to my master, that ever gentleman had. 11
Abig. Say, knave, why rail'st upon my father thus?
Itha. O, my master has the bravest policy.
Abig. Wherein?
Itha. Why, know you not?
Abig. Why, no.
Itha. Know you not of Matthias' and Don Lodowick's disaster?
Abig. No, what was it? 19
Itha. Why, the devil invented a challenge, my master writ it, and I carried it, first to Lodowick, and *imprimis* to Mathias.
And then they met, and, as the story says,
In doleful wise they ended both their days.
Abig. And was my father furtherer of their deaths?
Itha. Am I Ithamore?
Abig. Yes.
Itha. So sure did your father write, and I carry the challenge.
Abig. Well, Ithamore, let me request thee this. 30
Go to the new-made nunnery, and inquire
For any of the friars of Saint Jacques,[1].

[1] St. James.

And say, I pray them come and speak with me.
   Itha. I will, forsooth, mistress. |*Exit.*
   Abig. Hard-hearted father, unkind Barabas!
Was this the pursuit of thy policy!
To make me show them favour severally,
That by my favour they should both be slain?
Admit thou lov'dst not Lodowick for his sire,
Yet Don Mathias ne'er offended thee: 40
But thou wert set upon extreme revenge,
Because the prior dispossessed thee once,
And could'st not 'venge it, but upon his son
Nor on his son, but by Mathias' means;
Nor on Mathias, but by murdering me.
But I perceive there is no love on earth,
Pity in Jews, or piety in Turks.
But here comes cursed Ithamore, with the friar.

        Enter ITHAMORE *and* Friar JACOMO.

   F. Jac. Virgo, salve.
   Itha. When![1] duck you!   50
   Abig. Welcome, grave friar; Ithamore, begone!
                                   [*Exit* ITHAMORE.
Know, holy sir, I am bold to solicit thee.
   F. Jac. Wherein?
   Abig. To get me be admitted for a nun.
   F. Jac. Why, Abigail, it is not yet long since
That I did labour thy admission,
And then thou didst not like that holy life.
   Abig. Then were my thoughts so frail and unconfirmed,
And I was chained to follies of the world:
But now experience, purchasèd with grief,   60

        [1] Exclamation of impatience.

Has made me see the difference of things.
My sinful soul, alas, hath paced too long
The fatal labyrinth of misbelief,
Far from the sun that gives eternal life.
   F. Jac. Who taught thee this?
   Abig. The abbess of the house,
Whose zealous admonition I embrace:
O, therefore, Jacomo, let me be one,
Although unworthy, of that sisterhood.
   F. Jac. Abigail, I will, but see thou change no more,   70
For that will be most heavy to thy soul.
   Abig. That was my father's fault.
   F. Jac. Thy father's! how?
   Abig. Nay, you shall pardon me. (*Aside*) O Barabas,
Though thou deservest hardly at my hands,
Yet never shall these lips bewray thy life.
   F. Jac. Come, shall we go?
   Abig. My duty waits on you.   [*Exeunt.*

      Scene IV. — *A Room in* Barabas' *House.*

       Enter Barabas, *reading a letter.*

   Bar. What, Abigail become a nun again!
False and unkind; what, hast thou lost thy father?
And all unknown, and unconstrained of me,
Art thou again got to the nunnery?
Now here she writes, and wills me to repent.
Repentance! *Spurca!* what pretendeth[1] this?
I fear she knows — 'tis so — of my device
In Don Mathias' and Lodovico's deaths:

                [1] Portendeth.

If so, 'tis time that it be seen into :
For she that varies from me in belief 10
Gives great presumption that she loves me not;
Or loving, doth dislike of something done.—
But who comes here?

Enter ITHAMORE.

     O Ithamore, come near;
Come near, my love; come near, thy master's life,
My trusty servant, nay, my second self:
For I have now no hope but even in thee,
And on that hope my happiness is built.
When saw'st thou Abigail?
 Itha. To-day.
 Bar. With whom? 20
 Itha. A friar.
 Bar. A friar! false villain, he hath done the deed.
 Itha. How, sir?
 Bar. Why, made mine Abigail a nun.
 Itha. That's no lie, for she sent me for him.
 Bar. O unhappy day!
False, credulous, inconstant Abigail!
But let 'me go: and, Ithamore, from hence
Ne'er shall she grieve me more with her disgrace;
Ne'er shall she live to inherit aught of mine, 30
Be blest of me, nor come within my gates,
But perish underneath my bitter curse,
Like Cain by Adam for his brother's death.
 Itha. O master!
 Bar. Ithamore, entreat not for her, I am moved,
And she is hateful to my soul and me:
And 'less thou yield to this that I entreat,

I cannot think but that thou hat'st my life.

   Itha. Who, I, master? Why, I'll run to some rock,
And throw myself headlong into the sea;   40
Why, I'll do anything for your sweet sake.

   Bar. O trusty Ithamore, no servant, but my friend:
I here adopt thee for mine only heir,
All that I have is thine when I am dead,
And whilst I live use half; spend as myself;
Here take my keys, I'll give 'em thee anon:
Go buy thee garments: but thou shalt not **want**:
Only know this, that thus thou art to do:
But first go fetch me in the pot of rice
That for our supper stands upon the fire.   50

   Itha. (*aside*). I hold my head my master's hungry. I go,
     sir.   [*Exit.*

   Bar. Thus every villain ambles after wealth,
Although he ne'er be richer than in hope:
But, husht!

         Re-enter ITHAMORE *with the pot.*

   Itha. Here 'tis, master.

   Bar. Well said, Ithamore; what, hast thou brought
The ladle with thee too?

   Itha. Yes, sir, the proverb[1] says he that eats with the devil had need of a long spoon. I have brought you a ladle.

   Bar. Very well, Ithamore, then now be secret;   60
And for thy sake, whom I so dearly love,
Now shalt thou see the death of Abigail,
That thou may'st freely live to be my heir.

---

[1] This proverb is found in Chaucer's *Squiere's Tale*, in *A Comedy of Errors*, etc.

Itha. Why, master, will you poison her with a mess of rice porridge? that will preserve life, make her round and plump, and batten more than you are aware.

Bar. Ay, but, Ithamore, seest thou this?
It is a precious powder that I bought
Of an Italian, in Ancona, once,
Whose operation is to bind, infect, 70
And poison deeply, yet not appear
In forty hours after it is ta'en.

Itha. How, master?

Bar. Thus, Ithamore.
This even they use in Malta here, — 'tis called
Saint Jacques' Even, — and then I say they use
To send their alms into the nunneries:
Among the rest bear this, and set it there;
There's a dark entry where they take it in,
Where they must neither see the messenger, 80
Nor make inquiry who hath sent it them.

Itha. How so?

Bar. Belike there is some ceremony in't.
There, Ithamore, must thou go place this pot!
Stay, let me spice it first.

Itha. Pray do, and let me help you, master. Pray let me taste first.

Bar. Prythee do (ITHAMORE *tastes*): what say'st thou now?

Itha. Troth, master, I'm loth such a pot of pottage should be spoiled. 90

Bar. Peace, Ithamore, 'tis better so than spared.
Assure thyself thou shalt have broth by the eye,[1]
My purse, my coffer, and myself is thine.

---

[1] In abundance.

Itha. Well, master, I go.

Bar. Stay, first let me stir it, Ithamore.
As fatal be it to her as the draught
Of which great Alexander drunk and died:
And with her let it work like Borgia's wine,
Whereof his sire, the Pope, was poisonèd.
In few,[1] the blood of Hydra, Lerna's bane: 100
The juice of hebon,[2] and Cocytus' breath,
And all the poisons of the Stygian pool
Break from the fiery kingdom; and in this
Vomit your venom and invenom her
That like a fiend hath left her father thus.

Itha. (*aside*). What a blessing has he given't! was ever pot of rice porridge so sauced! What shall I do with it?

Bar. O, my sweet Ithamore, go set it down,
And come again so soon as thou hast done,
For I have other business for thee. 110

Itha. Here's a drench to poison a whole stable of Flanders mares: I'll carry't to the nuns with a powder.

Bar. And the horse pestilence to boot; away!

Itha. I am gone.
Pay me my wages, for my work is done.   [*Exit.*

Bar. I'll pay thee with a vengeance, Ithamore.   [*Exit.*

SCENE V. — *The Senate-house.*

Enter FERNEZE, MARTIN DEL BOSCO, Knights, *and* BASSO.

Fern. Welcome, great basso; how fares Calymath?
What wind drives you thus into Malta-road?

Bas. The wind that bloweth all the world besides, —
Desire of gold.

[1] In short.   [2] The juice of ebony, regarded as a deadly poison.

Fern. Desire of gold, great sir?
That's to be gotten in the Western Ind:
In Malta are no golden minerals.
    Bas. To you of Malta thus saith Calymath:
The time you took for respite is at hand,
For the performance of your promise passed,
And for the tribute-money I am sent.
    Fern. Basso, in brief, 'shalt have no tribute here.
Nor shall the heathens live upon our spoil:
First will we raze the city walls ourselves,
Lay waste the island, hew the temples down,
And, shipping off our goods to Sicily,
Open an entrance for the wasteful sea,
Whose billows beating the resistless [1] banks,
Shall overflow it with their refluence.
    Bas. Well, Governor, since thou hast broke the league
By flat denial of the promised tribute,
Talk not of razing down your city walls,
You shall not need trouble yourselves so far,
For Selim Calymath shall come himself,
And with brass bullets batter down your towers,
And turn proud Malta to a wilderness
For these intolerable wrongs of yours;
And so farewell.
    Fern. Farewell: [*Exit* Basso.
And now, ye men of Malta, look about,
And let's provide to welcome Calymath:
Close your portcullis, charge your basilisks,[2]
And as you profitably take up arms,
So now courageously encounter them;
For by this answer, broken is the league,

---

[1] Unable to resist.   [2] Immense cannon.

And naught is to be looked for now but wars,
And naught to us more welcome is than wars. [*Exeunt.*

SCENE VI. — *A Room in a Convent.*

Enter Friar JACOMO *and* Friar BARNARDINE.

F. Jac. O, brother, brother, all the nuns are sick,
And physic will not help them: they must die.
F. Barn. The abbess sent for me to be confessed:
O, what a sad confession will there be!
F. Jac. And so did fair Maria send for me:
I'll to her lodging: hereabouts she lies. [*Exit.*

Enter ABIGAIL.

F. Barn. What, all dead, save only Abigail?
Abig. And I shall die too, for I feel death coming.
Where is the friar that conversed with me?
F. Barn. O, he is gone to see the other nuns. 10
Abig. I sent for him, but seeing you are come,
Be you my ghostly father: and first know,
That in this house I lived religiously,
Chaste, and devout, much sorrowing for my sins;
But ere I came ——
F. Barn. What then?
Abig. I did offend high Heaven so grievously,
As I am almost desperate for my sins:
And one offence torments me more than all.
You knew Mathias and Don Lodowick? 20
F. Barn. Yes, what of them?
Abig. My father did contract me to 'em both:
First to Don Lodowick; him I never loved;

Mathias was the man that I held dear,
And for his sake did I become a nun.

F. Barn. So, say how was their end?

Abig. Both jealous of my love, envied[1] each other,
And by my father's practice,[2] which is there
Set down at large, the gallants were both slain.

[*Gives a written paper.*

F. Barn. O monstrous villainy! 30

Abig. To work my peace, this I confess to thee;
Reveal it not, for then my father dies.

F. Barn. Know that confession must not be revealed,
The canon law forbids it, and the priest
That makes it known, being degraded first,
Shall be condemned, and then sent to the fire.

Abig. So I have heard; pray, therefore keep it close.
Death seizeth on my heart: ah gentle friar,
Convert my father that he may be saved,
And witness that I die a Christian. [*Dies.* 40

F. Barn. Ay, and a virgin too; that grieves me most:
But I must to the Jew and exclaim on him,
And make him stand in fear of me.

Re-enter Friar JACOMO.

F. Jac. O brother, all the nuns are dead, let's bury them.

F. Barn. First help to bury this, then go with me
And help me to exclaim against the Jew.

F. Jac. Why, what has he done?

F. Barn. A thing that makes me tremble to unfold.

F. Jac. What, has he crucified a child?[3]

---

[1] Hated; the accent is on the second syllable. [2] Artifice.
[3] The Jews were often accused of this crime, especially when the **king** was in need of money.

F. Barn. No, but a worse thing: 'twas told to me in
    shrift, 50
Thou know'st 'tis death an if it be revealed.
Come, let's away. *[Exeunt.*

ACT IV.

Scene I. — *A Street.*

Enter Barabas *and* Ithamore. *Bells within.*

Bar. There is no music to[1] a Christian's knell:
How sweet the bells ring now the nuns are dead,
That sound at other times like tinker's pans!
I was afraid the poison had not wrought;
Or though it wrought, it would have done no good:
Now all are dead, not one remains alive.
    Itha. That's brave, master, but think you it will not be
        known?
    Bar. How can it, if we two be secret?
    Itha. For my part fear you not.
    Bar. I'd cut thy throat if I did. 10
    Itha. And reason too.
But here's a royal monastery hard by;
Good master, let me poison all the monks.
    Bar. Thou shalt not need, for now the nuns are dead
They'll die with grief.
    Itha. Do you not sorrow for your daughter's death?
    Bar. No, but I grieve because she lived so long.
An Hebrew born, and would become a Christian!
Cazzo, diabolo.

[1] Equal to.

Enter Friar JACOMO *and* Friar BARNARDINE.

Itha. Look, look, master, here come two religious caterpillars.

Bar. I smelt 'em ere they came.

Itha. God-a-mercy, nose! come, let's be gone.

F. Barn. Stay, wicked Jew, repent, I say, and stay.

F. Jac. Thou hast offended, therefore must be damned.

Bar. I fear they know we sent the poisoned broth.

Itha. And so do I, master; therefore speak 'em fair.

F. Barn. Barabas, thou hast ——

F. Jac. Ay, that thou hast ——

Bar. True, I have money, what though I have?

F. Barn. Thou art a ——

F. Jac. Ay, that thou art, a ——

Bar. What needs all this? I know I am a Jew.

F. Barn. Thy daughter ——

F. Jac. Ay, thy daughter ——

Bar. O speak not of her! then I die with grief.

F. Barn. Remember that ——

F. Jac. Ay, remember that ——

Bar. I must needs say that I have been a great usurer.

F. Barn. Thou hast committed ——

Bar. Fornication — but that was in another country;
And besides, the wench is dead.

F. Barn. Ay, but, Barabas,
Remember Mathias and Don Lodowick.

Bar. Why, what of them?

F. Barn. I will not say that by a forged challenge they
   met.

Bar. (*aside*). She has confest, and we are both undone,
My bosom inmate! but I must dissemble. —

O holy friars, the burthen of my sins
Lie heavy on my soul; then pray you tell me, 50
Is't not too late now to turn Christian?
I have been zealous in the Jewish faith,
Hard-hearted to the poor, a covetous wretch,
That would for lucre's sake have sold my soul.
A hundred for a hundred I have ta'en;
And now for store of wealth may I compare
With all the Jews of Malta; but what is wealth?
I am a Jew, and therefore am I lost.
Would penance serve to atone for this my sin,
I could afford to whip myself to death —— 60
　Itha. And so could I; but penance will not serve.
　Bar. To fast, to pray, and wear a shirt of hair,
And on my knees creep to Jerusalem.
Cellars of wine, and sollars[1] full of wheat,
Warehouses stuft with spices and with drugs,
Whole chests of gold, in bullion, and in coin,
Besides I know not how much weight in pearl,
Orient and round, have I within my house;
At Alexandria, merchandise unsold:[2]
But yesterday two ships went from this town, 70
Their voyage will be worth ten thousand crowns.
In Florence, Venice, Antwerp, London, Seville,
Frankfort, Lubeck, Moscow, and where not,
Have I debts owing; and in most of these,
Great sums of money lying in the banco;
All this I'll give to some religious house.
So I may be baptized, and live therein.

[1] Attics, or lofts (Latin *solarium*); still used in some parts of England, and in legal documents.
[2] Dyce suggests *untold*.

F. Jac. O good Barabas, come to our house.
F. Barn. O no, good Barabas, come to our house;
And, Barabas, you know —— 80
Bar. I know that I have highly sinned.
You shall convert me, you shall have all my wealth.
F. Jac. O Barabas, their laws are strict.
Bar. I know they are, and I will be with you.
F. Barn. They wear no shirts, and they go barefoot too.
Bar. (*to* BARN.). Then 'tis not for me; and I am resolved
You shall confess me, and have all my goods.
F. Jac. Good Barabas, come to me.
Bar. You see I answer him, and yet he stays;
Rid him away, and go you home with me. 90
F. Jac. I'll be with you to-night.
Bar. Come to my house at one o'clock this night.
F. Jac. You hear your answer, and you may be gone.
F. Barn. Why, go get you away.
F. Jac. I will not go for thee.
F. Barn. Not! then I'll make thee go.
F. Jac. How, dost call me rogue? [*They fight.*
Itha. Part 'em, master, part 'em.
Bar. This is mere frailty, brethren; be content.
(*Aside to* BARN.) Friar Barnardine, go you with Ithamore: 100
You know my mind, let me alone with him.
F. Jac. Why does he go to thy house? let him be gone.
Bar. I'll give him something and so stop his mouth.
[*Exit* ITHAMORE *with* Friar BARNARDINE.
I never heard of any man but he
Maligned the order of the Jacobins:
But do you think that I believe his words?
Why, brother, you converted Abigail;
And I am bound in charity to requite it,

And so I will. O Jacomo, fail not, but come.
  F. Jac. But, Barabas, who shall be your godfathers?   110
For presently you shall be shrived.
  Bar. Marry, the Turk[1] shall be one of my godfathers,
But not a word to any of your covent.[2]
  F. Jac. I warrant thee, Barabas.   [*Exit.*
  Bar. So, now the fear is past, and I am safe,
For he that shrived her is within my house;
What if I murdered him ere Jacomo comes?
Now I have such a plot for both their lives
As never Jew nor Christian knew the like:
One turned my daughter, therefore he shall die;   120
The other knows enough to have my life,
Therefore 'tis not requisite he should live.
But are not both these wise men to suppose
That I will leave my house, my goods, and all,
To fast and be well whipt? I'll none of that.
Now, Friar Barnardine, I come to you,
I'll feast you, lodge you, give you fair words,
And after that, I and my trusty Turk —
No more, but so: it must and shall be done.   [*Exit.*

Scene II. — *A Room in* Barabas' *House.*

Enter Barabas *and* Ithamore.

  Bar. Ithamore, tell me, is the friar asleep?
  Itha. Yes; and I know not what the reason is,
Do what I can he will not strip himself,
Nor go to bed, but sleeps in his own clothes;
I fear me he mistrusts what we intend.

---

[1] Ithamore.   [2] Convent; this form still appears in *Covent* Garden.

Bar. No, 'tis an order which the friars use :
Yet, if he knew our meanings, could he 'scape ?
    Itha. No, none can hear him, cry he ne'er so loud.
    Bar. Why, true, therefore did I place him there :
The other chambers open towards the street.
    Itha. You loiter, master ; wherefore stay we thus ?
O how I long to see him shake his heels.
    Bar. Come on, sirrah.
Off with your girdle, make a handsome noose.
        [ITHAMORE *takes off his girdle and ties a noose in it.*
Friar, awake !   [*They put the noose round the* Friar's *neck.*
    F. Barn. What, do you mean to strangle me ?
    Itha. Yes, 'cause you use to confess.
    Bar. Blame not us but the proverb, Confess and be hanged ; pull hard !
    F. Barn. What, will you have my life ?
    Bar. Pull hard, I say ; you would have had my goods.
    Itha. Ay, and our lives too, therefore pull amain.
                                              [*They strangle him.*
'Tis neatly done, sir, here's no print at all.
    Bar. Then it is as it should be ; take him up.
    Itha. Nay, master, be ruled by me a little. (*Stands the body upright against the wall and puts a staff in its hand.*) So, let him lean upon his staff ; excellent ! he stands as if he were begging of bacon.[1]
    Bar. Who would not think but that this friar lived ?
What time o' night is't now, sweet Ithamore ?
    Itha. Towards one.
    Bar. Then will not Jacomo be long from hence.
                                                      [*Exeunt*

---

[1] The body was stood up outside of the house.

SCENE III. — *Outside* BARABAS' *House.*

Enter Friar JACOMO.

F. Jac. This is the hour wherein I shall proceed,[1]
O happy hour wherein I shall convert
An infidel, and bring his gold into our treasury![2]
But soft, is not this Barnardine? it is;
And, understanding I should come this way,
Stands here a purpose, meaning me some wrong,
And intercept my going to the Jew. —
Barnardine!
Wilt thou not speak? thou think'st I see thee not;
Away, I'd wish thee, and let me go by: 10
No, wilt thou not? nay, then, I'll force my way;
And see, a staff stands ready for the purpose:
As thou lik'st that, stop me another time.

[*Takes the staff and strikes the body, which falls down.*

Enter BARABAS *and* ITHAMORE.

Bar. Why, how now, Jacomo, what hast thou done?
F. Jac. Why, stricken him that would have struck at me.
Bar. Who is it? Barnardine? now out, alas, he's slain!
Itha. Ay, master, he's slain; look how his brains drop out on's[3] nose.
F. Jac. Good sirs, I have done't, but nobody knows it but you two — I may escape. 20
Bar. So might my man and I hang with you for company.

---

[1] Succeed.

[2] Bullen rearranges these lines thus:

"O happy hour
Wherein I shall convert an infidel,
And bring his gold into our treasury."

[3] Of his.

Itha. No, let us bear him to the magistrates.
F. Jac. Good Barabas, let me go.
Bar. No, pardon me; the law must have its course.
I must be forced to give in evidence,
That being importuned by this Barnardine
To be a Christian, I shut him out,
And there he sat: now I, to keep my word,
And give my goods and substance to your house,
Was up thus early; with intent to go   30
Unto your friary, because you stayed.
Itha. Fie upon 'em, master; will you turn Christian when holy friars turn devils and murder one another?
Bar. No, for this example I'll remain a Jew:
Heaven bless me! what, a friar a murderer?
When shall you see a Jew commit the like?
Itha. Why, a Turk could ha' done no more.
Bar. To-morrow is the sessions; you shall to it.
Come, Ithamore, let's help to take him hence.
F. Jac. Villains, I am a sacred person; touch me not.   40
Bar. The law shall touch you, we'll but lead you, we:
'Las, I could weep at your calamity!
Take in the staff too, for that must be shown:
Law wills that each particular be known.   [*Exeunt.*

SCENE IV.—*A Veranda of* BELLAMIRA'S *House.*

Enter BELLAMIRA *and* PILIA-BORSA.

Bell. Pilia-Borsa, did'st thou meet with Ithamore?
Pilia. I did.
Bell. And did'st thou deliver my letter?
Pilia. I did.
Bell. And what think'st thou? will he come?

Pilia. I think so, but yet I cannot tell; for at the reading of the letter he looked like a man of another world.
Bell. Why so?
Pilia. That such a base slave as he should be saluted by such a tall[1] man as I am, from such a beautiful dame as you.
Bell. And what said he? 11
Pilia. Not a wise word, only gave me a nod, as who should say, "Is it even so?" and so I left him, being driven to a non-plus at the critical aspect of my terrible countenance.
Bell. And where didst meet him?
Pilia. Upon mine own freehold, within forty feet of the gallows, conning his neck-verse,[2] I take it, looking of[3] a friar's execution, whom I saluted with an old hempen proverb, *Hodie tibi, cras mihi,* and so I left him to the mercy of the hangman: but the exercise[4] being done, see where he comes.[5] 21

Enter ITHAMORE.

Itha. I never knew a man take his death so patiently as this friar; he was ready to leap off ere the halter was about his neck; and when the hangman had put on his hempen tippet, he made such haste to his prayers, as if he had had another cure to serve. Well, go whither he will, I'll be none of his followers in haste: and, now I think on't, going to the execution, a fellow met me with a muschatoes[6] like a raven's wing, and a dagger with a hilt like a warming-pan, and he gave me a letter from one Madam Bellamira, saluting me 30 in such sort as if he had meant to make clean my boots with

---

[1] Brave.
[2] The "neck-verse" which criminals had to read to secure the benefit of the clergy, was usually *Psalm* li, 1.
[3] On.   [5] Cf. *Richard III*, iii, 2.
[4] Sermon.   [6] Mustachios.

his lips; the effect was, that I should come to her house. I wonder what the reason is; it may be she sees more in me than I can find in myself: for she writes further, that she loves me ever since she saw me, and who would not requite such love? Here's her house, and here she comes, and now would I were gone; I am not worthy to look upon her.

Pilia. This is the gentleman you writ to.

Itha. (*aside*). Gentleman! he flouts me; what gentry can be in a poor Turk of tenpence?[1] I'll be gone. 40

Bell. Is't not a sweet-faced youth, Pilia?

Itha. (*aside*). Again, "sweet youth!" — Did not you, sir, bring the sweet youth a letter?

Pilia. I did, sir, and from this gentlewoman, who, as myself, and the rest of the family, stand or fall at your service.

Bell. Though woman's modesty should hale me back, I can withhold no longer; welcome, sweet love.

Itha. (*aside*). Now am I clean, or rather foully out of the way. 50

Bell. Whither so soon?

Itha. (*aside*). I'll go steal some money from my master to make me handsome. — Pray pardon me, I must go and see a ship discharged.

Bell. Canst thou be so unkind to leave me thus?

Pilia. An ye did but know how she loves you, sir!

Itha. Nay, I care not how much she loves me — Sweet Bellamira, would I had my master's wealth for thy sake!

Pilia. And you can have it, sir, an if you please. 59

Itha. If 'twere above ground, I could and would have it; but he hides and buries it up, as partridges do their eggs, under the earth.

---

[1] A contemptuous term, common at that time.

Pilia. And is't not possible to find it out?

Itha. By no means possible.

Bell. (*aside to* PILIA.). What shall we do with this base villain then?

Pilia. (*aside to* BELL.). Let me alone; do you but speak him fair. —
But, sir, you know some secrets of the Jew,
Which, if they were revealed, would do him harm. 70

Itha. Ay, and such as — Go to, no more! I'll make him send me half he has, and glad he 'scapes so too. I'll write unto him; we'll have money straight.

Pilia. Send for a hundred crowns at least.

Itha. Ten hundred thousand crowns. (*Writing*) "Master Barabas."

Pilia. Write not so submissively, but threatening him.

Itha. (*writing*). "Sirrah, Barabas, send me a hundred crowns."

Pilia. Put in two hundred at least. 80

Itha. (*writing*). "I charge thee send me three hundred by this bearer, and this shall be your warrant: if you do not — no more, but so."

Pilia. Tell him you will confess.

Itha. (*writing*). "Otherwise I'll confess all." — Vanish, and return in a twinkle.

Pilia. Let me alone; I'll use him in his kind.

[*Exit* PILIA-BORSA *with the letter.*

Itha. Hang him, Jew!

Bell. Now, gentle Ithamore,
Where are my maids? provide a running[1] banquet; 90
Send to the merchant, bid him bring me silks,
Shall Ithamore, my love, go in such **rags**?

[1] Hasty.

Itha. And bid the jeweller come hither too.
Bell. I have no husband, sweet; I'll marry thee.
Itha. Content: but we will leave this paltry land,
And sail from hence to Greece, to lovely Greece.
I'll be thy Jason, thou my golden fleece;
Where painted carpets o'er the meads are hurled,
And Bacchus' vineyards overspread the world;
Where woods and forests go in goodly green, 100
I'll be Adonis, thou shalt be Love's Queen.
The meads, the orchards, and the primrose-lanes,
Instead of sedge and reed, bear sugar-canes:
Thou in those groves, by Dis above,[1]
Shalt live with me and be my love.[2]
Bell. Whither will I not go with gentle Ithamore?

Re-enter PILIA-BORSA.

Itha. How now? hast thou the gold?
Pilia. Yes.
Itha. But came it freely? did the cow give down her milk freely? 110
Pilia. At reading of the letter, he stared and stamped and turned aside. I took him by the beard, and looked upon him thus; told him he were best to send it; then he hugged and embraced me.
Itha. Rather for fear than love.
Pilia. Then, like a Jew, he laughed and jeered, and told me he loved me for your sake, and said what a faithful servant you had been.

[1] This blunder is intentionally made.
[2] Marlowe's well-known lyric, *The Passionate Shepherd to his Love*, begins,—
 "Come live with me, and be my love,
 And we will all the pleasures prove
 That hills and valleys, dales and fields,
 Woods or steepy mountains, yields."

Itha. The more villain he to keep me thus; here's goodly 'parel, is there not? 120

Pilia. To conclude, he gave me ten crowns.

[*Gives the money to* ITHAMORE.

Itha. But ten? I'll not leave him worth a grey groat. Give me a ream[1] of paper; we'll have a kingdom of gold for't.

Pilia. Write for five hundred crowns.

Itha. (*writing*). "Sirrah, Jew, as you love your life send me five hundred crowns, and give the bearer one hundred." — Tell him I must have't.

Pilia. I warrant your worship shall have't.

Itha. And if he ask why I demand so much, tell him I scorn to write a line under a hundred crowns. 131

Pilia. You'd make a rich poet, sir. I am gone. [*Exit.*

Itha. Take thou the money; spend it for my sake.

Bell. 'Tis not thy money, but thyself I weigh;
Thus Bellamira esteems of gold. [*Throws it aside.*
But thus of thee. [*Kisses him.*

Itha. That kiss again! she runs division[2] of my lips. What an eye she casts on me! It twinkles like a star.

Bell. Come, my dear love, let's in! [*Exeunt.*

SCENE V. — *A Room in* BARABAS' *House.*

Enter BARABAS, *reading a letter.*

Bar. "Barabas, send me three hundred crowns." — Plain Barabas! O, that wicked courtesan!

---

[1] A play on the words *realm* and *kingdom*; *realm* was often written and pronounced *ream*.

[2] A musical term. "Divisions for the voice are intended to be sung in one breath to one syllable. The performance of this style of music is called running a division." — *Stainer and Barrett: Dict. of Musical Terms.*

He was not wont to call me Barabas.
"Or else I will confess:" ay, there it goes:
But, if I get him, *coupe de gorge* for that.
He sent a shaggy tattered staring slave,
That when he speaks draws out his grisly beard,
And winds it twice or thrice about his ear;
Whose face has been a grindstone for men's swords;[1]
His hands are hacked, some fingers cut quite off;　　10
Who, when he speaks, grunts like a hog, and looks
Like one that is employed in catzerie[2]
And crossbiting[3]—
And I by him must send three hundred crowns!
Well, my hope is, he will not stay there still;
And when he comes: O, that he were but here!

　　　　　　Enter PILIA-BORSA.

Pilia. Jew, I must have more gold.
Bar. Why, want'st thou any of thy tale?[4]
Pilia. No; but three hundred will not serve his turn.
Bar. Not serve his turn, sir?　　　　　　　　20
Pilia. No, sir; and, therefore, I must have five hundred more.
Bar. I'll rather ——
Pilia. O good words, sir, and send it you were best! see, there's his letter.　　　　　　　　[*Gives letter.*
Bar. Might he not as well come as send? pray bid him come and fetch it; what he writes for you, ye shall have straight.
Pilia. Ay, and the rest too, or else ——
Bar. (*aside*). I must make this villain away.　　30

---

[1] Cf. *Arden of Feversham.*　　[3] Swindling.
[2] Knavery.　　[4] Reckoning.

Please you dine with me, sir;—(*aside*) and you shall be most heartily poisoned.

Pilia. No, God-a-mercy. Shall I have these crowns?

Bar. I cannot do it, I have lost my keys.

Pilia. O, if that be all, I can pick ope your locks.

Bar. Or climb up to my counting-house window: you know my meaning.

Pilia. I know enough, and therefore talk not to me of your counting-house. The gold! or know, Jew, it is in my power to hang thee. 40

Bar. (*aside*). I am betrayed.—
'Tis not five hundred crowns that I esteem,
I am not moved at that: this angers me,
That he, who knows I love him as myself,
Should write in this imperious vein. Why, sir,
You know I have no child, and unto whom
Should I leave all but unto Ithamore?

Pilia. Here's many words, but no crowns: the crowns!

Bar. Commend me to him, sir, most humbly,
And unto your good mistress, as unknown. 50

Pilia. Speak, shall I have 'em, sir?

Bar. Sir, here they are.— [*Gives money.*
(*Aside*) O, that I should part with so much gold!
Here, take 'em, fellow, with as good a will——
(*Aside*) As I would see thee hanged; O, love stops my
 breath:
Never man servant loved as I do Ithamore!

Pilia. I know it, sir.

Bar. Pray, when, sir, shall I see you at my house?

Pilia. Soon enough, to your cost, sir. Fare you well.
[*Exit.*

Bar. Nay, to thine own cost, villain, if thou com'st! 60

Was ever Jew tormented as I am?
To have a shag-rag knave to come, force from me
Three hundred crowns, — and then five hundred crowns!
Well, I must seek a means to rid 'em all,
And presently; for in his villainy
He will tell all he knows, and I shall die for't.
I have it:
I will in some disguise go see the slave,
And how the villain revels with my gold. [*Exit.*

SCENE VI. — *Balcony of* BELLAMIRA'S *House.*

Enter BELLAMIRA, ITHAMORE, *and* PILIA-BORSA.

Bell. I'll pledge thee, love, and therefore drink it off.
Itha. Say'st thou me so? have at it; and do you hear?
[*Whispers.*
Bell. Go to, it shall be so.
Itha. Of[1] that condition I will drink it up.
Here's to thee!
Bell. Nay, I'll have all or none.
Itha. There, if thou lov'st me do not leave a drop.
Bell. Love thee! fill me three glasses.
Itha. Three and fifty dozen, I'll pledge thee.
Pilia. Knavely spoke, and like a knight-at-arms.   10
Itha. Hey, *Rivo Castiliano!*[2] a man's a man!
Bell. Now to the Jew.
Itha. Ha! to the Jew, and send me money he were best.
Pilia. What would'st thou do if he should send thee none?
Itha. Do nothing; but I know what I know; he's a murderer.

---

[1] On.   [2] Familiar refrain in drinking-songs; origin doubtful.

Bell. I had not thought he had been so brave a man.

Itha. You knew Mathias and the governor's son; he and I killed 'em both, and yet never touched 'em.

Pilia. O, bravely done.

Itha. I carried the broth that poisoned the nuns; and he and I, snickle hand too fast,[1] strangled a friar.

Bell. You two alone?

Itha. We two; and 'twas never known, nor never shall be for me.

Pilia. (*aside to* BELL.). This shall with me unto the governor.

Bell. (*aside to* PILIA.). And fit it should: but first let's ha' more gold, —
Come, gentle Ithamore.

Itha. Love me little, love me long.[2]

Enter BARABAS, *disguised as a French musician, with a lute, and a nosegay in his hat.*

Bell. A French musician! come, let's hear your skill.

Bar. Must tuna my lute for sound, twang, twang, first.

Itha. Wilt drink, Frenchman? here's to thee with a plague on this drunken hiccup!

Bar. Gramercy, monsieur.

Bell. Prythee, Pilia-Borsa, bid the fiddler give me the posy in his hat there.

Pilia. Sirrah, you must give my mistress your posy.

Bar. A votre commandement, madame.

---

[1] A corrupt passage: *snickle* is a noose, or slip-knot; commonly applied to the hangman's halter, and to snares for hares and rabbits. Cunningham suggests, "snickle hard and fast."

[2] This expression is found in Heywood's *Proverbs*, 1546.

Bell. How sweet, my Ithamore, the flowers smell!
Itha. Like thy breath, sweetheart; no violet like 'em.
Pilia. Foh! methinks they stink like a hollyhock.
Bar. (*aside*). So, now I am revenged upon 'em all.
The scent thereof was death; I poisoned it.
Itha. Play, fiddler, or I'll cut your cat's guts into chitter-
lings.
Bar. Pardonnez-moi, be no in tune yet; so now, now all
be in.
Itha. Give him a crown, and fill me out more wine. 50
Pilia. There's two crowns for thee; play.
Bar. (*aside*). How liberally the villain gives me mine own
gold! [*Plays.*
Pilia. Methinks he fingers very well.
Bar. (*aside*). So did you when you stole my gold.
Pilia. How swift he runs!
Bar. (*aside*). You run swifter when you threw my gold
out of my window.
Bell. Musician, hast been in Malta long?
Bar. Two, three, four month, madame. 60
Itha. Dost not know a Jew, one Barabas?
Bar. Very mush; monsieur, you no be his man?
Pilia. His man?
Itha. I scorn the peasant; tell him so.
Bar. (*aside*). He knows it already.
Itha. 'Tis a strange thing of that Jew, he lives upon
pickled grasshoppers and sauced mushrooms.
Bar. (*aside*). What a slave's this? the governor feeds not
as I do.
Itha. He never put on clean shirt since he was circum-
cised. 71
Bar. (*aside*). O rascal! I change myself twice a day.

Itha. The hat he wears, Judas left under the elder[1] when he hanged himself.

Bar. (*aside*). 'Twas sent me as a present from the great Cham.

Pilia. A musty slave he is; — Whither now, fiddler?

Bar. Pardonnez-moi, monsieur, me be no well.

Pilia. Farewell, fiddler! (*Exit* BARABAS.) One letter more to the Jew. 80

Bell. Prythee, sweet love, one more, and write it sharp.

Itha. No, I'll send by word of mouth now — Bid him deliver thee a thousand crowns, by the same token, that the nuns loved rice, that Friar Barnardine slept in his own clothes; any of 'em will do it.

Pilia. Let me alone to urge it, now I know the meaning.

Itha. The meaning has a meaning. Come, let's in:
To undo a Jew is charity, and not sin. [*Exeunt.*

ACT V.

SCENE I. — *The Council-house.*

Enter FERNEZE, Knights, MARTIN DEL BOSCO, *and* Officers.

Fern. Now, gentlemen, betake you to your arms,
And see that Malta be well fortified;
And it behooves you to be resolute;
For Calymath, having hovered here so long,
Will win the town, or die before the walls.

1st Knight. And die he shall, for we will never yield.

---

[1] Judas is said to have hanged himself on an elder-tree. When at Jerusalem in 1887, I saw in the field of Aceldama a blighted fig-tree, not above fifty years old, on which the natives say Judas hanged himself.

Enter BELLAMIRA *and* PILIA-BORSA.

Bell. O, bring us to the governor.
Fern. Away with her! she is a courtesan.
Bell. Whate'er I am, yet, governor, hear me speak;
I bring thee news by whom thy son was slain:
Mathias did it not; it was the Jew.
Pilia. Who, besides the slaughter of these gentlemen,
Poisoned his own daughter and the nuns,
Strangled a friar and I know not what
Mischief besides.
Fern. Had we but proof of this ——
Bell. Strong proof, my lord; his man's now at my lodging,
That was his agent; he'll confess it all.
Fern. Go fetch him straight (*exeunt* Officers). I always feared that Jew.

Enter Officers *with* BARABAS *and* ITHAMORE.

Bar. I'll go alone; dogs! do not hale me thus.
Itha. Nor me neither, I cannot outrun you, constable: —
O my belly!
Bar. (*aside*). One dram of powder more had made all sure;
What a damned slave was I!
Fern. Make fires, heat irons, let the rack be fetched.
1st Knight. Nay, stay, my lord; 't may be he will confess.
Bar. Confess! what mean you, lords? who should confess?
Fern. Thou and thy Turk; 'twas you that slew my son.
Itha. Guilty, my lord, I confess. Your son and Mathias were both contracted unto Abigail; he forged a counterfeit challenge.

Bar. Who carried that challenge?

Itha. I carried it, I confess; but who writ it? Marry, even he that strangled Barnardine, poisoned the nuns and his own daughter.

Fern. Away with him! his sight is death to me.

Bar. For what, you men of Malta? hear me speak:
She is a courtesan, and he a thief,
And he my bondman. Let me have [the] law,[1]
For none of this can prejudice my life. 40

Fern. Once more, away with him; you shall have law.

Bar. (*aside*). Devils, do your worst! I'll live in spite of you. —
As these have spoke, so be it to their souls! —
(*Aside*) I hope the poisoned flowers will work anon.

[*Exeunt* Officers *with* BARABAS *and* ITHAMORE, BELLAMIRA *and* PILIA-BORSA.

Enter KATHERINE.

Kath. Was my Mathias murdered by the Jew?
Ferneze, 'twas thy son that murdered him.

Fern. Be patient, gentle madam, it was he;
He forged the daring challenge made them fight.

Kath. Where is the Jew? where is that murderer?

Fern. In prison till the law has passed on him. 50

Re-enter First Officer.

1st Off. My lord, the courtesan and her man are dead:
So is the Turk and Barabas the Jew.

Fern. Dead!

1st Off. Dead, my lord, and here they bring his body.

Bosco. This sudden death of his is very strange.

---

[1] The metre requires the insertion of *the*.

Re-enter Officers *carrying* BARABAS *as dead.*

Fern. Wonder not at it, sir, the Heavens are just;
Their deaths were like their lives, then think not of 'em.
Since they are dead, let them be burièd;
For the Jew's body, throw that o'er the walls,
To be a pray for vultures and wild beasts. —   60
So now away, and fortify the town.
        [*Exeunt all, leaving* BARABAS *on the floor.*

SCENE II. — *Outside the City Walls.*

BARABAS *discovered rising.*

Bar. What, all alone? well fare, sleepy drink.
I'll be revenged on this accursèd town;
For by my means Calymath shall enter in.
I'll help to slay their children and their wives,
To fire the churches, pull their houses down,
Take my goods too, and seize upon my lands.
I hope to see the governor a slave,
And, rowing in a galley, whipt to death.

      Enter CALYMATH, Bassoes, *and* Turks.

Caly. Whom have we here, a spy?
Bar. Yes, my good lord, one that can spy a place   10
Where you may enter and surprise the town:
My name is Barabas: I am a Jew.
Caly. Art thou that Jew whose goods we heard were sold
For tribute-money?
Bar. The very same, my lord:
And since that time they have hired a slave, my man,
To accuse me of a thousand villainies;

I was imprisonèd, but 'scaped their hands.
   Caly. Did'st break prison?
   Bar. No, no;   20
I drank of poppy and cold mandrake juice:[1]
And being asleep, belike they thought me dead,
And threw me o'er the walls: so, or how else,
The Jew is here, and rests at your command.
   Caly. 'Twas bravely done: but tell me, Barabas,
Canst thou, as thou report'st, make Malta ours?
   Bar. Fear not, my lord, for here against the sluice,
The rock is hollow, and of purpose digged,
To make a passage for the running streams
And common channels[2] of the city.   30
Now, whilst you give assault unto the walls,
I'll lead five hundred soldiers through the vault,
And rise with them i' the middle of the town,
Open the gates for you to enter in;
And by this means the city is your own.
   Caly. If this be true, I'll make thee governor.
   Bar. And if it not be true, then let me die.
   Caly. Thou'st doomed thyself. Assault it presently.
                                                                 [*Exeunt.*

                SCENE III.—*A Square in the City.*

Alarums within.   *Enter* CALYMATH, Bassoes, Turks, *and*
      BARABAS, *with* FERNEZE *and* Knights *prisoners.*

   Caly. Now vail your pride, you captive Christians,
And kneel for mercy to your conquering foe:
Now where's the hope you had of haughty Spain?

---

   [1] Cf. *Othello*, iii, 3: ' not poppy, n r mandragora." *Mandrake* is a corruption of *mandragora.*
   [2] Kennels.—*Dyce.*

Ferneze, speak, had it not been much better
T'have kept thy promise than be thus surprised?
    Fern. What should I say? We are captives and must
        yield.
    Caly. Ay, villains, you must yield, and under Turkish
        yokes
Shall groaning bear the burden of our ire;
And, Barabas, as erst we promised thee,
For thy desert we make thee governor;   10
Use them at thy discretion.
    Bar. Thanks, my lord.
    Fern. O fatal day, to fall into the hands
Of such a traitor and unhallowed Jew!
What greater misery could Heaven inflict?
    Caly. 'Tis our command: and Barabas, we give
To guard thy person these our Janizaries:
Entreat[1] them well, as we have usèd thee.
And now, brave bassoes, come, we'll walk about
The ruined town, and see the wreck we made:—   20
Farewell, brave Jew; farewell, great Barabas!
    Bar. May all good fortune follow Calymath!
                    [*Exeunt* CALYMATH *and* Bassoes.
And now, as entrance to our safety,
To prison with the governor and these
Captains, his consorts and confederates.
    Fern. O villain! Heaven will be revenged on thee.
                [*Exeunt* Turks, *with* FERNEZE *and* Knights.
    Bar. Away! no more; let him not trouble me.[2]
Thus hast thou gotten, by thy policy,
No simple place, no small authority:

[1] Treat.
[2] The scene here is shifted to the governor's residence, inside the citadel.

I now am governor of Malta; true,— 30
But Malta hates me, and, in hating me,
My life's in danger, and what boots it thee,
Poor Barabas, to be the governor,
Whenas thy life shall be at their command?
No, Barabas, this must be looked into;
And since by wrong thou got'st authority,
Maintain it bravely by firm policy,
At least unprofitably lose it not:
For he that liveth in authority,
And neither gets him friends, nor fills his bags, 40
Lives like the ass, that Æsop speaketh of,
That labours with a load of bread and wine,
And leaves it off to snap on thistle-tops:
But Barabas will be more circumspect.
Begin betimes; occasion's bald behind;
Slip not thine opportunity, for fear too late
Thou seek'st for much, but canst not compass it.—
Within here!

    Enter FERNEZE *with a* Guard.

 Fern. My lord?
 Bar. Ay, "lord;" thus slaves will learn. 50
Now, governor;—stand by there, wait within.
           [*Exeunt* Guard.
This is the reason that I sent for thee;
Thou seest thy life and Malta's happiness
Are at my arbitrement; and Barabas
At his discretion may dispose of both;
Now tell me, governor, and plainly too,
What think'st thou shall become of it and thee?
 Fern. This, Barabas; since things are in thy power,

I see no reason but of Malta's wreck,
Nor hope of thee but extreme cruelty; 60
Nor fear I death, nor will I flatter thee.
   Bar. Governor, good words; be not so furious.
'Tis not thy life which can avail me aught;
Yet you do live, and live for me you shall:
And, as for Malta's ruin, think you not
'Twere slender policy for Barabas
To dispossess himself of such a place?
For sith, as once you said, 'tis in this isle,
In Malta here, that I have got my goods,
And in this city still have had success, 70
And now at length am grown your governor,
Yourselves shall see it shall not be forgot:
For, as a friend not known but in distress,
I'll rear up Malta, now remediless.
   Fern. Will Barabas recover Malta's loss?
Will Barabas be good to Christians?
   Bar. What wilt thou give me, governor, to procure
A dissolution of the slavish bands
Wherein the Turk hath yoked your land and you?
What will you give me if I render you 80
The life of Calymath, surprise his men
And in an outhouse of the city shut
His soldiers, till I have consumed 'em all with fire?
What will you give him that procureth this?
   Fern. Do but bring this to pass which thou pretendest,
Deal truly with us as thou intimatest,
And I will send amongst the citizens,
And by my letters privately procure
Great sums of money for thy recompense:
Nay more, do this, and live thou governor still. 90

Bar. Nay, do thou this, Ferneze, and be free;
Governor, I enlarge thee; live with me,
Go walk about the city, see thy friends:
Tush, send not letters to 'em, go thyself,
And let me see what money thou canst make;
Here is my hand that I'll set Malta free:
And thus we cast it: to a solemn feast
I will invite young Selim Calymath,
Where be thou present only to perform
One stratagem that I'll impart to thee,
Wherein no danger shall betide thy life,
And I will warrant Malta free for ever.
   Fern. Here is my hand; believe me, Barabas,
I will be there, and do as thou desirest.
When is the time?
   Bar. Governor, presently:
For Calymath, when he hath viewed the town,
Will take his leave and sail towards Ottoman.
   Fern. Then will I, Barbaras, about this coin,
And bring it with me to thee in the evening.
   Bar. Do so, but fail not; now farewell, Ferneze!—
                                       [*Exit* FERNEZE.
And thus far roundly goes the business:
Thus loving neither, will I live with both,
Making a profit of my policy;
And he from whom my most advantage comes
Shall be my friend.
This is the life we Jews are used to lead;
And reason too, for Christians do the like.
Well, now about effecting this device;
First to surprise great Selim's soldiers,
And then to make provision for the feast.

That at one instant all things may be done:
My policy detests prevention:
To what event my secret purpose drives,
I know; and they shall witness with their lives. [*Exit.*

SCENE IV. — *Outside the City Walls.*

Enter CALYMATH *and* BASSOES.

Caly. Thus have we viewed the city, seen the sack,
And caused the ruins to be new-repaired,
Which with our bombards'[1] shot and basilisks
We rent in sunder at our entry:
And now I see the situation,
And how secure this conquered island stands
Environed with the Mediterranean Sea,
Strong-countermined with other petty isles;
And, toward Calabria, backed by Sicily,
(Where Syracusian Dionysius reigned,)
Two lofty turrets that command the town;
I wonder how it could be conquered thus.

Enter a Messenger.

Mess. From Barabas, Malta's governor, I bring
A message unto mighty Calymath;
Hearing his sovereign was bound for sea,
To sail to Turkey, to great Ottoman,
He humbly would entreat your majesty
To come and see his homely citadel,
And banquet with him ere thou leav'st the isle.

Caly. To banquet with him in his citadel?
I fear me, messenger, to feast my train

[1] Large cannon.

Within a town of war so lately pillaged,
Will be too costly and too troublesome :
Yet would I gladly visit Barabas,
For well has Barabas deserved of us.

  Mess. Selim, for that, thus saith the governor,
That he hath in his store a pearl so big,
So precious, and withal so orient,
As, be it valued but indifferently,
The price thereof will serve to entertain   30·
Selim and all his soldiers for a month ;
Therefore he humbly would entreat your highness
Not to depart till he has feasted you.

  Caly. I cannot feast my men in Malta-walls,
Except he place his tables in the streets.

  Mess. Know, Selim, that there is a monastery
Which standeth as an outhouse to the town ;
There will he banquet them ; but thee at home,
With all thy bassoes and brave followers.

  Caly. Well, tell the governor we grant his suit,   40
We'll in this summer evening feast with him.

  Mess. I shall, my lord.   [*Exit.*

  Caly. And now, bold bassoes, let us to our tents,
And meditate how we may grace us best
To solemnize our governor's great feast.   [*Exeunt.*

Scene V. — *A Street.*

  Enter Ferneze, Knights, *and* Martin del Bosco.

  Fern. In this, my countrymen, be ruled by me,
Have special care that no man sally forth
Till you shall hear a culverin discharged

By him that bears the linstock,[1] kindled thus;
Then issue out and come to rescue me,
For happily I shall be in distress,
Or you releasèd of this servitude.

   1st Knight. Rather than thus to live as Turkish thralls,[2]
What will we not adventure?

   Fern. On then, begone.   10

   Knights. Farewell, grave governor!

      [*Exeunt on one side* Knights *and* MARTIN DEL BOSCO; *on the other* FERNEZE.

SCENE VI. — *A Hall in the Governor's Residence.*

Enter, above, BARABAS, *with a hammer, very busy; and* Carpenters.

   Bar. How stand the cords? How hang these hinges? fast?
Are all the cranes and pulleys sure?

   1st Carp. All fast.

   Bar. Leave nothing loose, all levelled to my mind.
Why now I see that you have art indeed.
There, carpenters, divide that gold amongst you:
                                   [*Gives money.*
Go swill in bowls of sack[3] and muscadine[4]!
Down to the cellar, taste of all my wines.

   1st Carp. We shall, my lord, and thank you.
                                  [*Exeunt* Carpenters.

   Bar. And, if you like them, drink your fill and die: 10
For so I live, perish may all the world!

---

[1] The stick which held the gunner's match.   [2] Slaves.
[3] A dry Spanish wine (Spanish *seco*, dry).
[4] A rich, fragrant wine; written also *muscatel* and *muscadel.*

Now Selim Calymath return me word
That thou wilt come, and I am satisfied.

Enter Messenger.

Now, sirrah, what, will he come?
  Mess. He will; and has commanded all his men
To come ashore, and march through Malta streets,
That thou mayest feast them in thy citadel.
  Bar. Then now are all things as my wish would have 'em,
There wanteth nothing but the governor's pelf,
And see, he brings it. 20

Enter FERNEZE.

Now, governor, the sum.
  Fern. With free consent, a hundred thousand pounds.
  Bar. Pounds say'st thou, governor? well, since it is no
    more,
I'll satisfy myself with that; nay, keep it still,
For if I keep not promise, trust not me.
And, governor, now partake my policy:
First, for his army; they are sent before,
Entered the monastery, and underneath
In several places are field-pieces pitched,
Bombards, whole barrels full of gunpowder 30
That on the sudden shall dissever it,
And batter all the stones about their ears,
Whence none can possibly escape alive.
Now as for Calymath and his consorts,
Here have I made a dainty gallery,
The floor whereof, this cable being cut,
Doth fall asunder; so that it doth sink
Into a deep pit past recovery.

Here, hold that knife (*throws down a knife*), and when
    thou seest he comes,
And with his bassoes shall be blithely set,   40
A warning-piece shall be shot off from the tower,
To give thee knowledge when to cut the cord
And fire the house: say, will not this be brave?
  Fern. O excellent! here, hold thee, Barabas,
I trust thy word, take what I promised thee.
  Bar. No, governor, I'll satisfy thee first,
Thou shalt not live in doubt of anything.
Stand close, for here they come (FERNEZE *retires*). Why,
    is not this
A kingly kind of trade to purchase towns
By treachery and sell 'em by deceit?   50
Now tell me, worldlings, underneath the sun
If greater falsehood ever has been done?

        Enter CALYMATH *and* Bassoes.

  Caly. Come, my companion bassoes; see, I pray,
How busy Barabas is there above
To entertain us in his gallery;
Let us salute him. Save thee, Barabas!
  Bar. Welcome, great Calymath!
  Fern. (*aside*). How the slave jeers at him.
  Bar. Will't please thee, mighty Selim Calymath,
To ascend our homely stairs?   60
  Caly. Ah, Barabas;—
Come, bassoes, ascend.
  Fern. (*coming forward*). Stay, Calymath!
For I will show thee greater courtesy
Than Barabas would have afforded thee.

Knight (*within*). Sound a charge there!
[*A charge sounded within.* FERNEZE *cuts the cord: the floor of the gallery gives way, and* BARABAS *falls into a caldron.*

Enter MARTIN DEL BOSCO *and* Knights.

Caly. How now! what means this?
Bar. Help, help me! Christians, help!
Fern. See, Calymath, this was devised for thee!
Caly. Treason! treason! bassoes, fly! 70
Fern. No, Selim, do not fly;
See his end first, and fly then if thou canst.
Bar. O help me, Selim! help me, Christians!
Governor, why stand you all so pitiless?
Fern. Should I in pity of thy plaints or thee,
Accursèd Barabas, base Jew, relent?
No, thus I'll see thy treachery repaid,
But wish thou hadst behaved thee otherwise.
Bar. You will not help me, then?
Fern. No, villain, no. 80
Bar. And, villains, know you cannot help me now.—
Then, Barabas, breathe forth thy latest hate,
And in the fury of thy torments strive
To end thy life with resolution.
Know, governor, 'twas I that slew thy son;
I framed the challenge that did make them meet:
Know, Calymath, I aimed thy overthrow,
And had I but escaped this stratagem,
I would have brought confusion on you all,
Damned Christian dogs! and Turkish infidels! 90
But now begins the extremity of heat

To pinch me with intolerable pangs:
Die, life! fly, soul! tongue, curse thy fill, and die! [*Dies.*
　Caly. Tell me, you Christians, what doth this portend?
　Fern. This train[1] he laid to have entrapped thy life;
Now, Selim, note the unhallowed deeds of Jews:
Thus he determined to have handled thee,
But I have rather chose to save thy life.
　Caly. Was this the banquet he prepared for us?
Let's hence, lest further mischief be pretended.[2]　　　100
　Fern. Nay, Selim, stay; for since we have thee here,
We will not let thee part so suddenly:
Besides, if we should let thee go, all's one,
For with thy galleys could'st thou not get hence,
Without fresh men to rig and furnish them.
　Caly. Tush, governor, take thou no care for that,
My men are all aboard,
And do attend my coming there by this.
　Fern. Why, heard'st thou not the trumpet sound a charge?
　Caly. Yes, what of that?　　　110
　Fern. Why then the house was fired,
Blown up, and all thy soldiers massacred.
　Caly. O monstrous treason!
　Fern. A Jew's courtesy:
For he that did by treason work our fall,
By treason hath delivered thee to us:
Know, therefore, till thy father hath made good
The ruins done to Malta and to us,
Thou canst not part; for Malta shall be freed,
Or Selim ne'er return to Ottoman.　　　120
　Caly. Nay, rather, Christians, let me go to Turkey,
In person there to meditate[3] your peace;

　　　1 Stratagem.　　2 Intended.　　3 *Query*, mediate.

To keep me here will not advantage you.
    Fern. Content thee, Calymath, here thou must stay,
And live in Malta prisoner; for come all the world
To rescue thee, so will we guard us now,
As sooner shall they drink the ocean dry
Than conquer Malta, or endanger us.
So march away and let due praise be given
Neither to Fate nor Fortune, but to Heaven. [*Exeunt.* 130

II.

THE ALCHEMIST.

By Ben Jonson.

Produced in 1610; dedicated to Lady Mary Wroth, niece of Sir Philip Sidney.

THE ALCHEMIST.[1]

TO THE READER.

IF thou beest more, thou art an understander, and then I trust thee. If thou art one that takest up, and but a pretender, beware of what hands thou receivest thy commodity; for thou wert never more fair in the way to be cozened than in this age, in poetry, especially in plays: wherein now the concupiscence of dances and of antics so reigneth, as to run away from Nature, and be afraid of her, is the only point of Art that tickles the spectators. But how out of purpose and place do I name Art? When the professors are grown so obstinate contemners of it, and presumers on their own naturals, as they are deriders of all diligence that way, and, by simple mocking at the terms, when they understand not the things, think to get off wittily with their ignorance. Nay, they are esteemed the more learned and sufficient for this, by the many, through their excellent vice of judgment. For they commend writers as they do fencers and wrestlers; who, if they come in robustuously, and put for it with a great deal of violence, are received for the braver fellows: when many times their own rudeness is the cause of their disgrace, and a little touch of their adversary gives all that boisterous force the foil. I deny not but that these men, who always seek to do more than enough, may sometime happen on something that is good and great; but very seldom: and when it comes it doth not recompense the rest of their ill. It sticks out, perhaps, and is more eminent, because all is sordid and vile about it; as lights are more discerned in a thick darkness than a faint shadow. I speak not this out of a hope to do good to any man against his will; for I know, if it were put to the question of theirs and mine, the worse would find more suffrages: because the most favour common errors. But I give thee this warning, that there is a great difference between those that, to gain the opinion of copy,[2] utter all they can, however unfitly; and those that use election and a mean. For it is only the disease of the unskilful to think rude things greater than polished, or scattered more numerous than composed.

[1] In a few places in the text of this play I have adopted slight verbal alterations, suggested by Professor Henry Morley.
[2] Reputation of being fertile writers.

DRAMATIS PERSONÆ.

SUBTLE, the Alchemist.
FACE, the Housekeeper.
DOL COMMON, their Colleague.
DAPPER, a Clerk.
DRUGGER, a Tobacco Man.
LOVEWIT, Master of the House.
SIR EPICURE MAMMON, a Knight.

PERTINAX SURLY, a Gamester.
TRIBULATION WHOLESOME, a Pastor of Amsterdam.
ANANIAS, a Deacon there.
KASTRIL, the angry Boy.
DAME PLIANT, his Sister, a Widow.
Neighbours, Officers, Mutes.

SCENE: *London.*

ARGUMENT.

T HE sickness[1] hot, a master quit, for fear,
H is house in town, and left one servant there.
E ase him corrupted, and gave means to know

A cheater and his punk[2]; who now brought low,
L eaving their narrow practice, were become
C ozeners at large; and only wanting some
H ouse to set up, with him they here contract,
E ach for a share, and all begin to act.
M uch company they draw, and much abuse,
I n casting figures,[3] telling fortunes, news,   10
S elling of flies,[4] false putting of the stone,
T ill it, and they, and all in fume are gone.

PROLOGUE.

FORTUNE, that favours fools, these two short hours
  We wish away, both for your sakes and ours,
Judging Spectators; and desire, in place,

[1] Plague.
[2] Coarse woman.
[3] Astrological divination.
[4] Familiar spirits.

To the author justice, to ourselves but grace.
Our scene is London, 'cause we would make known
   No country's mirth is better than our own:
No clime breeds better matter, for your bore,
   Shark, squire, impostor, many persons more,
Whose manners, now called humours, feed the stage;
   And which have still been subject for the rage   10
Or spleen of comic writers. Though this pen
   Did never aim to grieve, but better, men;
Howe'er the age he lives in doth endure
   The vices that she breeds, above their cure.
But when the wholesome remedies are sweet,
   And in their working gain and profit meet,
He hopes to find no spirit so much diseased
   But will with such fair corréctives be pleased:
For here he doth not fear who can apply.
   If there be any that will sit so nigh   20
Unto the stream, to look what it doth run,
   They shall find things they'd think or wish were done;
They are so natural follies, but so shown
   As even the doers may see, and yet not own.

ACT I.

SCENE I.—*A Room in* LOVEWIT'S *House.*

Enter FACE, *in a captain's uniform, with his sword drawn, and* SUBTLE *with a vial, quarrelling, and followed by* DOL COMMON.

  Face. Believe't, I will.
  Sub. Thy worst. I spit at thee.

Dol. Have you your wits? Why, gentlemen, for love ——
Face. Sirrah, I'll strip you ——
Dol. Nay, look ye, sovereign, general, are you madmen?
Sub. Oh, let the wild sheep loose. I'll gum your silks
With good strong water, an you come.
Dol. Will you have
The neighbours hear you? will you betray all?
Hark! I hear somebody. 10
Face. Sirrah ——
Sub. I shall mar
All that the tailor has made, if you approach.
Face. You most notorious whelp, you insolent slave,
Dare you do this?
Sub. Yes, faith; yes, faith.
Face. Why, who
Am I, my mongrel? Who am I?
Sub. I'll tell you,
Since you know not yourself. 20
Face. Speak lower, rogue.
Sub. Yes, you were once (time's not long past) the good,
Honest, plain, livery three pound thrum that kept
Your master's worship's house here in the Friars,
For the vacations ——
Face. Will you be so loud?
Sub. Since, by my means, translated suburb-captain.
Face. By your means, doctor dog!
Sub. Within man's memory,
All this I speak of. 30
Face. Why, I pray you, have I
Been countenanced by you, or you by me?
Do but collect, sir, where I met you first.
Sub. I do not hear well.

Face. Not of this, I think it.
But I shall put you in mind, sir;— at Pie-corner,
Taking your meal of steam in from cooks' stalls,
Where, like the father of hunger, you did walk
Piteously costive, with your pinch'd horn-nose,
And your complexion of the Roman wash,   40
Stuck full of black and melancholic worms,
Like powder corns shot at the artillery yard.
   Sub. I wish you could advance your voice a little.[1]
   Face. When you went pinn'd up in the several rags
You had raked and pick'd from dunghills, before day;
Your feet in mouldy slippers, for your kibes[2]:
A felt of rug,[3] and a thin threaden cloak,
That scarce would cover your no buttocks ——
   Sub. So, sir!
   Face. When all your alchemy and your algebra,   50
Your minerals, vegetals, and animals,
Your conjuring, cozening, and your dozen of trades,
Could not relieve your corps[4] with so much linen
Would make you tinder, but to see a fire,
I gave you countenance, credit for your coals,
Your stills, your glasses, your materials;
Built you a furnace, drew you customers,
Advanced all your black arts; lent you, beside,
A house to practise in ——
   Sub. Your master's house!   60
   Face. Where you have studied the more thriving skill
Of cozening since.
   Sub. Yes, in your master's house.
You and the rats here kept possession.

---

[1] A play on the word *voice*, which is used here for *reputation*.
[2] Chilblains.   [3] Hat of coarse woollen cloth.   [4] Body.

Make it not strange. I know you were one could keep
The buttery-hatch still lock'd, and save the chippings,
Sell the dole beer[1] to aquavitæ men,
The which, together with your Christmas vails[2]
At post-and-pair,[3] your letting out of counters,[4]
Made you a pretty stock, some twenty marks,[5]   70
And gave you credit to converse with cobwebs,
Here, since your mistress' death hath broke up house.
    Face. You might talk softlier, rascal.
    Sub. No, you scarab,
I'll thunder you in pieces : I will teach you
How to beware to tempt a Fury again,
That carries tempest in his hand and voice.
    Face. The place has made you valiant.
    Sub. No, your clothes.—
Thou vermin, have I ta'en thee out of dung,   80
So poor, so wretched, when no living thing
Would keep thee company, but a spider, or worse?
Rais'd thee from brooms, and dust, and watering-pots,
Sublimed thee, and exalted thee, and fix'd thee
In the third region, call'd our state of grace?
Wrought thee to spirit, to quintessence, with pains
Would twice have won me the Philosopher's work !
Put thee in words and fashion, made thee fit
For more than ordinary fellowships?
Giv'n thee thy oaths, thy quarrelling dimensions,   90
Thy rules to cheat at horse-race, cockpit, cards, dice,
Or whatever gallant tincture else?

---

[1] Beer furnished to the poor, from a rich man's buttery.
[2] Perquisites.   [3] A game at cards.
[4] The servant received a small fee for furnishing counters.
[5] A mark was worth 15*s.* 4*d.*

Made thee a second in mine own great art?
And have I this for thanks! Do you rebel,
Do you fly out in the projection?[1]
Would you be gone now?
   Dol. Gentlemen, what mean you?
Will you mar all?
   Sub. Slave, thou hadst no name ——
   Dol. Will you undo yourselves with civil war?   100
   Sub. Never been known, past *equi clibanum*,
The heat of horse-dung, under ground, in cellars,
Or an ale-house darker than deaf John's; been lost
To all mankind but laundresses and tapsters,
Had not I been.
   Dol. Do you know who hears you, sovereign?
   Face. Sirrah ——
   Dol. Nay, general, I thought you were civil.
   Face. I shall turn desperate if you grow thus loud.
   Sub. And hang thyself, I care not.   110
   Face. Hang thee, collier,
And all thy pots and pans, in picture, I will,
Since thou hast moved me ——
   Dol. Oh, this will o'erthrow all.
   Face. Write thee up bawd in Paul's, have all thy tricks,
Of cozening with a hollow coal, dust, scrapings,
Searching for things lost, with a sieve and shears,
Erecting figures in your rows of houses,[2]
And taking in of shadows with a glass,[3]
Told in red letters; and a face cut for thee   120

   [1] That is, fail at the last moment, when success is at hand.
   [2] Each *house*, in astrology, corresponded to one of the twelve signs of the zodiac.
   [3] Method of divination.

Worse than Gamaliel Ratsey's.[1]
  Dol. Are you sound?
Have you your senses, masters?
  Face. I will have
A book, but barely reckoning thy impostures,
Shall prove a true philosopher's stone to printers.
  Sub. Away, you trencher-rascal!
  Face. Out, you dog-leach!
The vomit of all prisons ——
  Dol. Will you be   130
Your own destructions, gentlemen?
  Face. Still spewed out
For lying too heavy on the basket.[2]
  Sub. Cheater!
  Face. Bawd!
  Sub. Cowherd!
  Face. Conjurer!
  Sub. Cut-purse!
  Face. Witch!
  Dol. O me!   140
We are ruin'd, lost! Have you no more regard
To your reputations? Where's your judgment? 'Slight,
Have yet some care of me, of your republic ——
  Face. Away this brach[3]! I'll bring thee, rogue, within
The statute of sorcery, tricesimo tertio
Of Harry the Eighth: ay, and perhaps thy neck
Within a noose, for laundring gold and barbing it.[4]
  Dol. (*snatches* FACE'S *sword*). You'll bring your head
    within a cockscomb, will you?

[1] A noted highwayman, executed at Bedford.
[2] For eating more than your share of the broken victuals sent in a basket to prisoners.
[3] Hunting-dog.   [4] Rolling and clipping gold.

And you, sir, with your menstrue.[1] (*Dashes* SUBTLE'S *vial out
of his hand.*) Gather it up. —
'Sdeath, you abominable pair of stinkards,[2]   150
Leave off your barking, and grow one again,
Or, by the light that shines, I'll cut your throats.
I'll not be made a prey unto the marshal
For ne'er a snarling dog-bolt of you both.
Have you together cozen'd all this while,
And all the world, and shall it now be said
You've made most courteous shift to cozen yourselves?
You will accuse him! you will *bring him in*   [*To* FACE.
Within the statute? Who shall take your word?
A rascal, upstart, apocryphal captain,   160
Whom not a Puritan in Blackfriars[3] will trust
So much as for a feather: and you, too,   [*To* SUBTLE.
Will give the cause, forsooth! you will insult,
And claim a primacy in the divisions!
You must be chief! as if you only had
The powder to project[4] with, and the work
Were not begun out of equality?
The venture tripartite? all things in common?
Without priority? 'Sdeath! you perpetual curs,
Fall to your couples again, and cozen kindly,   170
And heartily, and lovingly, as you should,
And lose not the beginning of a term,
Or, by this hand, I shall grow factious too,

---

[1] The fluid in which alchemists dissolved solid substances.

[2] Mean fellows.

[3] The Puritans, — the term was first current about 1564, — who are so cleverly ridiculed in this play, dwelt in the Blackfriars district in London; they dealt largely in feathers.

[4] The last, twelfth, process in alchemy, when the base metal was to be turned into gold.

And take my part, and quit you.
Face. 'Tis his fault;
He ever murmurs, and objects his pains,
And says, the weight of all lies upon him.
Sub. Why so it does.
Dol. How does it? Do not **we**
Sustain our parts?
Sub. Yes, but they are not **equal.**
Dol. Why, if your part exceed to-day, I hope
Ours may to-morrow match it.
Sub. Ay, they *may.*
Dol. May, murmuring mastiff! Ay, and do. Death on me!
Help me to throttle him.   [*Seizes* Sub. *by the throat.*
Sub. Dorothy! Mistress Dorothy!
'Ods precious, I'll do anything. What do you mean?
Dol. Because o' your fermentation and cibation[1]?
Sub. Not I, by heaven ——
Dol. Your Sol and Luna[2] —— Help me.   [*To* Face.
Sub. Would I were hang'd then! I'll conform myself.
Dol. Will you, sir? Do so then, and quickly: swear.
Sub. What should I swear?
Dol. To leave your faction, sir,
And labour kindly in the common work.
Sub. Let me not breathe if I meant aught beside.

[1] The sixth and seventh processes; *cibation* was the feeding of the matter in preparation with fresh substances; also, supplying what had been wasted by evaporation.

[2] The metals used by alchemists are thus enumerated by Chaucer, in *The Yeoman's Tale:*

"The bodies seven, lo! here hem anone,
Sol gold is, and *Luna* silver we threpe,
Mars yron, *Mercury* quicksilver we clepe,
Saturnus leade, and *Jupiter* is tinne,
And *Venus* copir."

I only used those speeches as a spur
To him.
 Dol. I hope we need no spurs, sir. Do we?
 Face. 'Slid, prove to-day who shall shark best.
 Sub. Agreed.
 Dol. Yes, and work close and friendly.
 Sub. 'Slight, the knot
Shall grow the stronger for this breach, with me.
        [*They shake hands.*
 Dol. Why, so, my good baboons! Shall we go make
A sort of sober, scurvy, precise neighbours,
That scarce have smiled twice since the king came in,
A feast of laughter at our follies? Rascals
Would run themselves from breath to see me ride,
Or you t' have but a hole to thrust your heads in,
For which you should pay ear-rent?[1] No, agree.
And may don Provost ride a feasting long
In his old velvet jerkin and stain'd scarfs,
My noble sovereign and worthy general,
Ere we contribute a new crewel garter
To his most worsted worship.[2]
 Sub. Royal Dol!
Spoken like Claridiana,[3] and thyself.
 Face. For which at supper thou shalt sit in triumph,
And not be styled Dol Common, but Dol Proper,
Dol Singular: the longest cut at night
Shall draw thee for his Doll Particular. [*Bell rings without.*
 Sub. Who's that? One rings. To the window, Dol.
 (*Exit* Dol.) Pray heaven

[1] Refers to the pillory.
[2] This punning on *crewel* and *worsted* was probably venerable even in Jonson's time.
[3] Heroine in *The Mirror of Knighthood.*

The master do not trouble us this quarter.
    Face. Oh, fear not him. While there dies one a week
O' the plague, he's safe from thinking toward London:
Beside, he's busy at his hop-yards now;
I had a letter from him. If he do,
He'll send such word for airing of the house   230
As you shall have sufficient time to quit it:
Though we break up a fortnight 'tis no matter.

          Re-enter DOL.

    Sub. Who is it, Dol?
    Dol. A fine young quodling.[1]
    Face. Oh,
My lawyer's clerk I lighted on last night
In Holborn, at the Dagger.[2] He would have
(I told you of him) a familiar,[3]
To rifle with at horses, and win cups.
    Dol. Oh, let him in.   240
    Sub. Stay. Who shall do't?
    Face. Get you
Your robes on: I will meet him as going out.
    Dol. And what shall I do?
    Face. Not be seen; away!   [*Exit* DOL.
Seem you very reserv'd.
    Sub. Enough.   [*Exit.*
    Face. (*aloud and retiring*). God be wi' you, sir.
I pray you, let him know that I was here:
His name is Dapper. I would gladly have staid, but —— 250
    Dap. (*within*). Captain, I am here.
    Face. Who's that?— He's come, I think, doctor.

---

[1] Slang; "young quill-driver."   [2] A low gambling-hell.
[3] A spirit who waited upon magicians.

Enter DAPPER.

Good faith, sir, I was going away.
  Dap. In truth,
I am very sorry, captain.
  Face. But I thought
Sure I should meet you.
  Dap. Ay, I am very glad.
I had a scurvy writ or two to make,
And I had lent my watch[1] last night to one   260
That dines to-day at the sheriff's, and so was robb'd
Of my pastime.
  Re-enter SUBTLE, *in his velvet cap and gown.*
Is this the cunning-man?
  Face. This is his worship.
  Dap. Is he a doctor?
  Face. Yes.
  Dop. And you have broke with him, captain?
  Face. Ay.
  Dap. And how?
  Face. Faith, he does make the matter, sir, so dainty   270
I know not what to say.
  Dap. Not so, good captain.
  Face. Would I were fairly rid of it, believe me.
  Dap. Nay, now you grieve me, sir. Why should you wish so? I dare assure you, I'll not be ungrateful.
  Face. I cannot think you will, sir. But the law
Is such a thing — and then he says, Read's matter[2]
Falling so lately —

---

[1] Watches were dear and scarce: *Dapper* pretends to a luxury above his condition.

[2] Simon Read, convicted of practising the black art, had been recently pardoned by James I.

Dap. Read ! he was an ass,
And dealt, sir, with a fool.   280
 Face. It was a clerk, sir.
 Dap. A clerk !
 Face. Nay, hear me, sir, you know the law
Better, I think ——
 Dap. I should, sir, and the danger :
You know, I showed the statute to you.
 Face. You did so.
 Dap. And will I tell then ! By this hand of flesh,
Would it might never write good court-hand more,
If I discover. What do you think of me,   290
That I am a chiaus[1]?
 Face. What's that?
 Dap. The Turk was here.
As one would say, do you think I am a Turk?
 Face. I'll tell the doctor so.
 Dap. Do, good sweet captain.
 Face. Come, noble doctor, pray thee, let's prevail;
This is the gentleman, and he's no chiaus.
 Sub. Captain, I have return'd you all my answer.
I would do much, sir, for your love ; but this   300
I neither may nor can.
 Face. Tut, do not say so.
You deal now with a noble fellow, doctor,
One that will thank you richly, and he is no chiaus.
Let that, sir, move you.
 Sub. Pray you, forbear——
 Face. He has

---

[1] A cheat. A Turkish *chiaus*, or interpreter, defrauded, in 1609, some Turkish merchants in England out of £4000: the fraud was famous at the time.

Four angels here.[1]
 Sub. You do me wrong, good sir.
 Face. Doctor, wherein? to tempt you with these spirits?
 Sub. To tempt my art and love, sir, to my peril.   311
'Fore heaven, I scarce can think you are my friend,
That so would draw me to apparent danger.
 Face. I draw you! A horse draw you, and a halter,
You, and your flies together ——
 Dap. Nay, good captain.
 Face. That know no difference of men.
 Sub. Good words, sir.
 Face. Good deeds, sir, Dr. Dogs-meat. 'Slight, I bring you
No cheating Clim o' the Cloughs,[2] or Claribels,   320
That look as big as five-and-fifty, and flush[3];
And spit out secrets like hot custard ——
 Dap. Captain!
 Face. Nor any melancholic under-scribe,
Shall tell the vicar, but a special gentle,
That is the heir to forty marks a year,
Consorts with the small poets of the time,
Is the sole hope of his old grandmother;
That knows the law, and writes you six fair hands,
Is a fine clerk, and has his cyphering perfect,   330
Will take his oath o' the Greek Testament,
If need be, in his pocket; and can court
His mistress out of Ovid.
 Dap. Nay, dear captain ——
 Face. Did you not tell me so?
 Dap. Yes; but I'd have you

[1] English gold coin, worth ten shillings.
[2] A North-country archer, often mentioned in the Robin Hood ballads.
[3] The highest counts at primero, a game of cards.

Use Master Doctor with some more respect.
　Face. Hang him, proud stag, with his broad velvet
　　head! ——
But for your sake I'd choke ere I would change
An article of breath with such a puckfist[1]:　　　340
Come, let's be gone.　　　　　　　　　　　[*Going.*
　Sub. Pray you, let me speak with you.
　Dap. His worship calls you, captain.
　Face. I am sorry
I e'er embark'd myself in such a business.
　Dap. Nay, good sir; he did call you.
　Face. Will he take then?
　Sub. First, hear me ——
　Face. Not a syllable, 'less you take.
　Sub. Pray you, sir ——　　　　　　　　350
　Face. Upon no terms, but an *assumpsit.*[2]
　Sub. Your humour must be law.
　　　　　　　　　　　[*He takes the four angels.*
　Face. Why, now, sir, talk.
Now I dare hear you with mine honour.　Speak.
So may this gentleman too.
　Sub. Why, sir ——　　　[*Offering to whisper* FACE.
　Face. No whispering.
　Sub. 'Fore heaven, you do not apprehend the loss
You do yourself in this.
　Face. Wherein? for what?　　　　　　　360
　Sub. Marry, to be so importunate for one
That when he has it, will undo you all;
He'll win up all the money in the town.

　　[1] Puff-ball, term of reproach.
　　[2] A voluntary promise, by word of mouth, to perform or pay anything to another.

Face. How!
Sub. Yes, and blow up gamester after gamester,
As they do crackers in a puppet play.
If I do give him a familiar,
Give you him all you play for; never set him:[1]
For he will have it.
   Face. You are mistaken, doctor. 370
Why, he does ask one but for cups and horses
A rifling fly; none of your great familiars.
   Dap. Yes, captain, I would have it for all games.
   Sub. I told you so.
   Face. (*taking* Dap. *aside*). 'Slight, that is a new business!
I understood you, a tame bird, to fly
Twice in a term, or so, on Friday nights,
When you had left the office, for a nag
Of forty or fifty shillings.
   Dap. Ay, 'tis true, sir; 380
But I do think now I shall leave the law,
And therefore——
   Face. Why, this changes quite the case.
Do you think that I dare move him?
   Dap. If you please, sir;
All's one to him, I see.
   Face. What! for that money?
I cannot with my conscience; nor should you
Make the request, methinks.
   Dap. No, sir; I mean 390
To add consideration.
   Face. Why, then, sir,
I'll try. (*Goes to* Subtle.) Say that it were for all games, doctor?

[1] Gamble with, lay a stake.

Sub. I say then, not a mouth shall eat for him
At any ordinary, but on the score,
That is a gaming mouth, conceive me.
    Face. Indeed!
    Sub. He'll draw you all the treasure of the realm,
If it be set him.
    Face. Speak you this from art?   400
    Sub. Ay, sir, and reason too, the ground of art.
He is of the only best complexion
The Queen of Fairy loves.
    Face. What! Is he?
    Sub. Peace.
He'll overhear you. Sir, should she but see him——
    Face. What?
    Sub. Do not you tell him.
    Face. Will he win at cards too?
    Sub. The spirits of dead Holland, living Isaac,[1]   410
You'd swear were in him; such a vigorous luck
As cannot be resisted. 'Slight, he'll put
Six of your gallants to a cloke, indeed.[2]
    Face. A strange success, that some man shall be born to.
    Sub. He hears you, man——
    Dap. Sir, I'll not be ungrateful!
    Face. Faith, I have confidence in his good nature:
You hear, he says he will not be ungrateful.
    Sub. Why, as you please; my venture follows yours.
    Face. Troth, do it, doctor; think him trusty, and make
        him.   420
He may make us both happy in a hour;
Win some five thousand pound, and send us two on't.
    Dap. Believe it, and I will, sir.

[1] Two adepts in alchemy at that period.   [2] Strip them.

Face. And you shall, sir.   [*Takes him aside.*
You have heard all?
    Dap. No, what was't?   Nothing, I, sir.
    Face. Nothing!
    Dap. A little, sir.
    Face. Well, a rare star
Reigned at your birth.   430
    Dap. At mine, sir! No.
    Face. The doctor
Swears that you are ——
    Sub. Nay, captain, you'll tell all now.
    Face. Allied to the Queen of Fairy.
    Dap. Who? that I am?
Believe it no such matter ——
    Face. Yes, and that
You were were born with a caul on your head.[1]
    Dap. Who says so?   440
    Face. Come,
You know it well enough, though you dissemble it.
    Dap. I' fac, I do not: you are mistaken.
    Face. How!
Swear by your fac?[2] And in a thing so known
Unto the doctor? How shall we, sir, trust you
In the other matter? can we ever think,
When you have won five or six thousand pound,
You'll send us shares in't, by this rate?
    Dap. By Jove, sir,   450
I'll win ten thousand pound, and send you half.
I' fac's no oath.
    Sub. No, no; he did but jest.

[1] The superstitious regarded this as a good omen, conferring power of second sight.
[2] A hit at the Puritans, who avoided oaths.

Face. Go to. Go thank the doctor: he's your friend,
To take it so.
    Dap. I thank his worship.
    Face. So!
Another angel.
    Dap. Must I?
    Face. Must you! 'Slight,   460
What else is thanks? Will you be trivial?—Doctor,
                  [DAPPER *gives him the money.*
When must he come for his familiar?
    Dap. Shall I not have it with me?
    Sub. Oh, good sir!
There must a world of ceremonies pass;
You must be bath'd and fumigated first:
Besides, the Queen of Fairy does not rise
Till it be noon.
    Face. Not, if she danced, to-night.
    Sub. And she must bless it.   470
    Face. Did you never see
Her royal grace yet?
    Dap. Whom?
    Face. Your aunt of Fairy?
    Sub. Not since she kissed him in the cradle, captain;
I can resolve you that.
    Face. Well, see her grace,
Whate'er it cost you, for a thing that I know.
It will be somewhat hard to compass; but
However, see her. You are made, believe it,   480
If you can see her. Her grace is a lone woman,
And very rich; and if she take a fancy,
She will do strange things. See her at any hand.
'Slid, she may hap to leave you all she has:

It is the doctor's fear.
 Dap. How will't be done, then?
 Face. Let me alone, take you no thought. Do you
But say to me, Captain, I'll see her grace.
 Dap. Captain, I'll see her grace.
 Face. Enough.   [*Knocking within.* 490
 Sub. Who's there?
Anon. (*Aside to* FACE.) Conduct him forth by the back way.
Sir, against one o'clock prepare yourself,
Till when you must be fasting; only take
Three drops of vinegar in at your nose,
Two at your mouth, and one at either ear;
Then bathe your fingers' ends and wash your eyes,
To sharpen your five senses, and cry *hum*
Thrice, and then *buz*,[1] as often; and then come. [*Exit.*
 Face. Can you remember this?   500
 Dap. I warrant you.
 Face. Well then away. It is but your bestowing
Some twenty nobles[2] 'mong her grace's servants,
And put on a clean shirt: you do not know
What grace her grace may do you in clean linen.[3]
      [*Exeunt* FACE *and* DAPPER.
 Sub. (*within*). Come in! Good wives, I pray you forbear
  me now;
Troth I can do you no good till afternoon.

   Re-enters, followed by DRUGGER.

What is your name, say you — Abel Drugger?
 Drug. Yes, sir.
 Sub. A seller of tobacco[4]?   510

---

[1] Words used in incantations.
[2] A noble was worth 6s. 8d.   [3] The fairies insisted on cleanliness.
[4] Tobacco was introduced into England before 1580.

Drug. Yes, sir.
Sub. Umph!
Free of the grocers[1]?
Drug. Ay, an't please you.
Sub. Well ——
Your business, Abel?
Drug. This, an't please your worship:
I am a young beginner, and am building
Of a new shop, an't like your worship, just
At corner of a street: — Here is the plot[2] on't — 520
And I would know by art, sir, of your worship,
Which way I should make my door, by necromancy,
And where my shelves: and which should be for boxes,
And which for pots. I would be glad to thrive, sir:
And I was wish'd[3] to your worship by a gentleman,
One Captain Face, that says you know men's planets,
And their good angels, and their bad.
Sub. I do.
If I do see them ——

Re-enter FACE.

Face. What! my honest Abel? 530
Thou art well met here.
Drug. Troth, sir, I was speaking,
Just as your worship came here, of your worship:
I pray you, speak for me to Master Doctor.
Face. He shall do anything. — Doctor, do you hear?
This is my friend, Abel, an honest fellow;
He lets me have good tobacco, and he does not
Sophisticate it with sack-lees or oil,
Nor washes it in muscadel and grains,

[1] Belonging to the grocers' guild.   [2] Plan.   [3] Recommended.

Nor buries it in gravel underground, 540
Wrapp'd up in greasy leather or sour clouts;
But keeps it in fine lily pots, that, open'd,
Smell like conserve of roses or French beans.
He has his maple block, his silver tongs,
Winchester pipes, and fire of juniper:[1]
A neat, spruce, honest fellow, and no goldsmith.[2]
   Sub. He is a fortunate fellow, that I am sure on.
   Face. Already, sir, have you found it? Lo thee, Abel!
   Sub. And in right way toward riches——
   Face. Sir! 550
   Sub. This summer
He will be of the clothing of his company,[3]
And next spring call'd to the scarlet;[4] spend what he can.
   Face. What, and so little beard?
   Sub. Sir, you must think
He may have a receipt to make hair come:
But he'll be wise, preserve his youth, and fine for't;
His fortune looks for him another way.
   Face. 'Slid, doctor, how canst thou know this so soon?
I am amused at that! 560
   Sub. By a rule, captain,
In metoposcopy,[5] which I do work by:
A certain star in the forehead, which you see not.
Your chestnut or your olive-colour'd face
Does never fail; and your long ear doth promise.
I knew't by certain spots, too, in his teeth,
And on the nail of his mercurial finger.

---

[1] These were to be found in every well-appointed tobacconist's **shop**: the weed was shredded on the *maple block;* the *tongs* held the live **coal**, which was of *juniper*, whose coals burned a long time.

[2] Usurer.   [3] Livery of the grocers.   [4] Be made sheriff

[5] Fortune-telling by examining the countenance.

Face. Which finger's that?
Sub. His little finger. Look.
You were born upon a Wednesday. 570
Drug. Yes, indeed, sir.
Sub. The thumb, in chiromancy, we give Venus;
The fore-finger to Jove; the midst to Saturn;
The ring to Sol; the least to Mercury,
Who was the lord, sir, of his horoscope,
His house of life being Libra; which fore-showed
He should be a merchant, and should trade with balance.
Face. Why, this is strange! Is it not, honest Nab?
Sub. There is a ship now coming from Ormus
That shall yield him such a commodity 580
Of drugs. This is the west, and this the south?
[*Pointing to the plan.*
Drug. Yes, sir.
Sub. And those are your two sides?
Drug. Ay, sir.
Sub. Make me your door, then, south; your broad side, west:
And on the east side of your shop, aloft,
Write Mathlai, Tarmiel, and Baraborat;
Upon the north part, Rael, Velel, Thiel.
They are the names of those mercurial spirits
That do fright flies[1] from boxes. 590
Drug. Yes, sir.
Sub. And
Beneath your threshold bury me a loadstone
To draw in gallants that wear spurs: the rest,
They'll seem to follow.
Face. That's a secret, Nab!

[1] Familiar spirits.

Sub. And on your stall, a puppet,[1] with a vice
And a court-fucus[2] to call city-dames:
You shall deal much with minerals.
  Drug. Sir, I have   600
At home, already——
  Sub. Ay, I know you have arsenic,
Vitriol, sal-tartar, argaile, alkali,
Cinoper: I know all. — This fellow, captain,
Will come, in time, to be a great distiller,
And give assay — I will not say directly,
But very fair — at the philosopher's stone.
  Face. Why, how now, Abel! is this true?
  Drug. (aside to FACE). Good captain,
What must I give?   610
  Face. Nay, I'll not counsel thee.
Thou hear'st what wealth—(he says, spend what thou
    canst)—
Thou'rt like to come to.
  Drug. I would gi' him a crown.
  Face. A crown! and toward such a fortune? Heart,
Thou shalt rather gi' him thy shop. No gold about thee?
  Drug. Yes, I have a portague[3] I have kept this half-year.
  Face. Out on thee, Nab! 'Slight, there was such an offer —
Shalt keep't no longer, I'll give't him for thee. Doctor,
Nab prays your worship to drink this, and swears   620
He will appear more grateful as your skill
Does raise him in the world.
  Drug. I would entreat
Another favour of his worship.
  Face. What is't, Nab?

---
[1] In the old morality plays a puppet was so dressed.
[2] Paint for the face.   [3] A Portuguese gold coin worth £3 12s.

Drug. But to look over, sir, my almanac,
And cross out my ill days, that I may neither
Bargain nor trust upon them.[1]
    Face. That he shall, Nab;
Leave it, it shall be done 'gainst afternoon.   630
    Sub. And a direction for his shelves.
    Face. Now, Nab,
Art thou well pleased, Nab?
    Drug. 'Thank, sir, both your worships.
    Face. Away. —   [*Exit* DRUGGER.
Why, now, you smoky persecutor of nature!
Now do you see that something's to be done
Beside your beech-coal and your corsive waters,
Your crosslets, crucibles, and cucurbites[2]?
You must have stuff brought home to you, to work on: 640
And yet you think I am at no expense
In searching out these veins, then following them,
Then trying them out. 'Fore God, my intelligence
Costs me more money than my share oft comes to,
In these rare works.
    Sub. You are pleasant, sir.

                 Re-enter DOL.

                       How now!
What says my Dainty Dolkin?
    Dol. Yonder fishwife
Will not away. And there's your giantess,
Come out of Lambeth.   650
    Sub. Heart, I cannot speak with them.
    Dol. Not afore night, I have told them in a voice,

   [2] In the almanacs of that period were set down the days propitious and unpropitious for business.
   [3] A gourd-shaped vessel for distilling.

Thorough the trunk, like one of your familiars.
But I have spied Sir Epicure Mammon——
  Sub. Where?
  Dol. Coming along, at far end of the lane,
Slow of his feet, but earnest of his tongue
To one that's with him.
  Sub. Face, go you, and shift.   [*Exit* FACE.
Dol, you must presently make ready too.   660
  Dol. Why, what's the matter?
  Sub. Oh, I did look for him
With the sun's rising: marvel he could sleep;
This is the day I am to perfect for him
The magisterium, our great work, the stone;
And yield it, made, into his hands: of which
He has this month talk'd as he were possess'd.
And now he's dealing pieces on't away.—
Methinks I see him entering ordinaries,
Dispensing for the pox and plaguy houses,   670
Reaching his dose, walking Moorfields for lepers,
And offering citizens' wives pomander bracelets.[1]
As his preservative, made of the elixir;
Searching the spital, to make old bones young;
And the highways for beggars to make rich ·
I see no end of his labours. He will make
Nature asham'd of her long sleep: when art,
Who's but a step-dame, shall do more than she,
In her best love to mankind, ever could:
If his dream lasts, he'll turn the age to gold. [*Exeunt.* 680

[1] A ball, or small box, of perfumes was carried in the pocket, or worn on a girdle or bracelet (French *pomme d'ambre*).

ACT II.

SCENE I. — *An Outer Room in* LOVEWIT'S *House.*

Enter SIR EPICURE MAMMON *and* SURLY.

Mam. Come on, sir. Now, you set your foot on shore
In *Novo Orbe;* here's the rich Peru :
And there within, sir, are the golden mines,
Great Solomon's Ophir ! he was sailing to't,
Three years, but we have reached it in ten months.
This is the day wherein, to all my friends,
I will pronounce the happy word, BE RICH ;
THIS DAY YOU SHALL BE SPECTATISSIMI.[1]
You shall no more deal with the hollow die
Or the frail card.[2] No more be at charge of keeping   10
The house of call for the young heir. No more
Shall thirst of satin, or the covetous hunger
Of velvet entrails for a rude-spun cloak,[3]
To be display'd at Madam Augusta's, make
The sons of Sword and Hazard fall before
The golden calf, and on their knees, whole nights,
Commit idolatry with wine and trumpets :
Or go a feasting, after drum and ensign.
No more of this. You shall start up young viceroys,
And unto thee I speak it first, BE RICH.   20
Where is my Subtle, there? Within, ho !
  Face (within). Sir, he'll come to you by and by.
  Mam. That is his fire-drake,

---

[1] Most illustrious.   [2] Used by dishonest gamblers.
[3] Cloaks of which the lining was richer than the material.

His Lungs,[1] his Zephyrus, he that puffs his coals,
Till he firk[2] nature up, in her own centre.
You are not faithful, sir. This night I'll change
All that is metal, in my house, to gold:
And early in the morning will I send
To all the plumbers and the pewterers,
And buy their tin and lead up; and to Lothbury[3]   30
For all the copper.
   Sur. What, and turn that too?
   Mam. Yes, and I'll purchase Devonshire and Cornwall,[4]
And make them perfect Indies! You admire now?
   Sur. No, faith.
   Mam. But when you see th' effects of the Great Medicine,
Of which one part projected on a hundred
Of Mercury, or Venus, or the moon,
Shall turn it to as many of the sun;
Nay, to a thousand, so *ad infinitum:*   40
You will believe me.
   Sur. Yes, when I see't I will.
But if my eyes do cozen me so, and I
Giving them no occasion, sure I'll have
A crow shall pluck them out next day.
   Mam. Ha! why?
Do you think I fable with you? I assure you,
He that has once the flower of the sun,
The perfect ruby, which we call elixir,

---

[1] The apprentice to an alchemist was called **Lungs**, because he blew the bellows.

[2] Stir, strike (Latin *ferio*).

[3] Stow, in his account of London (p. 287), says that Lothbury is "inhabited chiefly by founders, that cast candlesticks, chafing-dishes, spice mortars, and such-like copper works."

[4] That is, convert their minerals to gold.

Not only can do that, but by its virtue 50
Can confer honour, love, respect, long life;
Give safety, valour, yea, and victory,
To whom he will. In eight and twenty days,
I'll make an old man of fourscore a child.
    Sur. No doubt; he's that already.
    Mam. Nay, I mean,
Restore his years, renew him, like an eagle,
To the fifth age; make him get sons and daughters,
Young giants; as our philosophers have done,
The ancient patriarchs, afore the flood, 60
But taking, once a week, on a knife's point,
The quantity of a grain of mustard of it;
Become stout Marses, and beget young Cupids.
    Sur. The decay'd vestals of Pickt-hatch[1] would thank you,
That keep the fire alive there.
    Mam. 'Tis the secret
Of nature naturized[2] 'gainst all infections,
Cures all diseases coming of all causes;
A month's grief in a day, a year's in twelve;
And of what age soever, in a month: 70
Past all the doses of your drugging doctors.
I'll undertake, withal, to fright the plague[3]
Out of the kingdom in three months.
    Sur. And I'll

---

[1] A place of vile repute (in Trumbull Street, Cow Cross, Clerkenwell), where attacks of bullies made a pickt-hatch, or a half-door armed with spikes, a necessary defence. — *R. G. White.* Cf. *Merry Wives of Windsor*, ii, 2.

[2] The Schoolmen distinguished between *Natura naturans,* God the Creator, and *natura naturata,* the universe created.

[3] There had been a severe plague in 1602, and the theatres had been closed.

Be bound, the players shall sing your praises then,
Without their poets.
 Mam. Sir, I'll do't. Meantime,
I'll give away so much unto my man
Shall serve the whole city with preservative
Weekly; each house his dose, and at the rate —— 80
 Sur. As he that built the waterwork[1] does with water?
 Mam. You are incredulous.
 Sur. Faith, I have a humour
I would not willingly be gull'd. Your stone
Cannot transmute me.
 Mam. Pertinax Surly,
Will you believe antiquity? records?
I'll show you a book where Moses and his sister,
And Solomon have written of the art;[2]
Ay, and a treatise penn'd by Adam —— 90
 Sur. How!
 Mam. Of the philosopher's stone, and in High Dutch.
 Sur. Did Adam write, sir, in High Dutch?
 Mam. He did;[3]
Which proves it was the primitive tongue.
 Sur. What paper?
 Mam. On cedar board.
 Sur. Oh, that indeed, they say
Will last 'gainst worms.
 Mam. 'Tis like your Irish wood 100
'Gainst cobwebs. I have a piece of Jason's fleece too,
Which was no other than a book of alchemy,
Writ in large sheepskin, a good fat ram-vellum.

  [1] Bulmer constructed waterworks for London in 1595.
  [2] Fabricius, in a work on writers on chemistry, included these.
  [3] This absurdity was affirmed by Goropius Becanus.

Such was Pythagoras' thigh, Pandora's tub,
And all that fable of Medea's charms,
The manner of our work; the bulls, our furnace,
Still breathing fire; our argent-vive, the dragon:
The dragon's teeth, mercury sublimate,
That keeps the whiteness, hardness, and the biting;
And they are gather'd into Jason's helm, 110
The alembic, and then sow'd in Mars his field,
And thence sublimed so often, till they're fix'd.
Both this, the Hesperian garden, Cadmus' story,
Jove's shower, the boon of Midas, Argus' eyes,
Boccace his Demogorgon, thousands more,
All abstract riddles of our stone.—

Enter FACE *as a Servant.*

How now!
Do we succeed? Is our day come? and holds it?
   Face. The evening will set red upon you, sir;
You have colour for it, crimson[1]: the red ferment
Has done his office; three hours hence prepare you 120
To see projection.
   Mam. Pertinax, my Surly,
Again I say to thee aloud, Be rich.
This day thou shalt have ingots; and to-morrow
Give lords th' affront.[2]—Is it, my Zephyrus, right?
Blushes the bolt's head?
   Face. Aye.
   Mam. My only care is,

---

[1] Crimson was the color reached in the last stage before the base metal was projected.

[2] Meet, and look in the face.

Where to get stuff enough now to project on;
This town will not half serve me.
 Face. No, sir! Buy
The covering off o' churches.
 Mam. That's true.
 Face. Yes.
Let them stand bare, as do their auditory;
Or cap them, new, with shingles.
 Mam. No, good thatch:
Thatch will lie light upon the rafters, Lungs. —
Lungs, I will manumit thee from the furnace.
I will restore thee thy complexion, Puff,
Lost in the embers; and repair this brain,
Hurt with the fume o' the metals.
 Face. I have blown, sir,
Hard for your worship; thrown by many a coal,
When 'twas not beech[1]; weigh'd those I put in, just,
To keep your heat still even; these bleared eyes
Have waked to read your several colours, sir,
Of the pale citron, the green lion, the crow,
The peacock's tail, the plumed swan.[2]
 Mam. And, lastly,
Thou hast descried the flower, the sanguis agni?
 Face. Yes, sir.
 Mam. Where's master?
 Face. At his prayers, sir, he;
Good man, he's doing his devotions
For the success.
 Mam. Lungs, I will set a period
To all thy labours; thou shalt be the master

[1] Alchemists always used charcoal made from beechwood.
[2] Alchemists attributed peculiar virtues to these.

Of my seraglio.
    Face. Good, sir. 160
    Mam. For I do mean
To have a list of wives and concubines
Equal with Solomon, who had the stone
Alike with me; and I will make me a back
With the elixir, tough as Hercules.
Thou art sure thou saw'st it blood?[1]
    Face. Both blood and spirit, sir.
    Mam. I will have all my beds blown up, not stuft:
Down is too hard: and then, mine oval room
Fill'd with such pictures as Tiberius took 170
From Elephantis, and dull Aretine
But coldly imitated. Then, my glasses
Cut in more subtle angles, to disperse
And multiply the figures, as I walk.
My mists of perfume, vapoured 'bout the room,
To lose ourselves in; and my baths, like pits
To fall into; from whence we will come forth,
And roll us dry in gossamer and roses. —
Is it arrived at ruby?[1]—Where I spy
A wealthy citizen, or a rich lawyer, 180
Have a sublimed pure wife, unto that fellow
I'll send a thousand pound to make her mine.
    Face. And I shall carry it?
    Mam. No. I'll have no aids,[2]

---

[1] The propitious color.

[2] "The judgment is perfectly overwhelmed by the torrent of images, words, and book-knowledge with which Mammon confounds and stuns his incredulous hearer. They come pouring out like the successive strokes of Nilus. They 'doubly redouble strokes upon the foe.' Description outstrides proof. We are made to believe effects before we have testimony for their causes, as a lively description of the joys of heaven sometimes passes

But fathers and mothers; they will do it best,
Best of all others.   And my flatterers
Shall be the pure and gravest of divines
That I can get for money.   My mere fools,
Eloquent burgesses; and then my poets,   190
The same that writ so subtly of foul wind,
Whom I will entertain still for that subject.
The few that would give out themselves to be
Court and town rakes, and everywhere belie
Ladies who are known most innocent for them,
Those will I beg to make me eunuchs of;
And they shall fan me with ten ostrich tails
Apiece, made in a plume to gather wind.
We will be brave, Puff, now we have the med'cine.
My meat shall all come in in Indian shells,
Dishes of agate set in gold, and studded   200
With emeralds, sapphires, hyacinths and rubies.
The tongues of carps, dormice, and camels' heels,
Boiled in the spirit of Sol and dissolv'd pearl,
Apicius' diet, 'gainst the epilepsy:
And I will eat these broths with spoons of amber,[1]
Headed with diamond and carbuncle.

for an argument to prove the existence of such a place. If there be no one image which rises to the height of the sublime, yet the confluence and assemblage of them all produce an effect equal to the grandest poetry. Xerxes's army, that drank up whole rivers from their numbers, may stand for single Achilles. *Epicure Mammon* is the most determined offspring of the author. It has the whole 'matter and copy of the father, eye, nose, lip, and trick of his frown.' It is just such a swaggerer as contemporaries have described Ben to be. Mammon is arrogant pretension personified. What a 'tow'ring bravery' there is in his sensuality! He affects no pleasure under a sultan. It is as if 'Egypt with Assyria strove in luxury.'" — *Charles Lamb.*

[1] Spoons then had rich ornaments set in them.

My foot-boy shall eat pheasants, calvered[1] salmons,
Knots,[2] godwits,[2] lampreys : I myself will have
The beards of barbels served instead of salads ;
Oiled mushrooms, and the swelling unctuous paps   210
Of a fat pregnant sow, newly cut off,
Drest with an exquisite and poignant sauce ;
For which I'll say unto my cook, *There's gold:
Go forth, and be a knight.*[3]
    Face. Sir, I'll go look
A little how it heightens.   [*Exit.*
    Mam. Do. — My shirts
I'll have of taffeta-sarsnet, soft and light
As cobwebs ; and for all my other raiment,
It shall be such as might provoke the Persian,   220
Were he to teach the world riot anew.
My gloves of fishes' and birds' skins, perfumed
With gums of paradise and eastern air ——
    Sur. And do you think to have the stone with this?
    Mam. No, I do think t' have all this with the stone.
    Sur. Why, I have heard he must be *homo frugi*,
A pious, holy, and religious man,
One free from mortal sin, a very virgin.
    Mam. That makes it, sir ; he is so : but I buy it ;
My venture brings it me. He, honest wretch,   230
A notable, superstitious, good soul,
Has worn his knees bare and his slippers bald
With prayer and fasting for it : and, sir, let him
Do it alone, for me, still. Here he comes.

    [1] Cut in slices. See Walton's *Complete Angler.*
    [2] These were birds of the snipe species.
    [3] A hit at the recent creation of a large batch of knights by James I, at his accession to the throne in 1603.

Not a profane word afore him : 'tis poison. —

Enter SUBTLE.

Good-morrow, father.
 Sub. Gentle son, good-morrow.
And to your friend there. What is he, is with you?
 Mam. An heretic, that I did bring along,
In hope, sir, to convert him.   240
 Sub. Son, I doubt
You are covetous, that thus you meet your time
In the just point : prevent your day at morning.[1]
This argues something worthy of a fear
Of importune and carnal appetite.
Take heed you do not cause the blessing leave you,
With your ungovern'd haste. I should be sorry
To see my labours, now even at perfection,
Got by long watching and large patience,
Not prosper where my love and zeal hath placed them. 250
Which (heaven I call to witness, with yourself,
To whom I have poured my thoughts) in all my ends
Have look'd no way but unto public good,
To pious uses, and dear charity,
Now grown a prodigy with men. Wherein
If you, my son, should now prevaricate,
And to your own particular lusts employ
So great and catholic a bliss, be sure
A curse will follow, yea, and overtake
Your subtle and most secret ways.   260
 Mam. I know, sir ;
You shall not need to fear me : I but come
To have you confute this gentleman.

[1] Anticipate.

THE ALCHEMIST. [ACT II.

Sur. Who is,
Indeed, sir, somewhat costive of belief
Toward your stone ; would not be gulled.
Sub. Well, son,
All that I can convince him in is this,
The WORK IS DONE, bright Sol is in his robe.
We have a medicine of the triple soul, 270
The glorified spirit. Thanks be to heaven,
And make us worthy of it ! — 𝔈len Spiegel ![1]
Face (*within*). Anon, sir.
Sub. Look well to the register.
And let your heat still lessen by degrees,
To the aludels.[2]
Face (*within*). Yes, sir.
Sub. Did you look
O' the bolt's head[3] yet?
Face (*within*). Which? On D, sir? 280
Sub. Ay ;
What's the complexion?
Face (*within*). Whitish.
Sub. Infuse vinegar,
To draw his volatile substance and his tincture :
And let the water in glass E be filter'd,
And put into the gripe's-egg.[4] Lute him well,
And leave him closed in balneo.[5]
Face (*within*). I will, sir.

[1] A notorious rogue, lived in Saxony about 1480. The words mean *Owl Glass.*
[2] Subliming pots without bottoms, fitted into each other without luting.
[3] A long-necked vessel, conical in shape.
[4] A vessel shaped like a vulture's egg.
[5] *Balneum* means bath ; in alchemy, to heat a vessel by immersing it in hot water or sand.

Sur. What a brave language here is ! Next to canting. 290
Sub. I have another work, you never saw, son,
That three days since passed the philosopher's wheel [1]
In the lent [2] heat of Athanor, and's become
Sulphur of Nature.[3]
    Mam. But 'tis for me ?
    Sub. What need you ?
You have enough in that is perfect.
    Mam. Oh, but ——
    Sub. Why, this is covetise !
    Mam. No, I assure you, 300
I shall employ it all in pious uses,
Founding of colleges and grammar schools,
Marrying young virgins, building hospitals,
And now and then a church.

Re-enter FACE.

    Sub. How now !
    Face. Sir, please you,
Shall I not change the filter ?
    Sub. Marry, yes ;
And bring me the complexion of glass B. [*Exit* FACE.
    Mam. Have you another ? 310
    Sub. Yes, son ; were I assured
Your piety were firm, we would not want
The means to glorify it ; but I hope the best. —
I mean to tinct C in sand-heat to-morrow,
And give him imbibition.
    Mam. Of white oil ?

---

[1] To have passed this was a favorable sign.
[2] Slow.   [3] Digesting furnace.

Sub. No, sir, of red. F is come over to the helm too,
I thank my Maker, in St. Mary's bath,[1]
And shows *lac virginis*. Blessed be heaven!
I sent you of his fæces there calcined: 320
Out of that calx I have won the salt of mercury.
    Mam. By pouring on your rectified water?
    Sub. Yes, and reverberating[2] in Athanor.

Re-enter FACE.

How now! what colour says it?
    Face. The ground black, sir.
    Mam. That's your crow's head?[3]
    Sur. Your cock's-comb's, is it not?
    Sub. No, 'tis not perfect. Would it were the crow!
That work wants something.
    Sur. Oh, I looked for this. 330
The hay's[4] a pitching.
    Sub. Are you sure you loosed them
In their own menstrue?
    Face. Yes, sir, and then married them,
And put them in a bolt's-head nipp'd to digestion,
According as you bade me when I set
The liquor of Mars to circulation
In the same heat.
    Sub. The process then was right.
    Face. Yes, by the token, sir, the retort brake, 340
And what was saved was put into the pelican,

---

    [1] Where one vessel was placed in another containing water.
    [2] To heat, by beating back the flames from the top upon the material below.
    [3] Another hopeful sign.
    [4] A net for catching rabbits, by stretching it before their burrows.

And signed with Hermes' seal.[1]
   Sub. I think 'twas so.
We should have a new amalgama.
   Sur. (*aside*). Oh, this ferret[2]
Is rank as any pole-cat.
   Sub. But I care not:
Let him e'en die; we have enough beside,
In embrion. H has his white shirt on.
   Face. Yes, sir,   350
He's ripe for inceration, he stands warm
In his ash-fire. I would not you should let
Any die now, if I might counsel, sir,
For luck's sake to the rest: it is not good.
   Mam. He says right.
   Sur. (*aside*). Ay, are you bolted?[3]
   Face. Nay, I know't, sir,
I have seen the ill fortune. What is some three ounces
Of fresh materials?
   Mam. Is't no more?   360
   Face. No more, sir,
Of gold, t'amalgame with some six of mercury.
   Mam. Away, here's money. What will serve?
   Face. Ask him, sir.
   Mam. How much?
   Sub. Give him nine pound — you may give him ten.
   Sur. Yes, twenty, and be cozen'd — do.
   Mam. There 'tis.   [*Gives* FACE *the money.*
   Sub. This needs not; but that you will have it so,
To see conclusions of all; for two   370

---

[1] Made by heating the neck of a vessel, and then twisting it.
[2] *Face,* having just come from working over the fire, has red eyes.
[3] **Punning** allusion to the *rabbit-net* and *ferret.*

Of our inferior works are at fixation,[1]
A third is in ascension. Go your ways.
Have you set the oil of luna in kemia?
   Face. Yes, sir.
   Sub. And the philosopher's vinegar?
   Face. Ay.   [*Exit.*
   Sur. We shall have a salad!
   Mam. When do you make projection?
   Sub. Son, be not hasty, I exalt our med'cine,
By hanging him *in balneo vaporoso,*   380
And giving him solution; then congeal him;
And then dissolve him; then again congeal him:
For look, how oft I iterate the work
So many times I add unto his virtue.
As, if at first one ounce convert a hundred,
After his second loose, he'll turn a thousand;
His third solution, ten; his fourth, a hundred;
After his fifth, a thousand thousand ounces
Of any imperfect metal, into pure
Silver or gold, in all examinations,   390
As good as any of the natural mine.
Get you your stuff here against afternoon,
Your brass, your pewter, and your andirons.
   Mam. Not those of iron?
   Sub. Yes, you may bring them too:
We'll change all metals.
   Sur. I believe you in that.
   Mam. Then I may send my spits?
   Sub. Yes, and your racks.
   Sur. And dripping pans, and pot-hangers, and hooks, 400
Shall he not?

        [1] In a non-volatile state.

Sub. If he please.
Sur. — To be an ass.
Sub. How, sir!
Mam. This gentleman you must bear withal:
I told you he had no faith.
Sur. And little hope, sir;
But much less charity, should I gull myself.
Sub. Why, what have you observed, sir, in our art,
Seems so impossible? 410
Sur. But your whole work, no more.
That you should hatch gold in a furnace, sir,
As they do eggs in Egypt!
Sub. Sir, do you
Believe that eggs are hatched so?
Sur. If I should?
Sub. Why, I think that the greater miracle.
No egg but differs from a chicken more
Than metals in themselves.
Sur. That cannot be. 420
The egg's ordained by nature to that end,
And is a chicken *in potentia*.
Sub. The same we say of lead and other metals,
Which would be gold if they had time.
Mam. And that
Our art doth further.
Sub. Ay, for 'twere absurd
To think that nature in the earth bred gold
Perfect in the instant; something went before.
There must be remote matter. 430
Sur. Ay, what is that?
Sub. Marry, we say —
Mam. Ay, now it heats: stand, father,

Pound him to dust.
  Sub. It is, of the one part,
A humid exhalation, which we call
Materia liquida, or the unctuous water;
On the other part, a certain crass and vicious.
Portion of earth; both which, concorporate,
Do make the elementary matter of gold;   440
Which is not yet *propria materia,*
But common to all metals and all stones;
For, where it is forsaken of that moisture,
And hath more dryness, it becomes a stone;
Where it retains more of the humid fatness,
It turns to sulphur or to quicksilver,
Who are the parents of all other metals.
Nor can this remote matter suddenly
Progress so from extreme unto extreme,
As to grow gold, and leap o'er all the means.   450
Nature doth first beget the imperfect, then
Proceeds she to the perfect. Of that airy
And oily water, mercury is engendered;
Sulphur of the fat and earthy part; the one,
Which is the last, supplying the place of male,
The other of the female, in all metals.
Some do believe hermaphrodeity,
That both do act and suffer. But these two
Make the rest ductile, malleable, extensive.
And even in gold they are; for we do find   460
Seeds of them, by our fire, and gold in them;
And can produce the species of each metal
More perfect thence, than Nature doth in earth.
Beside, who doth not see in daily practice
Art can beget bees, hornets, beetles, wasps,

Out of the carcases and dung of creatures;
Yea, scorpions of an herb, being rightly placed?
And these are living creatures, far more perfect
And excellent than metals.
　Mam. Well said, father! 470
Nay, if he take you in hand, sir, with an argument,
He'll bray you in mortar.
　Sur. Pray you, sir, stay.
Rather than I'll be bray'd, sir, I'll believe
That Alchemy is a pretty kind of game,
Somewhat like tricks o' the cards, to cheat a man
With charming.
　Sub. Sir?
　Sur. What else are all your terms,
Whereon no one of your writers 'grees with other? 480
Of your elixir, your *lac virginis*,
Your stone, your med'cine, and your chrysosperme,
Your sal, your sulphur, and your mercury,
Your oil of height, your tree of life, your blood,
Your marchesite, your tutie, your magnesia,
Your toad, your crow, your dragon, and your panther;
Your sun, your moon, your firmament, your adrop,
Your lato, azoch, zernich, chibrit, heautarit,
And then your red man and your white woman,
With all your broths, your menstrues, and materials, 490
Of lye and egg-shells, women's terms, man's blood,
Hair o' the head, burnt clouts, chalk, merds, and clay,
Powder of bones, scalings of iron, glass,
And worlds of other strange ingredients,
Would burst a man to name?[1]

---

[1] It would be time wasted to rummage the old works on alchemy for an explanation of all these terms, which were doubtless as strange to the major-

Sub. And all these named,
Intending but one thing; which art our writers
Used to obscure their art.
  Mam. Sir, so I told him —
Because the simple idiot should not learn it, 500
And make it vulgar.
  Sub. Was not all the knowledge
Of the Egyptians writ in mystic symbols?
Speak not the Scriptures oft in parables?
Are not the choicest fables of the poets,
That were the fountains and first springs of wisdom,
Wrapp'd in perplexed allegories?
  Mam. I urged that,
And cleared to him that Sisyphus was damned
To roll the ceaseless stone, only because 510
He would have made ours common. [DOL *appears at the door.*
                    Who is this?
  Sub. 'Sprecious!— What do you mean? Go in, good lady,
Let me entreat you. (DOL *retires.*) Where's this varlet?

Re-enter FACE.

  Face. Sir.
  Sub. You very knave! do you use me thus?
  Face. Wherein, sir?
  Sub. Go in and see, you traitor. Go!   [*Exit* FACE.
  Mam. Who is it, sir?
  Sub. Nothing, sir; nothing.
  Mam. What's the matter, good sir? 520
I have not seen you thus distemper'd: who is't?
  Sub. All arts have still had, sir, their adversaries,
But ours the most ignorant.

ity of play-goers in Jonson's time as they are to us; the more common and important are explained in the course of the play.

Re-enter FACE.

What now?
    Face. 'Twas not my fault, sir; she would speak with you.
    Sub. Would she, sir! Follow me.   [*Exit.*
    Mam. (*stopping him*). Stay, Lungs.
    Face. I dare not, sir.
    Mam. Stay, man; what is she?
    Face. A lord's sister, sir.   530
    Mam. How! pray thee, stay.
    Face. She's mad, sir, and sent hither —
He'll be mad too——
    Mam. I warrant thee.
Why sent hither?
    Face. Sir, to be cured.
    Sub. (*within*). Why, rascal!
    Face. Lo you! — Here, sir!   [*Exit.*
    Mam. 'Fore God, a Bradamante,[1] a brave piece.
    Sur. Heart, this is an evil house! I will be burnt else. 540
    Mam. Oh, by this light, no; do not wrong him. He's
Too scrupulous that way: it is his vice.
No, he's a rare physician, do him right,
An excellent Paracelsian,[2] and has done
Strange cures with mineral physic. He deals all
With spirits, he; he will not hear a word
Of Galen or his tedious recipes.

Re-enter FACE.

How now, Lungs!

[1] A Christian amazon, sister to Rinaldo, and mistress of Ruggiero, in Boiardo's *Orlando Innamorato*, and Ariosto's *Orlando Furioso*. She possessed an irresistible spear, which unhorsed all her antagonists. — Wheeler: *Noted Names of Fiction*.

[2] Paracelsus was born in 1493 and died in 1541.

Face. Softly, sir; speak softly. I meant
To have told your worship all. This must not hear. 550
    Mam. No, he will not be " gull'd " : let him alone.
    Face. You are very right, sir; she is a most rare scholar,
And is gone mad with studying Broughton's works.[1]
If you but name a word touching the Hebrew
She falls into her fit, and will discourse
So learnedly of genealogies,
As you would run mad, too, to hear her, sir.
    Mam. How might one do t'have conference with her,
        Lungs?
    Face. Oh, divers have run mad upon the conference:
I do not know, sir. I am sent in haste 560
To fetch a vial.
    Sur. Be not gull'd, Sir Mammon.
    Mam. Wherein? Pray ye, be patient.
    Sur. Yes, as you are,
And trust confederate knaves and sharks and bawds.
    Mam. You are too foul, believe it.—Come here, Ulen,
One word.
    Face. I dare not, in good faith.   [*Going.*
    Mam. Stay, knave.
    Face. He is extreme angry that you saw her, sir. 570
    Mam. Drink that (*gives him money*). What is she when
        she's out of her fit?
    Face. Oh, the most affablest creature, sir! So merry!
So pleasant! She'll mount you up like quicksilver
Over the helm, and circulate like oil,
A very vegetal; discourse of state,
Of mathematics, frolic, anything ——
    Mam. Is she no way accessible? no means,

---

[1] A celebrated divine and Hebrew scholar in Elizabeth's time.

No trick to give a man a taste of her wit—
Or so?
   Sub. (*within*). Ulen! 580
   Face. I'll come to you again, sir. [*Exit.*
   Mam. Surly, I did not think one of your breeding
Would traduce personages of worth.
   Sur. Sir Epicure,
Your friend to use; yet still loth to be gulled:
I do not like your philosophical bawds.
Their stone is lechery enough to pay for
Without this bait.
   Mam. 'Heart, you abuse yourself.
I know the lady, and her friends, and means, 590
The original of this disaster. Her brother
Has told me all.
   Sur. And yet you never saw her
Till now!
   Mam. Oh yes, but I forgot. I have, believe it,
One of the treacherousest memories, I do think,
Of all mankind.
   Sur. What call you her brother?
   Mam. My lord ——
He will not have his name known, now I think on it. 600
   Sur. A very treacherous memory!
   Mam. On my faith ——
   Sur. Tut, if you have it not about you, pass it
Till we meet next.
   Mam. Nay, by this hand, 'tis true,
He's one I honour, and my noble friend;
And I respect his house.
   Sur. Heart! can it be
That a grave sir, a rich, that has no need,

A wise, sir, too, at other times, should thus, 610
With his own oaths and arguments, make hard means
To gull himself? An this be your elixir,
Your *lapis mineralis* and your lunary,
Give me your honest trick yet at primero,
Or gleek :[1] and take your *lutum sapientis*,
Your *menstruum simplex!* I'll have gold before you,
And with less danger of the quicksilver
Or the hot sulphur.

Re-enter FACE.

Face. Here's one from Captain Face, sir (*to* SURLY),
Desires you meet him in the Temple Church 620
Some half-hour hence, and upon earnest business.
Sir — (*whispers* MAMMON) — if you please to quit us now,
    and come
Again within two hours, you shall have
My master busy examining o' the works;
And I will steal you in unto the party,
That you may see her converse. Sir, shall I say
You'll meet the captain's worship?

Sur. Sir, I will.   [*Walks aside.*
But, by attorney and to a second purpose,
Now, I am sure I understand this house; 630
I'll swear it, were the marshal here to thank me:
The naming this commander doth confirm it.
Don Face ! why he's the most authentic dealer
In these commodities, the superintendent
To all the quainter traffickers in town !
He is the visitor, and does appoint
Who visits whom, and at what hour; what price;

[1] A game of cards.

Which gown, and in what smock ; what fall[1]; what tire.
Him will I prove, by a third person, to find
The subtleties of this dark labyrinth : 640
Which if I do discover, dear Sir Mammon,
You'll give your poor friend leave, though no philosopher,
To laugh : for you that are, 'tis thought, shall weep.
   Face. Sir, he does pray you'll not forget.
   Sur. I will not, sir.
Sir Epicure, I shall leave you.   [*Exit.*
   Mam. I follow you straight.
   Face. But do so, good sir, to avoid suspicion.
This gentleman has a parlous[2] head.
   Mam. But wilt thou, Ulen, 650
Be constant to thy promise?
   Face. As my life, sir.
   Mam. And wilt thou insinuate what I am, and praise me,
And say I am a noble fellow?
   Face. Oh, what else, sir?
And that you'll make her royal with the stone,
An empress : and yourself, King of Bantam.
   Mam. Wilt thou do this?
   Face. Will I, sir !
   Mam. Lungs, my Lungs ! 660
I love thee.
   Face. Send your stuff, sir, that my master
May busy himself about projection.
   Mam. Thou hast witch'd me, rogue : take, go.
                         [*Gives him money.*
   Face. Your jack,[3] and all, sir.
   Mam. Thou art a villain — I will send my jack,

---

[1] A ruff, or band, turned back on the shoulders.
[2] Perilous.   [3] Roasting-jack.

And the weights too. Slave, I could bite thine ear.
Away, thou dost not care for me.
    Face. Not I, sir!
    Mam. Come, I was born to make thee, my good weasel,
Set thee on a bench, and have thee twirl a chain   671
With the best lord's vermin of 'em all.
    Face. Away, sir.
    Mam. A count, nay, a count palatine ———
    Face. Good, sir, go.
    Mam. Shall not advance thee better: no, nor faster.
                                            [*Exit.*

        Re-enter SUBTLE *and* DOL.

    Sub. Has he bit? has he bit?
    Face. And swallowed too, my Subtle.
I have given him line, and now he plays, i' faith.
    Sub. And shall we twitch him?   680
    Face. Thorough both the gills.
For here is a rare bait, with which a man
No sooner's taken, but he straight firks mad.
    Sub. Dol, my Lord What's'hums sister, you must now
Bear yourself *statelich.*
    Dol. Oh, let me alone.
I'll not forget my race, I warrant you.
I'll keep my distance, laugh and talk aloud;
Have all the tricks of a proud scurvy lady,
And be as rude as her woman.   690
    Face. Well said, sanguine!
    Sub. But will he send his andirons?
    Face. His jack too,
And's iron shoeing-horn; I have spoke to him. Well,
I must not loose my wary gamester yonder.

Sub. Oh, Monsieur Caution, that *will not be gull'd.*
Face. Ay,
If I can strike a fine hook into him, now!
The Temple Church, there I have cast mine angle.
Well, pray for me. I'll about it. [*Knocking without.* 700
  Sub What, more gudgeons!
Dol, scout, scout! (DOL *goes to the window.*) Stay, Face,
  you must go to the door.
Pray God it be my Anabaptist. — Who is't, Dol?
  Dol. I know him not: he looks like a gold-endman.[1]
  Sub. Ods so! 'tis he, he said he would send — what
    call you him?
The sanctified elder, that should deal
For Mammon's jack and andirons. Let him in.
Stay, help me off, first, with my gown. (*Exit* FACE *with the
  gown.*) Away,
Madam, to your withdrawing chamber. (*Exit* DOL.) Now,
In a new tune, new gesture, but old language. —   710
This fellow is sent from one negotiates with me
About the stone too; for the holy brethren
Of Amsterdam, the exiled saints; that hope
To raise their discipline by it. I must use him
In some strange fashion, now, to make him admire me. —

Enter ANANIAS.

(*Aloud.*) Where is my drudge?

Re-enter FACE.

Face. Sir!
Sub. Take away the recipient,

---

[1] One who buys remnants of gold or silver; a goldsmith's apprentice.

And rectify your menstrue from the phlegma.¹
Then pour it on the Sol, in the cucurbite, 720
And let them macerate ² together.
 Face. Yes, sir.
And save the ground?
 Sub. No : *terra damnata*
Must not have entrance in the work. — Who are you?
 Ana. A faithful brother,³ if it please you.
 Sub. What's that?
A Lullianist?⁴ a Ripley!⁵ *Filius artis?*
Can you sublime and dulcify? calcine?
Know you the sapor pontic? sapor stiptic? 730
Or what is homogene, or heterogene?
 Ana. I understand no heathen language, truly.
 Sub. Heathen! you Knipper-doling?⁶ is Ars sacra,
Or chrysopœia, or spagyrica,⁷
Or the pamphysic, or panarchic knowledge,
A heathen language?
 Ana. Heathen Greek, I take it.
 Sub. How heathen Greek?
 Ana. All's heathen but the Hebrew.⁸
 Sub. Sirrah, my varlet, stand you forth and speak to him
Like a philosopher : answer in the language, 741
Name the vexations and the martyrizations

---

 ¹ Water of distillation.   ² Steep.
 ³ The Puritans called each other " faithful brothers."
 ⁴ Raymond Lully, one of the most famous philosophers of the Middle Age; b. about 1235, d. 1315.
 ⁵ George Ripley, canon of Bridlington in the fifteenth century, dedicated a great work on alchemy to King Edward IV. See Fuller's *Worthies.*
 ⁶ An Anabaptist, who raised a revolt in Münster in 1533.
 ⁷ Alchemical.
 ⁸ The Puritans, taking the Hebrew *Old Testament* for their guide, treated Greek, the language of the *New Testament*, scornfully.

Of metals in the work.
 Face. Sir, putrefaction,
Solution, ablution, sublimation,
Cohobation, calcination, ceration, and
Fixation.
 Sub. This is heathen Greek to you, now!—
And when comes vivification?
 Face. After mortification.
 Sub. What's cohobation?
 Face. 'Tis the pouring on
Your aqua regis,[1] and then drawing him off,
To the trine circle of the seven spheres.
 Sub. What's the proper passion of metals?
 Face. Malleation.
 Sub. What's your *ultimum supplicium auri?*
 Face. Antimonium.
 Sub. This is heathen Greek to you?—And what's your mercury?
 Face. A very fugitive, he will be gone, sir.
 Sub. How know you him?
 Face. By his viscosity,
His oleosity, and his suscitability.
 Sub. How do you sublime him?
 Face. With the calce of egg-shells,
White marble, talc.
 Sub. Your magisterium, now,
What's that?
 Face. Shifting, sir, your elements,
Dry into cold, cold into moist, moist into hot,
Hot into dry.
 Sub. This is heathen Greek to you still!

---

[1] Nitro-muriatic acid, to dissolve the gold.

Your *lapis philosophicus?*
    Face. 'Tis a stone,
And not a stone; a spirit, a soul, and a body:
Which if you do dissolve, it is dissolved;
If you coagulate, it is coagulated;
If you make it to fly, it flieth.
    Sub. Enough.   [*Exit* FACE.
This is heathen Greek to you! What are you, sir?
    Ana. Please you, a servant of the exiled brethren
That deal with widows and with orphans' goods:
And make a just account unto the saints:
A deacon.
    Sub. Oh, you are sent from Master Wholesome,
Your teacher?
    Ana. From Tribulation Wholesome,
Our very zealous pastor.
    Sub. Good! I have
Some orphans' goods to come here.
    Ana. Of what kind, sir?
    Sub. Pewter and brass, andirons and kitchenware,
Metals, that we must use our medicine on:
Wherein the brethren may have a pennyworth
For ready money.
    Ana. Were the orphans' parents
Sincere professors?
    Sub. Why do you ask?
    Ana. Because
We then are to deal justly, and give in truth
Their utmost value.
    Sub. 'Slid, you'd cozen else,
And if their parents were not of the faithful!—
I will not trust you, now I think on it,

Till I have talked with your pastor.   Have you brought
    money
To buy more coals?
   Ana. No, surely.
   Sub. No! how so?
   Ana. The brethren bid me say unto you, sir,   810
Surely they will not venture any more
Till they may see projection.
   Sub. How!
   Ana. You have had,
For the instruments, as bricks, and loam, and glasses,
Already thirty pound; and for materials,
They say, some ninety more: and they have heard since
That one at Heidelberg made it of an egg
And a small paper of pin-dust.
   Sub. What's your name?   820
   Ana. My name is Ananias.
   Sub. Out, the varlet
That cozen'd the apostles!   Hence, away,
Flee, mischief!   Had your holy consistory
No name to send me of another sound
Than wicked Ananias? send your elders
Hither to make atonement for you quickly,
And give me satisfaction; or out goes
The fire; and down th' alembics, and the furnace,
Piger Henricus, or what not.   Thou wretch!   830
Both sericon and bufo [1] shall be lost,
Tell them.   All hope of rooting out the bishops,
Or the antichristian hierarchy, shall perish,
If they stay threescore minutes: the aqueity,
Terreity, and sulphureity

              [1] Red tincture and black.

Shall run together again, and all be annulled,
Thou wicked Ananias! (*Exit* ANANIAS.) This will fetch 'em,
And make them haste towards their gulling more.
A man must deal like a rough nurse, and fright
Those that are froward to an appetite. 840

  Re-enter FACE *in his uniform, followed by* DRUGGER.

 Face. He is busy with his spirits, but we'll upon him.
 Sub. How now! what mates, what bayards[1] have we here?
 Face. I told you he would be furious.—Sir, here's Nab
Has brought you another piece of gold to look on—
We must appease him. Give it me—and prays you,
You would devise—what is it, Nab?
 Drug. A sign, sir.
 Face. Ay, a good lucky one, a thriving sign, doctor.
 Sub. I was devising now.
 Face. 'Slight, do not say so, 850
He will repent he gave you any more—
What say you to his constellation, doctor,
The Balance?
 Sub. No, that way is stale and common.
A townsman born in Taurus gives the bull,
Or the bull's head: in Aries, the ram,
A poor device! No, I will have his name
Formed in some mystic character; whose radii,
Striking the senses of the passers-by,
Shall, by a virtual influence, breed affections 860
That may result upon the party owns it:
As thus——
 Face. Nab!
 Sub. He shall have *a bel*, that's *Abel;*

---

[1] Bayard, a blind horse.

And by it standing one whose name is *Dee*,[1]
In a *rug* gown, there's *D*, and *Rug*, that's *drug:*
And right anenst him a dog snarling *er;*
There's *Drugger*, Abel Drugger. That's his sign.
And here's now mystery and hieroglyphic!
    Face. Abel, thou art made.   870
    Drug. Sir, I do thank his worship.
    Face. Six o' thy legs more will not do it, Nab.
He has brought you a pipe of tobacco, doctor.
    Drug. Yes, sir:
I have another thing I would impart ——
    Face. Out with it, Nab.
    Drug. Sir, there is lodged, hard by me,
A rich young widow ——
    Face. Good! a bona roba?
    Drug. But nineteen at the most.   880
    Face. Very good, Abel.
    Drug. Marry, she's not in fashion yet; she wears
A hood, but it stands a cop.[2]
    Face. No matter, Abel.
    Drug. And I do now and then give her a fucus —
    Face. What! dost thou deal, Nab?
    Sub. I did tell you, captain.
    Drug. And physic, too, sometime, sir; for which she
        trusts me
With all her mind. She's come up here of purpose
To learn the fashion.   890
    Face. Good (his match too!) — On, Nab.
    Drug. And she does strangely long to know her fortune.

---

[1] Dr. John Dee, alchemist and scholar, who modestly said that if he had found a Mæcenas, Britain would not have lacked an Aristotle.
[2] Ending in a point.

Face. Ods lid, Nab, send her to the doctor, hither.
Drug. Yes, I have spoke to her of his worship already;
But she's afraid it will be blown abroad,
And hurt her marriage.
    Face. Hurt it! 'tis the way
To heal it, if 'twere hurt; to make it more
Followed and sought; Nab, thou shalt tell her this.
She'll be more known, more talked of; and your widows 900
Are ne'er of any price till they be famous:
Their honour is their multitude of suitors:
Send her, it may be thy good fortune. What!
Thou dost not know.
    Drug. No, sir, she'll never marry
Under a knight: her brother has made a vow.
    Face. What! and dost thou despair, my little Nab,
Knowing what the doctor has set down for thee,
And seeing so many of the city dubbed?
One glass o' thy water, with a madam I know, 910
Will have it done, Nab; what's her brother — a knight?
    Drug. No, sir, a gentleman newly warm in his land, sir,
Scarce cold in his one-and-twenty, that does govern
His sister here; and is a man himself
Of some three thousand a year, and is come up
To learn to quarrel, and to live by his wits,
And will go down again, and die in the country.
    Face. How! to quarrel?
    Drug. Yes, sir, to carry quarrels,
As gallants do; to manage them by line.[1] 920
    Face. 'Slid, Nab, the doctor is the only man
In Christendom for him. He has made a table,
With mathematical demonstrations,

---

[1] Cf. Hamlet's "speak by the card."

Touching the art of quarrels: he will give him
An instrument to quarrel by. Go, bring them both,
Him and his sister. And, for thee, with her
The doctor haply may persuade. Go to:
Shalt give his worship a new damask suit
Upon the premises.
   Sub. Oh, good captain!   930
   Face. He shall;
He is the honestest fellow, doctor. — Stay not,
No offers; bring the damask, and the parties.
   Drug. I'll try my power, sir.
   Face. And thy will, too, Nab.
   Sub. 'Tis good tobacco, this! What is't an ounce?
   Face. He'll send you a pound, doctor.
   Sub. Oh, no.
   Face. He will do't.
It is the goodest soul Abel! — Abel, about it.   940
Thou shalt know more anon. Away, begone. — [*Exit* ABEL.
A miserable rogue, and lives with cheese,
And has the worms. That was the cause, indeed,
Why he came now: he dealt with me in private,
To get a med'cine for them.
   Sub. And shall, sir. This works.
   Face. A wife, a wife for one of us, my dear Subtle!
We'll e'en draw lots, and he that fails, shall have
The more in goods.
   Sub. Faith, best let's see her first, and then determine. 950
   Face. Content; but Dol must have no breath on't.
   Sub. Mum.
Away you, to your Surly yonder, catch him.
   Face. Pray God, I have not stayed too long.
   Sub. I fear it.   [*Exeunt*

ACT III.

SCENE I. — *The Lane before* LOVEWIT'S *House.*

Enter TRIBULATION WHOLESOME *and* ANANIAS.

Tri. These chastisements are common to the saints,
And such rebukes, we of the separation
Must bear with willing shoulders, as the trials
Sent forth to tempt our frailties.
    Ana. In pure zeal,
I do not like the man, he is a heathen,
And speaks the language of Canaan, truly.
    Tri. I think him a profane person indeed.
    Ana. He bears
The visible mark of the beast in his forehead.
And for his stone, it is a work of darkness,
And with philosophy blinds the eyes of man.
    Tri. Good brother, we must bend unto all means
That may give furtherance to the holy cause.
    Ana. Which his cannot: the sanctified cause
Should have a sanctified course.
    Tri. Not always necessary:
The children of perdition are ofttimes
Made instruments even of the greatest works:
Beside, we should give somewhat to man's nature,
The place he lives in, still about the fire,
And fume of metals, that intoxicate
The brain of man, and make him prone to passion.
Where have you greater atheists than your cooks?
Or more profane, or choleric than your glass-men?

More antichristian than your bell-founders?
What makes the devil so devilish, I would ask you,
Satan, our common enemy, but his being
Perpetually about the fire, and boiling
Brimstone and arsenic? We must give, I say, 30
Unto the motives, and the stirrers-up
Of humours in the blood. It may be so,
Whenas the work is done, the stone is made,
This heat of his may turn into a zeal,
And stand up for the beauteous discipline,
Against the filthy cloth and rag of Rome.
We must await his calling, and the coming
Of the good spirit. You did fault t'upbraid him
With the brethren's blessing of Heidelberg, weighing
What need we have to hasten on the work 40
For the restoring of the silenced saints,
Which ne'er will be, but by the philosopher's stone.
And so a learned elder, one of Scotland,
Assured me; *aurum potabile* being
The only med'cine for the civil magistrate
T'incline him to a feeling of the cause,
And must be daily used in the disease.
   Ana. I have not edified more, truly, by man;
Not since the beautiful light first shone on me:
And I am sad my zeal hath so offended. 50
  Tri. Let us call on him then.
  Ana. The motion's good,
And of the spirit; I will knock first. (*Knocks.*) Peace
     within!   [*The door is opened, and they enter.*

SCENE II. — *A Room in* LOVEWIT'S *House.*

Enter SUBTLE, *followed by* TRIBULATION *and* ANANIAS.

Sub. Oh, are you come? 'Twas time. Your threescore
 minutes
Were at last thread, you see; and down had gone
Furnus acediæ, turris circulatoris:
Lembec, bolt's-head, retort and pelican
Had all been cinders. — Wicked Ananias!
Art thou returned? Nay then, it goes down yet.
 Tri. Sir, be appeased; he is come to humble
Himself in spirit, and to ask your patience,
If too much zeal hath carried him aside
From the due path.   10
 Sub. Why, this doth qualify!
 Tri. The brethren had no purpose, verily,
To give you the least grievance: but are ready
To lend their willing hands to any project
The spirit and you direct.
 Sub. This qualifies more!
 Tri. And for the orphan's goods, let them be valued,
Or what is needful else to the holy work,
It shall be numbered; here, by me, the saints
Throw down their purse before you.   20
 Sub. This qualifies most!
Why, thus it should be, now you understand.
Have I discoursed so unto you of our stone,
And of the good that it shall bring your cause?
Showed you (beside the main of hiring forces
Abroad, drawing the Hollanders, your friends,
From the Indies, to serve you with all their fleet)

That even the med'cinal use shall make you a faction
And party in the realm? As, put the case,
That some great man in state, he have the gout,   30
Why, you but send three drops of your elixir,
You help him straight: there you have made a friend.
Another has the palsy or the dropsy,
He takes of your incombustible stuff,
He's young again: there you have made a friend.
A lady that is past the feat of body,
Though not of mind, and hath her face decayed
Beyond all cure of paintings, you restore
With the oil of talc: there you have made a friend,
And all her friends. A lord that is a leper,   40
A knight that has the bone-ache, or a squire
That hath both these, you make them smooth and sound
With a bare fricace of your med'cine: still
You increase your friends.
   Tri. Ay, it is very pregnant.
   Sub. And then the turning of this lawyer's pewter
To plate at Christmas——
   Ana. Christ-tide,[1] I pray you.
   Sub. Yet, Ananias!
   Ana. I have done.   50
   Sub. Or changing
His parcel gilt to massy gold. You cannot
But raise your friends. Withal to be of power
To pay an army in the field, to buy
The king of France out of his realms, or Spain
Out of his Indies. What can you not do
Against lords spiritual or temporal,

---

[1] The Puritans, scrupulous to avoid everything Romish, called Christ*mas* "Christ-*tide*."

That shall oppone you?
　Tri. Verily, 'tis true.
We may be temporal lords ourselves, I take it.　　60
　Sub. You may be anything, and leave off to make
Long-winded exercises; or suck up
Your *ha!* and *hum!* in a tune.　I not deny
But such as are not graced in a state,
May, for their ends, be adverse in religion,
And get a tune to call the flock together:
For, to say sooth, a tune does much with women
And other phlegmatic people; it is your bell.
　Ana. Bells are profane; a tune may be religious.
　Sub. No warning with you! then farewell my patience.　70
'Slight, it shall down: I will not be thus tortured.
　Tri. I pray you, sir.
　Sub. All shall perish.　I have spoke it.
　Tri. Let me find grace, sir, in your eyes: the man
He stands corrected: neither did his zeal,
But as yourself, allow a tune somewhere.
Which now, being tow'rd the stone, we shall not need.
　Sub. No, nor your holy vizard, to win widows
To give you legacies; or make zealous wives
To rob their husbands for the common cause:　　80
Nor take the start of bonds broke but one day,
And say they were forfeited by providence.
Nor shall you need o'ernight to eat huge meals,
To celebrate your next day's fast the better;
The whilst the brethren and the sisters humbled,
Abate the stiffness of the flesh.　Nor cast
Before your hungry hearers scrupulous bones;
As whether a Christian may hawk or hunt,
Or whether matrons of the holy assembly

May lay their hair out, or wear doublets,   90
Or have that idol starch about their linen.
  Ana. It is indeed an idol.
  Tri. Mind him not, sir.
I do command thee, spirit of zeal, but trouble,
To peace within him! Pray you, sir, go on.
  Sub. Nor shall you need to libel 'gainst the prelates,
And shorten so your ears against the hearing
Of the next wire-drawn grace. Nor of necessity
Rail against plays, to please the alderman
Whose daily custard you devour: nor lie   100
With zealous rage till you are hoarse. Not one
Of these so singular arts. Nor call yourselves
By names of Tribulation, Persecution,
Restraint, Long-patience, and such like, affected
By the whole family, or wood of you,
Only for glory, and to catch the ear
Of the disciple.
  Tri. Truly, sir, they are
Ways that the godly brethren have invented
For propagation of the glorious cause,   110
As very notable means, and whereby also
Themselves grow soon, and profitably, famous.
  Sub. Oh, but the stone, all's idle to it! Nothing!
The art of angels, nature's miracle,
The divine secret that doth fly in clouds
From east to west; and whose tradition
Is not from men, but spirits.
  Ana. I hate traditions;
I do not trust them. ——
  Tri. Peace!   120
  Ana. They are popish all.

I will not peace : I will not ——
    Tri. Ananias !
    Ana. Please the profane, to grieve the godly; I may not.
    Sub. Well, Ananias, thou shalt overcome.
    Tri. It is an ignorant zeal that haunts him, sir,
But truly, else, a very faithful brother,
A botcher, and a man, by revelation,
That hath a competent knowledge of the truth.
    Sub. Has he a competent sum there in the bag   130
To buy the goods within? I am made guardian,
And must, for charity, and conscience' sake,
Now see the most be made for my poor orphan;
Though I desire the brethren too good gainers;
There they are within. When you have view'd, and bought
        'em,
And ta'en the inventory of what they are,
They are ready for projection; there's no more
To do; cast on the med'cine so much silver
As there is tin there, so much gold as brass,
I'll give it you in, by weight.   140
    Tri. But how long time,
Sir, must the saints expect yet?
    Sub. Let me see.
How's the moon now? Eight, nine, ten days hence,
He will be silver potate; then three days
Before he citronise: some fifteen days,
The magisterium will be perfected.
    Ana. About the second day of the third week,
In the ninth month?
    Sub. Yes, my good Ananias.   150
    Tri. What will the orphans' goods arise to, think you?
    Sub. Some hundred marks, as much as filled three cars,

Unladed now : you'll make six millions of them.
But I must have more coals laid in.
   Tri. How !
   Sub. Another load,
And then we have finished. We must now increase
Our fire to *ignis ardens,* we are past
Fimus equinus, balnei, cineris,
And all those lenter heats. If the holy purse   160
Should with this draught fall low, and that the saints
Do need a present sum, I have a trick
To melt the pewter, you shall buy now, instantly,
And with a tincture make you as good Dutch dollars
As any are in Holland.
   Tri. Can you so ?
   Sub. Ay, and shall 'bide the third examination.
   Ana. It will be joyful tidings to the brethren.
   Sub. But you must carry it secret.
   Tri. Ay, but stay,   170
This act of coining, is it lawful?
   Ana. Lawful !
We know no magistrate ; or, if we did,[1]
This is foreign coin.
   Sub. It is no coining, sir,
It is but casting.
   Tri. Ha ! you distinguish well :
Casting of money may be lawful.
   Ana. 'Tis, sir.
   Tri. Truly, I take it so.   180
   Sub. There is no scruple,
Sir, to be made of it ; believe Ananias :

---

[1] A fine stroke ! The Puritans refused to recognize the then existing civil governments as being divinely sanctioned.

This case of conscience he is studied in.
   Tri. I'll make a question of it to the brethren.
   Ana. The brethren shall approve it lawful, doubt not.
Where shall it be done?   [*Knocking without.*
   Sub. For that we'll talk anon.
There's some to speak with me. Go in, I pray you,
And view the parcels.   That's the inventory.
I'll come to you straight.   [*Exeunt* TRIB. *and* ANA.[1]
                        Who is it? — Face ! appear.   190

   Enter FACE *in his uniform.*

How now ! Good prize?
   Face. Good plague ! Yond' costive cheater
Never came on.
   Sub. How then?
   Face. I have walked the round
Till now, and no such thing.
   Sub. And have you quit him?
   Face. Quit him ! an hell would quit him too, he were happy.
'Slight ! Would you have me stalk like a mill-jade,
All day, for one that will not yield us grains?   200
I know him of old.
   Sub. Oh, but to have gulled him
Had been a mastery.
   Face. Let him go, black boy !
And turn thee that some fresh news may possess thee.
A noble count, a don of Spain, my dear
Delicious compeer, and my party-bawd,
Who is come hither private for his conscience,

---

[1] It is well to remember, in reading Jonson's satires on the Puritans, that he was brought up in the Church of England, then joined the Catholic Church, and finally returned to Anglicanism.

And brought munition with him, six great slops,[1]
Bigger than three Dutch hoys,[2] beside round trunks,[3]   210
Furnished with pistolets, and pieces of eight,
Will straight be here, my rogue, to have thy bath
(That is the colour), and to make his battery
Upon our Dol, our castle, our Cinque-port,[4]
Our Dover pier, our what thou wilt.   Where is she?
She must prepare perfumes, delicate linen,
The bath in chief, a banquet, and her wit.
Where is the doxy?
   Sub. I'll send her to thee:
And but dispatch my brace of little John Leydens,[5]   220
And come again myself.
   Face. Are they within, then?
   Sub. Numbering the sum.
   Face. How much?
   Sub. A hundred marks, boy.   [*Exit.*
   Face. Why, this is a lucky day.   Ten pounds of Mammon!
Three of my clerk!   A portague of my grocer!
This of the brethren! beside reversions,
And states to come in the widow, and my count!
My share to-day will not be bought for forty ——   230

Enter DOL.

   Dol. What?
   Face. Pounds, dainty Dorothy!   Art thou so near?
   Dol. Yes; say, lord general, how fares our camp?

---

   [1] Large, loose breeches.   [2] Unwieldy Dutch ships.   [3] Hose.
   [4] The Cinque Ports were on the south coast of England, facing France, and under the government of a warden.   Originally there were five, as the name implies: Dover, Sandwich, Romney, Hastings, and Hithe; Winchelsea and Rye were added later.
   [5] The famous Anabaptist leader, put to death in 1536.

Face. As with the few that had entrenched themselves
Safe, by their discipline, against a world, Dol,
And laughed within those trenches, and grew fat
With thinking on the booties, Dol, brought in
Daily by their small parties. This dear hour
A doughty don is taken with my Dol;
And thou may'st make his ransom what thou wilt,
My Dousabel; he shall be brought here fettered
With thy fair looks, before he sees thee, — and thrown
In a down-bed, as dark as any dungeon;
Till he be tame
As the poor blackbirds were in the great frost,
Or bees are with a bason; and so hive him
My little God's-gift.[1]

 Dol. What is he, general?
 Face. An adalantado,
A grandee, girl. Was not my Dapper here yet?
 Dol. No.
 Face. Nor my Drugger?
 Dol. Neither.
 Face. A plague on 'em,
They are so long a-furnishing! Such stinkards
Would not be seen upon these festival days. —

Re-enter SUBTLE.

How now! have you done?
 Sub. Done. They are gone: the sum
Is here in bank, my Face. I would we knew
Another chapman now would buy 'em outright.
 Face. 'Slid, Nab shall do't against he have the widow
To furnish household.

[1] A play on Dol's name, *Dorothea* meaning *God's-gifts.*

Sub. Excellent, well thought on:
Pray God he come!
　Face. I pray he keep away
Till our new business be o'erpast.
　Sub. But, Face,
How cam'st thou by this secret don?
　Face. A spirit
Brought me th' intelligence in a paper here,　　　　270
As I was conjuring yonder in my circle
For Surly; I have my flies abroad. Your bath
Is famous, Subtle, by my means. Sweet Dol,
Tickle him with thy mother-tongue. His great
Verdugoship[1] has not a jot of language;
So much the easier to be cozened, my Dolly.
He will come here in a hired coach, obscure,
And our own coachman, whom I have sent as guide,
No creature else. (*Knocking without.*)　Who's that?
　　　　　　　　　　　　　　　　　　　[*Exit* DOL.
　Sub. It is not he?　　　　　　　　　　　　　　280
　Face. O no, not yet this hour.

Re-enter DOL.

　Sub. Who is't?
　Dol. Dapper,
Your clerk.
　Face. God's will then, Queen of Fairy,
On with your tire;—(*exit* DOL) — and doctor, with your robes.
Let's dispatch him, for God's sake.
　Sub. 'Twill be long.
　Face. I warrant you, take but the cue I give you,

---

[1] Verdugo was the name of a noble Spanish family.

It shall be brief enough. — (*Goes to the window.*)—'Slight,
　　here are more!
Abel, and I think the angry boy, the heir,
That fain would quarrel.
　　Sub. And the widow?
　　Face. No.
Not that I see. Away! 　　　　　　　　[*Exit* SUB.

　　　　　　Enter DAPPER.

　　　　　　　　Oh, sir, you are welcome.
The doctor is within a-moving for you;
I have had the most ado to win him to it!
He swears you'll be the darling of the dice:
He never heard her highness dote till now,
Your aunt has given you the most gracious words
That can be thought on.
　　Dap. Shall I see her grace?
　　Face. See her, and kiss her too. —

　　　　Enter ABEL, *followed by* KASTRIL.

　　　　　　　　What, honest Nab!
Hast brought the damask?
　　Drug. No, sir; here's tobacco.
　　Face. 'Tis well done, Nab: thou'lt bring the damask too?
　　Drug. Yes: here's the gentleman, captain, Master Kastril,
I have brought to see the doctor.
　　Face. Where's the widow?
　　Drug. Sir, as he likes, his sister, he says, shall come.
　　Face. Oh, is it so? Good time. Is your name Kastril, sir?
　　Kas. Ay, and the best of the Kastrils, I'd be sorry else,
By fifteen hundred a-year. Where is the doctor?
My mad tobacco-boy, here, tells me of one

That can do things: has he any skill?
   Face. Wherein, sir?
   Kas. To carry a business, manage a quarrel fairly,
Upon fit terms.
   Face. It seems, sir, you are but young
About the town, that can make that a question.   320
   Kas. Sir, not so young but I have heard some speech
Of the angry boys, and seen them take tobacco,
And in his shop; and I can take it too.
And I would fain be one of 'em, and go down
And practise in the country.
   Face. Sir, for the duello,
The doctor, I assure you, shall inform you,
To the least shadow of a hair, and show you
An instrument he has of his own making,
Wherewith no sooner shall you make report   330
Of any quarrel, but he will take the height on't
Most instantly, and tell in what degree
Of safety it lies in, or mortality.
And how it may be borne, whether in a right line,
Or a half-circle; or may else be cast
Into an angle blunt, if not acute:
All this he will demonstrate. And then, rules
To give and take the lie by.
   Kas. How! to take it?
   Face. Yes, in oblique he'll show you, or in circle;[1]   340
But never in diameter. The whole town
Study his theorems, and dispute them ordinarily
At the eating academies.
   Kas. But does he teach

---

[1] One critic remarks that Shakespeare, Fletcher, and Jonson tried to bring duelling into disrepute, by satirizing it; yet Jonson fought a duel, and killed his man.

Living by the wits too?
 Face. Anything whatever.
You cannot think that subtlety but he reads it.
He made me a captain. I was a stark pimp,
Just of your standing, 'fore I met with him;
It is not two months since. I'll tell you his method: 350
First, he will enter you at some ordinary.¹
 Kas. No, I'll not come there; you shall pardon me.
 Face. For why, sir?
 Kas. There's gaming there, and tricks.
 Face. Why, would you be
A gallant, and not game?
 Kas. Ay, 'twill spend a man.
 Face. Spend you! It will repair you when you are spent:
How do they live by their wits there, that have vented
Six times your fortunes? 360
 Kas. What, three thousand a year!
 Face. Ay, forty thousand.
 Kas. Are there such?
 Face. Ay, sir,
And gallants yet. Here's a young gentleman
Is born to nothing—(*points to* DAPPER) — forty marks a-year,
Which I count nothing:— he is to be initiated,
And have a fly of the doctor. He will win you,
By unresistible luck, within this fortnight,
Enough to buy a barony. They will set him 370
Upmost, at the groom porters, all the Christmas:
And for the whole year through, at every place
Where there is play, present him with the chair;
The best attendance, the best drink; sometimes
Two glasses of canary, and pay nothing;

   ¹ Eating-place.

The purest linen and the sharpest knife,
The partridge next his trencher; and somewhere
The dainty nook in private with the dainty.
You shall have your ordinaries bid for him,
As playhouses for a poet; and the master   380
Pray him aloud to name what dish he affects,
Which must be buttered shrimps; and those that drink
To no mouth else, will drink to his, as being
The goodly president mouth of all the board.
   Kas. Do you not gull one?
   Face. Ods, my life! do you think it?
You shall have a cast commander (can but get
In credit with a glover, or a spurrier,
For some two pair of either's ware aforehand),
Will by most swift posts, dealing with him,   390
Arrive at competent means to keep himself,
And be admired for't.
   Kas. Will the doctor teach this?
   Face. He will do more, sir: when your land is gone,
As men of spirit hate to keep earth long
In a vacation, when small money is stirring,
And ordinaries suspended till the term,
He'll show a perspective, where on one side
You shall behold the faces and the persons
Of all sufficient young heirs in town,   400
Whose bonds are current for commodity[1];
On th' other side, the merchants' forms, and others,
That without help of any second broker,
Who would expect a share, will trust such parcels:
In the third square, the very street and sign

---

[1] Young spendthrifts had to take in merchandise part of the sums they borrowed from usurers, who thus made a large profit.

Where the commodity dwells, and does but wait
To be delivered, be it pepper, soap,
Hops, or tobacco, oatmeal, wood, or cheeses.
All which you may so handle, to enjoy
To your own use, and never stand obliged.   410
    Kas. I' faith! is he such a fellow?
    Face. Why, Nab here knows him.
And then for making matches for rich widows,
Young gentlewomen, heirs, the fortunatest man!
He's sent to, far and near, all over England,
To have his counsel, and to know their fortunes.
    Kas. God's will, my suster shall see him.
    Face. I'll tell you, sir,
What he did tell me of Nab. It's a strange thing: —
By the way, you must eat no cheese, Nab, it breeds 420
    melancholy,
And that same melancholy breeds worms; but pass it: —
He told me honest Nab here was ne'er at tavern
But once in's life.
    Drug. Truth, and no more I was not.
    Face. And then he was so sick ——
    Drug. Could he tell you that too?
    Face. How should I know it?
    Drug. In troth we had been a-shooting,
And had a piece of fat ram mutton to supper,   430
That lay so heavy o' my stomach ——
    Face. And he has no head
To bear any wine; for what with the noise of the fiddlers
And care of his shop, for he dares keep no servants ——
    Drug. My head did so ache ——
    Face. As he was fain to be brought home,
The doctor told me: and then a good old woman ——

Drug. Yes, faith — she dwells in Sea-coal Lane — did cure me,
With sodden ale and pellitory[1] of the wall;
Cost me but twopence. — I had another sickness   440
Was worse than that.
   Face. Ay, that was with the grief
Thou took'st for being cessed[2] at eighteen-pence
For the waterwork.
   Drug. In truth, and it was like
T' have cost me almost my life.
   Face. Thy hair went off?
   Drug. Yes, sir; 'twas done for spite.
   Face. Nay, so says the doctor.
   Kas. Pray thee, tobacco boy, go fetch my suster;   450
I'll see this learned boy before I go,
And so shall she.
   Face. Sir, he is busy now;
But if you have a sister to fetch hither,
Perhaps your own pains may command her sooner,
And he by that time will be free.
   Kas. I go.   [*Exit.*
   Face. Drugger, she's thine: the damask!   [*Exit* ABEL.
                                   (*Aside*) Subtle and I
Must wrestle for her. — Come on, Master Dapper,
You see how I turn clients here away,   460
To give your cause dispatch; have you performed
The ceremonies were enjoined you?
   Dap. Yes, of the vinegar
And the clean shirt.
   Face. 'Tis well: that shirt may do you
More worship than you think. Your aunt's a-fire,

---

[1] A kind of weeds which grow on walls.   [2] Taxed.

But that she will not show it, t' have a sight of you.
Have you provided for her grace's servants?
  Dap. Yes, here are six score Edward shillings.
  Face. Good!
  Dap. And an old Harry's sovereign.
  Face. Very good!
  Dap. And three James shillings, and an Elizabeth groat;
Just twenty nobles.
  Face. Oh, you are too just.
I would you had had the other noble in Maries.
  Dap. I have some Philip and Maries.
  Face. Ay, those same
Are best of all: where are they?   Hark, the doctor.

Enter SUBTLE *disguised like a priest of Fairy, with a stripe of cloth.*

  Sub. (*in a feigned voice*).   Is yet her grace's cousin come?
  Face. He is come.
  Sub. And is he fasting?
  Face. Yes.
  Sub. And hath cried *hum?*
  Face. Thrice, you must answer.
  Dap. Thrice.
  Sub. And as oft *buz?*
  Face. If you have, say.
  Dap. I have.
  Sub. Then, to her cuz,
Hoping that he hath vinegared his senses,
As he was bid, the Fairy Queen dispenses,
By me, this robe, the petticoat of fortune;
Which that he straight put on, she doth importune.
And though to fortune near be her petticoat,

SCENE II.]   THE ALCHEMIST.   195

Yet nearer is her smock, the Queen doth note:
And therefore, even of that a piece she hath sent,
Which, being a child, to wrap him in was rent;
And prays him for a scarf he now will wear it,
With as much love as then her grace did tear it,   500
About his eyes — (*they bind him with the rag*) — to show he
   is fortunate.
And, trusting unto her to make his state,
He'll throw away all worldly pelf about him;
Which that he will perform, she doth not doubt him.
  Face. She need not doubt him, sir. Alas, he has nothing
But what he will part withal as willingly
Upon her grace's word — throw away your purse —
As she would ask it; — handkerchiefs and all —
              [*He throws away as they bid him.*
She cannot bid that thing but he'll obey. —
If you have a ring about you, cast it off,   510
Or a silver seal at your wrist; her grace will send
Her fairies here to search you, therefore deal
Directly with her highness: if they find
That you conceal a mite, you are undone.
  Dap. Truly, there's all.
  Face. All what?
  Dap. My money: truly.
  Face. Keep nothing that is transitory about you.
(*Aside to* SUBTLE.) Bid Dol play music. — Look, the elves
    are come   [DOL *plays on the cittern within.*
To pinch you, if you tell not truth. Advise you.   520
                    [*They pinch him.*
  Dap. Oh! I have a paper with a spur-ryal[1] in't.
  Face. Ti, ti.

      [1] A gold coin, valued at 15*s.* in 1606.

They knew't, they say.
  Sub. *Ti, ti, ti, ti.* He has more yet.
  Face. *Ti, ti-ti-ti.* In the other pocket.   [*Aside to* SUB.
  Sub. *Titi, titi, titi, titi, titi.*
They must pinch him or he will never confess, they say.
                                    [*They pinch him again.*
  Dap. Oh, oh!
  Face. Nay, pray you hold : he is her grace's nephew.
Ti, ti, ti? What care you? Good faith, you shall care. —
Deal plainly, sir, and shame the fairies. Show   531
You are innocent.
  Dap. By this good light, I have nothing.
  Sub. *Ti, ti, ti, ti, to, ta.* He does equivocate, she says :
Ti, ti, do ti, ti, ti, do, ti, da; and swears by the *light* when
he is blinded.
  Dap. By this good *dark*, I have nothing but a half-crown
Of gold about my wrist, that my love gave me ;
And a leaden heart I wore since she forsook me.
  Face. I thought 'twas something. And would you incur
Your aunt's displeasure for these trifles? Come,   540
I had rather you had thrown away twenty half-crowns.
                                              [*Takes it off.*
You may wear your leaden heart still. —

            Enter DOL *hastily.*

                              How now!
  Sub. What news, Dol?
  Dol. Yonder's your knight, Sir Mammon.
  Face. Ods lid, we never thought of him till now!
Where is he?
  Dol. Here hard by : he is at the door.
  Sub. And you are not ready, now! Dol, get his suit.
                                                [*Exit* DOL.

He must not be sent back.

Face. Oh, by no means. 550
What shall we do with this same puffin[1] here,
Now he's on the spit?

Sub. Why, lay him back awhile
With some device.

Re-enter DOL *with* FACE'S *clothes.*

— *Ti, ti, ti, ti, ti, ti.* Would her grace speak with me?
I come. — Help, Dol! [*Knocking without.*
 Face (*speaks through the key-hole*). Who's there? Sir Epicure,
My master's in the way. Please you to walk
Three or four turns, but till his back be turned,
And I am for you. Quickly, Dol! 560

Sub. Her grace
Commends her kindly to you, Master Dapper.

Dap. I long to see her grace.

Sub. She now is set
At dinner in her bed, and she has sent you
From her own private trencher a dead mouse,
And a piece of gingerbread, to be merry withal,
And stay your stomach, lest you faint with fasting.
Yet if you could hold out till she saw you, she says
It would be better for you. 570

Face. Sir, he shall
Hold out, an 'twere this two hours, for her highness;
I can assure you that. We will not lose
All we have done.

Sub. He must not see nor speak
To anybody till then.

[1] Kind of gull.

Face. For that we'll put, sir,
A stay in's mouth.
   Sub. Of what?
   Face. Of gingerbread. 580
Make you it fit.   He that hath pleased her grace
Thus far, shall not now crinkle¹ for a little. —
Gape, sir, and let him fit you.
            [*They thrust a gag of gingerbread in his mouth.*
   Sub. Come along, sir,
I now must show you Fortune's privy lodgings.
   Face. Are they perfumed, and his bath ready?
   Sub. All :
Only the fumigation's somewhat strong.
   Face (*speaking through the key-hole*). Sir Epicure, I am
      yours, sir, by-and-by.   [*Exeunt with* DAPPER.

ACT IV.

SCENE I. — *A Room in* LOVEWIT'S *House.*

Enter FACE *and* MAMMON.

   Face. Oh, sir, you are come in the only finest time.
   Mam. Where's master?
   Face. Now preparing for projection, sir.
Your stuff will be all changed shortly.
   Mam. Into gold?
   Face. To gold and silver, sir.
   Mam. Silver I care not for.
   Face. Yes, sir, a little to give beggars.
   Mam. Where's the lady?

¹ Bend, waver.

Face. At hand here. I have told her such brave things of
  you,
Touching your bounty and your noble spirit——
  Mam. Hast thou?
  Face. As she is almost in her fit to see you.
But, good sir, no divinity in your conference,
For fear of putting her in rage.
  Mam. I warrant thee.
  Face. Six men, sir, will not hold her down; and then
If the old man should hear or see you——
  Mam. Fear not.
  Face. The very house, sir, would run mad. You know it,
How scrupulous he is, and violent,
'Gainst the least act of sin.[1] Physic or mathematics,
Poetry, state, or frolic, as I told you,
She will endure, and never startle; but
No word of controversy.
  Mam. I am schooled, good Ulen.
  Face. And you must praise her house, remember that,
And her nobility.
  Mam. Let me alone:
No herald, no, nor antiquary, Lungs,
Shall do it better. Go.
  Face (*aside*). Why, this is yet
A kind of modern happiness to have
Dol Common for a great lady.   [*Exit.*
  Mam. Now, Epicure,
Heighten thyself, talk to her all in gold;
Rain her as many showers as Jove did drops
Unto his Danaë; show the god a miser
Compared with Mammon. What! The stone will do't.

[1] Alchemists pretended to lead spotless lives, in order to the success of their experiments.

She shall feel gold, taste gold, hear gold, sleep gold; 40
I will be puissant and mighty in my talk to her.

Re-enter FACE, *with* DOL *richly dressed.*

Here she comes.
    Face. To him, Dol, suckle him. This is the noble knight;
I told your ladyship ——
    Mam. Madam, with your pardon,
I kiss your vesture.
    Dol. Sir, I were uncivil
If I would suffer that; my lip to you, sir.
    Mam. I hope my lord, your brother, be in health, lady.
    Dol. My lord, my brother is, though I no lady, sir. 50
    Face (*aside*). Well said, my Guinea bird.
    Mam. Right noble madam ——
    Face (*aside*). Oh, we shall have most fierce idolatry.
    Mam. 'Tis your prerogative ——
    Dol. Rather your courtesy.
    Mam. Were there nought else to enlarge your virtues to me,
These answers speak your breeding and your blood.
    Dol. Blood we boast none, sir, a poor baron's daughter.
    Mam. Poor! And gat you? Profane not. Had your father
Slept all the happy remnant of his life 60
He had done enough to make himself, his issue,
And his posterity noble.
    Dol. Sir, although
We may be said to want the gilt and trappings,
The dress of honour, yet we strive to keep
The seeds and the materials.
    Mam. I do see

The old ingredient, virtue, was not lost,
Nor the drug money used to make your compound.
There is a strange nobility in your eye,   70
This lip, that chin !   Methinks you do resemble
One of the Austrian princes.¹
　Face (*aside*). Very like !
Her father was an Irish costermonger.²
　Mam. The House of Valois³ just had such a nose,
And such a forehead yet the Medici
Of Florence boast.
　Dol. Troth, and I have been likened
To all these princes.
　Face (*aside*). I'll be sworn I heard it.   80
　Mam. I know not how !   It is not any one,
But e'en the very choice of all their features.
　Face (*aside*). I'll in, and laugh.   [*Exit.*
　Mam. A certain touch, or air,
That sparkles a divinity beyond
An earthly beauty !
　Dol. Oh, you play the courtier.
　Mam. Good lady, give me leave ——
　Dol. In faith I may not,
To mock me, sir.   90
　Mam. To burn in this sweet flame ;
The phœnix never knew a nobler death.
　Dol. Nay, now you court the courtier, and destroy
What you would build : this art, sir, in your words
Calls your whole faith in question.

---

[1] The Hapsburgers were noted for "a sweet fulness of the lower lip." Swift assigned this feature to the Emperor of Lilliput.

[2] The hucksters in London were usually Irish.

[3] The characteristic feature of the Valois was a Roman nose.

Mam. By my soul ——
Dol. Nay, oaths are made of the same air, sir.
Mam. Nature
Never bestow'd upon mortality
A more unblamed, a more harmonious feature; 100
She played the step-dame in all faces else:
Sweet madam, let me be particular ——
  Dol. Particular, sir! I pray you know your distance.
  Mam. In no ill sense, sweet lady; but to ask
How your fair graces pass the hours? I see
You are lodged here in the house of a rare man,
An excellent artist; but what's that to you?
  Dol. Yes, sir; I study here the mathematics
And distillation.[1]
  Mam. Oh, I cry your pardon. 110
He's a divine instructor: can extract
The souls of all things by his art; call all
The virtues and the miracles of the sun
Into a temperate furnace; teach dull nature
What her own forces are. A man, the emperor
Has courted above Kelly[2]; sent his medals
And chains to invite him.
  Dol. Ay, and for his physic, sir, ——

[1] That is, astrology and alchemy.
[2] Edward Kelly, or Talbot, a notorious impostor of the sixteenth century, was born at Worcester, and apprenticed to an apothecary. Being convicted of fraud, his ears were cut off. Dee, another alchemist, took Kelly and Zaski, a young Pole, abroad. Kelly pretended to have discovered the philosopher's stone, and was patronized by the Emperor Rudolf II, who entertained him at Prague for a long time. But as the stone did not materialize, Kelly and his accomplices were thrown into prison. In attempting to escape, Kelly broke his leg, and died. Gifford remarks that this fraudulent trio — Kelly, Dee, and Zaski — may have suggested *Subtle*, *Face*, and *Dol*, to Jonson.

Mam. Above the art of Æsculapius,
That drew the envy of the Thunderer!   120
I know all this, and more.
 Dol. Troth, I am taken, sir,
Whole with these studies, that contemplate nature.
 Mam. It is a noble humour; but this form
Was not intended to so dark a use.
Had you been crooked, foul, of some coarse mould,
A cloister had done well; but such a feature
That might stand up the glory of a kingdom,
To live recluse, is a mere solecism,
Though in a nunnery. It must not be.   130
I muse, my lord your brother will permit it:
You should spend half my land first, were I he.
Does not this diamond better on my finger
Than in the quarry?
 Dol. Yes.
 Mam. Why, you are like it.
You were created, lady, for the light.
Here, you shall wear it; take it, the first pledge
Of what I speak, to bind you to believe me.
 Dol. In chains of adamant?   140
 Mam. Yes, the strongest bands.
And take a secret too — here, by your side,
Doth stand this hour the happiest man in Europe.
 Dol. You are contented, sir?
 Mam. Nay, in true being,
The envy of princes and the fear of states.
 Dol. Say you so, Sir Epicure?
 Mam. Yes, and thou shalt prove it,
Daughter of honour. I have cast mine eye
Upon thy form, and I will rear this beauty   150

Above all styles.
  Dol. You mean no treason, sir?
  Mam. No, I will take away that jealousy.
I am the lord of the philosopher's stone,
And thou the lady.
  Dol. How sir! Have you that?
  Mam. I am the master of the mastery.[1]
This day the good old wretch here o' the house
Has made it for us; now he's at projection.
Think therefore thy first wish now, let me hear it,   160
And it shall rain into thy lap, no shower,
But floods of gold, whole cataracts, a deluge,
To get a nation on thee.
  Dol. You are pleased, sir,
To work on the ambition of our sex.
  Mam. I am pleased the glory of her sex should know
This nook, here, of the Friars is no climate
For her to live obscurely in, to learn
Physic and surgery, for the constable's wife
Of some odd hundred in Essex; but come forth   170
And taste the air of palaces; eat, drink
The toils of empirics, and their boasted practice;
Tincture of pearl and coral, gold and amber;
Be seen at feasts and triumphs; have it asked,
What miracle she is; set all the eyes
Of court a-fire, like a burning glass,
And work them into cinders, when the jewels
Of twenty states adorn thee, and the light
Strikes out the stars! that when thy name is mentioned
Queens may look pale; and we but showing our love,   180
Nero's Poppæa may be lost in story!

               [1] Magisterium.

Thus will we have it.
 Dol. I could well consent sir.
But in a monarchy how will this be?
The prince will soon take notice, and both seize
You and your stone, it being a wealth unfit
For any private subject.
 Mam. If he knew it.
 Dol. Yourself do boast it, sir.
 Mam. To thee, my life.   190
 Dol. Oh, but beware, sir! you may come to end
The remnant of your days in a loathed prison,
By speaking of it.
 Mam. 'Tis no idle fear:
We'll therefore go withal, my girl, and live
In a free state, where we will eat our mullets
Soused in high-country wines, sup pheasants' eggs,
And have our cockles boiled in silver shells;
Our shrimps to swim again, as when they lived,
In a rare butter made of dolphins' milk,   200
Whose cream does look like opals: and with these
Delicate meats, set ourselves high for pleasure,
And take us down again, and then renew
Our youth and strength with drinking the elixir,
And so enjoy a perpetuity
Of life and lust! And thou shalt have thy wardrobe
Richer than nature's, still to change thyself,
And vary oftener, for thy pride, than she,
Or art, her wise and almost-equal servant.

Re-enter FACE.

 Face. Sir, you are too loud. I hear you every word   210
Into the laboratory. Some fitter place;

The garden or great chamber above. How like you her?
    Mam. Excellent! Lungs. There's for thee.
                                                            [Gives him money.
    Face. But do you hear?
Good sir, beware, no mention of the rabbins.
    Mam. We think not on 'em.   *[Exeunt* MAM. *and* DOL.
    Face. Oh, it is well, sir. — Subtle!

                     Enter SUBTLE.

Dost thou not laugh?
    Sub. Yes; are they gone?
    Face. All's clear.   220
    Sub. The widow is come.
    Face. And your quarrelling disciple?
    Sub. Ay.
    Face. I must to my captainship again, then.
    Sub. Stay, bring them in first.
    Face. So I meant. What is she?
A bonnibel?
    Sub. I know not.
    Face. We'll draw lots:
You'll stand to that?   230
    Sub. What else?
    Face. Oh, for a suit,
To fall now like a curtain, flap!
    Sub. To the door, man.
    Face. You'll have the first kiss, 'cause I am not ready.
                                                                          [Exit.
    Sub. Yes, and perhaps hit you through both the nostrils.
    Face (within). Who would you speak with?
    Kas. (within). Where's the captain?
    Face (within). Gone, sir,

About some business. 240
   Kas. (*within*). Gone!
   Face (*within*). He'll return straight.
But Master Doctor, his lieutenant, is here.

     Enter KASTRIL, *followed by* DAME PLIANT.

   Sub. Come near, my worshipful boy, my *terræ fili*,
That is, my boy of land; make thy approaches:
Welcome; I know thy lusts and thy desires,
And I will serve and satisfy them. Begin,
Charge me from thence, or thence, or in this line;
Here is my centre: ground thy quarrel.
   Kas. You lie. 250
   Sub. How, child of wrath and anger! the loud lie?
For what, my sudden boy?
   Kas. Nay, that look you to,
I am aforehand.
   Sub. Oh, this is no true grammar,
And as ill logic! You must render causes, child,
Your first and second intentions, know your canons
And your divisions, moods, degrees, and differences,
Your predicaments, substance, and accident,
Series, extern and intern, with their causes, 260
Efficient, material, formal, final,
And have your elements perfect?
   Kas. (*aside*). What is this!
The angry tongue he talks in?
   Sub. That false precept
Of being aforehand has deceived a number,
And made them enter quarrels, oftentimes
Before they were aware; and afterward
Against their wills.

Kas. How must I do then, sir? 270
Sub. I cry this lady mercy: she should first
Have been saluted. (*Kisses her.*) I do call you lady,
Because you are to be one ere't be long,
My soft and buxom widow.
Kas. Is she, i' faith?
Sub. Yes, or my art is an egregious liar.
Kas. How know you?
Sub. By inspection on her forehead,
And subtlety of her lip, which must be tasted
Often, to make a judgment. (*Kisses her again.*)
                        'Slight, she melts 280
Like a myrobolane [1]:—here is yet a line,
In *rivo frontis*, tells me he is no knight.
Dame P. What is he then, sir?
Sub. Let me see your hand.
Oh, your *linea fortunæ* makes it plain;
And stella here *in Monte Veneris*.
But, most of all, *junctura annularis*.[2]
He is a soldier, or a man of art, lady,
But shall have some great honour shortly.
Dame P. Brother, 290
He's a rare man, believe me!

    Re-enter FACE *in his uniform.*

Kas. Hold your peace.
Here comes the t'other rare man.—Save you, captain.
Face. Good Master Kastril! Is this your sister?
Kas. Ay, sir.
Please you to kuss her, and be proud to know her.
Face. I shall be proud to know you, lady. [*Kisses her.*

[1] A dried plum.   [2] See *Subtle's* speech, p. 138.

Dame P. Brother,
He calls me lady too.
   Kas. Ay, peace: I heard it.   *[Takes her aside.*
   Face. The count is come.
   Sub. Where is he?
   Face. At the door.
   Sub. Why, you must entertain him.
   Face. What will you do
With these the while?
   Sub. Why, have them up, and show them
Some fustian book, or the dark glass.
   Face. 'Fore God,
She is a delicate dab-chick[1]! I must have her. *[Exit.*
   Sub. Must you! ay, if your fortune will, you must. —
Come, sir, the captain will come to us presently:
I'll have you to my chamber of demonstrations,
Where I will show you both the grammar and logic
And rhetoric of quarrelling; my whole method
Drawn out in tables; and my instrument,
That hath the several scales upon't, shall make you
Able to quarrel at a straw's-breadth by moonlight.
And, lady, I'll have you look in a glass,
Some half an hour, but to clear your eyesight,
Against you see your fortune; which is greater
Than I may judge upon the sudden, trust me.
          [Exit, followed by Kas. *and* Dame P.

Re-enter Face.

   Face. Where are you, doctor?
   Sub. (*within*). I'll come to you presently.

[1] Small waterfowl.

Face. I will have this same widow, now I have seen her,
On any composition.

Re-enter SUBTLE.

Sub. What do you say?
Face. Have you disposed of them?
Sub. I have sent them up.
Face. Subtle, in troth, I needs must have this widow. 330
Sub. Is that the matter?
Face. Nay, but hear me.
Sub. Go to,
If you rebel once, Dol shall know it all:
Therefore be quiet, and obey your chance.
Face. Nay, thou art so violent now. Do but conceive
Thou art old and canst not serve——
Sub. Who cannot? I?
'Slight, I will serve her with thee, for a——
Face. Nay, 340
But understand: I'll give you composition.
Sub. I will not treat with thee: what! sell my fortune?
'Tis better than my birthright. Do not murmur:
Win her, and carry her. If you grumble, Dol
Knows it directly.
Face. Well, sir, I am silent.
Will you go help to fetch in Don in state? [*Exit.*
Sub. I follow you, sir: we must keep Face in awe,
Or he will overlook us like a tyrant.

Re-enter FACE, *introducing* SURLEY *disguised as a Spaniard.*

Brain of a tailor! who comes here? Don John[1]! 350

---

[1] Don John of Austria, hero of the battle of Lepanto in 1571; he was often represented in tapestries in Jonson's time.

Sur. *Señores, beso las manos a vuestras mercedes.*[1]
Sub. Stab me: I shall never hold, man.
He looks in that deep ruff like a head in a platter,
Served in by a short cloak upon two trestles.
   Face. Or, what do you say to a collar of brawn, cut down
Beneath the souse,[2] and wriggled with a knife?
   Sub. 'Slud, he does look too fat to be a Spaniard.
   Face. Perhaps some Fleming or some Hollander got him
In D'Alva's time; Count Egmont's bastard.[3]
   Sub. Don,   360
Your scurvy, yellow, Madrid face is welcome.
   Sur. *Gratia.*
   Sub. He speaks out of a fortification.
Pray God he have no squibs in those deep sets.[4]
   Sur. *Por dios, señores, muy linda casa!*[5]
   Sub. What says he?
   Face. Praises the house, I think;
I know no more but's action.
   Sub. Yes, the *casa,*
My precious Diego will prove fair enough   370
To cozen you in. Do you mark? You shall
Be cozened, Diego.
   Face. Cozened, do you see,
My worthy Donzel, cozened.
   Sur. *Entiendo.*[6]

[1] Usual Spanish salutation; "Gentlemen, I kiss your hands."
[2] Ear.
[3] Alva, the atrocious Spanish governor of the Netherlands, from 1567 to 1573, who put to death Egmont, a Flemish noble, in 1568.
[4] Plaits in his ruff.
[5] "Gad, sirs, a very pretty house."   [6] "I understand."

Sub. Do you intend it? So do we, dear Don.
Have you brought pistolets[1] or portagues,
My solemn Don? — Dost thou feel any?
    Face (*feels his pockets*). Full.
    Sub. You shall be emptied, Don, pumped and drawn   380
Dry, as they say.
    Face. Milked, in troth, sweet Don.
    Sub. See all the monsters; the great lion of all, Don.
    Sur. Con licencia, se puede ver a esta señora ?[2]
    Sub. What talks he now?
    Face. Of the senora.
    Sub. Oh, Don,
That is the lioness, which you shall see
Also, my Don.
    Face. 'Slid, Subtle, how shall we do?   390
    Sub. For what?
    Face. Why Dol's employed, you know.
    Sub. That's true,
'Fore heaven I know not: he must stay, that's all.
    Face. Stay! that he must not by no means.
    Sub. No! Why?
    Face. Unless you'll mar all. 'Slight, he will suspect it:
And then he will not pay, not half so well.
This is a travelled master, and does know
All the delays; a notable hot rascal,   400
And looks already rampant.
    Sub. 'Sdeath, and Mammon must not be troubled.
    Face. Mammon! in no case.
    Sub. What shall we do then?
    Face. Think: you must be sudden.

---

[1] Coins.   [2] "If you please, may I see the lady?"

Sur. *Entiendo que la señora es tan hermosa, que codicio tan verla, como la bien aventurança de mi vida.*[1]

    Face. *Mi vida!* 'Slid, Subtle, he puts me in mind o' the widow.
What dost thou say to draw her to it, ha!
And tell her 'tis her fortune? All our venture   410
Now lies upon't. It is but one man more,
Which of us chance to have her: and beside, —
What dost thou think on't, Subtle?

    Sub. Who, I? Why ——

    Face. The credit of our house too is engaged.

    Sub. You made me an offer for my share erewhile.
What wilt thou give me i' faith?

    Face. Oh, by that light
I'll not buy now: you know your doom to me.
E'en take your lot, obey your chance, sir; win her,   420
And wear her out, for me.

    Sub. 'Slight, I'll not have her then.

    Face. It is the common cause; therefore bethink you.
Dol else must know it as you said.

    Sub. I care not.

    Sur. *Señores, porque se tarda tanto?*[2]

    Sub. Faith, I am not fit, I am old.

    Face. That's now no reason, sir.

    Sur. *Puede ser, de hacer burla de mi amor?*[3]

    Face. You hear the Don too? by this air I call,   430
And loose the hinges: Dol!

    Sub. A plague of hell ——

    Face. Will you then do?

---

[1] "I hear the lady is so handsome, that I am eager to see her, as the best fortune of my life."
[2] "Why this long delay, sirs?"
[3] "Can it be to make sport of my love?"

Sub. You are a terrible rogue!
I'll think of this: will you, sir, call the widow?
　Face. Yes, and I'll take her too with all her faults,
Now I do think on't better.
　Sub. With all my heart, sir;
Am I discharged o' the lot?
　Face. As you please.   440
　Sub. Hands.   [*They take hands.*
　Face. Remember now, that upon any change
You never claim her.
　Sub. Much good joy and health to you, sir.
Marry her so! Fate, let me wed a witch first.
　Sur. Por estas honradas barbas¹ ——
　Sub. He swears by his beard.
Dispatch, and call the brother too.   [*Exit* FACE.
　Sur. Tengo duda, señores, que no me hagan alguna
traycion.²   450
　Sub. How, issue on? yes, præsto, senor. Please you
Enthratha the *chambratha*, worthy Don:
Where if you please the fates, in your *bathada*,
You shall be soaked, and stroked, and tubbed, and rubbed,
And scrubbed, and fubbed, dear Don, before you go.
You shall in faith, my scurvy baboon Don,
Be curried, clawed, and flawed, and tawed indeed.
I will the heartilier go about it now,
And make the widow yours so much the sooner,
To be revenged on this impetuous Face: 460
The quickly doing of it is the grace.
　　　　　　　　　　　[*Exeunt* SUB. *and* SURLY.³

　¹ "By these honored beards."
　² "I suspect, sirs, that you are playing a trick on me."
　³ "The Spanish speeches smack of a Conversation Book. Jonson seems to have borrowed this device from Plautus, in *Pœnulus*." — *Gifford.*

SCENE II.—*Another Room in the same.*

Enter FACE, KASTRIL, *and* DAME PLIANT.

Face. Come, lady : I knew the doctor would not leave
Till he had found the very nick of her fortune.
   Kas. To be a countess, say you, a Spanish countess, sir?
   Dame P. Why, is that better than an English countess?
   Face. Better! 'Slight, make you that a question, lady?[1]
   Kas. Nay, she is a fool, captain, you must pardon her.
   Face. Ask from your courtier, to your Inns-of-Court man,
To your mere milliner ; they will tell you all,
Your Spanish gennet is the best horse ; your Spanish
Stoup[2] is the best garb ; your Spanish beard   10
Is the best cut ; your Spanish ruffs are the best
Wear ; your Spanish pavin[3] the best dance ;
Your Spanish titillation in a glove
The best perfume : and for your Spanish pike
And Spanish blade, let your poor captain speak—
Here comes the doctor.

Enter SUBTLE, *with a paper.*

   Sub. My most honoured lady,
For so I am now to style you, having found
By this my scheme you are to undergo
An honourable fortune very shortly,   20
What will you say now, if some ——
   Face. I have told her all, sir ;
And her right worshipful brother here, that she shall be

---

[1] In the early years of James I's reign, Spanish influence and Spanish fashions were paramount in English court society.

[2] No commentator nor dictionary explains this word.

[3] The *pavane*, a grave and stately dance, so called from the city of Pavia.

A countess; do not delay them, sir: a Spanish countess.

Sub. Still, my scarce-worshipful captain, you can keep
No secret! Well, since he has told you, madam,
Do you forgive him, and I do.

Kas. She shall do that, sir;
I'll look to't, 'tis my charge.

Sub. Well then; nought rests 30
But that she fit her love now to her fortune.

Dame P. Truly, I shall never brook a Spaniard.

Sub. No!

Dame P. Never since eighty-eight[1] could I abide them,
And that was some three years afore I was born, in truth.

Sub. Come, you must love him, or be miserable;
Choose which you will.

Face. By this good rush, persuade her.

Kas. Ods lid, you shall love him, or I'll kick you.

Dame P. Why, 40
I'll do as you will have me, brother.

Kas. Do,
Or by this hand I'll maul you.

Face. Nay, good sir,
Be not so fierce.

Sub. No, my enraged child;
She will be ruled. What, when she comes to taste
The pleasures of a countess! to be courted ——

Face. And kissed, and then come forth in pomp.

Sub. And know her state! 50

Face. Of keeping all the idolators of the chamber
Barer to her than at their prayers!

Sub. Is served
Upon the knee!

---

[1] 1588; when the English defeated the Spanish Armada.

Face. And has her pages, ushers,
Footmen, and coaches ——
  Sub. Her six mares ——
  Face. Nay, eight!
  Sub. To hurry her through London, to the Exchange,
Bethlem,[1] the china-houses ——
  Face. Yes, and have
The citizens gape at her, and praise her tires,
And my lord's humble bands, that ride with her.
  Kas. Most brave! By this hand, you are not my suster
If you refuse.
  Dame P. I will not refuse, brother.

          Enter SURLY.

  Sur. Que es esto, señores, que non venga? Esta tardanza me mata![2]
  Face. It is the Count come:
The doctor knew he would be here, by his art.
  Sub. En gallanta madama, Don! gallantissima!
  Sur. Por todos los dioses, la mas acabada hermosura, que he visto en mi vida![3]
  Face. Is't not a gallant language that they speak?
  Kas. An admirable language! Is't not French?
  Face. No, Spanish, sir.
  Kas. It goes like law-French,
And that, they say, is the courtliest language.
  Face. List, sir.
  Sur. El sol ha perdido su lumbre, con el esplandor que trae esta dama! Valgame dios![4]

---

[1] Bedlam, the madhouse.
[2] "Why doesn't she come, sirs? This delay kills me."
[3] "By all the gods, the most perfect beauty I ever saw!"
[4] "The sun has lost its light, from the splendor this lady brings."

Face. He admires your sister.
Kas. Must not she make curtsey?
Sub. Ods will, she must go to him, man, and kiss him!
It is the Spanish fashion for the women
To make first court.
Face. 'Tis true he tells you, sir:
His art knows all.
Sur. Porque no se acude?[1]
Kas. He speaks to her, I think. 90
Face. That he does, sir.
Sur. Por el amor de dios, que es esto que se tarda?[2]
Kas. Nay, see: she will not understand him! Gull, Noddy.[3]
Dame P. What say you, brother?
Kas. Ass, my suster.
Go kuss him, as the cunning man would have you;
I'll thrust a pin in you else.
Face. Oh no, sir.
Sur. Señora mia, mi persona està muy indigna de allegar a tanta hermosura.[4] 101
Face. Does he not use her bravely?
Kas. Bravely, i' faith!
Face. Nay, he will use her better.
Kas. Do you think so?
Sur. Señora, si serà servida entremonos.[5]

[*Exit with* DAME PLIANT.

Kas. Where does he carry her?
Face. Into the garden, sir;

---

[1] "Why don't you obey?"
[2] "Why this delay?"   [3] Simpleton.
[4] "Madam, I am very unworthy to approach such beauty."
[5] "Madam, you shall be obeyed; let us enter."

Take you no thought; I must interpret for her.
  Sub. (*aside to* FACE, *who goes out*).   Give Dol the word.[1]
    — Come, my fierce child, advance,   110
We'll to our quarrelling lesson again.
  Kas. Agreed.
I love a Spanish boy with all my heart.
  Sub. Nay, and by this means, sir, you shall be brother
To a great count.
  Kas. Ay, I knew that at first.
This match will advance the house of the Kastrils.
  Sub. Pray God your sister prove but pliant!
  Kas. Why,
Her name is so, by her other husband.   120
  Sub. How?
  Kas. The Widow Pliant.   Knew you not that?
  Sub. No, faith, sir;
Yet, by erection of her figure, I guessed it.
Come, let's go practise.
  Kas. Yes, but do you think, doctor,
I e'er shall quarrel well?
  Sub. I warrant you.   [*Exeunt.*

SCENE III.—*Another Room in the same.*

Enter DOL *in her fit of raving, followed by* MAMMON.

  Dol. For after Alexander's death ——
  Mam. Good lady ——
  Dol. That Perdiccas and Antigonus were slain,
The two that stood, Seleuc', and Ptolemy ——
  Mam. Madam.

[1] To begin her counterfeit frenzy.

Dol. Made up the two legs, and the fourth beast,
That was Gog-north and Egypt-south: which after
Was called Gog-iron-leg and South-iron-leg ——
   Mam. Lady ——
   Dol. And then Gog-horned. So was Egypt too:
Then Egypt-clay-leg and Gog-clay-leg ——
   Mam. Sweet madam ——
   Dol. And last Gog-dust and Egypt-dust, which fall
In the last link of the fourth chain. And these
Be stars in story, which none see or look at ——
   Mam. What shall I do?
   Dol. For, as he says, except
We call the rabbins, and the heathen Greeks ——
   Mam. Dear lady ——
   Dol. To come from Salem and from Athens,
And teach the people of Great Britain ——

    Enter FACE, *hastily, in his Servant's dress.*

   Face. What's the matter, sir?
   Dol. To speak the tongue of Eber and Javan ——
   Mam. Oh,
She's in her fit.
   Dol. We shall know nothing ——
   Face. Death, sir,
We are undone!
   Dol. Where then a learned linguist
Shall see the ancient used communion
Of vowels and consonants ——
   Face. My master will hear!
   Dol. A wisdom which Pythagoras held most **high** ——
   Mam. Sweet honourable lady!
   Dol. To comprise

All sounds of voices, in few marks of letters ——
  Face. Nay, you must never hope to lay her now.
                                    [*They all speak.*
  Dol. And so we may arrive by Talmud skill
And profane Greek, to raise the building up
Of Helen's house against the Ishmaelite,   40
King of Thogarma, and his habergions
Brimstony, blue, and fiery; and the force
Of King Abaddon, and the beast of Cittim:
Which Rabbi David Kimchi, Onkelos,
And Aben Ezra do interpret Rome.
  Face. How did you put her into't?
  Mam. Alas! I talked
Of a fifth monarchy I would erect,
With the philosopher's stone, by chance, and she
Falls on the other four straight.[1]   50
  Face. Out of Broughton!
I told you so. 'Slid, stop her mouth.
  Mam. Is't best?
  Face. She'll never leave else. If the old man hear her——
  Sub. (*within*). What's to do there?
  Face. Oh, we are lost! Now she hears him, she is quiet.

      Enter SUBTLE; *they run different ways.*

  Mam. Where shall I hide me!
  Sub. How! what sight is here?
Close deeds of darkness, and that shun the light!
Bring him again. Who is he? What, my son?   60
Oh, I have lived too long.

[1] From Broughton's *Concert of Scripture.* Broughton was educated by Bernard Gilpin, and sent by him to Cambridge. Later, he quitted the Church of England and joined the Brownists at Amsterdam; died in 1612.

Mam. Nay, good, dear father,
There was no evil purpose.
 Sub. Not! and flee me,
When I come in?
 Mam. That was my error.
 Sub. Error!
Guilt, guilt, my son: give it the right name. No marvel
If I found check in our great work within,
When such affairs as these were managing. 70
 Mam. Why, have you so?
 Sub. It has stood still this half-hour:
And all the rest of our less works gone back.
Where is the instrument of wickedness,
My lewd false drudge?
 Mam. Nay, good sir, blame not him;
Believe me, 'twas against his will or knowledge:
I saw her by chance.
 Sub. Will you commit more sin,
To excuse a varlet? 80
 Mam. By my hope, 'tis true, sir.
 Sub. Nay, then I wonder less, if you, for whom
The blessing was prepared, would so tempt heaven,
And lose your fortunes.
 Mam. Why, sir?
 Sub. This will retard
The work a month at least.
 Mam. Why, if it do,
What remedy? But think it not, good father:
Our purposes were honest. 90
 Sub. As they were,
So the reward will prove —   [*A loud explosion within.*
            How now! Ah me!

God and all saints be good to us.

Re-enter FACE.

What's that?

Face. Oh, sir, we are defeated! All the works
Are flown *in fumo*, every glass is burst:
Furnace and all rent down; as if a bolt
Of thunder had been driven through the house.
Retorts, receivers, pelicans, bolt-heads,
All struck in shivers! [SUBTLE *falls down as in a swoon.*
Help, good sir! Alas,
Coldness and death invades him. Nay, Sir Mammon,
Do the fair offices of a man! You stand
As you were readier to depart than he. [*Knocking within.*
Who's there? My lord her brother is come.

Mam. Ha, Lungs!

Face. His coach is at the door. Avoid his sight,
For he's as furious as his sister's mad.

Mam. Alas!

Face. My brain is quite undone with fume, sir,
I ne'er must hope to be mine own man again.

Mam. Is all lost, Lungs? Will nothing be preserved
Of all our cost?

Face. Faith, very little, sir;
A peck of coals or so, which is cold comfort, sir.

Mam. Oh, my voluptuous mind! I am justly punished.

Face. And so am I, sir.

Mam. Cast forth from all my hopes ——

Face. Nay, certainties, sir.

Mam. By mine own base affections.

Sub. (*seeming to come to himself*). Oh, the curst fruits of
vice and lust!

Mam. Good father,
It was my sin.   Forgive it.

Sub. Hangs my roof
Over us still, and will not fall, O justice,
Upon us, for this wicked man!

Face. Nay, look, sir,
You grieve him now with staying in his sight;
Good sir, the nobleman will come too, and take you,
And that may breed a tragedy.

Mam. I'll go.

Face. Ay, and repent at home, sir.   It may be,
For some good penance you may have it yet;
A hundred pound to the box at Bethlem——

Mam. Yes.

Face. For the restoring such as have their wits.

Mam. I'll do't.

Face. I'll send one to you to receive it.

Mam. Do.
Is no projection left?

Face. All flown, or stinks, sir.

Mam. Will nought be saved that's good for med'cine,
   think'st thou?

Face. I cannot tell, sir.   There will be perhaps
Something about the scraping of the shards
Will cure the itch —(*aside*) though not your itch of mind,
   sir.
It shall be saved for you, and sent home.   Good sir,
This way for fear the lord should meet you.
                                [*Exit* MAMMON.

Sub. (*raising his head*).   Face!

Face. Ay.

Sub. Is he gone?

Face. Yes, and as heavily
As all the gold he hoped for were in's blood.
Let us be light, though. 150
    Sub. (*leaping up*). Ay, as balls, and bound
And hit our heads against the roof for joy:
There's so much of our care now cast away.
    Face. Now to our Don.
    Sub. Yes, your young widow by this time
Is made a countess, Face.
    Face. Good, sir.
    Sub. Off with your case,
And greet her kindly, as a bridegroom should,
After these common hazards. 160
    Face. Very well, sir,
Will you go fetch Don Diego off, the while?
    Sub. And fetch him over too, if you'll be pleased, sir:
Would Dol were in her place, to pick his pockets now!
    Face. Why, you can do't as well, if you would set to't.
I pray you prove your virtue.
    Sub. For your sake, sir. [*Exeunt.*

SCENE IV.— *Another Room in the same.*

Enter SURLY *and* DAME PLIANT.

   Sur. Lady, you see into what hands you are fallen;
'Mongst what a nest of villains! and how near
Your honour was to have catched a certain flaw,
Through your credulity, had I but been
So punctually forward, as place, time,
And other circumstances would have made a man;
For you're a handsome woman: would you were wise too!

I am a gentleman come here disguised,
Only to find the knaveries of this citadel;
And where I might have wronged your honour, and have not,
I claim some interest in your love. You are, 11
They say, a widow, rich; and I'm a bachelor,
Worth nought: your fortunes may make me a man,
As mine have preserved you a woman. Think upon it,
And whether I have deserved you or no.
   Dame P. I will, sir.
   Sur. And for these household rogues, let me alone
To treat with them.

Enter SUBTLE.

   Sub. How doth my noble Diego,
And my dear Madam Countess? Hath the Count 20
Been courteous, lady? liberal and open?
Donzel, methinks you look melancholic
After your interview, and scurvy: truly
I do not like the dulness of your eye;
It hath a heavy cast, 'tis upsee Dutch,[1]
And says you are a lumpish cavalier.
Be lighter, I will make your pockets so.
                                     [*Attempts to pick them.*
   Sur. (*throws open his cloak*). Will you, Don Bawd and
       Pick-purse? (*Strikes him down.*) How now! Reel
       you?
Stand up, sir; you shall find, since I am so heavy,
I'll give you equal weight. 30
   Sub. Help! murder!
   Sur. No, sir,

---

[1] From the Dutch *opzee*, over sea. A thick Dutch beer was much drunk in England.

There's no such thing intended : a good cart
And a clean whip shall ease you of that fear.
I am the Spanish Don *that should be cozen'd —
Do you see, cozen'd!* Where's your Captain Face,
That parcel broker, and whole-bawd, all rascal !

Enter FACE *in his uniform.*

Face. How, Surly !
Sur. Oh, make your approach, good captain.
I have found from whence your copper rings and spoons   40
Come, now, wherewith you cheat abroad in taverns.
'Twas here you learned t' anoint your boot with brimstone,
Then rub men's gold on't for a kind of touch,
And say 'twas nought, when you had changed the colour,
That you might have 't for nothing. And this doctor,
Your sooty, smoky-bearded compeer, he
Will close you so much gold, in a bolt's-head,
And, on a turn, convey in the stead another
With sublimed mercury, that shall burst in the heat,
And fly out all *in fumo!* Then weeps Mammon ;   50
Then swoons his worship. (FACE *slips out.*)   Or, he is the
      Faustus
That casteth figures and can conjure, cures
Plagues, piles, and pox, by the ephemerides,[1]
And holds intelligence while you send in —
Captain — what ! is he gone?
              [*Seizes* SUBTLE *as he is retiring.*
                    Nay, you must tarry,
Though he be 'scaped, and answer by the ears, sir.

Re-enter FACE *with* KASTRIL.

Face. Why, now's the time, if ever you will quarrel

[1] Astronomical almanacs.

Well, as they say, and be a true-born child:
The doctor and your sister both are abused.

   Kas. Where is he? Which is he? He is a slave,   60
Whate'er he is, and he must answer me. — Are you
The man, sir, I would know?

   Sur. I should be loth, sir,
To confess so much.

   Kas. Then you lie in your throat.

   Sur. How!

   Face (*to* KASTRIL). A very errant rogue, sir, and a cheater,
Employed here by another conjurer,
That does not love the doctor, and would cross him
If he knew how.   70

   Sur. Sir, you are abused.

   Kas. You lie;
And 'tis no matter.

   Face. Well said, sir! He is
The impudentest rascal ——

   Sur. You are indeed: will you hear me, sir?

   Face. By no means: bid him begone.

   Kas. Begone, sir, quickly.

   Sur. This is strange! — Lady, do you inform your brother.

   Face. There is not such a foist[1] in all the town,   80
The doctor had him presently; and finds yet
The Spanish count will come here. (*Aside*) Bear up,
   Subtle.

   Sub. Yes, sir, he must appear within this hour.

   Face. And yet this rogue would come in a disguise,
By the temptation of another spirit,
To trouble our art, though he could not hurt it!

   Kas. Ay,

---

[1] Cheating rogue.

I know — Away — (*to his sister*) — you talk like a foolish
  mauther.[1]
 Sur. Sir, all is truth she says.
 Face. Do not believe him, sir.   90
He is the lyingest swabber! Come your ways, sir.
 Sur. You are valiant out of company!
 Kas. Yes; how then, sir.

   Enter DRUGGER *with a piece of damask.*

 Face. Nay, here's an honest fellow too, that knows him
And all his tricks. (*Aside to* DRUG.) Make good what I say,
  Abel;
This cheater would have cozened thee o' the widow.
He owes this honest Drugger here, seven pound,
He has had on him, in twopen'orths of tobacco.
 Drug. Yes, sir.
And he has damned himself three terms to pay me.   100
 Face. And what does he owe for lotium?
 Drug. Thirty shillings, sir;
And for six syringes.
 Sur. Hydra of villainy!
 Face. Nay, sir; you must quarrel him out o' the house.
 Kas. I will:
— Sir, if you get not out o' doors, you lie!
And you are a pimp.
 Sur. Why, this is madness, sir,
Not valour in you; I must laugh at this.   110
 Kas. It is my humour; you are a pimp and a trig,
And an Amadis de Gaul or a Don Quixote.
 Drug. Or a knight o' the curious coxcomb, do you see?

---

[1] An awkward, rustic woman; the term is still used in Norfolkshire.

Enter ANANIAS.

Ana. Peace to the household!
Kas. I'll keep peace for no man.
Ana. Casting of dollars is concluded lawful.
Kas. Is he the constable?
Sub. Peace, Ananias.
Face. No, sir.
Kas. Then you are an otter, a shad, a whit, a very tim. 120
Sur. You'll hear me, sir?
Kas. I will not.
Ana. What is the motive?
Sub. Zeal in the young gentleman
Against his Spanish slops.
　Ana. They are profane,
Lewd, superstitious, and idolatrous breeches.
　Sur. New rascals!
Kas. Will you begone, sir?
Ana. Avoid, Satan!　　　　　　　　　　　130
Thou art not of the light: that ruff of pride
About thy neck betrays thee; and is the same
With that which the unclean birds, in seventy-seven,[1]
Were seen to prank it with on divers coasts:
Thou look'st like Antichrist, in that lewd hat.
　Sur. I must give way.
Kas.　Begone, sir.
Sur.　But I'll take
A course with you ——
　Ana. Depart, proud Spanish fiend!　　　140
Sur. Captain and Doctor.
Ana. Child of perdition!

[1] Probably refers to depredations of Spaniards, but in what localities is not clear.

Kas. Hence, sir! [*Exit* SURLY.
Did I not quarrel bravely?
　Face. Yes, indeed, sir.
　Kas. Nay, and I give my mind to't, I shall do't.
　Face. Oh, you must follow, sir, and threaten him tame:
He'll turn again else.
　Kas. I'll re-turn him then. [*Exit.*
[SUBTLE *takes* ANANIAS *aside.*
　Face. Drugger, this rogue prevented us for thee: 150
We had determined that thou should'st have come
In a Spanish suit, and have carried her so; and he,
A brokerly slave! goes, puts it on himself.
Hast brought the damask?
　Drug. Yes, sir.
　Face. Thou must borrow
A Spanish suit: hast thou no credit with the players?
　Drug. Yes, sir; did you never see me play the fool?
　Face. I know not, Nab: — (*aside*) Thou shalt, if I can
　　help it. —
Hieronymo's[1] old cloak, ruff, and hat will serve; 160
I'll tell thee more when thou bring'st 'em. [*Exit* DRUGGER.
　Ana. Sir, I know
The Spaniard hates the brethren, and hath spies
Upon their actions: and that this was one
I make no scruple. — But the holy synod
Have been in prayer and meditation for it;
And 'tis revealed, no less to them than me,
That casting of money is most lawful.
　Sub. True,
But here I cannot do it; if the house 170

　Chief character in Thomas Kyd's *Spanish Tragedy*, a play much ridiculed by Elizabethan dramatists.

Should chance to be suspected, all would out,
And we be locked up in the Tower for ever,
To make gold there for the state, never come out;
And then are you defeated.
 Ana. I will tell
This to the elders and the weaker brethren,
That the whole company of the separation
May join in humble prayer again.
 Sub. And fasting.
 Ana. Yea, for some fitter place. The peace of mind
Rest with these walls!   [*Exit.*
 Sub. Thanks, courteous Ananias.
 Face. What did he come for?
 Sub. About casting dollars,
Presently out of hand. And so I told him
A Spanish minister came here to spy
Against the faithful ——
 Face. I conceive. Come, Subtle,
Thou art so down upon the least disaster!
How wouldst thou ha' done, if I had not helped thee out?
 Sub. I thank thee, Face, for the angry boy, i' faith.
 Face. Who would have looked it should have been that rascal
Surly? he had dyed his beard and all. Well, sir,
Here's damask come to make you a suit.
 Sub. Where's Drugger?
 Face. He is gone to borrow me a Spanish habit;
I'll be the count, now.
 Sub. But where's the widow?
 Face. Within, with my lord's sister; Madam Dol
Is entertaining her.
 Sub. By your favour, Face,

Now she is honest, I will stand again.
   Face. You will not offer it.
   Sub. Why?
   Face. Stand to your word,
Or — here comes Dol, she knows ——
   Sub. You are tyrannous still.

Enter DOL, hastily.

   Face. Strict for my right. — How now, Dol! Hast [thou] told her,
The Spanish Count will come?
   Dol. Yes; but another is come   210
You little looked for!
   Face. Who is that?
   Dol. Your master;
The master of the house.
   Sub. How, Dol!
   Face. She lies,
This is some trick. Come, leave your quiblins,[1] Dorothy.
   Dol. Look out and see.   [FACE *goes to the window.*
   Sub. Art thou in earnest?
   Dol. 'Slight,   220
Forty o' the neighbours are about him, talking.
   Face. 'Tis he, by this good day.
   Dol. 'Twill prove ill day
For some on us.
   Face. We are undone, and taken.
   Dol. Lost, I'm afraid.
   Sub. You said he would not come
While there died one a week within the liberties
   Face. No: 'twas within the walls.

---

[1] Petty duplicities.

Sub. Was't so! cry you mercy.   230
I thought the liberties.   What shall we do now, Face?
 Face. Be silent: not a word, if he call or knock,
I'll into mine own shape again and meet him,
Of Jeremy, the butler.   In the meantime,
Do you two pack up all the goods and purchase [1]
That we can carry in the two trunks.   I'll keep him
Off for to-day, if I cannot longer: and then
At night I'll ship you both away to Ratcliff,
Where we will meet to-morrow, and there we'll share.
Let Mammon's brass and pewter keep the cellar;   240
We'll have another time for that.   But, Dol,
Prythee go heat a little water quickly;
Subtle must shave me: all my captain's beard
Must off, to make me appear smooth Jeremy.
You'll do it?
 Sub. Yes, I'll shave you, as well as I can.
 Face. And not cut my throat, but trim me?
 Sub. You shall see, sir.[2]   [*Exeunt.*

ACT V.

SCENE I. — *Before* LOVEWIT'S *Door.*

Enter LOVEWIT, *with several of the* Neighbours.

Love. Has there been much resort, say you?
1st Nei. Daily, sir.

---

[1] Cant word for stolen goods.   Cf. *Henry V*, iii, 2: "They will steal anything and call it — purchase."

[2] "I do not believe that any scene in the whole compass of the English Drama is worked up with so much comic skill and knowledge of effect as the conclusion of this masterly act." — *Gifford.*

2d Nei. And nightly, too.
3d Nei. Ay, some as brave as lords.
4th Nei. Ladies and gentlewomen.
5th Nei. Citizens' wives.
1st Nei. And knights.
6th Nei. In coaches.
2d Nei. Yes, and oyster women.
1st Nei. Beside other gallants.
3d Nei. Sailors' wives.
4th Nei. Tobacco men.
5th Nei. Another Pimlico[1]!
Love. What should my knave advance,
To draw this company? He hung out no banners
Of a strange calf with five legs to be seen,
Or a huge lobster with six claws?
6th Nei. No, sir.
3d Nei. We had gone in then, sir.
Love. He has no gift
Of teaching in the nose that e'er I knew of.
You saw no bills set up that promised cure
Of agues, or the tooth-ache?
2d Nei. No such thing, sir.
Love. Nor heard a drum struck for baboons or puppets?
5th Nei. Neither, sir.
Love. What device should he bring forth now?
I love a teeming wit as I love my nourishment;
'Pray God he have not kept such open house
That he hath sold my hangings and my bedding!
I left him nothing else. If he have eat them,
A plague o' the moth, say I! Sure he has got
Some tempting pictures to call all this ging[2]!

---

[1] A resort near Hogsden, noted for its cakes and ale.   [2] Gang.

Or't may be he has the fleas that run at tilt
Upon a table, or some dog to dance.
When saw you him?
 1st Nei. Who, sir, Jeremy?
 2d Nei. Jeremy Butler?
We saw him not this month.
 Love. How!   40
 4th Nei. Not these five weeks, sir.
 6th Nei. These six weeks at the least.
 Love. You amaze me, neighbours!
 5th Nei. Sure, if your worship know not where he is
He's slipped away.
 6th Nei. Pray God, he be not made away.
 Love. Ha! it's no time to question, then.
           [*Knocks at the door.*
 6th Nei. About
Some three weeks since, I heard a doleful cry,
As I sat up a-mending my wife's stockings.   50
 Love. 'Tis strange that none will answer! Didst thou hear
A cry, say'st thou?
 6th Nei. Yes, sir, like unto a man
That had been strangled an hour, and could not speak.
 2d Nei. I heard it too, just this day three weeks, at two
  o'clock
Next morning.
 Love. These be miracles, or you make them so.
A man an hour strangled, and could not speak,
And both you heard him cry?
 3d Nei. Yes, downward, sir.   60
 Love. Thou art a wise fellow. Give me thy hand, I pray
  thee,
What trade art thou on?

3d Nei. A smith, an't please your worship.

Love. A smith! then lend me thy help to get this door open.

3d Nei. That I will presently, sir, but fetch my tools.

[*Exit.*

1st Nei. Sir, best to knock again, afore you break it.

Love. (*knocks again*). I will.

Enter FACE, *in his butler's livery.*

Face. What mean you, sir?

1st, 2d, 4th Nei. Oh, here's Jeremy!

Face. Good sir, come from the door.

Love. Why, what's the matter?

Face. Yet farther, you are too near yet.

Love. In the name of wonder,
What means the fellow!

Face. The house, sir, has been visited.

Love. What, with the plague? stand thou then farther.

Face. No, sir,
I had it not.

Love. Who had it then? I left
None else but thee in the house.

Face. Yes, sir, my fellow,
The cat that kept the buttery, had it on her
A week before I spied it; but I got her
Conveyed away in the night: and so I shut
The house up for a month ——

Love. How!

Face. Purposing then, sir,
To have burnt rose-vinegar, treacle, and tar,
And have made it sweet, that you should ne'er have known it;
Because I knew the news would but afflict you, sir.

Love. Breathe less, and farther off! Why this is stranger:
The neighbours tell me all here that the doors
Have still been open ——
  Face. How, sir!
  Love. Gallants, men and women,
And of all sorts, tag-rag, been seen to flock here
In threaves,[1] these ten weeks, as to a second Hogsden,
In days of Pimlico and Eyebright.[2]
  Face. Sir,
Their wisdoms will not say so.   100
  Love. To-day they speak
Of coaches and gallants; one in a French hood
Went in, they tell me; and another was seen
In a velvet gown at the window: divers more
Pass in and out.
  Face. They did pass through the doors then,
Or walls, I assure their eyesights, and their spectacles;
For here, sir, are the keys, and here have been,
In this my pocket, now above twenty days:
And for before, I kept the fort alone there.   110
But that 'tis yet not deep in the afternoon,
I should believe my neighbours had seen double
Through the black pot, and made these apparitions!
For, on my faith to your worship, for these three weeks
And upwards the door has not been opened.
  Love. Strange!
  1st Nei. Good faith, I think I saw a coach.

---

[1] Droves; so Jonson in *The Sad Shepherd:* "They come in threaves, to frolic with him"; so also Chapman, *Gent. Usher*, Act ii, 1. But Skeat says that the word means "a number of sheaves of wheat, generally twelve or twenty-four."

[2] Perhaps a cant term for a kind of malt liquor then popular.

2d Nei. And I too,
I'd have been sworn.
　Love. Do you but think it now?
And but one coach?
　4th Nei. We cannot tell, sir: Jeremy
Is a very honest fellow.
　Face. Did you see me at all?
　1st Nei. No; that we are sure on.
　2d Nei. I'll be sworn o' that.
　Love. Fine rogues to have your testimonies built on!

Re-enter Third Neighbour, *with his Tools.*

　3d Nei. Is Jeremy come?
　1st Nei. Oh, yes; you may leave your tools.
We were deceived, he says.
　2d Nei. He has had the keys;
And the door has been shut these three weeks.
　3d Nei. Like enough.
　Love. Peace and get hence, you changelings.

Enter SURLY *and* MAMMON.

　Face (aside). Surly come!
And Mammon made acquainted! They'll tell all.
How shall I beat them off? what shall I do?
Nothing's more wretched than a guilty conscience.[1]
　Sur. No, sir, he was a great physician. This,
It was no evil house, but a mere chancel!
You knew the lord and his sister.
　Mam. Nay, good Surly ——
　Sur. The happy word, BE RICH ——
　Mam. Play not the tyrant ——

---

[1] Quoted from Plautus.

Sur. Should be to-day pronounced to all your friends.
And where be your andirons now? and your brass pots,
That should have been golden flagons, and great wedges?
    Mam. Let me but breathe. What, they have shut their doors,
Methinks!
    Sur. Ay, now 'tis holiday with them.
    Mam. Rogues,   [He *and* SURLY *knock.* 150
Cozeners, rascals, cheats!
    Face. What mean you, sir!
    Mam. To enter if we can.
    Face. Another man's house!
Here is the owner, sir; turn you to him,
And speak your business.
    Mam. Are you, sir, the owner?
    Love. Yes, sir.
    Mam. And are those knaves within, your cheaters!
    Love. What knaves, what cheaters?   160
    Mam. Subtle and his Lungs.
    Face. The gentleman is distracted, sir! No lungs,
Nor lights have been seen here these three weeks, sir,
Within these doors, upon my word.
    Sur. Your word,
Groom arrogant!
    Face. Yes, sir, I am the housekeeper,
And know the keys have not been out of my hands.
    Sur. This is a new Face.
    Face. You do mistake the house, sir: 170
What sign was't at?
    Sur. You rascal! this is one
Of the confederacy. Come, let's get officers,
And force the door.

Love. Pray you, stay, gentlemen.
Sur. No, sir, we'll come with warrant.
Mam. Ay, and then
We shall have your doors open. [*Exeunt* MAM. *and* SUR.
Love. What means this?
Face. I cannot tell, sir.   180
1st Nei. These are two of the gallants
That we do think we saw.
Face. Two of the fools!
You talk as idly as they. Good faith, sir,
I think the moon has crazed 'em all.[1] Oh, me!

Enter KASTRIL.

(*Aside*) The angry boy come too! He'll make a noise,
And ne'er away till he have betrayed us all.
Kas. (*knocking*). What rogues, cheats, slaves, you'll open
    the door anon!
What, cockatrice, my suster! But this light
I'll fetch the marshal to you. You are a toad   190
To keep your castle ——
Face. Who would you speak with, sir?
Kas. The dirty doctor and the cozening captain,
And puss my suster.
Love. This is something, sure.
Face. Upon my trust, the doors were never open, sir.
Kas. I have heard all their tricks told me twice over,
By the fat knight and the lean gentleman.
Love. Here comes another.

Enter ANANIAS *and* TRIBULATION.

Face. Ananias too!   200

[1] A very ancient and wide-spread superstition, the origin of the word *lunatic*.

And his pastor!
 Tri. (*beating at the door*). The doors are shut against us.
 Ana. Come forth, you seed of sulphur, sons of fire!
Your stench it is broke forth; abomination
Is in the house.
 Kas. Ay, my suster's there.
 Ana. The place,
It is become a cage of unclean birds.
 Kas. Yes, I will fetch the scavenger and the constable.
 Tri. You shall do well.   210
 Ana. We'll join to weed them out.
 Kas. You will not come, then, cockatrice,[1] my suster!
 Ana. Call her not sister; she's a harlot, verily.
 Kas. I'll raise the street.
 Love. Good gentleman, a word.
 Ana. Satan avoid, and hinder not our zeal!
        [*Exeunt* ANA., TRIB., *and* KAS.
 Love. The world's turned Bethlem.
 Face. These are all broke loose,
Out of St. Katherine's, where they use to keep
The better sort of mad-folks.   220
 1st Nei. All these persons
We saw go in and out here.
 2d Nei. Yes, indeed, sir.
 3d Nei. These were the parties.
 Face. Peace, you drunkards! Sir,
I wonder at it: please you to give me leave
To touch the door, I'll try an the lock be changed.
 Love. It mazes me!

---

[1] A fabulous serpent, said to come from a cock's egg, and to have wings, legs, and crest like a cock. It was deemed so venomous as to be able to kill with its look. Same as the basilisk.

Face (*goes to the door*). Good faith, sir, I believe
There's no such thing: 'tis all *deceptio visus* —   230
    (*Aside*) Would I could get him away.
    Dap. (*within*). Master Captain! Master Doctor!
    Love. Who's that?
    Face (*aside*). Our clerk within, that I forgot! — I know
        not, sir.
    Dap. (*within*). For God's sake, when will her grace be
        at leisure?
    Face. Ha!
Illusions, some spirit o' the air! (*Aside*) His gag is melted,
And now he sets out the throat.
    Dap. (*within*). I am almost stifled ——
    Face (*aside*). Would you were altogether.   240
    Love. 'Tis in the house.
Ha! list.
    Face. Believe it, sir, in the air.
    Love. Peace, you.
    Dap. (*within*). Mine aunt's grace does not use me well.
    Sub. (*within*). You fool,
Peace, you'll mar all.
    Face (*speaks through the key-hole, while* LOVEWIT *advances unobserved to the door*). Or you will else, you
        rogue.
    Love. Oh, is it so? Then you converse with spirits!
Come, sir. No more of your tricks, good Jeremy,
The truth, the shortest way.   250
    Face. Dismiss this rabble, sir, —
    (*Aside*) What shall I do? I am catched.
    Love. Good neighbours,
I thank you all. You may depart. (*Ex.* Neigh.) Come, sir,
You know that I am an indulgent master,

And therefore conceal nothing. What's your medicine,
To draw so many several sorts of wild-fowl?
 Face. Sir, you were wont to affect mirth and wit,
But here's no place to talk on't in the street.
Give me but leave to make the best of my fortune,   260
And only pardon me the abuse of your house :
It's all I beg. I'll help you to a widow,
In recompense, that you shall give me thanks for,
Will make you seven years younger, and a rich one.
'Tis but your putting on a Spanish cloak :
I have her within. You need not fear the house ;
It was not visited.
 Love. But by me, who came
Sooner than you expected.
 Face. It is true, sir.   270
Pray you, forgive me.
 Love. Well, let's see your widow.   [*Exeunt.*

Scene II.—*A Room in the same.*

Enter Subtle, *leading in* Dapper *with his eyes bound as before.*

 Sub. How! have you eaten your gag?
 Dap. Yes, faith, it crumbled
Away in my mouth.
 Sub. You have spoiled all, then.
 Dap. No!
I hope my aunt of Fairy will forgive me.
 Sub. Your aunt's a gracious lady; but in troth
You were to blame.
 Dap. The fume did overcome me,
And I did do't to stay my stomach. Pray you   10

So satisfy her grace.
    Enter FACE *in his uniform.*
Here comes the Captain.
 Face. How now! Is his mouth down?
 Sub. Ay, he has spoken!
 Face. A plague, I heard him, and you too. He's undone
  then.
I have been fain to say the house is haunted
With spirits, to keep churl back.
 Sub. And hast thou done it?
 Face. Sure, for this night.
 Sub. Why, then triumph and sing   20
Of Face so famous, the precious king
Of present wits.
 Face. Did you not hear the coil
About the door?
 Sub. Yes, and I dwindled with it.
 Face. Show him his aunt, and let him be dispatched;
I'll send her to you.   [*Exit* FACE.
 Sub. Well, sir, your aunt her grace
Will give you audience presently, on my suit,
And the captain's word that you did not eat your gag   30
In any contempt of her highness.   [*Unbinds his eyes.*
 Dap. Not I, in troth, sir.
    Enter DOL, *like the Queen of Fairy.*
 Sub. Here she is come. Down o' your knees and wriggle:
She has a stately presence. (DAPPER *kneels, and shuffles
  towards her.*) Good! Yet nearer,
And bid, God save you!
 Dap. Madam!
 Sub. And your aunt.

Dap. And my most gracious aunt, God save your grace.
Dol. Nephew, we thought to have been angry with you;
But that sweet face of yours hath turned the tide, 40
And made it flow with joy, that ebb'd of love.
Arise, and touch our velvet gown.
  Sub. The skirts,
And kiss 'em. So!
  Dol. Let me now stroke that head.
Much, nephew, shalt thou win, much shalt thou spend,
Much shalt thou give away, much shalt thou lend.
  Sub. (*aside*). Ay, much indeed! Why do you not thank
    her grace?
  Dap. I cannot speak for joy.
  Sub. See the kind wretch! 50
Your grace's kinsman right.
  Dol. Give me the bird.
Here is your fly in a purse, about your neck, cousin;
Wear it, and feed it about this day seven-night,
On your right wrist ——
  Sub. Open a vein with a pin,
And let it suck but once a week; till then
You must not look on't.
  Dol. No: and, kinsman,
Bear yourself worthy of the blood you come on. 60
  Sub. Her grace would have you eat no more Woolsack pies,
Nor Dagger frumety.[1]
  Dol. Nor break his fast
In Heaven and Hell.[2]

---

[1] Frumety was food made of wheat boiled in milk. The Woolsack and Dagger were two taverns of low repute.
[2] Two mean alehouses abutting on Westminster Hall. There was a third called Purgatory.

Sub. She's with you everywhere!
Nor play with costomongers at mum-chance,[1] trey-trip,[2]
God-make-you-rich[3] (when as your aunt has done it);
But keep
The gallant'st company and the best games——
   Dap. Yes, sir. 70
   Sub. Gleek and primero: and what you get, be true to us.
   Dap. By this hand, I will.
   Sub. You may bring's a thousand pound
Before to-morrow night, if but three thousand
Be stirring, an you will.
   Dap. I swear I will, then.
   Sub. Your fly will learn you all games.
   Face (within). Have you done there?
   Sub. Your grace will command him no more duties?
   Dol. No! 80
But come and see me often. I may chance
To leave him three or four hundred chests of treasure,
And some twelve thousand acres of Fairyland,
If he game well and comely with good gamesters.
   Sub. There's a kind aunt! Kiss her departing part.
But you must sell your forty mark a-year, now.
   Dap. Ay, sir, I mean.
   Sub. Or give't away; plague on't!
   Dap. I'll give't mine aunt: I'll go and fetch the writings.
                                                     [*Exit.*
   Sub. 'Tis well — away! 90

Re-enter FACE.

   Face. Where's Subtle?

---

[1] A rude game with dice.
[2] A game with draughts, to win which a trey must be thrown.
[3] A game.

Sub. Here: what news?

Face. Drugger is at the door; go take his suit,
And bid him fetch a parson, presently:
Say he shall marry the widow. Thou shalt spend
A hundred pound by the service! (*Ex.* SUB.) Now, Queen Dol,
Have you packed up all?

Dol. Yes.

Face. And how do you like
The Lady Pliant? 100

Dol. A good dull innocent.

Re-enter SUBTLE.

Sub. Here's your Hieronymo's cloak and hat.

Face. Give me them.

Sub. And the ruff too?

Face. Yes; I'll come to you presently. [*Exit.*

Sub. Now he is gone about his project, Dol,
I told you of, for the widow.

Dol. 'Tis direct
Against our articles.

Sub. Well, we will fit him, wench. 110
Hast thou gulled her of her jewels or her bracelets?

Dol. No; but I will do't.

Sub. Soon at night, my Dolly,
When we are shipped, and all our goods aboard,
Eastward for Ratcliff; we will turn our course
To Brainford, westward, if thou say'st the word,
And take our leaves of this o'er-weening rascal,
This peremptory Face.

Dol. Content, I'm weary of him.

Sub. Thou'st cause, when the slave will run a-wiving, Dol,

Against the instrument that was drawn between us.
   Dol. I'll pluck his bird as bare as I can.
   Sub. Yes, tell her
She must by any means address some present
To the cunning man, make him amends for wronging
His art with her suspicion; send a ring
Or chain of pearl; she will be tortured else
Extremely in her sleep, say, and have strange things
Come to her. Wilt thou?
   Dol. Yes.
   Sub. My fine flitter-mouse,[1]
My bird o' the night! we'll revel at the Pigeons,[2]
When we have all, and may unlock the trunks,
And say, this is mine, and thine; and thine, and mine.
                                                        [*They kiss.*

                    Re-enter FACE.

   Face. What now! a-billing?
   Sub. Yes, a little exalted
In the good passage of our stock-affairs.
   Face. Drugger has brought his parson; take him in, Subtle,
And send Nab back again to wash his face.
   Sub. I will: and shave himself.   [*Exit.*
   Face. If you can get him.
   Dol. You are hot upon it, Face, whate'er it is!
   Face. A trick that Dol shall spend ten pound a month by.

                    Re-enter SUBTLE.
Is he gone?
   Sub. The chaplain waits you in the hall, sir.

---

[1] Bat; German *fledermaus.*
[2] The Three Pigeons: an inn at Brentford; afterwards kept by the noted actor Lowin, when the Puritans shut up the theatres.

Face. I'll go bestow him.　　　　　　　　　　*[Exit.*

Dol. He'll now marry her, instantly.

Sub. He cannot yet, he is not ready. Dear Dol,
Cozen her of all thou canst. To deceive him
Is no deceit, but justice, that would break　　　150
Such an inextricable tie as ours was.

Dol. Let me alone to fit him.

Re-enter FACE.

Face. Come, my venturers,
You have packed up all? Where be the trunks? Bring forth.

Sub. Here.

Face. Let us see them. Where's the money?

Sub. Here,
In this.

Face. Mammon's ten pound; eight score before;
The brethren's money this. Drugger's and Dapper's.　　160
What paper's that?

Dol. The jewel of the waiting-maid's,
That stole it from her lady, to know certain ——

Face. If she should have precedence of her mistress?

Dol. Yes.

Face. What box is that?

Sub. The fish-wives' rings, I think,
And the ale-wives' single money.[1] Is't not, Dol?

Dol. Yes; and the whistle that the sailor's wife
Brought you to know an her husband were with Ward.[2]　170

Face. We'll wet it to-morrow; and our silver-beakers
And tavern cups. Where be the French petticoats,
And girdles and hangers?

[1] Money of small value, requiring no change.
[2] A notorious pirate.

Sub. Here, in the trunk,
And the bolts of lawn.
　Face. Is Drugger's damask there,
And the tobacco?
　Sub. Yes.
　Face. Give me the keys.
　Dol. Why you the keys? 180
　Sub. No matter, Dol; because
We shall not open them before he comes.
　Face. 'Tis true, you shall not open them, indeed;
Nor have them forth, do you see? not forth, Dol.
　Dol. No!
　Face. No, my smock rampant. The right is, my master
Knows all, has pardoned me, and he will keep them;
Doctor, 'tis true — you look — for all your figures:
I sent for him indeed.[1] Wherefore, good partners,
Both he and she be satisfied: for here 190
Determines the indenture tripartite
'Twixt Subtle, Dol, and Face. All I can do
Is to help you over the wall, o' the back-side,
Or lend you a sheet to save your velvet gown, Dol.
Here will be officers presently, bethink you
Of some course suddenly to 'scape the dock[2]:
For thither you will come else. — (*Loud knocking.*) — Hark
　　you, thunder.
　Sub. You are a precious fiend!
　Off. (*without*). Open the door.
　Face. Dol, I am sorry for thee, i' faith; but hear'st thou?
It shall go hard but I will place thee somewhere: 201
Thou shalt have my letter to Mistress Amo ——

　　　　[1] A characteristic lie.
　　　　[2] An apartment in Newgate, or Bridewell, prison.

Dol. Hang you!
Face. Or Madam Cæsarean.[1]
Dol. Out upon you, rogue!
Would I had but time to beat thee!
Face. Subtle,
Let's know where you set up next; I will send you
A customer now and then, for old acquaintance:
What new course have you? 210
Sub. Rogue, I'll hang myself,
That I may walk a greater devil than thou,
And haunt thee in the flock-bed and the buttery. [*Exeunt.*

SCENE III.—*An outer Room in the same.*

Enter LOVEWIT *in the Spanish dress, with the* Parson.

[*Loud knocking at the door.*]

Love. What do you mean, my masters?
Mam. (*without*). Open your door,
Cheaters, thieves, conjurors.
Off. (*without*). Or we will break it open.
Love. What warrant have you?
Off. (*without*). Warrant enough, sir, doubt not,
If you'll not open it.
Love. Is there an officer, there?
Off. (*without*). Yes, two or three for failing.[2]
Love. Have but patience, 10
And I will open it straight.

Enter FACE *as butler.*

Face. Sir, have you done?

---

[1] The nicknames of two notorious women.   [2] For fear of failing.

SCENE III.] THE ALCHEMIST. 253

Is it a marriage? perfect?
  Love. Yes, my brain.
  Face. Off with your ruff and cloak then; be yourself, sir.
  Sur. (*without*). Down with the door.
  Kas. (*without*). 'Slight, ding[1] it open.
  Love. (*opening the door*). Hold,
Hold, gentleman, what means this violence?

MAMMON, SURLY, KASTRIL, ANANIAS, TRIBULATION, *and*
        Officers *rush in.*

  Mam. Where is this collier?   20
  Sur. And my Captain Face?
  Mam. These day owls.
  Sur. That are birding[2] in men's purses.
  Mam. Madam Suppository.
  Kas. Doxy, my suster.
  Ana. Locusts
Of the foul pit.
  Tri. Profane as Bel and the Dragon.
  Ana. Worse than the grasshoppers or the lice of Egypt.
  Love. Good gentlemen, hear me. Are you officers,   30
And cannot stay this violence?
  1st Off. Keep the peace.
  Love. Gentlemen, what is the matter? Whom do you seek?
  Mam. The chemical cozener.
  Sur. And the captain pander.
  Kas. The nun, my suster.
  Mam. Madam Rabbi——
  Ana. Scorpions
And caterpillars.
  Love. Fewer at once, I pray you.   40

---

[1] Break; still common in Scotland.   [2] Pilfering.

2d Off. One after another, gentlemen, I charge you,
By virtue of my staff.
    Ana. They are the vessels
Of pride, lust, and the cart.[1]
    Love. Good zeal, lie still
A little while.
    Tri. Peace, Deacon Ananias.
    Love. The house is mine here, and the doors are open:
If there be any such persons as you seek for,
Use your authority, search on, o' God's name.   50
I am but newly come to town, and finding
This tumult 'bout my door, to tell you true,
It somewhat mazed me; till my man here, fearing
My more displeasure, told me he had done
Somewhat an insolent part, let out my house
(Belike, presuming on my known aversion
From any air o' the town while there was sickness)
To a doctor and a captain: who, what they are,
Or where they be, he knows not.
    Mam. Are they gone?   60
    Love. You may go in and search, sir. (MAMMON, ANA.
        and TRIB. *go in.*)   Here, I find
The empty walls worse than I left them, smoked,
A few cracked pots and glasses, and a furnace:
The ceiling filled with poesies of the candle,
And madam with a dildo[1] writ o' the walls:
Only one gentlewoman, I met here,
That is within, that said she was a widow ——
    Kas. Ay, that's my suster: I'll go thump her. Where is
        she?   [*Goes in.*

---

[1] Hangman's cart.
[2] The refrain of a coarse old song; cf. *Winter's Tale*, iv, 3: "dildos and faldings."

Love. And should have married a Spanish Count, but he,
When he came to't neglected her so grossly, 70
That I, a widower, am gone through with her.
 Sur. How! have I lost her then?
 Love. Were you the don, sir!
Good faith, now, she does blame you extremely, and says
You swore, and told her you had taken the pains
To dye your beard, and umbre o'er your face,
Borrowed a suit, and ruff, all for her love;
And then did nothing. What an oversight,
And want of putting forward, sir, was this!
Well fare an old harquebuzier, yet, 80
Could prime his powder, and give fire, and hit,
All in a twinkling!

    Re-enter MAMMON.

 Mam. The whole nest are fled!
 Love. What sort of birds were they?
 Mam. A kind of choughs,[1]
Or thievish daws, sir, that have pick'd my purse
Of eight score and ten pound within these five weeks,
Beside my first materials; and my goods,
That lie in the cellar, which I am glad they have left,
I may have home yet. 90
 Love. Think you so, sir?
 Mam. Ay.
 Love. By order of law, sir, but not otherwise.
 Mam. Not mine own stuff!
 Love. Sir, I can take no knowledge
That they are yours, but by public means.
If you can bring certificate that you were gull'd of them,

---

[1] Kind of crow.

Or any formal writ out of a court,
That you did cozen yourself, I will not hold them.
    Mam. I'll rather lose them.   100
    Love. That you shall not, sir,
By me, in troth: upon these terms they are yours.
What! should they have been, sir, turn'd into gold, all?
    Mam. No,
I cannot tell — It may be they should — What then?
    Love. What a great loss in hope have you sustain'd!
    Mam. Not I, the commonwealth has.
    Face. Ay, he would have built
The city new; and made a ditch about it
Of silver, should have run with cream from Hogsden;   110
That, every Sunday, in Moor-fields, the younkers,[1]
And tits and tom-boys should have fed on, gratis.
    Mam. I will go mount a turnip-cart and preach
The end of the world, within these two months. Surly,
What! in a dream?
    Sur. Must I needs cheat myself,
With that same foolish vice of honesty!
Come, let us go and hearken out the rogues:
That Face I'll mark for mine, if e'er I meet him.
    Face. If I can hear of him, sir, I'll bring you word,   120
Unto your lodging; for in troth, they were strangers
To me, I thought them honest as myself, sir.
                                      [Exeunt MAM. *and* SUR.

            Re-enter ANANIAS *and* TRIBULATION.

    Tri. 'Tis well, the saints shall not lose all yet. Go,

---

[1] Rich, **well-born youths** (German *Junker*); cf. *Merchant of Venice,* ii, 6: —
        "How like a younker, or a prodigal,
        The scarfèd bark puts from her native bay."

And get some carts ——
   Love. For what, my zealous friends?
   Ana. To bear away the portion of the righteous
Out of this den of thieves.
   Love. What is that portion?
   Ana. The goods sometimes the orphan's, that the brethren
Bought with their silver pence.   130
   Love. What, those in the cellar,
The knight Sir Mammon claims?
   Ana. I do defy
The wicked Mammon, so do all the brethren,
Thou profane man! I ask thee with what conscience
Thou canst advance that idol against us,
That have the seal? were not the shillings number'd,
That made the pounds; were not the pounds told out,
Upon the second day of the fourth week,
In the eighth month, upon the table dormant,   140
The year of the last patience of the saints,
Six hundred and ten?
   Love. Mine earnest vehement botcher,
And deacon also, I cannot dispute with you:
But if you get you not away the sooner,
I shall confute you with a cudgel.
   Ana. Sir!
   Tri. Be patient, Ananias.
   Ana. I am strong,
And will stand up, well girt, against an host   150
That threaten Gad in exile.
   Love. I shall send you
To Amsterdam, to your cellar.
   Ana. I will pray there,
Against thy house: may dogs defile thy walls,

And wasps and hornets breed beneath thy roof,
This seat of falsehood, and this cave of cozenage!
                                      [*Exeunt* ANA. *and* TRIB.
                    Enter DRUGGER.

  Love. Another too?
  Drug. Not I, sir, I am no brother.
  Love. (*beats him*). Away, you Harry Nicholas[1]! do you
    talk?   [*Exit* DRUGGER. 160
  Face. No, this was Abel Drugger. Good sir, go,
                                      [*To the* Parson.
And satisfy him; tell him all is done:
He staid too long a-washing of his face.
The doctor, he shall hear of him at West-chester;
And of the captain, tell him, at Yarmouth, or
Some good port-town else, lying for a wind. [*Exit* Parson.
If you can get off the angry child, now, sir ——

          Enter KASTRIL, *dragging in his sister.*

  Kas. Come on, you ewe, you have match'd most sweetly,
    have you not?
'Slight, you are a mammet[2]! O, I could touse you, now.
Death, mun' you marry, with a plague!   170
  Love. You lie, boy;
As sound as you; and I'm aforehand with you.
  Kas. Anon!
  Love. Come, will you quarrel? I will feize[3] you, sirrah;
Why do you not buckle to your tools?

    [1] A fanatic of Leyden, supposed to be the founder of the sect called
"The Family of Love."
    [2] Puppet; the word is a corruption of Mahomet, and was applied to
effigies of him.
    [3] Chastise, beat; still used in the West of England.

Kas. Ods light,
This is a fine old boy as e'er I saw!
Love. What, do you change your copy now? Proceed,
Here stands my dove: stoop[1] at her, if you dare.
Kas. 'Slight, I must love him! I cannot choose, i' faith,
An I should be hang'd for't! Suster, I protest,
I honour thee for this match.
Love. O, do you so, sir?
Kas. Yes, and thou canst take tobacco and drink, old boy,
I'll give her five hundred pound more to her marriage,
Than her own state.
Love. Fill a pipe full, Jeremy.
Face. Yes; but go in and take it, sir.
Love. We will —
I will be ruled by thee in anything, Jeremy.
Kas. 'Slight, thou art not hide-bound, thou art a jovy[2] boy!
Come, let us in, I pray thee, and take our whiffs.
Love. Whiff in with your sister, brother boy.
(*Exeunt* KAS. *and* DAME P.) That master
That had received such happiness by a servant,
In such a widow, and with so much wealth,
Were very ungrateful, if he would not be
A little indulgent to that servant's wit,
And help his fortune, though with some small strain
Of his own candour.[3] — (*Advancing.*) Therefore, gentlemen,
And kind spectators, if I have outstript
An old man's gravity, or strict canon, think
What a young wife and a good brain may do;
Stretch age's truth sometimes, and crack it too.

---

[1] Pounce upon; a term in falconry.
[2] Merry.   [3] Fair reputation, honor.

Speak for thyself, knave.

Face. So I will, sir.—(*Advancing to the front of the stage.*)
Gentlemen,
My part a little fell in this last scene,
Yet 'twas decorum. And though I am clean
Got off from Subtle, Surly, Mammon, Dol,
Hot Ananias, Dapper, Drugger, all
With whom I traded : yet I put myself   210
On you that are my country : and this pelf,
Which I have got, if you do quit me, rests
To feast you often, and invite new guests.   [*Exeunt.*[1]

[1] "The manifold harmony of inventive combination and imaginative contrast, the multitudinous unity of various and concordant effects, the complexity and the simplicity of action and impression, which hardly allow the reader's mind to hesitate between enjoyment and astonishment, laughter and wonder, admiration and diversion — all the distinctive qualities which the alchemic cunning of the poet has fused together in the crucible of dramatic satire for the production of a flawless work of art, have given us the most perfect model of imaginative realism and satirical comedy that the world has ever seen; the most wonderful work of its kind that can ever be run upon the same lines." — *Swinburne : A Study of Ben Jonson.* Coleridge " thought the *Œdipus Tyrannus*, *The Alchemist*, and *Tom Jones*, the three most perfect plots ever planned."

III.

PHILASTER;

OR,

LOVE LIES A-BLEEDING.

BY FRANCIS BEAUMONT AND JOHN FLETCHER

Probably first represented in 1608.

PHILASTER;

OR,

LOVE LIES A-BLEEDING.

DRAMATIS PERSONÆ.

KING.
PHILASTER, Heir to the Crown of Sicily.
PHARAMOND, Prince of Spain.
DION, a Lord.
CLEREMONT. } Noble Gentlemen.
THRASILINE. }
An old Captain.
Citizens.
A Country Fellow.

Two Woodmen.
Guard, Attendants.
ARETHUSA, Daughter of the King.
EUPHRASIA, Daughter of DION, disguised as a Page under the name of BELLARIO.
MEGRA, a Court Lady.
GALATEA, a Lady attending the Princess.
Two other Ladies.

SCENE: *Messina and its neighbourhood.*

ACT I.

SCENE I. — *The Presence Chamber in the Palace.*

Enter DION, CLEREMONT, *and* THRASILINE.

Cle. Here's nor lords nor ladies.

Dion. Credit me, gentlemen, I wonder at it. They received strict charge from the King to attend here: besides, it was boldly published, that no officer should forbid any gentleman that desired to attend and hear.

Cle. Can you guess the cause?

Dion. Sir, it is plain, about the Spanish Prince, that's come to marry our kingdom's heir and be our sovereign.

Thra. Many, that will seem to know much, say she looks not on him like a maid in love. 10

Dion. Oh, sir, the multitude, that seldom know any thing but their own opinions, speak that they would have; but the prince, before his own approach, received so many confident messages from the state, that I think she's resolved to be ruled.

Cle. Sir, it is thought, with her he shall enjoy both these kingdoms of Sicily and Calabria.

Dion. Sir, it is without controversy so meant. But 'twill be a troublesome labour for him to enjoy both these kingdoms with safety, the right heir to one of them living, and living so virtuously; especially, the people admiring the bravery of his mind and lamenting his injuries. 22

Cle. Who? Philaster?

Dion. Yes; whose father, we all know, was by our late King of Calabria unrighteously deposed from his fruitful Sicily. Myself drew some blood in those wars, which I would give my hand to be washed from.

Cle. Sir, my ignorance in state-policy will not let me know why, Philaster being heir to one of these kingdoms, the King should suffer him to walk abroad with such free liberty. 30

Dion. Sir, it seems your nature is more constant than to inquire after state-news. But the King, of late, made a hazard of both the kingdoms, of Sicily and his own, with offering but to imprison Philaster; at which the city was in arms, not to be charmed down by any state-order or proclamation, till they saw Philaster ride through the streets pleased and without a guard; at which they threw their hats and their arms from them; some to make bonfires, some to drink, all for his deliverance: which, wise men say, is the cause the King labours to bring in the power of a foreign nation to awe his own with. 41

Enter GALATEA, *a* Lady, *and* MEGRA.

Thra. See, the ladies! What's the first?

Dion. A wise and modest gentlewoman that attends the princess.

Cle. The second?

Dion. She is one that may stand still discreetly enough, and ill-favouredly dance her measure; simper when she is courted by her friend, and slight her husband.

Cle. The last? 49

Dion. Marry, I think she is one whom the state keeps for the agents of our confederate princes: she'll cog[1] and lie with a whole army, before the league shall break. Her name is common through the kingdom, and the trophies of her dishonour advanced beyond Hercules' Pillars.

Cle. She's a profitable member.

Lady. Peace, if you love me: you shall see these gentlemen stand their ground and not court us.

Gal. What if they should?

Megra. What if they should! 59

Lady. Nay, let her alone. — What if they should! Why, if they should, I say they were never abroad: what foreigner would do so? it writes them directly untravelled.

Gal. Why, what if they be?

Megra. What if they be!

[1] Cheat, cajole.

Lady. Good madam, let her go on.—What if they be! why, if they be, I will justify, they cannot maintain discourse with a judicious lady, nor make a leg[1] nor say " **excuse me.**"
Gal. Ha, ha, ha!
Lady. Do you laugh, madam?
Dion. Your desires upon you, ladies! 70
Lady. Then you must sit beside us.
Dion. I shall sit near you then, lady.
Lady. Near me, perhaps; but there's a lady endures no stranger; and to me you appear a very strange fellow.
Megra. Methinks he's not so strange; he would quickly be acquainted.
Thra. Peace, the King!

Enter KING, PHARAMOND, ARETHUSA, *and* Attendants.

King. To give a stronger testimony of love
Than sickly promises (which commonly
In princes find both birth and burial 80
In one breath) we have drawn you, worthy sir,
To make your fair endearments to our daughter,
And worthy services known to our subjects,
Now loved and wondered at; next, our intent
To plant you deeply, our immediate heir
Both to our blood and kingdoms. For this lady,
(The best part of your life, as you confirm me,
And I believe,) though her few years and sex
Yet teach her nothing but her fears and blushes,
Desires without desire, discourse and knowledge 90
Only of what herself is to herself,
Make her feel moderate health; and when she sleeps,
In making no ill day, knows no ill dreams:

[1] Bow.

Think not, dear sir, these undivided parts,
That must mould up a virgin, are put on
To show her so, as borrowed ornaments,
To speak her perfect love to you, or add
An artificial shadow to her nature —
No, sir; I boldly dare proclaim her yet
No woman. But woo her still, and think her modesty
A sweeter mistress than the offered language
Of any dame, were she a queen, whose eye
Speaks common loves and comforts to her servants.[1]
Last, noble son (for so I now must call you),
What I have done thus public, is not only
To add a comfort in particular
To you or me, but all; and to confirm
The nobles and the gentry of these kingdoms
By oath to your succession, which shall be
Within this month at most.

 Thra. This will be hardly done.
 Cle. It must be ill done, if it be done.
 Dion. When 'tis at best, 'twill be but half done, whilst
So brave a gentleman is wronged and flung off.
 Thra. I fear.
 Cle. Who does not?
 Dion. I fear not for myself, and yet I fear too:
Well, we shall see, we shall see. No more.
 Pha. Kissing your white hand, mistress, I take leave
To thank your royal father; and thus far
To be my own free trumpet. Understand,
Great King, and these your subjects, mine that must be,
(For so deserving you have spoke me, sir,
And so deserving I dare speak myself,)

[1] Suitors.

To what a person. of what eminence,
Ripe expectation, of what faculties,
Manners and virtues, you would wed your kingdoms;
You in me have your wishes. Oh, this country!
By more than all my hopes, I hold it happy;
Happy in their dear memories that have been   130
Kings great and good; happy in yours that is;
And from you (as a chronicle to keep
Your noble name from eating age) do I
Opine myself most happy. Gentlemen,
Believe me in a word, a prince's word,
There shall be nothing to make up a kingdom
Mighty and flourishing, defencèd, feared,
Equal to be commanded and obeyed,
But through the travails of my life I'll find it,
And tie it to this country. And I vow   140
My reign shall be so easy to the subject,
That every man shall be his prince himself
And his own law — yet I his prince and law.
And, dearest lady, to your dearest self
(Dear in the choice of him whose name and lustre
Must make you more and mightier) let me say,
You are the blessed'st living; for, sweet princess,
You shall enjoy a man of men to be
Your servant; you shall make him yours, for whom
Great queens must die.   150
   Thra. Miraculous!
   Cle. This speech calls him Spaniard, being nothing
But a large inventory of his own commendations.
   Dion. I wonder what's his price; for certainly
He'll sell himself, he has so praised his shape.
But here comes one more worthy those large speeches,

Enter PHILASTER.

Than the large speaker of them.
Let me be swallowed quick, if I can find,
In all the anatomy of yon man's virtues,
One sinew sound enough to promise for him,   160
He shall be constable. By this sun, he'll ne'er make king
Unless it be for trifles, in my poor judgment.
    Phi. (*kneeling*). Right noble sir, as low as my obedience,
And with a heart as loyal as my knee,
I beg your favour.
    King. Rise; you have it, sir.   [PHILASTER *rises.*
    Dion. Mark but the King, how pale he looks with fear!
Oh, this same nettle conscience, how it jades us!
    King. Speak your intents, sir.
    Phi. Shall I speak 'em freely?   170
Be still my royal sovereign.
    King. As a subject,
We give you freedom.
    Dion. Now it heats.
    Phi. Then thus I turn
My language to you, prince; you, foreign man!
Ne'er stare nor put on wonder, for you must
Endure me, and you shall. This earth you tread upon
(A dowry, as you hope, with this fair princess),
By my dead father (oh, I had a father,   180
Whose memory I bow to!) was not left
To your inheritance, and I up and living —
Having myself about me and my sword,
The souls of all my name and memories,
These arms and some few friends beside the gods —
To part so calmly with it, and sit still

And say, " I might have been." I tell thee, Pharamond,
When thou art king, look I be dead and rotten,
And my name ashes : for, hear me, Pharamond !
This very ground thou goest on, this fat earth, 190
My father's friends made fertile with their faiths,
Before that day of shame shall gape and swallow
Thee and thy nation, like a hungry grave,
Into her hidden bowels ; prince, it shall ;
By Nemesis, it shall !

   Pha. He's mad ; beyond cure, mad.

   Dion. Here is a fellow has some fire in's veins :
The outlandish prince looks like a tooth-drawer.

   Phi. Sir, prince of popinjays,[1] I'll make it well
Appear to you I am not mad. 200

   King. You displease us :
You are too bold.

   Phi. No, sir, I am too tame,
Too much a turtle, a thing born without passion,
A faint shadow, that every drunken cloud
Sails over and makes nothing.

   King. I do not fancy this.
Call our physicians : sure, he's somewhat tainted.

   Thra. I do not think 'twill prove so.

   Dion. He has given him a general purge already, 210
For all the right he has ; and now he means
To let him blood. Be constant, gentlemen :
By these hilts, I'll run his hazard,
Although I run my name out of the kingdom !

   Cle. Peace, we are all one soul.

   Pha. What you have seen in me to stir offence,

---

[1] Parrots; a mark like a parrot put on a pole to be shot at; hence a coxcomb.

I cannot find, unless it be this lady,
Offered into mine arms, with the succession;
Which I must keep, (though it hath pleased your fury
To mutiny within you,) without disputing
Your genealogies, or taking knowledge
Whose branch you are: the King will leave it me,
And I dare make it mine. You have your answer.

Phi. If thou wert sole inheritor to him
That made the world his, and couldst see no sun
Shine upon anything but thine; were Pharamond
As truly valiant as I feel him cold,
And ringed among the choicest of his friends
(Such as would blush to talk such serious follies,
Or back such bellied commendations),
And from this presence, spite of all these bugs,[1]
You should hear further from me.

King. Sir, you wrong the prince; I gave you not this freedom
To brave our best friends: you deserve our frown.
Go to; be better tempered.

Phi. It must be, sir, when I am nobler used.

Gal. Ladies,
This would have been a pattern of succession,
Had he ne'er met this mischief. By my life,
He is the worthiest the true name of man
This day within my knowledge.

Meg. I cannot tell what you may call your knowledge;
But the other is the man set in mine eye:
Oh, 'tis a prince of wax![2]

Gal. A dog it is.

[1] Bugbears. In Welsh, *bwg* means spectre, a hobgoblin.
[2] Handsome, elegant.

King. Philaster, tell me
The injuries you aim at in your riddles.
    Phi. If you had my eyes, sir, and sufferance,
My griefs upon you and my broken fortunes,   250
My wants great, and now nought but hopes and fears,
My wrongs would make ill riddles to be laughed at.
Dare you be still my king, and right me not?
    King. Give me your wrongs in private.
    Phi. Take them,
And ease me of a load would bow strong Atlas.
                                            [They talk apart.
    Cle. He dares not stand the shock.
    Dion. I cannot blame him; there's danger in't.   258
Every man in this age has not a soul of crystal, for all men
to read their actions through: men's hearts and faces are so
far asunder, that they hold no intelligence. Do but view yon
stranger well, and you shall see a fever through all his bravery,
and feel him shake like a true recreant: if he give not back
his crown again upon the report of an elder-gun, I have no
augury.
    King. Go to;
Be more yourself, as you respect our favour;
You'll stir us else. Sir, I must have you know,
That you are, and shall be, at our pleasure,
What fashion we will put upon you. Smooth   .   270
Your brow, or by the gods ——
    Phi. I am dead, sir; you're my fate. It was not I
Said, I was wronged: I carry all about me
My weak stars lead me to, all my weak fortunes.
Who dares in all this presence speak, (that is
But man of flesh, and may be mortal,) tell me,
I do not most entirely love this prince,

And honour his full virtues!
King. Sure, he's possessed.
Phi. Yes, with my father's spirit. It's here, O King! 280
A dangerous spirit. Now he tells me, King,
I was a king's heir, bids me be a king,
And whispers to me, these are all my subjects.
'Tis strange he will not let me sleep, but dives
Into my fancy, and there gives me shapes
That kneel and do me service, cry me king:
But I'll suppress him; he's a factious spirit,
And will undo me. Noble sir, your hand;
I am your servant.
King. Away! I do not like this: 290
I'll make you tamer, or I'll dispossess you
Both of your life and spirit. For this time
I pardon your wild speech, without so much
As your imprisonment.
[*Exeunt* KING, PHARAMOND, ARETHUSA, *and* Attendants.

Dion. I thank you, sir! you dare not for the people.
Gal. Ladies, what think you now of this brave fellow?
Meg. A pretty talking fellow, hot at hand. But eye yon stranger: is he not a fine complete gentleman? Oh, these strangers, I do affect them strangely! As I live, I could love all the nation over and over for his sake. 300
Gal. Pride comfort your poor head-piece, lady! 'tis a weak one, and had need of a night-cap.
[*Exeunt* GALATEA, MEGRA, *and* Lady.
Dion. See, how his fancy labours! Has he not
Spoke home and bravely? what a dangerous train
Did he give fire to! how he shook the King,
Made his soul melt within him, and his blood

Run into whey! it stood upon his brow
Like a cold winter-dew.
   Phi. Gentlemen,
You have no suit to me? I am no minion: 310
You stand, methinks, like men that would be courtiers,
If I could well be flattered at a price,
Not to undo your children. You're all honest:
Go, get you home again, and make your country
A virtuous court, to which your great ones may,
In their diseased age, retire and live recluse.
   Cle. How do you, worthy sir?
   Phi. Well, very well;
And so well that, if the King please, I find
I may live many years. 320
   Dion. The King must please,
Whilst we know what you are and who you are,
Your wrongs and virtues. Shrink not, worthy sir,
But add your father to you; in whose name
We'll waken all the gods, and conjure up
The rods of vengeance, the abusèd people,
Who, like to raging torrents, shall swell high,
And so begirt the dens of these male-dragons,
That, through the strongest safety, they shall beg
For mercy at your sword's point. 330
   Phi. Friends, no more;
Our ears may be corrupted; 'tis an age
We dare not trust our wills to. Do you love me?
   Thra. Do we love Heaven and honour?
   Phi. My Lord Dion, you had
A virtuous gentlewoman called you father;
Is she yet alive?
   Dion. Most honoured sir, she is;

And, for the penance but of an idle dream,
Has undertook a tedious pilgrimage. 340

Enter a Lady.

Phi. Is it to me
Or any of these gentlemen you come?
  Lady. To you, brave lord; the princess would entreat
Your present company.
  Phi. The princess send for me! you are mistaken.
  Lady. If you be called Philaster, 'tis to you.
  Phi. Kiss her fair hand, and say I will attend her.
                                              [*Exit* Lady.
  Dion. Do you know what you do?
  Phi. Yes; go to see a woman.
  Cle. But do you weigh the danger you are in? 350
  Phi. Danger in a sweet face!
By Jupiter, I must not fear a woman!
  Thra. But are you sure it was the princess sent?
It may be some foul train to catch your life.
  Phi. I do not think it, gentlemen; she's noble.
Her eye may shoot me dead, or those true red
And white friends in her face may steal my soul out;
There's all the danger in't: but, be what may,
Her single name hath armèd me.   [*Exit.*
  Dion. Go on,   360
And be as truly happy as thou'rt fearless!
Come, gentlemen, let's make our friends acquainted,
Lest the King prove false.   [*Exeunt*

SCENE II. — ARETHUSA'S *Apartment in the Palace.*

Enter ARETHUSA *and a* Lady.

Are. Comes he not?
Lady. Madam?
Are. Will Philaster come?
Lady. Dear madam, you were wont to credit me
At first.
Are. But didst thou tell me so?
I am forgetful, and my woman's strength
Is so o'ercharged with dangers like to grow
About my marriage, that these under-things
Dare not abide in such a troubled sea.   10
How looked he when he told thee he would come?
Lady. Why, well.
Are. And not a little fearful?
Lady. Fear, madam! sure, he knows not what it is.
Are. You are all of his faction; the whole court
Is bold in praise of him; whilst I
May live neglected, and do noble things,
As fools in strife throw gold into the sea,
Drowned in the doing. But, I know he fears.
Lady. Fear, madam! methought, his looks hid more   20
Of love than fear.
Are. Of love! to whom? to you?
Did you deliver those plain words I sent,
With such a winning gesture and quick look
That you have caught him?
Lady. Madam, I mean to you.
Are. Of love to me! alas, thy ignorance
Lets thee not see the crosses of our births!

Nature, that loves not to be questioned
Why she did this or that, but has her ends, 30
And knows she does well, never gave the world
Two things so opposite, so contrary,
As he and I am: if a bowl of blood,
Drawn from this arm of mine, would poison thee,
A draught of his would cure thee. Of love to me!
   Lady. Madam, I think I hear him.
   Are. Bring him in.   [*Exit* Lady.
You gods, that would not have your dooms withstood,
Whose holy wisdoms at this time it is,
To make the passion of a feeble maid 40
The way unto your justice, I obey.

       Re-enter Lady *with* PHILASTER.

   Lady. Here is my Lord Philaster.
   Are. Oh, 'tis well.
Withdraw yourself.   [*Exit* Lady.
   Phi. Madam, your messenger
Made me believe you wished to speak with me.
   Are. 'Tis true, Philaster; but the words are such
I have to say, and do so ill beseem
The mouth of woman, that I wish them said,
And yet am loath to speak them. Have you known 50
That I have aught detracted from your worth?
Have I in person wronged you? or have set
My baser instruments to throw disgrace
Upon your virtues?
   Phi. Never, madam, you.
   Are. Why, then, should you, in such a public place,
Injure a princess, and a scandal lay
Upon my fortunes, famed to be so great,

Calling a great part of my dowry in question?
　Phi. Madam, this truth which I shall speak will be　60
Foolish: but, for your fair and virtuous self,
I could afford myself to have no right
To anything you wished.
　Are. Philaster, know,
I must enjoy these kingdoms.
　Phi. Madam, both?
　Are. Both, or I die: by fate, I die, Philaster,
If I not calmly may enjoy them both.
　Phi. I would do much to save that noble life:
Yet would be loath to have posterity　70
Find in our stories, that Philaster gave
His right unto a sceptre and a crown
To save a lady's longing.
　Are. Nay, then, hear:
I must and will have them, and more ——
　Phi. What more?
　Are. Or lose that little life the gods prepared
To trouble this poor piece of earth withal.
　Phi. Madam, what more?
　Are. Turn, then, away thy face.　80
　Phi. No.
　Are. Do.
　Phi. I can endure it. Turn away my face!
I never yet saw enemy that looked
So dreadfully, but that I thought myself
As great a basilisk as he; or spake
So horrible, but that I thought my tongue
Bore thunder underneath, as much as his;
Nor beast that I could turn from: shall I then
Begin to fear sweet sounds? a lady's voice,　90

Whom I do love? Say, you would have my life;
Why, I will give it you; for 'tis to me
A thing so loathed, and unto you that ask
Of so poor use, that I shall make no price:
If you entreat, I will unmovedly hear.
 Are. Yet, for my sake, a little bend thy looks.
 Phi. I do.
 Are. Then know, I must have them and thee.
 Phi. And me?
 Are. Thy love; without which, all the land   100
Discovered yet will serve me for no use
But to be buried in.
 Phi. Is't possible?
 Are. With it, it were too little to bestow
On thee. Now, though thy breath do strike me dead,
(Which, know, it may) I have unript my breast.
 Phi. Madam, you are too full of noble thoughts,
To lay a train for this contemnèd life,
Which you may have for asking: to suspect
Were base, where I deserve no ill. Love you!   110
By all my hopes, I do, above my life!
But how this passion should proceed from you
So violently, would amaze a man
That would be jealous.
 Are. Another soul into my body shot
Could not have filled me with more strength and spirit
Than this thy breath. But spend not hasty time
In seeking how I came thus: 'tis the gods,
The gods, that make me so; and, sure, our love
Will be the nobler and the better blest,   120
In that the secret justice of the gods
Is mingled with it. Let us leave, and kiss;

Lest some unwelcome guest should fall betwixt us,
And we should part without it.
   Phi. 'Twill be ill
I should abide here long.
   Are. 'Tis true; and worse
You should come often. How shall we devise
To hold intelligence, that our true loves,
On any new occasion, may agree   130
What path is best to tread?
   Phi. I have a boy,
Sent by the gods, I hope, to this intent,
Not yet seen in the court. Hunting the buck,
I found him sitting by a fountain's side,
Of which he borrowed some to quench his thirst,
And paid the nymph again as much in tears.
A garland lay him by, made by himself
Of many several flowers bred in the vale,
Stuck in that mystic order that the rareness   140
Delighted me: but ever when he turned
His tender eyes upon 'em, he would weep,
As if he meant to make 'em grow again.
Seeing such pretty helpless innocence
Dwell in his face, I asked him all his story:
He told me that his parents gentle died,
Leaving him to the mercy of the fields,
Which gave him roots; and of the crystal springs,
Which did not stop their courses; and the sun,
Which still, he thanked him, yielded him his light.   150
Then took he up his garland, and did show
What every flower, as country-people hold,
Did signify, and how all, ordered thus,
Expressed his grief; and, to my thoughts, did read

The prettiest lecture of his country art
That could be wished: so that, methought, I could
Have studied it. I gladly entertained
Him, who was as glad to follow; and have got
The trustiest, loving'st, and the gentlest boy
That ever master kept.[1] Him will I send   160
To wait on you, and bear our hidden love.

Re-enter Lady.

Are. 'Tis well; no more.
Lady. Madam, the prince is come to do his service.
Are. What will you do, Philaster, with yourself?
Phi. Why, that which all the gods have pointed out for me.
Are. Dear, hide thyself. —
Bring in the prince.   [*Exit* Lady.
Phi. Hide me from Pharamond!
When thunder speaks, which is the voice of Jove,
Though I do reverence, yet I hide me not;   170
And shall a stranger-prince have leave to brag
Unto a foreign nation, that he made
Philaster hide himself?
Are. He cannot know it.
Phi. Though it should sleep for ever to the world,
It is a simple sin to hide myself,
Which will for ever on my conscience lie.
Are. Then, good Philaster, give him scope and way
In what he says; for he is apt to speak
What you are loath to hear: for my sake, do.   180
Phi. I will.

[1] This pretty and picturesque passage — probably by Fletcher — is a good specimen of that romantic quality in Beaumont and Fletcher's works to which reference has been made in the Preface.

Re-enter Lady *with* Pharamond.

Pha. My princely mistress, as true lovers ought,
I come to kiss these fair hands, and to show, [*Exit* Lady.
In outward ceremonies, the dear love
Writ in my heart.
    Phi. If I shall have an answer no directlier,
I am gone.
    Pha. To what would he have answer?
    Are. To his claim unto the kingdom.
    Pha. Sirrah, I forbare you before the King ——   190
    Phi. Good sir, do so still: I would not talk with you.
    Pha. But now the time is fitter: do but offer
To make mention of right to any kingdom,
Though it be scarce habitable ——
    Phi. Good sir, let me go.
    Pha. And by my sword ——
    Phi. Peace, Pharamond! if thou ——
    Are. Leave us, Philaster.
    Phi. I have done.   [*Going.*
    Pha. You are gone! by Heaven I'll fetch you back.   200
    Phi. You shall not need.   [*Returning.*
    Pha. What now?
    Phi. Know, Pharamond,
I loathe to brawl with such a blast as thou,
Who art nought but a valiant voice; but if
Thou shalt provoke me further, men shall say,
"Thou wert," and not lament it.
    Pha. Do you slight
My greatness so, and in the chamber of
The princess?   210
    Phi. It is a place to which I must confess

I owe a reverence; but were't the church,
Ay, at the altar, there's no place so safe,
Where thou dar'st injure me, but I dare kill thee:
And for your greatness, know, sir, I can grasp
You and your greatness thus, thus into nothing.
Give not a word, not a word back! Farewell. [*Exit*.

Pha. 'Tis an odd fellow, madam; we must stop
His mouth with some office when we are married.

Are. You were best make him your controller. 220

Pha. I think he would discharge it well. But, madam,
I hope our hearts are knit; and yet, so slow
The ceremonies of state are, that 'twill be long
Before our hands be so. If then you please,
Being agreed in heart, let us not wait
For dreaming form, but take a little stolen
Delights, and so prevent[1] our joys to come.

Are. If you dare speak such thoughts,
I must withdraw in honour. [*Exit*.

Pha. The constitution of my body will never hold out
till the wedding; I must seek elsewhere. [*Exit*. 231

ACT II.

SCENE I. — *An Apartment in the Palace.*

Enter PHILASTER *and* BELLARIO.

Phi. And thou shalt find her honourable, boy;
Full of regard unto thy tender youth,
For thine own modesty; and, for my sake,

[1] Outstrip, forestall, anticipate; cf. *Twelfth Night*, iii, 1, 94; *Hamlet*, ii, 2, 305.

Apter to give than thou wilt be to ask,
Ay, or deserve.
　Bel. Sir, you did take me up
When I was nothing; and only yet am something
By being yours.　You trusted me unknown;
And that which you were apt to conster [1]
A simple innocence in me, perhaps
Might have been craft, the cunning of a boy
Hardened in lies and theft: yet ventured you
To part my miseries and me; for which,
I never can expect to serve a lady
That bears more honour in her breast than you.
　Phi. But, boy, it will prefer thee.　Thou art young,
And bear'st a childish overflowing love
To them that clap thy cheeks and speak thee fair yet;
But when thy judgment comes to rule those passions,
Thou wilt remember best those careful friends
That placed thee in the noblest way of life.
She is a princess I prefer thee to.
　Bel. In that small time that I have seen the world,
I never knew a man hasty to part with
A servant he thought trusty: I remember,
My father would prefer the boys he kept
To greater men than he; but did it not
Till they were grown too saucy for himself.
　Phi. Why, gentle boy, I find no fault at all
In thy behaviour.
　Bel. Sir, if I have made
A fault in ignorance, instruct my youth:
I shall be willing, if not apt, to learn;
Age and experience will adorn my mind

[1] Construe.

With larger knowledge ; and if I have done
A wilful fault, think me not past all hope
For once. What master holds so strict a hand
Over his boy, that he will part with him
Without one warning? Let me be corrected,
To break my stubbornness, if it be so,   40
Rather than turn me off; and I shall mend.
   Phi. Thy love doth plead so prettily to stay,
That, trust me, I could weep to part with thee.
Alas, I do not turn thee off! thou know'st
It is my business that doth call thee hence ;
And when thou art with her, thou dwell'st with me.
Think so, and 'tis so : and when time is full,
That thou hast well discharged this heavy trust,
Laid on so weak a one, I will again
With joy receive thee ; as I live, I will!   50
Nay, weep not, gentle boy. 'Tis more than time
Thou didst attend the princess.
   Bel. I am gone.
But since I am to part with you, my lord,
And none knows whether I shall live to do
More service for you, take this little prayer :
Heaven bless your loves, your fights, all your designs !
May sick men, if they have your wish, be well ;
And Heaven hate those you curse, though I be one !
                                                            [*Exit.*
   Phi. The love of boys unto their lords is strange ;   60
I have read wonders of it : yet this boy
For my sake (if a man may judge by looks
And speech) would out-do story. I may see
A day to pay him for his loyalty.   [*Exit.*

Scene II. — *A Gallery in the Palace.*

Enter Pharamond.

Pha. Why should these ladies stay so long? They must come this way: I know the queen employs 'em not; for the reverend mother sent me word, they would all be for the garden. If they should all prove honest[1] now, I were in a fair taking; I was never so long without sport in my life, and, in my conscience, 'tis not my fault. Oh, for our country ladies!

Enter Galatea.

(*Aside*) Here's one bolted; I'll hound at her. Madam!
Gal. Your grace!
Pha. Shall I not be a trouble? 10
Gal. Not to me, sir.
Pha. Nay, nay, you are too quick. By this sweet hand —
Gal. You'll be forsworn, sir; 'tis but an old glove. If you will talk at distance, I am for you: but, good prince, be not ribald, nor do not brag; these two I bar; and then, I think, I shall have sense enough to answer all the weighty apophthegms your royal blood shall manage.
Pha. Dear lady, can you love? 18
Gal. Dear prince! how dear? I ne'er cost you a coach yet, nor put you to the dear repentance of a banquet. Here's no scarlet, sir, to blush the sin out it was given for. This wire[2] mine own hair covers; and this face has been so far from being dear to any, that it ne'er cost penny painting; and, for the rest of my poor wardrobe, such as you see, it leaves no handle behind it, to make the jealous mercer's wife curse our good doings.

[1] Chaste. [2] Women then used wire frames in their head-dresses.

Pha. You mistake me, lady.

Gal. Lord, I do so: would you or I could help it!

Pha. You're very dangerous bitter, like a potion.

Gal. No, sir, I do not mean to purge you, though I mean to purge a little time on you.

Pha. Do ladies of this country use to give No more respect to men of my full being?

Gal. Full being! I understand you not, unless your grace means growing to fatness; and then your only remedy (upon my knowledge, prince) is, in a morning, a cup of neat white wine brewed with carduus,[1] then fast till supper; about eight you may eat; use exercise, and keep a sparrow-hawk; you can shoot in a tiller[2]: but, of all, your grace must fly phlebotomy,[3] fresh pork, conger, and clarified whey; they are all dullers of the vital spirits.

Pha. Lady, you talk of nothing all this while.

Gal. 'Tis very true, sir; I talk of you.

Pha. (*aside*). This is a crafty wench; I like her wit well; 'twill be rare to stir up a leaden appetite: she's a Danaë, and must be courted in a shower of gold. — Madam, look here; all these, and more than ——

Gal. What have you there, my lord? gold! now, as I live, 'tis fair gold! You would have silver for it, to play with the pages: you could not have taken me in a worse time; but, if you have present use, my lord, I'll send my man with silver and keep your gold for you. [*Takes gold.*

Pha. Lady, lady!

Gal. She's coming, sir, behind, will take white money.[4] — (*Aside*) Yet for all this I'll match ye.

[*Exit behind the hangings.*

[1] Thistle.
[2] The handle of a cross-bow.
[3] Blood-letting.
[4] Cant term for silver money.

Pha. If there be but two such more in this kingdom, and near the court, we may even hang up our harps. Ten such camphire constitutions[1] as this would call the golden age again in question; and what a mischief that would breed let all consider! 60

Enter MEGRA.

(*Aside*) Here's another: if she be of the same last, the devil shall pluck her on. — Many fair mornings, lady.
 Meg. As many mornings bring as many days,
Fair, sweet and hopeful to your grace!
 Pha. (*aside*). She gives good words yet; sure this wench
  is free. —
If your more serious business do not call you,
Let me hold quarter with you; we will talk
An hour out quickly.
 Meg. What would your grace talk of?
 Pha. Of some such pretty subject as yourself: 70
I'll go no further than your eye, or lip;
There's theme enough for one man for an age.
 Meg. Sir, they stand right, and my lips are yet even,
Smooth, young enough, ripe enough, and red enough,
Or my glass wrongs me.
 Pha. Oh, they are two twinned cherries dyed in blushes,
Which those fair suns above with their bright beams
Reflect upon and ripen. Sweetest beauty,
Bow down those branches, that the longing taste
Of the faint looker-on may meet those blessings, 80
And taste and live.
 Meg. Oh, delicate sweet prince! —
(*Aside*) She that hath snow enough about her heart

---

[1] Cold-blooded.

To take the wanton spring of ten such lines off,
May be a nun without probation. — Sir,
You have in such neat poetry gathered a kiss,
That if I had but five lines of that number,
Such pretty begging blanks, I should commend
Your forehead or your cheeks, and kiss you too.

Pha. Do it in prose; you cannot miss it, madam. 90

Meg. I shall, I shall.

Pha. By my life, but you shall not;
I'll prompt you first. (*Kisses her.*) Can you do it now?

Meg. Methinks 'tis easy, now you ha' done't before me;
But yet I should stick at it.

Pha. Stick till to-morrow;
I'll never part you, sweetest. But we lose time:
Can you love me?

Meg. Love you, my lord! how would you have me love you? 99

Pha. I'll teach you in a short sentence, 'cause I will not load your memory: this is all; love me, and go with me.

Meg. 'Tis impossible.

Pha. Not to a willing mind, that will endeavour.

Meg. Why, prince, you have a lady of your own
That yet wants teaching.

Pha. I'll sooner teach a mare the old measures,[1] than teach her.

Meg. By my honour, that's a foul fault, indeed;
But time and your good help will wear it out, sir.
Has your grace seen the court-star, Galatea? 110

Pha. Out upon her! she's as cold of her favour as an apoplex: she sailed by but now.

Meg. And how do you hold her wit, sir?

[1] Stately dances.

Pha. I hold her wit? The strength of all the guard cannot hold it, if they were tied to it; she would blow 'em out of the kingdom. They talk of Jupiter; he's but a squib-cracker to her: look well about you, and you may find a tongue-bolt. But speak, sweet lady, shall I be freely welcome?

Meg. Whither? 120

Pha. To your room. If you mistrust my faith, you do me the unnoblest wrong.

Meg. I dare not, prince, I dare not.

Pha. Make your own conditions, my purse shall seal 'em; and what you dare imagine you can want, I'll furnish you withal: give two hours to your thoughts every morning about it. Come, I know you are bashful;
Speak in my ear, will you be mine? Keep this,
And with it me: soon I will visit you. [*Gives her a ring.*

Meg. My lord, 130
My chamber's most unsafe; but when 'tis night,
I'll find some means to slip into your lodging;
Till when——

Pha. Till when, this and my heart go with thee!
[*Exeunt severally.*

Re-enter GALATEA.

Gal. Oh, thou pernicious petticoat prince! are these your virtues? Well, if I do not lay a train to blow your sport up, I am no woman: and, Lady Towsabel, I'll fit you for't. [*Exit.*

SCENE III. — ARETHUSA'S *Apartment in the Palace.*

Enter ARETHUSA *and a* Lady.

Are. Where's the boy?
Lady. Within, madam.
Are. Gave you him gold to buy him clothes?
Lady. I did.
Are. And has he done't?
Lady. Yes, madam.
Are. 'Tis a pretty sad-talking boy, is it not?
Asked you his name?
Lady. No, madam.

Enter GALATEA.

Are. Oh, you are welcome. What good news? 10
Gal. As good as any one can tell your grace,
That says, she has done that you would have wished.
Are. Hast thou discovered?
Gal. I have strained a point
Of modesty for you.
Are. I prithee, how?
Gal. In listening after scandal. I see, let a lady live never so modestly, she shall be sure to find a lawful time to hearken after scandal. Your prince, brave Pharamond, was so hot on't! 20
Are. With whom?
Gal. Why, with the lady I suspected:
I can tell the time and place.
Are. Oh, when, and where?
Gal. To-night, his lodging.
Are. Run thyself into the presence; mingle there again

With other ladies; leave the rest to me.   [*Exit* GALATEA.
(*Aside*) If destiny (to whom we dare not say,
"Why didst thou this?") have not decreed it so,
In lasting leaves (whose smallest characters   30
Were never altered yet), this match shall break.
Where's the boy?
    Lady. Here, madam.

    Enter BELLARIO, *richly dressed.*

    Are. Sir,
You are sad to change your service; is't not so?
    Bel. Madam, I have not changed; I wait on you,
To do him service.
    Are. Thou disclaim'st[1] in me.
Tell me thy name.
    Bel. Bellario.   40
    Are. Thou canst sing and play?
    Bel. If grief will give me leave, madam, I can.
    Are. Alas, what kind of grief can thy years know?
Hadst thou a curst[2] master when thou went'st to school?
Thou art not capable of other grief,
Thy brows and cheeks are smooth as waters be
When no breath troubles them: believe me, boy,
Care seeks out wrinkled brows and hollow eyes,
And builds himself caves, to abide in them.
Come, sir, tell me truly, does your lord love me?   50
    Bel. Love, madam! I know not what it is.
    Are. Canst thou know grief, and never yet knew'st love?
Thou art deceived, boy.   Does he speak of me
As if he wished me well?
    Bel. If it be love

---

[1] Renounce any claim in.   [2] Cross.

To forget all respect of his own friends
In thinking of your face ; if it be love
To sit crossed-armed and sigh away the day,
Mingled with starts, crying your name as loud
And hastily as men i' the streets do fire ; 60
If it be love to weep himself away
When he but hears of any lady dead
Or killed, because it might have been your chance ;
If, when he goes to rest (which will not be),
'Twixt every prayer he says, to name you once,
As others drop a bead, be to be in love,
Then, madam, I dare swear he loves you.
 Are. Oh, you're a cunning boy, and taught to lie
For your lord's credit ! but thou know'st a lie
That bears this sound is welcomer to me 70
Than any truth that says he loves me not.
Lead the way, boy. — Do you attend me too. —
'Tis thy lord's business hastes me thus. Away ! [*Exeunt.*

 SCENE IV. — *Before* PHARAMOND'S *Lodging in the Court of the Palace.*

Enter DION, CLEREMONT, THRASILINE, MEGRA, *and* GALATEA.

 Dion. Come, ladies, shall we talk a round ? As men
Do walk a mile, women should talk an hour
After supper : 'tis their exercise.
 Gal. 'Tis late.
 Meg. 'Tis all
My eyes will do to lead me to my bed.
 Gal. I fear, they are so heavy, you'll scarce find
The way to your own lodging with 'em to-night.

Enter PHARAMOND.

Thra. The prince!

Pha. Not a-bed, ladies? you're good sitters-up: What think you of a pleasant dream, to last
Till morning?

Meg. I should choose, my lord, a pleasing wake before it.

Enter ARETHUSA *and* BELLARIO.

Are. 'Tis well, my lord; you're courting of these ladies.—
Is't not late, gentlemen?

Cle. Yes, madam.

Are. Wait you there. [*Exit.*

Meg. (*aside*). She's jealous, as I live. Look you on, my lord,
The princess has a Hylas,[1] an Adonis.

Pha. His form is angel-like.

Meg. Why, this is he that must, when you are wed,
Sit by your pillow, like young Apollo, with
His hand and voice binding your thoughts in sleep;
The princess does provide him for you and for herself.

Pha. I find no music in these boys.

Meg. Nor I:
They can do little, and that small they do,
They have not wit to hide.

Dion. Serves he the princess?

Thra. Yes.

Dion. 'Tis a sweet boy: how brave[2] she keeps him!

Pha. Ladies all, good rest; I mean to kill a buck
To-morrow morning, ere you've done your dreams.

---

[1] A beautiful youth, beloved by Hercules, whom he accompanied on the Argonautic expedition
[2] Finely dressed.

Meg. All happiness attend your grace! (*Exit* PHARA-
MOND.) Gentlemen, good rest. — Come, shall we go to bed?
Gal. Yes. — All good night.
Dion. May your dreams be true to you! —
                    [*Exeunt* GALATEA *and* MEGRA.
What shall we do, gallants? 'tis late. The King
Is up still: see, he comes; a guard along with him.   40

   Enter KING *with* ARETHUSA, Guards *and* Attendants.

King. Look your intelligence be true.
Are. Upon my life, it is: and I do hope
Your highness will not tie me to a man
That in the heat of wooing throws me off,
And takes another.
Dion. What should this mean?
King. If it be true,
That lady had better have embraced
Cureless diseases. Get you to your rest:
You shall be righted. [*Exeunt* ARETHUSA *and* BELLARIO. 50
                    — Gentlemen, draw near;
We shall employ you. Is young Pharamond
Come to his lodging?
Dion. I saw him enter there.
King. Haste, some of you, and cunningly discover
If Megra be in her lodging.   [*Exit.*
Cle. Sir,
She parted hence but now, with other ladies.
King. If she be there, we shall not need to make
A vain discovery of our suspicion.   60
(*Aside*) You gods, I see that who unrighteously
Holds wealth or state from others shall be cursed
In that which meaner men are blest withal:

Ages to come shall know no male of him
Left to inherit, and his name shall be
Blotted from earth; if he have any child,
It shall be crossly matched; the gods themselves
Shall sow wild strife betwixt her lord and her.
Yet, if it be your wills, forgive the sin
I have committed; let it not fall 70
Upon this under-standing child of mine !
She has not broke your laws. But how can I
Look to be heard of gods that must be just,
Praying upon the ground I hold by wrong?

Re-enter DION.

Dion. Sir, I have asked, and her women swear she is within; but they, I think, are wicked. I told 'em, I must speak with her; they laughed, and said, their lady lay speechless. I said, my business was important; they said, their lady was about it. I grew hot, and cried, my business was a matter that concerned life and death; they answered, so was sleeping, at which their lady was. I urged again, she had scarce time to be so since last I saw her: they smiled again, and seemed to instruct me that sleeping was nothing but lying down and winking. Answers more direct I could not get: in short, sir, I think she is not there.

King. 'Tis then no time to dally. — You o' the guard,
Wait at the back door of the prince's lodging,
And see that none pass thence, upon your lives. —

[*Exeunt* Guards.

Knock, gentlemen; knock loud; louder yet.
What, has their pleasure taken off their hearing? — 90
I'll break your meditations. — Knock again. —
Not yet? I do not think he sleeps, having this

'Larum by him. — Once more. — Pharamond ! prince !
[PHARAMOND *appears at a window.*
Pha. What saucy groom knocks at this dead of night?
Where be our waiters? By my vexèd soul,
He meets his death that meets me, for this boldness.
  King. Prince, prince, you wrong your thoughts; we are
    your friends :
Come down.
  Pha. The King! 100
  King. The same, sir. Come down, sir:
We have cause of present counsel with you.

Enter PHARAMOND *below.*

  Pha. If your grace please
To use me, I'll attend you to your chamber.
  King. No, 'tis too late, prince ; I'll make bold with yours.
  Pha. I have some private reasons to myself
Make me unmannerly, and say you cannot.—
Nay, press not forward, gentlemen ; he must
Come through my life that comes here.
  King. Sir, be resolved [1] I must and will come. — Enter.
  Pha. I will not be dishonoured : 111
He that enters, enters upon his death.
Sir, 'tis a sign you make no stranger of me,
To bring these renegadoes to my chamber
At these unseasoned hours.
  King. Why do you
Chafe yourself so? you are not wronged nor shall be ;
Only I'll search your lodging, for some cause
To ourself known. — Enter, I say.
  Pha. I say, no. [MEGRA *appears at a window.*

[1] Persuaded.

Meg. Let 'em enter, prince, let 'em enter; 121
I know their business;
'Tis the poor breaking of a lady's honour
They hunt so hotly after; let 'em enjoy it. —
You have your business, gentlemen; I was here. —
Oh, my lord the King, this is not noble in you
To make public the weakness of a woman!
   King. Come down.
   Meg. I dare, my lord. Your hootings and your clamours,
Your private whispers and your broad fleerings, 130
Can no more vex my soul than this base carriage:
But I have vengeance yet in store for some
Shall, in the most contempt you can have of me,
Be joy and nourishment.
   King. Will you come down?
   Meg. Yes, to laugh at your worst; but I shall wring you,
If my skill fail me not.   [*Exit above.*
   King. Sir, I must dearly chide you for this looseness;
You have wronged a worthy lady: but, no more. —
Conduct him to my lodging and to bed. 140
      [*Exeunt* PHARAMOND *and* Attendants.

    Enter MEGRA *below.*

   King. Now, lady of honour, where's your honour now?
No man can fit your palate but the prince:
Thou most ill-shrouded rottenness, thou piece
Made by a painter and a 'pothecary,
Thou troubled sea of lust, thou wilderness
Inhabited by wild thoughts, thou swoln cloud
Of infection, thou ripe mine of all diseases,
Thou all-sin, all-hell, and last, all-devils, tell me,
Had you none to pull on with your courtesies

But he that must be mine, and wrong my daughter? 150
By all the gods! all these, and all the pages,
And all the court, shall hoot thee through the court,
Fling rotten oranges, make ribald rhymes,
And sear thy name with candles upon walls!
Do you laugh, Lady Venus?

  Meg. Faith, sir, you must pardon me;
I cannot choose but laugh to see you merry.
If you do this, O King! nay, if you dare do it,
By all those gods you swore by, and as many
More of mine own, I will have fellows, and such 160
Fellows in it, as shall make noble mirth!
The princess, your dear daughter, shall stand by me
On walls, and sung in ballads, any thing:
Urge me no more; I know her and her haunts,
Her lays, leaps, and outlays, and will discover all;
Nay, will dishonour her. I know the boy
She keeps; a handsome boy, about eighteen;
Know what she does with him, where, and when.
Come, sir, you put me to a woman's madness,
The glory of a fury; and if I do not 170
Do't to the height——

  King. What boy is this she raves at?

  Meg. Alas! good-minded prince, you know not these things!
I am loath to reveal 'em. Keep this fault,
As you would keep your health, from the hot air
Of the corrupted people, or, by Heaven,
I will not fall alone. What I have known
Shall be as public as a print; all tongues
Shall speak it as they do the language they
Are born in, as free and commonly; I'll set it, 180

Like a prodigious star, for all to gaze at,
And so high and glowing, that other kingdoms far and foreign
Shall read it there, nay, travel with 't, till they find
No tongue to make it more, nor no more people;
And then behold the fall of your fair princess![1]

King. Has she a boy?

Cle. So please your grace, I have seen a boy wait on her,
A fair boy.

King. Go, get you to your quarter:
For this time I will study to forget you.   190

Meg. Do you study to forget me, and I'll study
To forget you.   [*Exeunt* KING *and* MEGRA, *severally*.

Cle. Why, here's a male spirit fit for Hercules. If ever there be Nine Worthies of women, this wench shall ride astride and be their captain.

Dion. Sure, she has a garrison of devils in her tongue, she uttereth such balls of wild-fire: she has so nettled the King, that all the doctors in the country will scarce cure him. That boy was a strange-found-out antidote to cure her infection; that boy, that princess' boy; that brave, chaste, virtuous lady's boy; and a fair boy, a well-spoken boy! All these considered, can make nothing else — but there I leave you, gentlemen.   203

Thra. Nay, we'll go wander with you.   [*Exeunt.*

---

[1] "This passage is one of those instances of a magnificent idea spoiled by mislocation, which are too often found in Beaumont and Fletcher. And observe the consequent anti-climax. A bad woman is threatening a father with defamation of his child; and she raises a phenomenon in the heavens which of itself is truly grand and awful, a spectacle for a world, in order to represent what at the utmost could be nothing but a scandal confined to a particular country. A comet leads kingdoms forth to travel by its light, in order to arrive at nothing greater than the fall of a princess, by a lie about a boy." — *Leigh Hunt.*

ACT III.

SCENE I. — *The Court of the Palace.*

Enter DION, CLEREMONT, *and* THRASILINE.

Cle. Nay, doubtless, 'tis true.
Dion. Ay ; and 'tis the gods
That raised this punishment, to scourge the King
With his own issue. Is it not a shame
For us that should write noble in the land,
For us that should be freemen, to behold
A man that is the bravery of his age,
Philaster, pressed down from his royal right
By this regardless King? and only look
And see the sceptre ready to be cast
Into the hands of that lascivious lady
That dotes on that smooth boy, now to be married
To yon strange prince, who, but that people please
To let him be a prince, is born a slave
In that which should be his most noble part,
His mind?
Thra. That man that would not stir with you
To aid Philaster, let the gods forget
That such a creature walks upon the earth !
Cle. Philaster is too backward in't himself.
The gentry do await it, and the people,
Against their nature, are all bent for him,
And like a field of standing corn, that's moved
With a stiff gale, their heads bow all one way.

Dion. The only cause that draws Philaster back
From this attempt is the fair princess' love,
Which he admires, and we can now confute.
   Thra. Perhaps he'll not believe it.
   Dion. Why, gentlemen,
'Tis without question so.
   Cle. Ay, 'tis past speech,
She lives dishonestly : but how shall we,
If he be curious,[1] work upon his faith?
   Thra. We are all satisfied within ourselves.
   Dion. Since it is true, and tends to his own good,
I'll make this new report to be my knowledge ;
I'll say I know it; nay, I'll swear I saw it.
   Cle. It will be best.
   Thra. 'Twill move him.
   Dion. Here he comes.

           Enter PHILASTER.

Good morrow to your honour : we have spent
Some time in seeking you.
   Phi. My worthy friends,
You that can keep your memories to know
Your friend in miseries, and cannot frown
On men disgraced for virtue, a good day
Attend you all ! What service may I do
Worthy your acceptation?
   Dion. My good lord,
We come to urge that virtue, which we know
Lives in your breast, forth. Rise, and make a head :
The nobles and the people are all dulled
With this usurping King ; and not a man,

---

[1] Scrupulous.

That ever heard the word, or knew such a thing
As virtue, but will second your attempts.
  Phi. How honourable is this love in you
To me that have deserved none ! Know, my friends,
(You, that were born to shame your poor Philaster
With too much courtesy,) I could afford
To melt myself in thanks : but my designs   60
Are not yet ripe : suffice it, that ere long
I shall employ your loves ; but yet the time
Is short of what I would.
  Dion. The time is fuller, sir, than you expect ;
That which hereafter will not, perhaps, be reached
By violence may now be caught. As for the King,
You know the people have long hated him ;
But now the princess, whom they loved ——
  Phi. Why, what of her?
  Dion. Is loathed as much as he.   70
  Phi. By what strange means?
  Dion. She's known unchaste.
  Phi. Thou liest.
  Dion. My lord ——
  Phi. Thou liest,
          [*Offers to draw his sword : they hold him.*
And thou shalt feel it ! I had thought thy mind
Had been of honour. Thus to rob a lady
Of her good name, is an infectious sin
Not to be pardoned : be it false as hell,
'Twill never be redeemed, if it be sown   80
Amongst the people, fruitful to increase
All evil they shall hear. Let me alone
That I may cut off falsehood whilst it springs !
Set hills on hills betwixt me and the man

That utters this, and I will scale them all,
And from the utmost top fall on his neck,
Like thunder from a cloud.
 Dion. This is most strange :
Sure, he does love her.
 Phi. I do love fair truth :
She is my mistress, and who injures her
Draws vengeance from me. Sirs, let go my arms.
 Thra. Nay, good my lord, be patient.
 Cle. Sir, remember this is your honoured friend,
That comes to do his service, and will show you
Why he uttered this.
 Phi. I ask you pardon, sir ;
My zeal to truth made me unmannerly :
Should I have heard dishonour spoke of you,
Behind your back, untruly, I had been
As much distempered and enraged as now.
 Dion. But this, my lord, is truth.
 Phi. Oh, say not so !
Good sir, forbear to say so ; 'tis then truth,
That all womankind is false : urge it no more ;
It is impossible. Why should you think
The princess light?
 Dion. Why, she was taken at it.
 Phi. 'Tis false ! by Heaven, 'tis false ! it cannot be !
Can it? Speak, gentlemen ; for love of truth, speak !
It's possible? Can women all be damned?
 Dion. Why, no, my lord.
 Phi. Why, then, it cannot be.
 Dion. And she was taken with her boy.
 Phi. What boy?
 Dion. A page, a boy that serves her.

Phi. Oh, good gods !
A little boy?
Dion. Ay ; know you him my lord?
Phi. (aside). Hell and sin know him ! — Sir, you are
    deceived ;   120
You are abused, and so is she, and I.
    Dion. How you, my lord?
    Phi. Why, all the world's abused
In an unjust report.
    Dion. Oh, noble sir, your virtues
Cannot look into the subtle thoughts of woman !
In short, my lord, I took them ; I myself.
    Phi. Now, all the devils, thou didst ! Fly from my rage !
'Would thou hadst ta'en devils engendering plagues,
When thou did'st take them ! Hide thee from my eyes ! 130
Would thou hadst taken thunder on thy breast,
When thou didst take them ; or been strucken dumb
For ever ; that this foul deed might have slept
In silence !
    Thra. Have you known him so ill-tempered?
    Cle. Never before.
    Phi. The winds, that are let loose
From the four several corners of the earth,
And spread themselves all over sea and land,
Kiss not a chaste one. What friend bears a sword   140
To run me through?
    Dion. Why, my lord, are you
So moved at this?
    Phi. When any fall from virtue,
I am distract ; I have an interest in't.
    Dion. But, good my lord, recall yourself, and think
What's best to be done.

Phi. I thank you; I will do it:
Please you to leave me; I'll consider of it.
To-morrow I will find your lodging forth,	150
And give you answer.
   Dion. All the gods direct you
The readiest way!
   Thra. He was extreme impatient.
   Cle. It was his virtue and his noble mind.
             [*Exeunt* DION, CLEREMONT, *and* THRASILINE.
   Phi. I had forgot to ask him where he took them;
I'll follow him. Oh, that I had a sea
Within my breast, to quench the fire I feel!
More circumstances will but fan this fire:
It more afflicts me now, to know by whom	160
This deed is done, than simply that 'tis done;
And he that tells me this, is honourable,
As far from lies as she is far from truth.
Oh, that, like beasts, we could not grieve ourselves
With that we see not! Bulls and rams will fight
To keep their females, standing in their sight;
But take 'em from them, and you take at once
Their spleens away; and they will fall again
Unto their pastures, growing fresh and fat;
And taste the waters of the springs as sweet	170
As 'twas before, finding no start in sleep:
But miserable man——

         Enter BELLARIO.

     (*Aside*) See, see, you gods,
He walks still; and the face you let him wear
When he was innocent is still the same,
Not blasted! Is this justice? do you mean

To intrap mortality, that you allow
Treason so smooth a brow? I cannot now
Think he is guilty.
　Bel. Health to you, my lord!
The princess doth commend her love, her life, 180
And this, unto you. [*Gives a letter.*
　Phi. Oh, Bellario,
Now I perceive she loves me! she does show it
In loving thee, my boy: she has made thee brave.
　Bel. My lord, she has attired me past my wish,
Past my desert; more fit for her attendant,
Though far unfit for me who do attend.
　Phi. Thou art grown courtly, boy. — Oh, let all women,
That love black deeds, learn to dissemble here,
Here, by this paper! She does write to me 190
As if her heart were mines of adamant
To all the world besides; but, unto me,
A maiden-snow that melted with my looks. —
Tell me, my boy, how doth the princess use thee?
For I shall guess her love to me by that.
　Bel. Scarce like her servant, but as if I were
Something allied to her, or had preserved
Her life three times by my fidelity;
As mothers fond do use their only sons,
As I'd use one that's left unto my trust, 200
For whom my life should pay if he met harm,
So she does use me.
　Phi. Why, this is wondrous well:
But what kind language does she feed thee with?
　Bel. Why, she does tell me she will trust my youth
With all her loving secrets, and does call me
Her pretty servant; bids me weep no more

For leaving you; she'll see my services
Regarded: and such words of that soft strain,
That I am nearer weeping when she ends   210
Than ere she spake.
   Phi. This is much better still.
   Bel. Are you not ill, my lord?
   Phi. Ill? no, Bellario.
   Bel. Methinks your words
Fall not from off your tongue so evenly,
Nor is there in your looks that quietness
That I was wont to see.
   Phi. Thou art deceived, boy:
And she strokes thy head?   220
   Bel. Yes.
   Phi. And she does clap thy cheeks?
   Bel. She does, my lord.
   Phi. And she does kiss thee, boy? ha!
   Bel. How, my lord?
   Phi. She kisses thee?
   Bel. Not so, my lord.
   Phi. Come, come, I know she does.
   Bel. No, by my life.
   Phi. Why then she does not love me. Come, she does,
I bade her do it; I charged her, by all charms   231
Of love between us, by the hope of peace
We should enjoy, to yield thee all delights.
Tell me, gentle boy,
Is she not parallelless? is not her breath
Sweet as Arabian winds when fruits are ripe?
Are not her breasts two liquid ivory balls?
Is she not all a lasting mine of joy?
   Bel. Ay, now I see why my disturbèd thoughts

Were so perplexed: when first I went to her,
My heart held augury.   You are abused;
Some villain has abused you: I do see
Whereto you tend.   Fall rocks upon his head
That put this to you! 'tis some subtle train
To bring that noble frame of yours to nought.
   Phi. Thou think'st I will be angry with thee.   Come,
Thou shalt know all my drift: I hate her more
Than I love happiness, and placed thee there
To pry with narrow eyes into her deeds.
Hast thou discovered? is she fallen to lust,
As I would wish her?   Speak some comfort to me.
   Bel. My lord, you did mistake the boy you sent:
Had she the lust of sparrows or of goats,
Had she a sin that way, hid from the world,
Beyond the name of lust, I would not aid
Her base desires: but what I came to know
As servant to her, I would not reveal,
To make my life last ages.
   Phi. Oh, my heart!
This is a salve worse than the main disease.
Tell me thy thoughts; for I will know the least
                                         [*Draws his sword.*
That dwells within thee, or will rip thy heart
To know it: I will see thy thoughts as plain
As I do now thy face.
   Bel. Why, so you do.
She is (for aught I know) by all the gods,   [*Kneels.*
As chaste as ice! but were she foul as hell,
And I did know it thus, the breath of kings,
The points of swords, tortures, nor bulls of brass,
Should draw it from me.

Phi. Then it is no time
To dally with thee; I will take thy life,
For I do hate thee: I could curse thee now.
    Bel. If you do hate, you could not curse me worse;
The gods have not a punishment in store
Greater for me than is your hate.
    Phi. Fie, fie,
So young and so dissembling! Tell me when
And where thou didst betray her, or let plagues
Fall on me, if I destroy thee not!   280
    Bel. Heaven knows I never did; and when I lie
To save my life, may I live long and loathed!
Hew me asunder, and, whilst I can think,
I'll love those pieces you have cut away
Better than those that grow, and kiss those limbs
Because you made 'em so.
    Phi. Fear'st thou not death?
Can boys contemn that?
    Bel. Oh, what boy is he
Can be content to live to be a man,   290
That sees the best of men thus passionate,
Thus without reason?
    Phi. Oh, but thou dost not know
What 'tis to die.
    Bel. Yes, I do know, my lord:
'Tis less than to be born; a lasting sleep;
A quiet resting from all jealousy,
A thing we all pursue; I know, besides,
It is but giving over of a game
That must be lost.[1]   300

[1] The references to death, in the plays of Beaumont and Fletcher, are almost invariably noble. Cf. *Thierry and Theodoret*, iv, 1; *Valentinian*, i, 3, and iv, 4.

Phi. But there are pains, false boy,
For perjured souls: think but on these, and then
Thy heart will melt, and thou wilt utter all.
　Bel. May they fall all upon me whilst I live,
If I be perjured, or have ever thought
Of that you charge me with! If I be false,
Send me to suffer in those punishments
You speak of; kill me!
　Phi. Oh, what should I do?
Why, who can but believe him? he does swear　　　310
So earnestly, that if it were not true,
The gods would not endure him. (*Sheathes his sword.*)
　　Rise, Bellario:　　　　　　[BELLARIO *rises.*
Thy protestations are so deep, and thou
Dost look so truly when thou utter'st them,
That, though I know 'em false as were my hopes,
I cannot urge thee further. But thou wert
To blame to injure me, for I must love
Thy honest looks, and take no revenge upon
Thy tender youth: a love from me to thee
Is firm, what'er thou dost: it troubles me　　　320
That I have called the blood out of thy cheeks,
That did so well become thee. But, good boy,
Let me not see thee more: something is done
That will distract me, that will make me mad,
If I behold thee. If thou tender'st me,
Let me not see thee.
　Bel. I will fly as far
As there is morning, ere I give distaste
To that most honoured mind. But through these tears,
Shed at my hopeless parting, I can see　　　330
A world of treason practised upon you,

And her, and me. Farewell for evermore!
If you shall hear that sorrow struck me dead,
And after find me loyal, let there be
A tear shed from you in my memory,
And I shall rest at peace.
   Phi. Blessing be with thee,
Whatever thou deserv'st! — (*Exit* BELLARIO.) Oh, where shall I
Go bathe this body? Nature too unkind;
That made no medicine for a troubled mind! [*Exit.* 340

SCENE II. — ARETHUSA'S *Apartment in the Palace.*

Enter ARETHUSA.

   Are. I marvel my boy comes not back again:
But that I know my love will question him
Over and over, — how I slept, waked, talked,
How I remembered him when his dear name
Was last spoke, and how, when I sighed, wept, sung,
And ten thousand such, — I should be angry at his stay.

Enter KING.

   King. What, at your meditations! Who attends you?
   Are. None but my single self: I need no guard;
I do no wrong, nor fear none.
   King. Tell me, have you not a boy?   10
   Are. Yes, sir.
   King. What kind of boy?
   Are. A page, a waiting boy.
   King. A handsome boy?
   Are. I think he be not ugly:

Well qualified and dutiful I know him;
I took him not for beauty.
   King. He speaks and sings and plays?
   Are. Yes, sir.
   King. About eighteen?   20
   Are. I never asked his age.
   King. Is he full of service?
   Are. By your pardon, why do you ask?
   King. Put him away.
   Are. Sir!
   King. Put him away. He has done you that good service
Shames me to speak of.
   Are. Good sir, let me understand you.
   King. If you fear me,
Show it in duty; put away that boy.   30
   Are. Let me have reason for it, sir, and then
Your will is my command.
   King. Do not you blush to ask it? Cast him off,
Or I shall do the same to you. You're one
Shame with me, and so near unto myself,
That, by my life, I dare not tell myself
What you, myself, have done.
   Are. What have I done, my lord?
   King. 'Tis a new language, that all love to learn:
The common people speak it well already;   40
They need no grammar. Understand me well;
There be foul whispers stirring. Cast him off,
And suddenly: do it! Farewell.   [*Exit.*
   Are. Where may a maiden live securely free,
Keeping her honour fair? Not with the living;
They feed upon opinions, errors, dreams,
And make 'em truths; they draw a nourishment

Out of defamings, grow upon disgraces:
And, when they see a virtue fortified
Strongly above the battery of their tongues, 50
Oh, how they cast to sink it! and, defeated,
(Soul-sick with poison) strike the monuments
Where noble names lie sleeping, till they sweat,
And the cold marble melt.

Enter PHILASTER.

Phi. Peace to your fairest thoughts, dearest mistress!
Are. Oh, my dearest servant,[1] I have a war within me!
Phi. He must be more than man that makes these crystals
Run into rivers. Sweetest fair, the cause?
And, as I am your slave, tied to your goodness,
Your creature, made again from what I was 60
And newly spirited, I'll right your honour.
Are. Oh, my best love, that boy!
Phi. What boy?
Are. That pretty boy you gave me ——
Phi. What of him?
Are. Must be no more mine.
Phi. Why?
Are. They are jealous of him.
Phi. Jealous! who?
Are. The King. 70
Phi. (*aside*). Oh, my fortune!
Then 'tis no idle jealousy. — Let him go.
Are. Oh, cruel!
Are you hard-hearted too? who shall now tell you
How much I loved you? who shall swear it to you,
And weep the tears I send? who shall now bring you

[1] Lover.

Letters, rings, bracelets? lose his health in service?
Wake tedious nights in stories of your praise?
Who shall now sing your crying elegies,
And strike a sad soul into senseless pictures, 80
And make them mourn? who shall take up his lute,
And touch it till he crown a silent sleep
Upon my eyelids, making me dream, and cry,
"Oh, my dear, dear Philaster!"
   Phi. (*aside*). Oh, my heart!
Would he had broken thee, that made me know
This lady was not loyal!— Mistress,
Forget the boy; I'll get thee a far better.
   Are. Oh, never, never such a boy again
As my Bellario! 90
   Phi. 'Tis but your fond affection.
   Are. With thee, my boy, farewell for ever
All secrecy in servants! Farewell faith,
And all desire to do well for itself!
Let all that shall succeed thee for thy wrongs
Sell and betray chaste love!
   Phi. And all this passion for a boy?
   Are. He was your boy, and you put him to me,
And the loss of such must have a mourning for.
   Phi. Oh, thou forgetful woman! 100
   Are. How, my lord?
   Phi. False Arethusa!
Hast thou a medicine to restore my wits,
When I have lost 'em? If not, leave to talk,
And do thus.
   Are. Do what, sir? would you sleep?
   Phi. For ever, Arethusa. Oh, you gods,
Give me a worthy patience! Have I stood

Naked, alone, the shock of many fortunes?
Have I seen mischiefs numberless and mighty
Grow like a sea upon me? Have I taken
Danger as stern as death into my bosom,
And laughed upon it, made it but a mirth,
And flung it by? Do I live now like him,
Under this tyrant King, that languishing
Hears his sad bell and sees his mourners? Do I
Bear all this bravely, and must sink at length
Under a woman's falsehood? Oh, that boy,
That cursèd boy!

Are. Nay, then, I am betrayed:
I feel the plot cast for my overthrow.
Oh, I am wretched!

Phi. Now you may take that little right I have
To this poor kingdom: give it to your joy;
For I have no joy in it. Some far place,
Where never womankind durst set her foot
For bursting with her poisons, must I seek,
And live to curse you:
There dig a cave, and preach to birds and beasts
What woman is, and help to save them from you:
How heaven is in your eyes, but in your hearts
More hell than hell has; how your tongues, like scorpions,
Both heal and poison; how your thoughts are woven
With thousand changes in one subtle web,
And worn so by you; how that foolish man,
That reads the story of a woman's face
And dies believing it, is lost for ever:
How all the good you have is but a shadow,
I' the morning with you, and at night behind you
Past and forgotten; how your vows are frosts,

Fast for a night, and with the next sun gone;
How you are, being taken all together,
A mere confusion, and so dead a chaos,
That love cannot distinguish. These sad texts,
Till my last hour, I am bound to utter of you.
So, farewell all my woe, all my delight! [*Exit.*

Are. Be merciful, ye gods, and strike me dead!
What way have I deserved this? Make my breast
Transparent as pure crystal, that the world,
Jealous of me, may see the foulest thought 150
My heart holds. Where shall a woman turn her eyes,
To find out constancy?

Enter BELLARIO.

Save me, how black
And guiltily, methinks, that boy looks now!
Oh, thou dissembler, that, before thou spak'st,
Wert in thy cradle false, sent to make lies
And betray innocents! Thy lord and thou
May glory in the ashes of a maid
Fooled by her passion; but the conquest is
Nothing so great as wicked. Fly away!
Let my command force thee to that which shame 160
Would do without it. If thou understood'st
The loathèd office thou hast undergone,
Why, thou wouldst hide thee under heaps of hills,
Lest men should dig and find thee.

Bel. Oh, what god,
Angry with men, hath sent this strange disease
Into the noblest minds! Madam, this grief
You add unto me is no more than drops
To seas, for which they are not seen to swell·

My lord hath struck his anger through my heart, 170
And let out all the hope of future joys.
You need not bid me fly; I came to part,
To take my latest leave. Farewell for ever!
I durst not run away in honesty
From such a lady, like a boy that stole
Or made some grievous fault. The power of gods
Assist you in your sufferings! Hasty time
Reveal the truth to your abusèd lord
And mine, that he may know your worth; whilst I 179
Go seek out some forgotten place to die! [*Exit* BELLARIO.
 Are. Peace guide thee! Thou hast overthrown me once;
Yet, if I had another Troy to lose,
Thou, or another villain with thy looks,
Might talk me out of it, and send me naked,
My hair dishevelled, through the fiery streets.

Enter a Lady.

 Lady. Madam, the King would hunt, and calls for you
With earnestness.
 Are. I am in tune to hunt!
Diana, if thou canst rage with a maid
As with a man,[1] let me discover thee 190
Bathing, and turn me to a fearful hind,
That I may die pursued by cruel hounds,
And have my story written in my wounds! [*Exeunt.*[2]

---

[1] Actæon, who, having caught sight of Diana bathing, was torn to pieces by his own dogs.

[2] The skill with which this third act is composed is excellent. What could be more natural than the art with which the King, the Princess, and Philaster are enmeshed in mutual misunderstandings, not a loophole for explanations visible?

ACT IV.

SCENE I. — *Before the Palace.*

Enter KING, PHARAMOND, ARETHUSA, GALATEA, MEGRA, DION, CLEREMONT, THRASILINE, *and* Attendants.

King. What, are the hounds before and all the woodmen, Our horses ready and our bows bent?
Dion. All, sir.
King (*to* PHARAMOND). You are cloudy, sir: come, we have forgotten
Your venial trespass; let not that sit heavy
Upon your spirit: here's none dare utter it.
Dion. He looks dull as a dormouse. See how he sinks!
Thra. He needs no teaching, he strikes sure enough: his greatest fault is, he hunts too much in the purlieus; would he would leave off poaching! 10
Dion. And for his horn, h'as left it at the lodge where he lay late. Oh, he's a precious limehound[1]! turn him loose upon the pursuit of a lady, and if he lose her, hang him up i' the slip.
King. Is your boy turned away?
Are. You did command, sir,
And I obeyed you.
King. 'Tis well done. Hark ye further.
[*They talk apart.*

---

[1] Hunting-dog; from the collar, and thong (*leam, lyam, lime*) **used in leading** him.

Cle. Is't possible this fellow should repent? methinks, that were not noble in him; and yet he looks like a mortified member, as if he had a sick man's salve[1] in's mouth. If a worse man had done this fault now, some physical justice or other would presently (without the help of an almanack) have opened the obstructions of his liver, and let him blood with a dogwhip. 25

Dion. See, see how modestly yon lady looks, as if she came from churching with her neighbour! Why, what a devil can a man see in her face but that she's honest!

Thra. Troth, no great matter to speak of; a foolish twinkling with the eye, that spoils her coat; but he must be a cunning herald that finds it. 31

Dion. See how they muster one another! Oh, there's a rank regiment where the devil carries the colours and his dam drum-major! now the world and the flesh come behind with the carriage.[2]

Cle. Sure this lady has a good turn done her against her will. Her face looks like a warrant, willing and commanding all tongues, as they will answer it, to be tied up and bolted when this lady means to let herself loose. As I live, she has got her a goodly protection and a gracious: Oh, if they were to be got for money, what a great sum would come out of the city for these licenses! 42

King. To horse, to horse! we lose the morning, gentlemen. [*Exeunt.*

---

[1] A religious work, *The Sick Man's Salve*, was often ridiculed by the early dramatists.

[2] Baggage.

Scene II. — *A Forest.*

Enter two Woodmen.

1st Wood. What, have you lodged the deer?
2d Wood. Yes, they are ready for the bow.
1st Wood. Who shoots?
2d Wood. The princess.
1st Wood. No, she'll hunt.
2d Wood. She'll take a stand, I say.
1st Wood. Who else?
2d Wood. Why, the young stranger-prince.

1st Wood. He shall shoot in a stone-bow[1] for me. I never loved his beyond-sea-ship since he forsook the say,[2] for paying ten shillings. I think he should love venery; he is an old Sir Tristrem,[3] for if you be remembered, he forsook the stag once to strike a rascal miching[4] in a meadow, and her he killed in the eye. Who shoots else? 14

2d Wood. The Lady Galatea.

1st Wood. She's liberal, and, by my bow, they say she's honest; and whether that be a fault, I have nothing to do. There's all?

2d Wood. No, one more; Megra.

1st Wood. That's a firker[5] i 'faith, boy! I have known her lose herself three times in one afternoon (if the woods have been answerable), and it has been work enough for one man to find her, and he has sweat for it. She rides well and she pays well. Hark! let's go. [*Exeunt.* 24

---

1 Cross-bow for shooting stones.
2 The assay, or slitting of the deer, in order to test the quality of his flesh, which involved a fee of ten shillings to the keeper.
3 Sir Tristram, one of the knights of the Round Table.
4 Lurking, skulking; cf. *Hamlet*, iii, 2, 146.   5 Slasher.

Enter PHILASTER.

Phi. Oh, that I had been nourished in these woods
With milk of goats and acorns, and not known
The right of crowns nor the dissembling trains
Of women's looks; but digged myself a cave,
Where I, my fire, my cattle, and my bed,
Might have been shut together in one shed;   30
And then had taken me some mountain-girl,
Beaten with winds, chaste as the hardened rocks
Whereon she dwells, that might have strewed my bed
With leaves and reeds, and with the skins of beasts,
Our neighbours, and have borne at her big breasts
My large coarse issue![1] This had been a life
Free from vexation.

Enter BELLARIO.

Bel. Oh, wicked men!
An innocent may walk safe among beasts;
Nothing assaults me here. (*Aside*) See, my grieved lord
Sits as his soul were searching out a way   40
To leave his body!—Pardon me, that must
Break thy last commandment; for I must speak:
You that are grieved can pity; hear, my lord!
    Phi. Is there a creature yet so miserable,
That I can pity?
    Bel. Oh, my noble lord,
View my strange fortune, and bestow on me,
According to your bounty (if my service
Can merit nothing), so much as may serve
To keep that little piece I hold of life   50

[1] Cf. Tennyson's *Locksley Hall.*

From cold and hunger!
    Phi. Is it thou? begone!
Go, sell those misbeseeming clothes thou wear'st,
And feed thyself with them.
    Bel. Alas, my lord, I can get nothing for them!
The silly country-people think 'tis treason
To touch such gay things.
    Phi. Now, by my life, this is
Unkindly done, to vex me with thy sight.
Thou'rt fallen again to thy dissembling trade: 60
How shouldst thou think to cozen me again?
Remains there yet a plague untried for me?
Even so thou wept'st, and looked'st, and spok'st when first
I took thee up:
Curse on the time! If thy commanding tears
Can work on any other, use thy art;
I'll not betray it. Which way wilt thou take?
That I may shun thee, for thine eyes are poison
To mine, and I am loath to grow in rage:
This way, or that way?   70
    Bel. Any will serve; but I will choose to have
That path in chase that leads unto my grave.
                        [*Exeunt severally.*

Enter on one side DION, *and on the other the two* Woodmen.

    Dion. This is the strangest sudden chance! You, woodmen!
    1st Wood. My Lord Dion?
    Dion. Saw you a lady come this way on a sable horse studded with stars of white?
    2d Wood. Was she not young and tall?
    Dion. Yes. Rode she to the wood or to the plain?

2d Wood. Faith my lord, we saw none.
                                    [*Exeunt* Woodmen.
  Dion. Plague of your questions then!   80

            Enter CLEREMONT.
What, is she found?
  Cle. Nor will be, I think.
  Dion. Let him seek his daughter himself. She cannot stray about a little, but the whole court must be in arms.
  Cle. There's already a thousand fatherless tales amongst us. Some say, her horse ran away with her; some, a wolf pursued her; others, it was a plot to kill her, and that armed men were seen in the wood: but, questionless, she rode away willingly.

        Enter KING, THRASILINE, *and* Attendants.

  King. Where is she?   90
  Cle. Sir, I cannot tell.
  King. How's that?
Answer me so again!
  Cle. Sir, shall I lie?
  King. Yes, lie and damn, rather than tell me that.
I say again, where is she? Mutter not! —
Sir, speak you; where is she?
  Dion. Sir, I do not know.
  King. Speak that again so boldly, and, by Heaven,
It is thy last! — You, fellows, answer me;   100
Where is she? Mark me, all; I am your King:
I wish to see my daughter; show her me;
I do command you all, as you are subjects,
To show her me! What! am I not your King?
If ay, then am I not to be obeyed?
  Dion. Yes, if you command things possible and honest.

King. Things possible and honest! Hear me, thou,
Thou traitor, that dar'st confine thy King to things
Possible and honest! show her me,
Or, let me perish, if I cover not   110
All Sicily with blood!
   Dion. Indeed I cannot,
Unless you tell me where she is.
   King. You have betrayed me; you have let me lose
The jewel of my life. Go, bring her to me,
And set her here before me: 'tis the King
Will have it so; whose breath can still the winds,
Uncloud the sun, charm down the swelling sea,
And stop the floods of heaven. Speak, can it not?
   Dion. No.   120
   King. No! cannot the breath of kings do this?
   Dion. No; nor smell sweet itself, if once the lungs
Be but corrupted.
   King. Is it so? Take heed!
   Dion. Sir, take you heed how you dare the powers
That must be just.
   King. Alas! what are we kings!
Why do you, gods, place us above the rest,
To be served, flattered, and adored, till we
Believe we hold within our hands your thunder, 130
And when we come to try the power we have,
There's not a leaf shakes at our threatenings?
I have sinned, 'tis true, and here stand to be punished;
Yet would not thus be punished: let me choose
My way, and lay it on!
   Dion (*aside*). He articles with the gods. Would somebody would draw bonds for the performance of covenants betwixt them!

Enter PHARAMOND, GALATEA, *and* MEGRA.

King. What, is she found?
Pha. No; we have ta'en her horse; 140
He galloped empty by. There is some treason.
You, Galatea, rode with her into the wood;
Why left you her?
Gal. She did command me.
King. Command! you should not.
Gal. 'Twould ill become my fortunes and my birth
To disobey the daughter of my King.
King. You're all cunning to obey us for our hurt;
But I will have her.
Pha. If I have her not, 150
By this hand, there shall be no more Sicily.
Dion (*aside*). What, will he carry it to Spain in's pocket?
Pha. I will not leave one man alive, but the King,
A cook, and a tailor.
King (*aside*). I see
The injuries I have done must be revenged.
Dion. Sir, this is not the way to find her out.
King. Run all, disperse yourselves. The man that finds her,
Or (if she be killed), the traitor, I'll make him great.
Dion (*aside*). I know some would give five thousand pounds to find her. 161
Pha. Come, let us seek.
King. Each man a several way;
Here I myself.
Dion. Come, gentlemen, we here.
Cle. Lady, you must go search too.
Meg. I had rather be searched myself. [*Exeunt severally.*

Scene III. — *Another Part of the Forest.*

Enter ARETHUSA.

Are. Where am I now? Feet, find me out a way,
Without the counsel of my troubled head:
I'll follow you boldly about these woods,
O'er mountains, through brambles, pits, and floods.
Heaven, I hope, will ease me: I am sick. [*Sits down.*

Enter BELLARIO.

Bel. (*aside*). Yonder's my lady. Heaven knows I want
Nothing, because I do not wish to live;
Yet I will try her charity. — Oh, hear,
You that have plenty! from that flowing store
Drop some on dry ground. — See, the lively red
Is gone to guard her heart! I fear she faints. —
Madam, look up! — She breathes not. — Open once more
Those rosy twins, and send unto my lord
Your latest farewell! — Oh, she stirs. — How is it,
Madam? speak comfort.

Are. 'Tis not gently done,
To put me in a miserable life,
And hold me there: I prithee, let me go;
I shall do best without thee; I am well.

Enter PHILASTER.

Phi. I am to blame to be so much in rage:
I'll tell her coolly when and where I heard
This killing truth. I will be temperate
In speaking, and as just in hearing. ——
Oh, monstrous! Tempt me not, ye gods! good gods,

Tempt not a frail man! What's he, that has a heart,
But he must ease it here!
   Bel. My lord, help, help!
The princess!
   Are. I am well: forbear.
   Phi. (aside). Let me love lightning, let me be embraced
And kissed by scorpions, or adore the eyes   31
Of basilisks, rather than trust the tongues
Of hell-bred women! Some good god look down,
And shrink these veins up; stick me here a stone,
Lasting to ages in the memory
Of this damned act! — Hear me, you wicked ones!
You have put hills of fire into this breast,
Not to be quenched with tears; for which may guilt
Sit on your bosoms! at your meals and beds
Despair await you! What, before my face?   40
Poison of asps between your lips! diseases
Be your best issues! Nature make a curse,
And throw it on you!
   Are. Dear Philaster, leave
To be enraged, and hear me.
   Phi. I have done;
Forgive my passion. Not the calmèd sea,
When Æolus locks up his windy brood,
Is less disturbed than I: I'll make you know it.
Dear Arethusa, do but take this sword,   50
                     [*Offers his drawn sword.*
And search how temperate a heart I have;
Then you and this your boy may live and reign
In lust without control. Wilt thou, Bellario?
I prithee kill me; thou art poor, and may'st
Nourish ambitious thoughts; when I am dead,

Thy way were freer. Am I raging now?
If I were mad, I should desire to live.
Sirs,[1] feel my pulse, whether you have known
A man in a more equal tune to die.
    Bel. Alas, my lord, your pulse keeps madman's time!
So does your tongue.   61
    Phi. You will not kill me, then?
    Are. Kill you!
    Bel. Not for a world.
    Phi. I blame not thee,
Bellario: thou hast done but that which gods
Would have transformed themselves to do. Be gone,
Leave me without reply; this is the last
Of all our meetings —(*Exit* BELLARIO.) Kill me with this
    sword;
Be wise, or worse will follow: we are two   70
Earth cannot bear at once. Resolve to do,
Or suffer.
    Are. If my fortune be so good to let me fall
Upon thy hand, I shall have peace in death.
Yet tell me this, will there be no slanders,
No jealousies in the other world; no ill there?
    Phi. No.
    Are. Show me, then, the way.
    Phi. Then guide my feeble hand,
You that have power to do it, for I must   80
Perform a piece of justice!— If your youth
Have any way offended Heaven, let prayers
Short and effectual reconcile you to it.
    Are. I am prepared.

---

[1] Women, as well as men, were formerly addressed as *sirs.*

Enter a Country Fellow.

C. Fell. (*aside*). I'll see the King, if he be in the forest; I have hunted him these two hours; if I should come home and not see him, my sisters would laugh at me. I can see nothing but people better horsed than myself, that outride me; I can hear nothing but shouting. These kings had need of good brains; this whooping is able to put a mean man out of his wits. There's a courtier with his sword drawn; by this hand, upon a woman, I think! 92

Phi. Are you at peace?

Are. With heaven and earth.

Phi. May they divide thy soul and body! [*Wounds her.*

C. Fell. Hold, dastard! strike a woman! Thou'rt a craven, I warrant thee: thou wouldst be loath to play half a dozen venies¹ at wasters² with a good fellow for a broken head.

Phi. Leave us, good friend. 100

Are. What ill-bred man art thou, to intrude thyself Upon our private sports, our recreations?

C. Fell. God 'uds me,³ I understand you not; but I know the rogue has hurt you.

Phi. Pursue thy own affairs: it will be ill To multiply blood upon my head; which thou Wilt force me to.

C. Fell. I know not your rhetoric; but I can lay it on, if you touch the woman.

Phi. Slave, take what thou deservest! [*They fight.* 110

Are. Heavens guard my lord!

C. Fell. Oh, do you breathe?

Phi. (*aside*). I hear the tread of people. I am hurt:

¹ A turn or bout, at fencing; French *venue.*
² Singlestick, or cudgels.   ³ God judge me.

The gods take part against me: could this boor
Have held me thus else? I must shift for life,
Though I do loathe it. I would find a course
To lose it rather by my will than force. [*Exit.*

C. Fell. I cannot follow the rogue. I pray thee, wench, come and kiss me now.

Enter PHARAMOND, DION, CLEREMONT, THRASILINE, *and* Woodmen.

Pha. What art thou? 120

C. Fell. Almost killed I am for a foolish woman; a knave has hurt her.

Pha. The princess, gentlemen!— Where's the wound, madam!
Is it dangerous?

Are. He has not hurt me.

C. Fell. I' faith, she lies; h'as hurt her in the breast; look else.

Pha. O, sacred spring of innocent blood!

Dion. 'Tis above wonder! who should dare this?

Are. I felt it not. 130

Pha. Speak, villain, who has hurt the princess?

C. Fell. Is it the princess?

Dion. Ay.

C. Fell. Then I have seen something yet.

Pha. But who has hurt her?

C. Fell. I told you, a rogue; I ne'er saw him before, I.

Pha. Madam, who did it?

Are. Some dishonest wretch;
Alas, I know him not, and do forgive him!

C. Fell. He's hurt too; he cannot go far; I made my father's old fox[1] fly about his ears. 141

[1] Sword.

Pha. How will you have me kill him?
Are. Not at all;
'Tis some distracted fellow.
Pha. By this hand,
I'll leave ne'er a piece of him bigger than a nut,
And bring him all to you in my hat.
Are. Nay, good sir,
If you do take him, bring him quick[1] to me,
And I will study for a punishment 150
Great as his fault.
Pha. I will.
Are. But swear.
Pha. By all my love, I will. —
Woodmen, conduct the princess to the King,
And bear that wounded fellow to dressing. —
Come, gentlemen, we'll follow the chase close.
  [*Exeunt on one side* PHARAMOND, DION, CLEREMONT,
  and THRASILINE; *on the other* ARETHUSA *attended by the First* Woodman.
C. Fell. I pray you, friend, let me see the King.
2d Wood. That you shall, and receive thanks.
C. Fell. If I get clear with this, I'll go see no more gay
  sights. [*Exeunt.* 160

SCENE IV.—*Another Part of the Forest.*

Enter BELLARIO.

Bel. A heaviness near death sits on my brow,
And I must sleep. Bear me, thou gentle bank,
For ever, if thou wilt. You sweet ones all, [*Lies down.*
Let me unworthy press you: I could wish

[1] Alive.

SCENE IV.] PHILASTER. 333

I rather were a corse strewed o'er with you
Than quick above you. Dulness shuts mine eyes,
And I am giddy: oh, that I could take
So sound a sleep that I might never wake! [*Sleeps*.

Enter PHILASTER.

Phi. I have done ill; my conscience calls me false,
To strike at her that would not strike at me. 10
When I did fight, methought I heard her pray
The gods to guard me. She may be abused,
And I a loathèd villain: if she be,
She will conceal who hurt her. He has wounds
And cannot follow; neither knows he me.
Who's this? Bellario sleeping! If thou be'st
Guilty, there is no justice that thy sleep
Should be so sound, and mine, whom thou hast wronged,
[*Cry within.*
So broken. Hark! I am pursued. Ye gods,
I'll take this offered means of my escape: 20
They have no mark to know me but my blood,
If she be true; if false, let mischief light
On all the world at once! Sword, print my wounds
Upon this sleeping boy! I have none, I think,
Are mortal, nor would I lay greater on thee.
[*Wounds* BELLARIO.[1]
Bel. Oh, death, I hope, is come! Blest be that hand!
It meant me well. Again, for pity's sake!
Phi. I have caught myself; [*Falls.*
The loss of blood hath stayed my flight. Here, here,

---

[1] Dryden justly condemns these pinkings of Arethusa and Bellario by Philaster. "It is as if the jealous but naturally gentle lover wished to do a little bit of murder without actually committing it," says Leigh Hunt.

Is he that struck thee: take thy full revenge; 30
Use me, as I did mean thee, worse than death;
I'll teach thee to revenge. This luckless hand
Wounded the princess; tell my followers [1]
Thou didst receive these hurts in staying me,
And I will second thee; get a reward.
 Bel. Fly, fly, my lord, and save yourself!
 Phi. How's this?
Wouldst thou I should be safe?
 Bel. Else were it vain
For me to live. These little wounds I have 40
Have not bled much: reach me that noble hand;
I'll help to cover you.
 Phi. Art thou then true to me?
 Bel. Or let me perish loathed! Come, my good lord,
Creep in amongst those bushes: who does know
But that the gods may save your much-loved breath?
 Phi. Then I shall die for grief, if not for this,
That I have wounded thee. What wilt thou do?
 Bel. Shift for myself well. Peace! I hear 'em come.
        [PHILASTER *creeps into a bush.*
(*Voices within.*) Follow, follow, follow! that way they
  went. 50
 Bel. With my own wounds I'll bloody my own sword.
I need not counterfeit to fall; Heaven knows
That I can stand no longer.   [*Falls.*

 Enter PHARAMOND, DION, CLEREMONT, *and* THRASILINE.

 Pha. To this place we have tracked him by his blood.
 Cle. Yonder, my lord, creeps one away.
 Dion. Stay, sir! what are you?

---

[1] Pursuers.

Bel. A wretched creature, wounded in these woods
By beasts: relieve me, if your names be men,
Or I shall perish.
   Dion. This is he, my lord,
Upon my soul, that hurt her: 'tis the boy,
That wicked boy, that served her.
   Pha. Oh, thou damned
In thy creation! what cause couldst thou shape
To hurt the princess?
   Bel. Then I am betrayed.
   Dion. Betrayed! no, apprehended.
   Bel. I confess,
(Urge it no more) that big with evil thoughts,
I set upon her, and did take my aim,
Her death. For charity let fall at once
The punishment you mean, and do not load
This weary flesh with tortures.
   Pha. I will know
Who hired thee to this deed.
   Bel. Mine own revenge.
   Pha. Revenge! for what?
   Bel. It pleased her to receive
Me as her page, and, when my fortunes ebbed,
That men strid o'er them careless, she did shower
Her welcome graces on me, and did swell
My fortunes till they overflowed their banks,
Threatening the men that crossed 'em; when, as swift
As storms arise at sea, she turned her eyes
To burning suns upon me, and did dry
The streams she had bestowed, leaving me worse
And more contemned than other little brooks,
Because I had been great. In short, I knew

I could not live, and therefore did desire
To die revenged. 90
   Pha. If tortures can be found
Long as thy natural life, resolve to feel
The utmost rigour.
   Cle. Help to lead him hence.
                [PHILASTER *creeps out of the bush.*
   Phi. Turn back, you ravishers of innocence!
Know ye the price of that you bear away
So rudely?
   Pha. Who's that?
   Dion. 'Tis the Lord Philaster.
   Phi. 'Tis not the treasure of all kings in one, 100
The wealth of Tagus, nor the rocks of pearl
That pave the court of Neptune, can weigh down
That virtue. It was I that hurt the princess.
Place me, some god, upon a pyramis[1]
Higher than hills of earth, and lend a voice
Loud as your thunder to me, that from thence
I may discourse to all the under-world
The worth that dwells in him!
   Pha. How's this?
   Bel. My lord, some man 110
Weary of life, that would be glad to die.
   Phi. Leave these untimely courtesies, Bellario.
   Bel. Alas, he's mad! Come, will you lead me on?
   Phi. By all the oaths that men ought most to keep,
And gods do punish most when men do break,
He touched her not. — Take heed, Bellario,
How thou dost drown the virtues thou hast shown
With perjury. — By all that's good, 'twas I!

            [1] Pyramid.

You know she stood betwixt me and my right.
  Pha. Thy own tongue be thy judge! 120
  Cle. It was Philaster.
  Dion. Is't not a brave boy?
Well, sirs, I fear me we were all deceived.
  Phi. Have I no friend here?
  Dion. Yes.
  Phi. Then show it: some
Good body lend a hand to draw us nearer.
Would you have tears shed for you when you die?
Then lay me gently on his neck, that there
I may weep floods and breathe forth my spirit. 130
'Tis not the wealth of Plutus, nor the gold   [*Embraces* BEL.
Locked in the heart of earth, can buy away
This arm-full from me: this had been a ransom
To have redeemed the great Augustus Cæsar,
Had he been taken. You hard-hearted men,
More stony than these mountains, can you see
Such clear pure blood drop, and not cut your flesh
To stop his life? to bind whose bitter wounds,
Queens ought to tear their hair, and with their tears
Bathe 'em. — Forgive me, thou that art the wealth 140
Of poor Philaster!

        Enter KING, ARETHUSA, *and* Guard.

  King. Is the villain ta'en?
  Pha. Sir, here be two confess the deed; but sure
It was Philaster.
  Phi. Question it no more;
It was.
  King. The fellow that did fight with him,
Will tell us that.

Are. Aye me! I know he will.
King. Did not you know him? 150
Are. Sir, if it was he,
He was disguised.
Phi. (*aside*). I was so. Oh, my stars,
That I should live still.
King. Thou ambitious fool,
Thou that hast laid a train for thy own life!—
Now I do mean to do, I'll leave to talk.
Bear them to prison.
Are. Sir, they did plot together to take hence
This harmless life; should it pass unrevenged, 160
I should to earth go weeping: grant me, then,
By all the love a father bears his child,
Their custodies, and that I may appoint
Their tortures and their death.
Dion. Death! Soft; our law will not reach that for this fault.
King. 'Tis granted; take 'em to you with a guard.—
Come, princely Pharamond, this business past,
We may with more security go on
To your intended match.

[*Exeunt all except* DION, CLEREMONT, *and* THRASILINE.

Cle. I pray that this action lose not Philaster the hearts of the people. 171
Dion. Fear it not; their over-wise heads will think it but a trick. [*Exeunt.*

ACT V.

Scene I. — *Before the Palace.*

Enter Dion, Cleremont, *and* Thrasiline.

Thra. Has the King sent for him to death?
Dion. Yes; but the King must know 'tis not in his power to war with Heaven.
Cle. We linger time; the King sent for Philaster and the headsman an hour ago.
Thra. Are all his wounds well?
Dion. All; they were but scratches; but the loss of blood made him faint.
Cle. We dally, gentlemen.
Thra. Away! 10
Dion. We'll scuffle hard before he perish. [*Exeunt.*

Scene II. — *A Prison.*

Enter Philaster, Arethusa, *and* Bellario.

Are. Nay, dear Philaster, grieve not; we are well.
Bel. Nay, good my lord, forbear; we are wondrous well.
Phi. Oh, Arethusa, oh, Bellario,
Leave to be kind!
I shall be shut from Heaven, as now from earth,
If you continue so. I am a man
False to a pair of the most trusty ones
That ever earth bore: can it bear us all?
Forgive and leave me. But the King hath sent

To call me to my death : oh, show it me,
And then forget me ! and for thee, my boy,
I shall deliver words will mollify
The hearts of beasts to spare thy innocence.
   Bel. Alas, my lord, my life is not a thing
Worthy your noble thoughts ! 'tis not a life,
'Tis but a piece of childhood thrown away.[1]
Should I outlive you, I should then outlive
Virtue and honour ; and when that day comes,
If ever I shall close these eyes but once,
May I live spotted for my perjury,
And waste my limbs to nothing !
   Are. And I (the woful'st maid that ever was,
Forced with my hands to bring my lord to death)
Do by the honour of a virgin swear
To tell no hours beyond it !
   Phi. Make me not hated so.
   Are. Come from this prison all joyful to our deaths !
   Phi. People will tear me, when they find you true
To such a wretch as I ; I shall die loathed.
Enjoy your kingdoms peaceably, whilst I
For ever sleep forgotten with my faults :
Every just servant, every maid in love,
Will have a piece of me, if you be true.
   Are. My dear lord, say not so.
   Bel. A piece of you !
He was not born of woman that can cut
It and look on.
   Phi. Take me in tears betwixt you, for my heart
Will break with shame and sorrow.
   Are. Why, 'tis well.

[1] One of the loveliest touches in the play.

Bel. Lament no more.
Phi. Why, what would you have done
If you had wronged me basely, and had found
Your life no price compared to mine? for love, sirs,
Deal with me truly.
Bel. 'Twas mistaken, sir.
Phi. Why, if it were?
Bel. Then, sir, we would have asked
You pardon.
Phi. And have hope to enjoy it? 50
Are. Enjoy it! ay.
Phi. Would you indeed? be plain.
Bel. We would, my lord.
Phi. Forgive me, then.
Are. So, so.
Bel. 'Tis as it should be now.
Phi. Lead to my death. [*Exeunt.*

SCENE III. — *A State-room in the Palace.*

Enter KING, DION, CLEREMONT, THRASILINE, *and* Attendants.

King. Gentlemen, who saw the prince?
Cle. So please you, sir, he's gone to see the city
And the new platform, with some gentlemen
Attending on him.
King. Is the princess ready
To bring her prisoner out?
Thra. She waits your grace.
King. Tell her we stay. [*Exit* THRASILINE.
Dion. King, you may be deceived yet:
The head you aim at cost more setting on 10
Than to be lost so lightly. — (*Aside*) If it must off;

Like a wild overflow, that swoops before him
A golden stack, and with it shakes down bridges,
Cracks the strong hearts of pines, whose cable-roots
Held out a thousand storms, a thousand thunders,
And, so made mightier, takes whole villages
Upon his back, and in that heat of pride
Charges strong towns, towers, castles, palaces,
And lays them desolate; so shall thy head,
Thy noble head, bury the lives of thousands, 20
That must bleed with thee like a sacrifice,
In thy red ruins.

Enter ARETHUSA, PHILASTER, BELLARIO *in a robe and garland, and* THRASILINE.

King. How now? what masque is this?
Bel. Right royal sir, I should
Sing you an epithalamium of these lovers,
But having lost my best airs with my fortunes,
And wanting a celestial harp to strike
This blessèd union on, thus in glad story
I give you all. These two fair cedar-branches
The noblest of the mountain where they grew, 30
Straightest and tallest, under whose still shades
The worthier beasts have made their lairs, and slept
Free from the fervour of the Sirian star
And the fell thunder-stroke, free from the clouds,
When they were big with humour, and delivered,
In thousand spouts their issues to the earth;
Oh, there was none but silent quiet there!
Till never-pleasèd Fortune shot up shrubs,
Base under-brambles, to divorce these branches;
And for a while they did so, and did reign 40

Over the mountain, and choke¹ up his beauty
With brakes, rude thorns and thistles, till the sun
Scorched them even to the roots and dried them there:
And now a gentle gale hath blown again,
That made these branches meet and twine together,
Never to be divided. The god that sings
His holy numbers over marriage-beds
Hath knit their noble hearts; and here they stand
Your children, mighty King: and I have done.
  King. How, how? 50
  Are. Sir, if you love it in plain truth,
(For now there is no masquing in't,) this gentleman,
The prisoner that you gave me, is become
My keeper, and through all the bitter throes
Your jealousies and his ill fate have wrought him,
Thus nobly hath he struggled, and at length
Arrived here my dear husband.
  King. Your dear husband!—
Call in the Captain of the Citadel.—
There you shall keep your wedding. I'll provide 60
A masque shall make your Hymen² turn his saffron
Into a sullen coat, and sing sad requiems
To your departing souls;
Blood shall put out your torches; and, instead
Of gaudy flowers about your wanton necks,
An axe shall hang like a prodigious meteor,
Ready to crop your loves' sweets. Hear, ye gods!
From this time do I shake all title off
Of father to this woman, this base woman;
And what there is of vengeance in a lion 70

¹ Another reading is *cloak*.
² In old masques and pageants, Hymen was clothed in saffron.

Chafed[1] among dogs or robbed of his dear young,
The same, enforced more terrible, more mighty,
Expect from me!
   Are. Sir, by that little life I have left to swear by,
There's nothing that can stir me from myself.
What I have done, I have done without repentance;
For death can be no bugbear unto me,
So long as Pharamond is not my headsman.
   Dion (aside). Sweet peace upon thy soul, thou worthy
      maid,
Whene'er thou diest! For this time I'll excuse thee,   80
Or be thy prologue.
   Phi. Sir, let me speak next;
And let my dying words be better with you
Than my dull living actions. If you aim
At the dear life of this sweet innocent,
You are a tyrant and a savage monster,
That feeds upon the blood you gave a life to;
Your memory shall be as foul behind you,
As you are, living; all your better deeds
Shall be in water writ, but this in marble;[2]   90
No chronicle shall speak you, though your own,
But for the shame of men. No monument,
Though high and big as Pelion, shall be able
To cover this base murder: make it rich
With brass, with purest gold and shining jasper,
Like the Pyramides; lay on epitaphs
Such as make great men gods; my little marble

---

[1] Variation, *cast*.

[2] Cf. *Henry VIII*, iv, 2, — a play in which Fletcher collaborated with Shakespeare: —
      "Men's evil manners live in brass; their virtues
      We write in water."

That only clothes my ashes, not my faults,
Shall far outshine it.   And for after-issues,
Think not so madly of the heavenly wisdoms, 100
That they will give you more for your mad rage
To cut off, unless it be some snake, or something
Like yourself, that in his birth shall strangle you.
Remember my father, King! there was a fault,
But I forgive it: let that sin persuade you
To love this lady; if you have a soul,
Think, save her, and be savèd.   For myself,
I have so long expected this glad hour,
So languished under you, and daily withered,
That, Heaven knows, it is a joy to die; 110
I find a recreation in't.

Enter a Gentleman.

Gent. Where is the King?
King. Here.
Gent. Get you to your strength,
And rescue the Prince Pharamond from danger;
He's taken prisoner by the citizens,
Fearing [1] the Lord Philaster.
Dion (*aside*). Oh, brave followers!
Mutiny, my fine dear countrymen, mutiny!
Now, my brave valiant foremen, shew your weapons 120
In honor of your mistresses!

Enter a Second Gentleman.

2d Gent. Arm, arm, arm, arm!
King. A thousand devils take 'em!
Dion (*aside*). A thousand blessings on 'em!

[1] Fearing for.

2d Gent. Arm, O King! The city is in mutiny,
Led by an old grey ruffian, who comes on
In rescue of the Lord Philaster.
  King. Away to the citadel! I'll see them safe,
And then cope with these burghers. Let the guard
And all the gentlemen give strong attendance.   130
    [*Exeunt all except* DION, CLEREMONT, *and* THRASILINE.
  Cle. The city up! this was above our wishes.
  Dion. Ay, and the marriage too. By my life,
This noble lady has deceived us all.
A plague upon myself, a thousand plagues,
For having such unworthy thoughts of her dear honour!
Oh, I could beat myself! or do you beat me,
And I'll beat you; for we had all one thought.
  Cle. No, no, 'twill but lose time.
  Dion. You say true. Are your swords sharp? — Well, my
dear countrymen What-ye-lacks,[1] if you continue, and fall not
back upon the first broken shin, I'll have you chronicled and
chronicled, and cut and chronicled, and sung in all-to-be-
praised sonnets, and bawled in new brave ballads, that all
tongues shall troul[2] you in *sæcula sæculorum*, my kind can-
carriers.   145
  Thra. What if a toy[3] take 'em i' the heels now, and they
run all away, and cry, "the devil take the hindmost"?
  Dion. Then the same devil take the foremost too, and
souse him for his breakfast! If they all prove cowards, my
curses fly amongst them, and be speeding! May they have
murrains rain to keep the gentlemen at home unbound in
easy frieze! may the moths branch[4] their velvets, and their

---

[1] Shop-keepers used to stand before their doors and cry, "What-d'ye-lack?" to the passers-by.
[2] Troll, sing a catch.   [3] Freak.   [4] Eat off the nap.

silks only to be worn before sore eyes ! may their false lights undo 'em, and discover presses, holes, stains, and oldness in their stuffs, and make them shop-rid ! may they live mewed up with necks of beef and turnips ! may they have many children, and none like the father ! may they know no language but that gibberish they prattle to their parcels, unless it be the goatish[1] Latin they write in their bonds — and may they write that false, and lose their debts !   160

Re-enter KING.

King. Now the vengeance of all the gods confound them ! How they swarm together ! what a hum they raise ! — Devils choke your wild throats ! If a man had need to use their valours, he must pay a brokage[2] for it, and then bring 'em on, and they will fight like sheep. 'Tis Philaster, none but Philaster, must allay this heat : they will not hear me speak, but fling dirt at me and call me tyrant. Oh, run, dear friend, and bring the Lord Philaster ! speak him fair ; call him prince ; do him all the courtesy you can ; commend me to him. Oh, my wits, my wits ! [*Exit* CLEREMONT. 170

Dion (*aside*). Oh, my brave countrymen ! as I live, I will not buy a pin out of your walls for this ; nay, you shall cozen me, and I'll thank you, and send you brawn and bacon, and soil you every long vacation a brace of foremen,[3] that at Michaelmas shall come up fat and kicking.

King. What they will do with this poor prince, the gods know, and I fear.

Dion. Why, sir, they'll flay him, and make church-buck-

---

[1] Barbarous; another reading is *Gothic*.

[2] A commission allowed to the middleman in a commercial transaction.

[3] Fatten a brace of geese; cf. "soiled horse," in *King Lear*, iv, 6, 124. Better spelt *soul*, from the Old French *saoler*, Mod. French *soûler*.

ets of's skin, to quench rebellion; then clap a rivet in's
sconce, and hang him up for a sign.

Enter PHILASTER *and* CLEREMONT.

King. Oh, worthy sir, forgive me! do not make
Your miseries and my faults meet together,
To bring a greater danger. Be yourself,
Still sound amongst diseases. I have wronged you;
And though I find it last, and beaten to it,
Let first your goodness know it. Calm the people,
And be what you were born to: take your love,
And with her my repentance, all my wishes
And all my prayers. By the gods, my heart speaks this;
And if the least fall from me not performed,
May I be struck with thunder!

Phi. Mighty sir,
I will not do your greatness so much wrong,
As not to make your word truth. Free the princess
And the poor boy, and let me stand the shock .
Of this mad sea-breach, which I'll either turn,
Or perish with it.

King. Let your own word free them.

Phi. Then thus I take my leave, kissing your hand,
And hanging on your royal word. Be kingly,
And be not moved, sir: I shall bring you peace
Or never bring myself back.

King. All the gods go with thee. [*Exeunt.*

Scene IV. — *A Street.*

Enter an old Captain *and* Citizens *with* Pharamond *prisoner.*

Cap. Come, my brave myrmidons, let us fall on !
Let your caps swarm, my boys, and your nimble tongues
Forget your mother gibberish of " what do you lack,"
And set your mouths ope, children, till your palates
Fall frighted half a fathom past the cure
Of bay-salt and gross pepper, and then cry
" Philaster, brave Philaster ! " Let Philaster
Be deeper in request, my ding-a-dings,
My pairs of dear indentures, kings of clubs,[1]
Than your cold water-camlets, or your paintings   10
Spitted with copper. Let not your hasty silks,
Or your branched cloth of bodkin, or your tissues,
Dearly belovèd of spiced cake and custard,
Your Robin Hoods, Scarlets, and Johns, tie your affections
In darkness to your shops. No, dainty duckers[2]
Up with your three-piled spirits, your wrought valours[3] :
And let your uncut cholers make the King feel
The measure of your mightiness. Philaster !
Cry, my rose-nobles,[4] cry !

   All. Philaster ! Philaster !   20

   Cap. How do you like this, my lord-prince ?
These are mad boys, I tell you ; these are things

---

[1] London shop-keepers and their apprentices commonly used clubs as weapons.

[2] Cringers.   [3] Play on the word *velours*, velvet.

[4] Another pun ; rose-nobles were gold coins stamped with a rose, and worth sixteen shillings.

That will not strike their top-sails to a foist,[1]
And let a man of war, an argosy,
Hull and cry cockles.[2]
  Pha. Why, you rude slave, do you know what you do?
  Cap. My pretty prince of puppets, we do know;
And give your greatness warning that you talk
No more such bug's-words,[3] or that soldered crown
Shall be scratched with a musket.[4]   30
— Let him loose, my spirits:
Make us a round ring with your bills,[5] my Hectors,
And let us see what this trim man dares do.
Now, sir, have at you! here I lie;
And with this swashing blow (do you see, sweet prince?)
I could hock[6] your grace, and hang you up cross-legged,
Like a hare at a poulter's, and do this with this wiper.
  Pha. You will not see me murdered, wicked villains?
  1st Cit. Yes, indeed, will we, sir; we have not seen one
For a great while.   40
  Cap. He would have weapons, would he?
Give him a broadside, my brave boys, with your pikes;
Branch[7] me his skin in flowers like a satin,
And between every flower a mortal cut. —
Your royalty shall ravel! — Jag him, gentlemen;
I'll have him cut to the kell,[8] then down the seams.
O for a whip to make him galloon-laces!
I'll have a coach-whip.
  Pha. Oh, spare me, gentlemen!
  Cap. Hold, hold;   50

---

[1] A small craft; Italian *fusta*.   [2] Crow over them.
[3] Bombastic.   [4] A small hawk.   [5] Battle-axes, halberds.
[6] Ham-string.   [7] See note, p. 346.
[8] The omentum, or adipose membrane attached to the stomach.

The man begins to fear and know himself;
He shall for this time only be seeled up,[1]
With a feather through his nose, that he may only
See heaven, and think whither he is going. Nay,
Nay, my beyond-sea sir, we will proclaim you:
You would be king!
Thou tender heir apparent to a church-ale,[2]
Thou slight prince of single sarcenet,
Thou royal ring-tail,[3] fit to fly at nothing
But poor men's poultry, and have every boy 60
Beat thee from that too with his bread and butter!

Pha. Gods keep me from these hell-hounds!

1st Cit. I'll have a leg, that's certain.

2d Cit. I'll have an arm.

3d Cit. I'll have his nose, and at mine own charge build
A college and clap it upon the gate.[4]

4th Cit. Good captain, let me have his liver to feed ferrets.

Cap. Who will have parcels else? speak.

Pha. Good gods, consider me! I shall be tortured.

1st Cit. Captain, I'll give you the trimming of your two-hand sword, 70
And let me have his skin to make false scabbards.

2d Cit. He had no horns, sir, had he?

Cap. No, sir, he's a pollard:
What wouldst thou do with horns?

2d Cit. Oh, if he had had,
I would have made rare hafts and whistles of 'em;

---

[1] To close the eyelids, as of a hawk, by passing a fine thread through them.

[2] Festival at the dedication of a church.   [3] Female of the hen harrier.

[4] Allusion to Brazen Nose College, Oxford.

But his shin-bones, if they be sound, shall serve me.

Enter PHILASTER.

All. Long live Philaster, the brave Prince Philaster!
Phi. I thank you, gentlemen. But why are these
Rude weapons brought abroad, to teach your hands   80
Uncivil trades?
  Cap. My royal Rosicleer,[1]
We are thy myrmidons, thy guard, thy roarers[2];
And when thy noble body is in durance,
Thus do we clap our musty murrions[3] on,
And trace the streets in terror. Is it peace,
Thou Mars of men? is the King sociable,
And bids thee live? art thou above thy foemen,
And free as Phœbus? speak. If not, this stand
Of royal blood shall be a-broach, a-tilt,   90
And run even to the lees of honour.
  Phi. Hold, and be satisfied: I am myself
Free as my thoughts are: by the gods, I am!
  Cap. Art thou the dainty darling of the King?
Art thou the Hylas to our Hercules?
Do the lords bow, and the regarded scarlets
Kiss their gummed golls,[4] and cry "We are your servants"?
Is the court navigable, and the presence stuck
With flags of friendship? If not, we are thy castle,
And this man sleeps.   100
  Phi. I am what I desire to be, your friend;
I am what I was born to be, your prince.

---

[1] A character in *The Mirror of Knighthood.*
[2] Cant name for street ruffians.
[3] Morions, steel caps.   [4] Hands rubbed with gum or perfume.

Pha. Sir, there is some humanity in you;
You have a noble soul: forget my name,
And know my misery: set me safe aboard
From these wild cannibals, and, as I live,
I'll quit this land for ever. There is nothing, —
Perpetual prisonment, cold, hunger, sickness
Of all sorts, of all dangers, and all together,
The worst company of the worst men, madness, age,   110
To be as many creatures as a woman,
And do as all they do, nay, to despair, —
But I would rather make it a new nature,
And live with all those, than endure one hour
Amongst these wild dogs.
   Phi. I do pity you. — Friends, discharge your fears;
Deliver me the prince: I'll warrant you
I shall be old enough to find my safety.
   3d Cit. Good sir, take heed he does not hurt you;
He is a fierce man, I can tell you, sir.   120
   Cap. Prince, by your leave, I'll have a surcingle,
And mail[1] you like a hawk.
   Phi. Away, away, there is no danger in him:
Alas, he had rather sleep to shake his fit off!
Look you, friends, how gently he leads! Upon my word,
He's tame enough, he needs no further watching.
Good my friends, go to your houses,
And by me have your pardons and my love;
And know there shall be nothing in my power
You may deserve, but you shall have your wishes: 130
To give you more thanks, were to flatter you.
Continue still your love; and, for an earnest,
Drink this.   *[Gives money.*

[1] To tie up a falcon's pinions.

All. Long mayst thou live, brave prince, brave prince,
brave prince! [*Exeunt* PHIL. *and* PHAR.
Cap. Go thy ways, thou art the king of courtesy!
Fall off again, my sweet youths. Come,
And every man trace to his house again,
And hang his pewter up; then to the tavern,
And bring your wives in muffs. We will have music;
And the red grape shall make us dance and rise, boys. 140
[*Exeunt.*[1]

SCENE V. — *An Apartment in the Palace.*

Enter KING, ARETHUSA, GALATEA, MEGRA, DION, CLERE-
MONT, THRASILINE, BELLARIO, *and* Attendants.

King. Is it appeased?
Dion. Sir, all is quiet as this dead of night,
As peaceable as sleep. My lord Philaster
Brings on the prince himself.
King. Kind gentleman!
I will not break the least word I have given
In promise to him: I have heaped a world
Of grief upon his head, which yet I hope
To wash away.

Enter PHILASTER *and* PHARAMOND.

Cle. My lord is come. 10
King. My son!
Blest be the time that I have leave to call
Such virtue mine! Now thou art in mine arms,

[1] The speeches of the Captain, with their puns and strained metaphors, may have seemed witty once, but their wit evaporated long ago. Fashion in fun varies from age to age; wisdom, pathos, sublimity, are more permanent.

Methinks I have a salve unto my breast
For all the stings that dwell there. Streams of grief
That I have wronged thee, and as much of joy
That I repent it, issue from mine eyes:
Let them appease thee. Take thy right; take her;
She is thy right too; and forget to urge
My vexèd soul with that I did before. 20
 Phi. Sir, it is blotted from my memory,
Past and forgotten. — For you, prince of Spain,
Whom I have thus redeemed, you have full leave
To make an honourable voyage home.
And if you would go furnished to your realm
With fair provision, I do see a lady,
Methinks, would gladly bear you company:
How like you this piece?
 Meg. Sir, he likes it well.
I know your meaning. 30
Can shame remain perpetually in me,
And not in others? or have princes salves
To cure ill names, that meaner people want?
 Phi. What mean you?
 Meg. You must get another ship,
To bear the princess and her boy together.
 Dion. How now!
 Meg. Ship us all four, my lord; we can endure
Weather and wind alike.
 King. Clear thou thyself, or know not me for father. 40
 Are. This earth, how false it is! What means is left
  for me
To clear myself? It lies in your belief:
My lords, believe me; and let all things else
Struggle together to dishonour me.

Bel. Oh, stop your ears, great King, that I may speak
As freedom would! then I will call this lady
As base as are her actions: hear me, sir;
Believe your heated blood when it rebels
Against your reason, sooner than this lady.
 Meg. By this good light, he bears it handsomely.   50
 Phi. This lady! I will sooner trust the wind
With feathers, or the troubled sea with pearl,
Than her with any thing. Believe her not.
Why, think you, if I did believe her words,
I would outlive 'em? Honour cannot take
Revenge on you; then what were to be known
But death?
 King. Forget her, sir, since all is knit
Between us. But I must request of you
One favour, and will sadly be denied.   60
 Phi. Command, whate'er it be.
 King. Swear to be true
To what you promise.
 Phi. By the powers above,
Let it not be the death of her or him,
And it is granted!
 King. Bear away that boy
To torture: I will have her cleared or buried.
 Phi. Oh, let me call my word back, worthy sir!
Ask something else: bury my life and right   70
In one poor grave; but do not take away
My life and fame at once.
 King. Away with him! It stands irrevocable.
 Phi. Turn all your eyes on me: here stands a man,
The falsest and the basest of this world.
Set swords against this breast, some honest man,

For I have lived till I am pitied !
My former deeds were hateful ; but this last
Is pitiful, for I unwillingly
Have given the dear preserver of my life   80
Unto his torture. Is it in the power
Of flesh and blood to carry this, and live?
                    [*Offers to stab himself.*
   Are. Dear sir, be patient yet !   Oh, stay that hand !
   King. Sirs, strip that boy.
   Dion. Come, sir, your tender flesh
Will try your constancy.
   Bel. Oh, kill me, gentlemen !
   Dion. No.— Help, sirs.
   Bel. Will you torture me?
   King. Haste there ;   90
Why stay you?
   Bel. Then I shall not break my vow,
You know, just gods, though I discover all.
   King. How's that? will he confess?
   Dion. Sir, so he says.
   King. Speak then.
   Bel. Great King, if you command
This lord to talk with me alone, my tongue,
Urged by my heart, shall utter all the thoughts
My youth hath known ; and stranger things than these   100
You hear not often.
   King. Walk aside with him.
                    [DION *and* BELLARIO *walk apart*
   Dion. Why speak'st thou not?
   Bel. Know you this face, my lord?
   Dion. No.
   Bel. Have you not seen it, nor the like?

Dion. Yes, I have seen the like, but readily
I know not where.
   Bel. I have been often told
In court of one Euphrasia, a lady, 110
And daughter to you; betwixt whom and me
They that would flatter my bad face would swear
There was such strange resemblance, that we two
Could not be known asunder, drest alike.
   Dion. By Heaven, and so there is!
   Bel. For her fair sake,
Who now doth spend the spring-time of her life
In holy pilgrimage, move to the King,
That I may scape this torture.
   Dion. But thou speak'st 120
As like Euphrasia as thou dost look.
How came it to thy knowledge that she lives
In pilgrimage?
   Bel. I know it not, my lord;
But I have heard it, and do scarce believe it.
   Dion. Oh, my shame! is it possible? Draw near,
That I may gaze upon thee. Art thou she,
Or else her murderer?[1] where wert thou born?
   Bel. In Syracusa.
   Dion. What's thy name? 130
   Bel. Euphrasia.
   Dion. Oh, 'tis just, 'tis she!
Now I do know thee. Oh, that thou hadst died,
And I had never seen thee nor my shame!
How shall I own thee? shall this tongue of mine
E'er call thee daughter more?

   [1] In some countries the superstitious believed that the murderer inherited the form and qualities of his victim.

Bel. Would I had died indeed! I wish it too:
And so I must have done by vow, ere published
What I have told, but that there was no means
To hide it longer. Yet I joy in this, 140
The princess is all clear.
 King. What, have you done?
 Dion. All is discovered.
 Phi. Why then hold you me? [*Offers to stab himself.*
All is discovered! Pray you, let me go.
 King. Stay him.
 Are. What is discovered?
 Dion. Why, my shame.
It is a woman: let her speak the rest.
 Phi. How? that again! 150
 Dion. It is a woman.
 Phi. Blessed be you powers that favour innocence!
 King. Lay hold upon that lady. [MEGRA *is seized.*
 Phi. It is a woman, sir! — Hark, gentlemen,
It is a woman! — Arethusa, take
My soul into thy breast, that would be gone
With joy. It is a woman! Thou art fair,
And virtuous still to ages, in despite
Of malice.
 King. Speak you, where lies his shame? 160
 Bel. I am his daughter.
 Phi. The gods are just.
 Dion. I dare accuse none; but, before you two,
The virtue of our age, I bend my knee
For mercy. [*Kneels.*
 Phi. (*raising him*). Take it freely; for I know,
Though what thou didst were undiscreetly done,
'Twas meant well.

Are. And for me,
I have a power to pardon sins, as oft 170
As any man has power to wrong me.
   Cle. Noble and worthy!
   Phi. But, Bellario,
(For I must call thee still so,) tell me why
Thou didst conceal thy sex. It was a fault,
A fault, Bellario, though thy other deeds
Of truth outweighed it: all these jealousies
Had flown to nothing, if thou hadst discovered
What now we know.
   Bel. My father oft would speak 180
Your worth and virtue; and, as I did grow
More and more apprehensive, I did thirst
To see the man so praised. But yet all this
Was but a maiden-longing, to be lost
As soon as found; till, sitting in my window,
Printing my thoughts in lawn, I saw a god,
I thought, (but it was you,) enter our gates:
My blood flew out and back again, as fast
As I had puffed it forth and sucked it in
Like breath: then was I called away in haste 190
To entertain you. Never was a man,
Heaved from a sheep-cote to a sceptre, raised
So high in thoughts as I: you left a kiss
Upon these lips then, which I mean to keep
From you for ever: I did hear you talk,
Far above singing. After you were gone,
I grew acquainted with my heart, and searched
What stirred it so: alas, I found it love!
Yet far from lust; for, could I but have lived
In presence of you, I had had my end. 200

For this I did delude my noble father
With a feigned pilgrimage, and dressed myself
In habit of a boy; and, for I knew
My birth no match for you, I was past hope
Of having you; and, understanding well
That when I made discovery of my sex
I could not stay with you, I made a vow,
By all the most religious things a maid
Could call together, never to be known,
Whilst there was hope to hide me from men's eyes, 210
For other than I seemed, that I might ever
Abide with you. Then sat I by the fount,
Where first you took me up.
 King. Search out a match
Within our kingdom, where and when thou wilt,
And I will pay thy dowry; and thyself
Wilt well deserve him.
 Bel. Never, sir, will I
Marry; it is a thing within my vow:
But, if I may have leave to serve the princess, 220
To see the virtues of her lord and her,
I shall have hope to live.
 Are. I, Philaster,
Cannot be jealous, though you had a lady
Drest like a page to serve you; nor will I
Suspect her living here. — Come, live with me;
Live free as I do. She that loves my lord,
Cursed be the wife that hates her!
 Phi. I grieve such virtue should be laid in earth
Without an heir. — Hear me, my royal father: 230
Wrong not the freedom of our souls so much,
To think to take revenge of that base woman;

Her malice cannot hurt us. Set her free
As she was born, saving from shame and sin.
  King. Set her at liberty. But leave the court;
This is no place for such. — You, Pharamond,
Shall have free passage, and a conduct home
Worthy so great a prince. When you come there,
Remember 'twas your faults that lost you her,
And not my purposed will.   240
  Pha. I do confess,
Renownèd sir.
  King. Last, join your hands in one. Enjoy, Philaster,
This kingdom, which is yours, and, after me,
Whatever I call mine. My blessing on you!
All happy hours be at your marriage-joys,
That you may grow yourselves over all lands,
And live to see your plenteous branches spring
Wherever there is sun! Let princes learn
By this to rule the passions of their blood;   250
For what Heaven wills can never be withstood.
                                        [*Curtain falls.*[1]

---

[1] **Of** Euphrasia, disguised as Bellario, Dyce says: "She is one of our authors' most perfect creations,— unequalled in the romantic tenderness and the deep devotedness of her affection by any character which at all resembles her in the wide range of fiction, from her supposed prototype, the Viola of Shakespeare, down to the Constance of Scott and the Kaled of Byron."

IV.

THE TWO NOBLE KINSMEN.

BY JOHN FLETCHER AND WILLIAM SHAKESPEARE.

Probably written between 1608 and 1612. The story is borrowed from *The Knighte's Tale* of Chaucer, who took it from Boccaccio's *Teseide*.

THE TWO NOBLE KINSMEN.

DRAMATIS PERSONÆ.

THESEUS, Duke of Athens.
PIRITHOUS, an Athenian General.
ARTESIUS, an Athenian Captain.
PALAMON, } Nephews to Creon,
ARCITE,   }   King of Thebes.
VALERIUS, a Theban Nobleman.
Six Knights.
A Herald.
A Gaoler.
Wooer to the Gaoler's Daughter.
A Doctor.
Brother to the Gaoler.
Friends to the Gaoler.

A Gentleman.
GERROLD, a Schoolmaster.
HIPPOLYTA, Bride to Theseus.
EMILIA, her Sister.
Three Queens.
The Gaoler's Daughter.
Waiting-woman to Emilia.
Countrymen, Messengers, a Man personating Hymen, Boy, Executioners, Guard, and Attendants, Country Wenches, and Women personating Nymphs.

SCENE: *Athens and the neighbourhood; and in part of the first act, Thebes and the neighbourhood.*

PROLOGUE.

Chaucer, of all admir'd, the story gives;
There constant to eternity it lives.
If we let fall the nobleness of this,
And the first sound this child hear be a hiss,
How will it shake the bones of that good man,

And make him cry from under ground, " O, fan
From me the witless chaff of such a writer
That blasts my bays, and my fam'd works makes lighter
Than Robin Hood ! " This is the fear we bring ;
For, to say truth, it were an endless thing, 10
And too ambitious, to aspire to him.
Weak as we are, and almost breathless swim
In this deep water, do but you hold out
Your helping hands, and we shall tack about,
And something do to save us : you shall hear
Scenes, though below his art, may yet appear
Worth two hours' travail. To his bones sweet sleep !
Content to you ! — If this play do not keep
A little dull time from us, we perceive
Our losses fall so thick, we needs must leave. [*Flourish.* 20

ACT I.[1]

SCENE I. — *Athens. Before a Temple.*

Enter HYMEN, *with a torch burning*; *a* Boy, *in a white robe, before, singing and strewing flowers ; after* HYMEN, *a* Nymph, *encompassed in her tresses,*[2] *bearing a wheaten garland; then* THESEUS, *between two other* Nymphs *with wheaten chaplets on their heads ; then* HIPPOLYTA, *the bride, led by* PIRITHOUS, *and another holding a garland over her head, her tresses likewise hanging; after her,* EMILIA, *holding up her train ;* ARTESIUS *and* Attendants.

[1] The First Act is attributed to *Shakespeare* by most of the critics.
[2] Emblem of virginity.

The Song. [*Music.*

*Roses, **their sharp** spines being gone,*
Not royal in their smells alone,
   But in their hue;
Maiden[1] *pinks, of odour faint,*
Daisies smell-less, yet most quaint,
   And sweet thyme true;

Primrose, first-born child of Ver,
Merry spring-time's harbinger,
   With her bells dim;
Oxlips in their cradles growing,   10
Marigolds on death-beds blowing,
   Larks'-heels[2] *trim;*

All dear Nature's children sweet,
Lie 'fore bride and bridegroom's feet,
   Blessing their sense! [Strewing flowers.
Not an angel of the air,—
Bird melodious, or bird fair,—
   Be absent hence!

The crow, the slanderous cuckoo, nor
The boding raven, nor chough hoar,   20
   Nor chattering pie,
May on our bride-house perch or sing,
Or with them any discord bring,
   But from it fly![3]

---

[1] Fresh; also used for strewing on the grave of a maiden, or faithful wife.

[2] Small Indian cress, or nasturtium.

[3] Dowden, Nicholson, Hargrove, and Furnivall think *Shakespeare* did not write this song; Littledale is in doubt.

Enter three Queens, *in black, with veils stained, and with imperial crowns. The* First Queen *falls down at the foot of* THESEUS; *the* Second *falls down at the foot of* HIPPOLYTA; *the* Third *before* EMILIA.

1st Queen. For pity's sake and true gentility's,
Hear and respect me!
   2d Queen.   For your mother's sake,
And as you wish yourself may thrive with fair ones,
Hear and respect me!
   3d Queen. Now for the love of him whom Jove hath
      mark'd
The honour of your bed, and for the sake   30
Of clear virginity, be advocate
For us, and our distresses! This good deed
Shall raze[1] you out o' the book of trespasses
All you are set down there.
   Theseus. Sad lady, rise.
   Hippolyta.   Stand up.
   Emilia.   No knees to me!
What woman I may stead,[2] that is distress'd
Does bind me to her.
   Theseus. What's your request? Deliver you for all.
   1st Queen. We are three queens, whose sovereigns fell
      before
The wrath of cruel Creon; who endure   40
The beaks of ravens, talons of the kites,
And pecks of crows, in the foul fields of Thebes.
He will not suffer us to burn their bones,
To urn their ashes, nor to take the offence
Of mortal loathsomeness from the blest eye

---

[1] Erase for you.   [2] Help.

Of holy Phœbus, but infects the winds
With stench of our slain lords. O, pity, duke!
Thou purger of the earth, draw thy fear'd sword,
That does good turns to the world; give us the bones
Of our dead kings, that we may chapel them!
And, of thy boundless goodness, take some note
That for our crowned heads we have no roof
Save this, which is the lion's and the bear's,
And vault to everything!
   Theseus.   Pray you, kneel not;
I was transported with your speech, and suffer'd
Your knees to wrong themselves. I have heard the fortunes
Of your dead lords, which gives me such lamenting
As wakes my vengeance and revenge for 'em.
King Capanëus[1] was your lord: the day
That he should marry you, at such a season
As now it is with me, I met your groom
By Mars's altar; you were that time fair,
Not Juno's mantle fairer than your tresses,
Nor in more bounty spread her; your wheaten wreath
Was then nor thresh'd nor blasted; Fortune at you
Dimpled her cheek with smiles; Hercules our kinsman —
Then weaker than your eyes — laid by his club;
He tumbled down upon his Nemean hide,
And swore his sinews thaw'd. O grief and time,
Fearful consumers, you will all devour!
   1st Queen. O, I hope some god,
Some god hath put his mercy in your manhood,
Whereto he'll infuse power, and press you **forth**
Our undertaker!
   Theseus.   O, no knees, none, widow!

---

[1] One of the seven heroes who marched from Argos against Thebes.

Unto the helmeted Bellona[1] use them,
And pray for me, your soldier. —
Troubled I am. [*Turns away*.
   2d Queen.   Honour'd Hippolyta,
Most dreaded Amazonian, that hast slain
The scythe-tusk'd boar; that, with thy arm as strong
As it is white, wast near to make the male   80
To thy sex captive, but that this thy lord —
Born to uphold creation in that honour
First nature styl'd it in — shrunk thee into
The bound thou wast o'erflowing, at once subduing
Thy force and thy affection; soldieress,
That equally canst poise sternness with pity;
Who, now, I know, hast much more power on him
Than e'er he had on thee; who ow'st his strength
And his love too, who is a servant[2] for
The tenour of thy speech; dear glass of ladies,   90
Bid him that we, whom flaming war doth scorch,
Under the shadow of his sword may cool us;
Require him he advance it o'er our heads.
Speak't in a woman's key, like such a woman
As any of us three; weep ere you fail;
Lend us a knee;
But touch the ground for us no longer time
Than a dove's motion when the head's pluck'd off;
Tell him, if he i' the blood-siz'd[3] field lay swoln,
Showing the sun his teeth, grinning at the moon,   100
What you would do!
   Hippolyta.   Poor lady, say no more;
I had as lief trace this good action with you

---

[1] The Roman goddess of war.
[2] Obedient lover.   [3] Made sticky with blood.

As that whereto I'm going, and ne'er yet
Went I so willing way. My lord is taken
Heart-deep with your distress: let him consider;
I'll speak anon.
 3d Queen. O, my petition was [*Kneels to* EMILIA.
Set down in ice, which by hot grief uncandied,[1]
Melts into drops; so sorrow, wanting form,
Is press'd with deeper matter.
 Emilia. Pray stand up;
Your grief is written in your cheek.
 3d Queen. O, woe! 110
You cannot read it there; there, through my tears,
Like wrinkled pebbles in a glassy stream,
You may behold 'em! Lady, lady, alack,
He that will all the treasure know o' the earth,
Must know the centre too; he that will fish
For my least minnow, let him lead his line
To catch one at my heart. O, pardon me!
Extremity, that sharpens sundry wits,
Makes me a fool.
 Emilia. Pray you, say nothing, pray you;
Who cannot feel nor see the rain, being in't 120
Knows neither wet nor dry. If that you were
The ground-piece of some painter, I would buy you,
T' instruct me 'gainst a capital grief indeed, —
Such heart-pierc'd demonstration! — but, alas,
Being a natural[2] sister of our sex,
Your sorrow beats so ardently upon me,
That it shall make a counter-reflect 'gainst
My brother's heart, and warm it to some pity
Though it were made of stone; pray have good comfort!

   [1] Dissolved. [2] Real, not feigned.

Theseus. Forward to the temple! leave not out a jot   130
O' the sacred ceremony.
 1st Queen.   O, this celebration
Will longer last, and be more costly, than
Your suppliants' war! Remember that your fame
Knolls in the ear o' the world. What you do quickly
Is not done rashly; your first thought is more
Than others' labour'd meditance; your premeditating
More than their actions; but — O Jove! — your actions,
Soon as they move, as ospreys do the fish,[1]
Subdue before they touch. Think, dear duke, think
What beds our slain kings have!
 2d Queen.   What griefs our beds,   140
That our dear lords have none!
 3d Queen.   None fit for the dead!
Those that, with cords, knives, drams, precipitance,[2]
Weary of this world's light, have to themselves
Been death's most horrid agents, human grace
Affords them dust and shadow —
 1st Queen.   But our lords
Lie blistering 'fore the visiting[3] sun,
And were good kings when living.
 Theseus.   It is true:
And I will give you comfort,
To give your dead lords graves; the which to do
Must make some work with Creon.   150

---

[1] Cf. *Coriolanus*, iv, 7:
  "I think he'll be to Rome,
  As is the osprey to the fish, who takes it
  By sovereignty of nature."

[2] Those who take their own lives by hanging, stabbing, poison, and throwing themselves from a height.

[3] Surveying; cf. *Tempest*, i, 2, 308.

1st Queen.   And that work now presents itself to the
      doing;
Now 'twill take form; the heats are gone to-morrow.
Then bootless toil must recompense itself
With its own sweat; now he's secure,
Not dreams we stand before your puissance,
Rinsing our holy begging in our eyes,
To make petition clear.
  2d Queen.   Now you may take him,
Drunk with his victory —
  3d Queen.   And his army full
Of bread and sloth.
  Theseus.   Artesius, that best know'st
How to draw out, fit to this enterprise,   160
The prim'st for this proceeding, and the number
To carry such a business, forth and levy
Our worthiest instruments; whilst we despatch
This grand act of our life, this daring deed
Of fate in wedlock!
  1st Queen.   Dowagers, take hands!
Let us be widows to our woes!   Delay
Commends us to a famishing hope.
  All the Queens.   Farewell!
  2d Queen. We come unseasonably; but when could grief
Cull forth, as unpang'd judgment can, fitt'st time
For best solicitation?
  Theseus.   Why, good ladies,   170
This is a service, whereto I am going,
Greater than any war; it more imports me
Than all the actions that I have foregone,
Or futurely can cope.
  1st Queen.   The more proclaiming

Our suit shall be neglected. When her arms,
Able to lock Jove from a synod,¹ shall
By warranting moonlight corslet thee, O, when
Her twinning cherries shall their sweetness fall
Upon thy tasteful lips, what wilt thou think
Of rotten kings or blubber'd ² queens? what care 180
For what thou feel'st not, what thou feel'st being able
To make Mars spurn his drum? O, if thou couch
But one night with her, every hour in't will
Take hostage of thee for a hundred, and
Thou shalt remember nothing more than what
That banquet bids ³ thee to!
    Hippolyta (*kneeling to* THESEUS). Though much unlike
You should be so transported, as much sorry
I should be such a suitor, yet I think,
Did I not, by the abstaining of my joy,
Which breeds a deeper longing, cure their surfeit ⁴ 190
That craves a present medicine, I should pluck
All ladies' scandal on me. Therefore, sir,
As I shall here make trial of my prayers,
Either presuming them to have some force,
Or sentencing for aye their vigour dumb,
Prorogue this business we are going about, and hang
Your shield afore your heart, about that neck
Which is my fee,⁵ and which I freely lend
To do these poor queens service.
    All Queens.   O, help now! [*To* EMILIA.

    ¹ Assembly of the gods; so *Cymbeline*, v, 4, 89.
    ² Disfigured by weeping. "The reader ought to recollect that formerly this word did not convey the somewhat ludicrous idea which it does at present." — *Dyce.*
    ³ Invites.   ⁴ Excess of grief.   ⁵ Property.

Our cause cries for your knee.
   Emilia (*kneeling to* THESEUS). If you grant not   200
My sister her petition, in that force,
With that celerity and nature, which
She makes it in, from henceforth I'll not dare
To ask you anything, nor be so hardy
Ever to take a husband.
   Theseus.   Pray stand up!
                   [HIPPOLYTA *and* EMILIA *rise.*
I am entreating of myself to do
That which you kneel to have me. — Pirithous,
Lead on the bride. Get you¹ and pray the gods
For success and return; omit not anything
In the pretended² celebration. — Queens,   210
Follow your soldier. — As before, hence you, [*To* ARTESIUS.
And at the banks of Aulis meet us with
The forces you can raise, where we shall find
The moiety of a number, for a business
More bigger look'd. — (*To* HIPPOLYTA) Since that our theme is haste,
I stamp this kiss upon thy currant lip;
Sweet, keep it as my token! — (*To* ARTESIUS) Set you forward;
For I will see you gone. —   [*Exit* ARTESIUS.
Farewell, my beauteous sister! — Pirithous,
Keep the feast full; bate not an hour on't!
   Pirithous.   Sir,   220
I'll follow you at heels; the feast's solemnity
Shall want³ till you return.
   Theseus.   Cousin, I charge you,
Budge not from Athens; we shall be returning

¹ Get you hence.   ² Intended.   ³ Be incomplete.

Ere you can end this feast, of which, I pray you,
Make no abatement. — Once more, farewell all !
 [HIPPOLYTA, EMILIA, PIRITHOUS, HYMEN, Boy, Nymphs,
   and Attendants *enter the temple.*
 1st Queen. Thus dost thou still make good
The tongue o' the world —
 2d Queen. And earn'st a deity
Equal with Mars —
 3d Queen. If not above him ; for,
Thou, being but mortal, mak'st affections bend
To godlike honours ; they themselves, some say, 230
Groan under such a mastery.
 Theseus. As we are men,
Thus should we do ; being sensually subdued,[1]
We lose our human title. Good cheer, ladies !
Now turn we towards your comforts. [*Flourish. Exeunt.*[2]

[1] Overcome by our passions.

[2] This scene " has sometimes Shakespeare's identical images and words; it has his quaint force and sententious brevity, crowding thoughts and fancies into the narrowest space, and submitting to obscurity in preference to feeble dilation; it has sentiments enunciated with reference to subordinate relations, which other writers would have expressed with less grasp of thought; it has even Shakespeare's alliteration, and one or two of his singularities in conceit; it has clearness in the images taken separately, and confusion from the prodigality with which one is poured out after another, in the heat and hurry of imagination; it has both fulness of illustration, and a variety which is drawn from the most distant sources; and it has, thrown over all, that air of originality and that character of poetry, the principle of which is often hid when their presence and effect are most quickly and instinctively perceptible." — *Spalding.*

" The first thing that seems to indicate the presence of the mind of Shakespeare is the clearness with which, in the first scene, we are put in possession of the exact state of affairs at the opening of the play, without any circumlocution or long-winded harangues, but naturally and dramatically. And, indeed, one of the most striking characteristics of Shakespeare is, **if we may so express it, the downright honesty of his genius, that**

Scene II. — *Thebes. The Court of the Palace.*

Enter PALAMON *and* ARCITE.

Arcite. Dear Palamon, dearer in love than blood,
And our prime cousin, yet unharden'd in
The crimes of nature, let us leave the city,
Thebes, and the temptings in't, before we further
Sully our gloss of youth :
And here to keep in abstinence we shame
As in incontinence ; for not to swim
I' the aid o' the current were almost to sink,
At least to frustrate striving ; and to follow
The common stream, 'twould bring us to an eddy   10
Where we should turn or drown ; if labour through,[1]
Our gain but life and weakness.
 Palamon.   Your advice
Is cried up with example. What strange ruins,[2]
Since first we went to school, may we perceive
Walking in Thebes ! scars and bare weeds,
The gain o' the martialist, who did propound
To his bold ends honour and golden ingots,

---

disdains anything like trick or mystery. This is almost peculiar to Shakespeare. Where, in his works, as much is revealed at the very opening as is necessary to the understanding of the plot, we find, in the works of other dramatists, as much kept back as possible; and we are continually greeted with some surprise or startled with some unexpected turn in the conduct of the piece." — *Hickson.*

[1] If we should labor through it.

[2] "Not material ruins of houses, but wrecks of men, that is, men who are but wrecks of their former selves. Palamon is following up the idea started by Arcite, that the men in Thebes were mostly coming to ruin." — *Skeat.*

Which though he won, he had not; and now flurted[1]
By Peace, for whom he fought! Who then shall offer
To Mars's so-scorn'd altar? I do bleed
When such I meet, and wish great Juno would
Resume her ancient fit of jealousy,[2]
To get the soldier work, that Peace might purge
For her repletion, and retain anew
Her charitable heart, now hard, and harsher
Than strife or war could be.
    Arcite.   Are you not out?
Meet you no ruin but the soldier in
The cranks and turns of Thebes? You did begin
As if you met decays of many kinds,
Perceive you none that do arouse your pity
But the unconsider'd soldier?
    Palamon.   Yes; I pity
Decays where'er I find them; but such most
That, sweating in an honourable toil,
Are paid with ice to cool 'em.
    Arcite.   'Tis not this
I did begin to speak of; this is virtue
Of no respect in Thebes. I spake of Thebes,
How dangerous, if we will keep our honours,
It is for our residing; where every evil
Hath a good colour; where every seeming good's
A certain evil; where not to be even jump[3]
As they are here, were to be strangers, and
Such things to be mere monsters.
    Palamon.   It is in our power—
Unless we fear that apes can tutor 's — to

[1] Scorned.
[2] Refers to the cause of the Trojan war.   [3] Precisely.

Be masters of our manners. What need I
Affect another's gait, which is not catching
Where there is faith¹? or to be fond upon
Another's way of speech, when by mine own
I may be reasonably conceiv'd,² sav'd too,
Speaking it truly? Why am I bound
By any generous bond to follow him   50
Follows his tailor, haply so long until
The follow'd make pursuit? Or let me know
Why mine own barber is unbless'd, with him
My poor chin too, for 'tis not scissar'd just
To such a favourite's glass? What canon is there
That does command my rapier from my hip,
To dangle't in my hand, or to go tip-toe
Before the street be foul! Either I am
The fore-horse in the team, or I am none
That draw i' the sequent trace. These poor slight sores   60
Need not a plantain; that which rips my bosom,
Almost to the heart, 's —
   Arcite.   Our uncle Creon.
   Palamon.   He,
A most unbounded tyrant, whose successes
Makes heaven unfear'd, and villainy assur'd
Beyond its power there's nothing; almost puts
Faith in a fever, and deifies alone
Voluble chance; who only attributes
The faculties of other instruments
To his own nerves and act; commands men's service,
And what they win in't, boot and glory; one   70
That fears not to do harm, good dares not. Let
The blood of mine that's sib³ to him be suck'd

      ¹ Self-reliance.   ² Understood.   ³ Related to.

From me with leeches ! let them break and fall
Off me with that corruption !
    Arcite.   Clear-spirited cousin,
Let's leave his court, that we may nothing share
Of his loud infamy ; for our milk
Will relish of the pasture, and we must
Be vile or disobedient, not his kinsmen
In blood, unless in quality.
    Palamon.   Nothing truer !
I think the echoes of his shames have deaf'd   80
The ears of heavenly justice ; widows' cries
Descend again into their throats, and have not
Due audience of the gods. — Valerius !

            Enter VALERIUS.

    Valerius. The king calls for you ; yet be leaden-footed
Till his great rage be off him. Phœbus, when
He broke his whipstock and exclaim'd against
The horses of the sun,[1] but whisper'd, to [2]
The loudness of his fury.
    Palamon.   Small winds shake him ;
But what's the matter?
    Valerius. Theseus — who, where he threats, appals — hath sent   90
Deadly defiance to him, and pronounces
Ruin to Thebes ; who is at hand to seal
The promise of his wrath.
    Arcite.   Let him approach !
But that we fear the gods in him, he brings not
A jot of terror to us ; yet what man

    [1] Perhaps alludes to Phœbus's wrath after the death of Phaëthon.
    [2] Compared to.

Thirds his own worth — the case is each of ours —
When that his action's dregg'd with mind assur'd
'Tis bad he goes about?[1]
 Palamon.   Leave that unreason'd;
Our services stand now for Thebes, not Creon.
Yet to be neutral to him were dishonour,   100
Rebellious to oppose; therefore we must
With him stand to the mercy of our fate,
Who hath bounded our last minute.
 Arcite.   So we must. —
Is't said this war's afoot? or it shall be,
On fail of some condition?
 Valerius.   'Tis in motion;
The intelligence[2] of state came in the instant
With the defier.
 Palamon. Let's to the king, who, were he
A quarter carrier of that honour which
His enemy comes in, the blood we venture
Should be as for our health; which were not spent, 110
Rather laid out for purchase: but, alas,
Our hands advanc'd before our hearts, what will
The fall o' the stroke do damage?
 Arcite.   Let the event,
That never-erring arbitrator, tell us
When we know all ourselves; and let us follow
The becking of our chance.   [*Exeunt.*[3]

 [1] "What man can exert a third part of his powers when his mind is clogged with a consciousness that he fights in a bad cause?" — *Mason.*
 [2] Messenger; cf. *King John,* iv, 2, 116.
 [3] Of this scene *Spalding* says: "Its broken versification points out Shakespeare; the quaintness of some conceits is his; and several of the phrases and images have much of his pointedness, brevity, or obscurity. The scene, though not lofty in tone, does not want interest, and contains

SCENE III. — *Before the Gates of Athens.*

Enter PIRITHOUS, HIPPOLYTA, *and* EMILIA.

Pirithous. No further!
Hippolyta.   Sir, farewell! Repeat my wishes
To our great lord, of whose success I dare not
Make any timorous question; yet I wish him
Excess and overflow of power, an't might be,
To dare ill-dealing fortune. Speed to him;
Store [1] never hurts good governors.
    Pirithous.   Though I know
His ocean needs not my poor drops, yet they
Must yield their tribute there. — My precious maid,
Those best affections that the heavens infuse
In their best-temper'd pieces keep enthron'd   10
In your dear heart!
    Emilia.   Thanks, sir. Remember me
To our all-royal brother, for whose speed
The great Bellona I'll solicit; and
Since, in our terrene state, petitions are not
Without gifts understood, I'll offer to her
What I shall be advis'd she likes. Our hearts
Are in his army, in his tent.
    Hippolyta.   In's bosom!

some extremely original illustrations." *Hickson* thinks " that either Shakespeare and Fletcher wrote the scene in conjunction, or that it was originally written by Fletcher, and afterwards revised and partly re-written by Shakespeare." *Littledale* asks: " Does it not therefore appear more likely that the view put forward by Spalding, and upheld by Dyce, Skeat, and Swinburne — that Shakespeare was the first sketcher of the piece, Fletcher the ' padder '; that the play is ' gilt o'er-dusted,' rather than ' dust that is a little gilt' gives after all the true explanation of the mystery ? "

[1] Abundance of men or money.

We have been soldiers, and we cannot weep
When our friends don their helms or put to sea,
Or tell of babes broach'd on the lance, or women　　20
That have sod[1] their infants in — and after eat them —
The brine they wept at killing 'em; then if
You stay to see of us such spinsters, we
Should hold you here for ever.
　　Pirithous.　　　　　　　　Peace be to you,
As I pursue this war! which shall be then
Beyond further requiring.　　　　　　　　　[*Exit.*
　　Emilia.　　　　　　　How his longing
Follows his friend! Since his depart his sports,
Though craving seriousness and skill, pass'd slightly
His careless execution, where nor gain
Made him regard, or loss consider; but　　30
Playing one business in his hand, another
Directing in his head, his mind nurse equal
To these so differing twins. Have you observ'd him
Since our great lord departed?
　　Hippolyta.　　　　　　　With much labour,
And I did love him for't. They two have cabin'd
In many as dangerous as poor a corner,
Peril and want contending; they have skiff'd
Torrents, whose roaring tyranny and power
I' the least of these was dreadful; and they have
Fought out together, where death's self was lodg'd,　　40
Yet fate hath brought them off. Their knot of love
Tied, weav'd, entangled, with so true, so long,
And with a finger of so deep a cunning,
May be outworn, never undone. I think
Theseus cannot be umpire to himself,

[1] Seethed, boiled.

Cleaving his conscience into twain, and doing
Each side like justice, which he loves best.
  Emilia.   Doubtless
There is a best, and reason has no manners
To say it is not you. I was acquainted
Once with a time, when I enjoy'd a playfellow;   50
You were at wars when she the grave enrich'd,
Who made too proud the bed, took leave o' the moon —
Which then look'd pale at parting — when our count
Was each eleven.
  Hippolyta.   'Twas Flavina.
  Emilia.   Yes.
You talk of Pirithous' and Theseus' love :
Theirs has more ground, is more maturely season'd,
More buckled with strong judgment, and their needs
The one of th' other may be said to water
Their intertangled roots of love ; but I
And she I sigh and spoke of were things innocent,   60
Lov'd for we did, and, like the elements
That know not what nor why, yet do effect
Rare issues by their operance,[1] our souls
Did so to one another. What she lik'd,
Was then of me approv'd ; what not, condemn'd,
No more arraignment. The flower that I would pluck
And put between my breasts — then but beginning
To swell about the blossom — she would long
Till she had such another, and commit it
To the like innocent cradle, where phœnix-like   70
They died in perfume. On my head no toy[2]
But was her pattern ; her affections — pretty,
Though happily her careless wear — I follow'd

    [1] Operation.   [2] Head-dress.

For my most serious decking. Had mine ear
Stol'n some new air, or at adventure humm'd one
From musical coinage, why, it was a note
Whereon her spirits would sojourn — rather dwell on —
And sing it in her slumbers. This rehearsal —
Which, every innocent wots well, comes in
Like old importment's bastard — has this end,   80
That the true love 'tween maid and maid may be
More than in sex dividual.[1]
    Hippolyta.   You're out of breath;
And this high-speeded pace is but to say,
That you shall never, like the maid Flavina,
Love any that's call'd man.
    Emilia.   I am sure I shall not.
    Hippolyta. Now, alack, weak sister,
I must no more believe thee in this point —
Though in't I know thou dost believe thyself —
Than I will trust a sickly appetite,
That loathes even as it longs. But sure, my sister,   90
If I were ripe for your persuasion, you
Have said enough to shake me from the arm
Of the all-noble Theseus; for whose fortunes
I will now in and kneel, with great assurance,
That we, more than his Pirithous, possess
The high throne in his heart.
    Emilia.   I am not
Against your faith; yet I continue mine.[2]   *[Exeunt.*

1 " The end of this long relation, as every innocent is aware, comes in like the ' illegitimate conclusion ' of a long story told very consequentially." — *Littledale.*

2 This scene " has Shakespeare's stamp deeply cut upon it," and is " probably all his." — *Spalding.* " The friendship of Theseus and Pirithous becomes a natural introduction to the object of friendship in general, and

SCENE IV. *A Field before Thebes.*

Cornets. A battle struck within; then a retreat; then a flourish. Then enter THESEUS, *victor; the three* Queens *meet him and fall on their faces before him.*

1st Queen. To thee no star be dark!
2d Queen.   Both heaven and earth
Friend thee for ever!
3d Queen.   All the good that may
Be wish'd upon thy head, I cry amen to't!
Theseus. The impartial gods, who from the mounted heavens
View us their mortal herd, behold who err,
And in their time chastise. Go and find out
The bones of your dead lords, and honour them
With treble ceremony. Rather than a gap
Should be in their dear rites, we would supply't.
But those we will depute which shall invest   10
You in your dignities, and even each thing
Our haste does leave imperfect. So adieu,
And heaven's good eyes look on you!—What are those?
                    [*Exeunt* Queens.

female friendship in particular; and, in this light, the character of Emilia is shown so simple, so pure, yet so **fervent,** that we **justify** and account for her irresolution and inability to **decide between** the rivals, both of whom she admires without actually loving **either.** It is a scene, in fact, necessary to that perfection of character and **consistency** of purpose which but one writer of the age attained. Struck out, the play would still be intelligible, as no part of the action would thereby be lost; but Emilia would straightway sink into one of those conventional characters that strange circumstances throw into the power of the dramatist, and, judged by any other than his own peculiar standard, would certainly have little claim upon **our** respect." — *Hickson.*

Herald. Men of great quality, as may be judg'd
By their appointment; some of Thebes have told's
They are sisters' children, nephews to the king.
  Theseus. By the helm of Mars, I saw them in the war,
Like to a pair of lions smear'd with prey,
Make lanes in troops aghast; I fix'd my note
Constantly on them, for they were a mark   20
Worth a god's view   What was't that prisoner told me,
When I inquir'd their names?
  Herald.   We learn, they're call'd
Arcite and Palamon.
  Theseus.   'Tis right; those, those.
They are not dead?
  Herald. Nor in a state of life: had they been taken
When their last hurts were given, 'twas possible
They might have been recover'd; yet they breathe,
And have the name of men.
  Theseus.   Then like men use 'em;
The very lees of such, millions of rates
Exceed the wine of others.   All our surgeons   30
Convent in their behoof; our richest balms,
Rather than niggard, waste: their lives concern us
Much more than Thebes is worth.   Rather than have 'em
Freed of this plight, and in their morning state,
Sound and at liberty, I would 'em dead;
But, forty thousand fold, we had rather have 'em
Prisoners to us than death.   Bear 'em speedily
From our kind air — to them unkind — and minister
What man to man may do; for our sake, more:
Since I have known fight's fury, friends' behests,   40
Love's provocations, zeal, a mistress' task,
Desire of liberty, a fever, madness,

Hath set a mark — which nature could not reach to
Without some imposition, — sickness in will,
Or wrestling strength in reason. For our love
And great Apollo's mercy, all our best
Their best skill tender![1] — Lead into the city;
Where having bound things scatter'd, we will post
To Athens 'fore our army. [*Flourish. Exeunt.*

SCENE V. — *Another Part of the Field.*

Enter the Queens *with the hearses of their husbands in a funeral solemnity, etc.*

Song.

Urns and odours bring away!
Vapours, sighs, darken the day!

---

[1] This corrupt passage has puzzled all the commentators. *Skeat* says: "It is clear that *friends* should be a genitive case, coupled as it is with *Love's provocations;* and the suggestion *fight's fury* is a great improvement upon the *fright's fury* of the old editions. The introduction of *in* after *zeal*, as proposed by Mr. Dyce, is also a happy thought. But there we may as well stop. I understand the word *that* before *Hath*, nothing being commoner in our dramatists than the omission of the relative: and I retain *Hath*, without altering it, as some have done, to *Have*. I interpret it thus: 'For I have known the fury of fight, the requisitions of friends, the provocations of love, the zeal employed in executing a mistress's task, or the desire of liberty — to be (or, to amount to) a fever or a madness, which has proposed an aim (for endeavours) which the man's natural strength could not attain to, without at least some forcing, or some fainting of the will, or some severe struggle in the mind.' This is at least as good as any previous explanations, and further discussion of so difficult a passage would be useless. *Imposition* means demand or requirement, in an excessive degree." *Littledale* adds: "Theseus directs that the prisoners shall be removed from all sights that might be suggestive of their captivity and so hinder their recovery, since he knows that, among other causes, *desire of liberty* hath sometimes produced a degree of mental apathy or delirium (*set a mark of sickness of will or wrestling strength in reason*) which could only be combated by practising some deception (*nature could not reach to*, etc.)."

> *Our dole*[1] *more deadly looks than dying;*
> *Balms, and gums, and heavy cheers,*[2]
> *Sacred vials fill'd with tears,*
> *And clamours through the wild air flying!*
> *Come, all sad and solemn shows,*
> *That are quick-eyed pleasure's foes!*
> *We convent*[3] *nought else but woes.*
>   *We convent,* etc. 10

3d Queen. This funeral path brings to your household's grave.
Joy seize on you again! Peace sleep with him!
  2d Queen. And this to yours!
  1st Queen.   Yours this way! Heavens lend
A thousand differing ways to one sure end!
  3d Queen. This world's a city full of straying streets,
And death's the market-place, where each one meets.[4]
                                [*Exeunt severally.*[5]

---

[1] Sorrow.   [2] Sad mien.   [3] Bring together.
[4] An old epitaph in the churchyard of Abernethy, Scotland, runs thus:—

> " The world's a city
> Full of streets,
> And death's a market
> That every one meets;
> But if life were a thing
> That money could buy,
> The poor could not live
> And the rich would not die."

[5] *Littledale* doubts that Shakespeare wrote this scene.

ACT II.

SCENE I.[1] — *Athens. A Garden, with a Castle in the Background.*

Enter Gaoler *and* Wooer.

Gaoler. I may depart with little, while I live; something I may cast to you, not much. Alas, the prison I keep, though it be for great ones, yet they seldom come; before one salmon, you shall take a number of minnows. I am given out to be better lined than it can appear to me report is a true speaker; I would I were really that I am delivered to be! Marry, what I have — be it what it will — I will assure upon my daughter at the day of my death.

Wooer. Sir, I demand no more than your own offer; and I will estate your daughter in what I have promised. 10

Gaoler. Well, we will talk more of this when the solemnity is past. But have you a full promise of her? When that shall be seen, I tender my consent.

Wooer. I have, sir. Here she comes.

Enter Gaoler's Daughter, *with rushes.*

Gaoler. Your friend and I have chanced to name you here, upon the old business: but no more of that now. So soon as the court-hurry is over, we will have an end of it. I' the mean time, look tenderly to the two prisoners. I can tell you they are princes. 19

---

[1] *Hickson, Coleridge* and *Littledale* attribute this scene to Shakespeare; *Weber, Spalding,* and *Dyce* to Fletcher.

SCENE I.] THE TWO NOBLE KINSMEN. 391

Daughter. These strewings are for their chamber. 'Tis pity they are in prison, and 'twere pity they should be out. I do think they have patience to make any adversity ashamed; the prison itself is proud of 'em, and they have all the world in their chamber.

Gaoler. They are famed to be a pair of absolute men.

Daughter. By my troth, I think fame but stammers 'em; they stand a grise[1] above the reach of report.

Gaoler. I heard them reported in the battle to be the only doers.

Daughter. Nay, most likely; for they are noble sufferers. I marvel how they would have looked, had they been victors, that with such a constant nobility enforce a freedom out of bondage, making misery their mirth, and affliction a toy to jest at. 34

Gaoler. Do they so?

Daughter. It seems to me, they have no more sense of their captivity, than I of ruling Athens; they eat well, look merrily, discourse of many things, but nothing of their own restraint and disasters. Yet sometime a divided sigh, martyred as 'twere i' the deliverance, will break from one of them; when the other presently gives it so sweet a rebuke, that I could wish myself a sigh to be so chid, or at least a sigher to be comforted. 43

Wooer. I never saw 'em.

Gaoler. The duke himself came privately in the night, and so did they; what the reason of it is, I know not. — (PALAMON *and* ARCITE *appear at a window, above.*) Look, yonder they are! that's Arcite looks out.

Daughter. No, sir, no; that's Palamon. Arcite is the lower of the twain; you may perceive a part of him. 50

[1] Step.

Gaoler. Go to, leave your pointing! They would not make us their object; out of their sight!

Daughter. It is a holiday to look on them! Lord, the difference of men! [*Exeunt.*

SCENE II.[1] — *A Room in the Prison.*

Enter PALAMON *and* ARCITE.

Palamon. How do you, noble cousin?
Arcite.   How do you, sir?
Palamon. Why, strong enough to laugh at misery,
And bear the chance of war yet. We are prisoners
I fear for ever, cousin.
    Arcite.   I believe it;
And to that destiny have patiently
Laid up my hour to come.
    Palamon.   O cousin Arcite,
Where is Thebes now? where is our noble country?
Where are our friends and kindreds? Never more
Must we behold those comforts; never see
The hardy youths strive for the games of honour,   10
Hung with the painted favours of their ladies,
Like tall ships under sail; then start amongst 'em,
And, as an east wind, leave 'em all behind us
Like lazy clouds, whilst Palamon and Arcite,
Even in the wagging of a wanton leg,
Outstripp'd the people's praises, won the garlands,
Ere they have time to wish 'em ours. O, never
Shall we two exercise, like twins of honour,

[1] *Weber, Dyce,* and *Skeat* make no separation between this scene and the preceding; but the Quarto does.

Our arms again, and feel our fiery horses
Like proud seas under us ! Our good swords now—   20
Better the red-eyed god of war ne'er wore —
Ravish'd[1] our sides, like age, must run to rust,
And deck the temples of those gods that hate us ;
These hands shall never draw 'em out like lightning,
To blast whole armies, more !
   Arcite.   No, Palamon,
Those hopes are prisoners with us : here we are,
And here the graces of our youths must wither,
Like a too-timely spring ; here age must find us,
And, which is heaviest, Palamon, unmarried ;
The sweet embraces of a loving wife,   30
Loaden with kisses, arm'd with thousand Cupids,
Shall never clasp our necks ; no issue know us,
No figures of ourselves shall we e'er see,
To glad our age, and like young eagles teach 'em
Boldly to gaze against bright arms, and say,
" Remember what your fathers were, and conquer ! "
The fair-eyed maids shall weep our banishments,
And in their songs curse ever-blinded Fortune,
Till she for shame see what a wrong she has done
To youth and nature. This is all our world ;   40
We shall know nothing here but one another,
Hear nothing but the clock that tells our woes ;
The vine shall grow, but we shall never see it ;
Summer shall come, and with her all delights,
But dead-cold winter must inhabit here still.
   Palamon. 'Tis too true, Arcite. To our Theban hounds,
That shook the aged forest with their echoes,
No more now must we halloo ; no more shake

[1] Torn from.

Our pointed javelins, whilst the angry swine
Flies like a Parthian quiver from our rages, 50
Stuck with our well-steel'd darts! All valiant uses —
The food and nourishment of noble minds —
In us two here shall perish; we shall die —
Which is the curse of honour — lazily,
Children of grief and ignorance.
  Arcite.   Yet, cousin,
Even from the bottom of these miseries,
From all that fortune can inflict upon us,
I see two comforts rising, two mere blessings,
If the gods please to hold here, — a brave patience,
And the enjoying of our griefs together. 60
Whilst Palamon is with me, let me perish
If I think this our prison.
  Palamon.   Certainly,
'Tis a main goodness, cousin, that our fortunes
Were twin'd together: 'tis most true, two souls
Put in two noble bodies, let 'em suffer
The gall of hazard, so they grow together,
Will never sink; they must not; say they could,
A willing man dies sleeping, and all's done.
  Arcite. Shall we make worthy uses of this place,
That all men hate so much?
  Palamon.   How, gentle cousin? 70
  Arcite. Let's think this prison holy sanctuary,
To keep us from corruption of worse men.
We are young, and yet desire the ways of honour,
That liberty and common conversation,
The poison of pure spirits, might, like women,
Woo us to wander from. What worthy blessing
Can be, but our imaginations
May make it ours? and here being thus together,

We are an endless mine to one another;
We are one another's wife, ever begetting   80
New births of love; we are father, friends, acquaintance;
We are, in one another, families;
I am your heir, and you are mine; this place
Is our inheritance; no hard oppressor
Dare take this from us; here, with a little patience,
We shall live long, and loving; no surfeits seek us;
The hand of war hurts none here, nor the seas
Swallow their youth. Were we at liberty,
A wife might part us lawfully, or business;
Quarrels consume us; envy of ill men   90
Grave¹ our acquaintance; I might sicken, cousin,
Where you should never know it, and so perish
Without your noble hand to close mine eyes,
Or prayers to the gods: a thousand chances,
Were we from hence, would sever us.
  Palamon.   You have made me—
I thank you, cousin Arcite — almost wanton
With my captivity; what a misery
It is to live abroad, and everywhere!
'Tis like a beast, methinks! I find the court here,
I am sure, a more content; and all those pleasures,   100
That woo the wills of men to vanity,
I see through now; and am sufficient
To tell the world, 'tis but a gaudy shadow,
That old Time, as he passes by, takes with him.
What had we been, old in the court of Creon,
Where sin is justice, lust and ignorance
The virtues of the great ones! Cousin Arcite,
Had not the loving gods found this place for us.

¹ Bury.

We had died as they do, ill old men, unwept,
And had their epitaphs, the peoples' curses. 110
Shall I say more?
   Arcite.   I would hear you still.
   Palamon.   Ye shall.
Is there record of any two that lov'd
Better than we do, Arcite?
   Arcite.   Sure, there cannot.
   Palamon. I do not think it possible our friendship
Should ever leave us.
   Arcite.   Till our deaths it cannot;
And after death our spirits shall be led
To those that love eternally. Speak on, sir.

        Enter EMILIA *and* Waiting-woman, *below.*

   Emilia. This garden has a world of pleasures in't.
What flower is this?
   Waiting-woman. 'Tis call'd narcissus, madam.
   Emilia. That was a fair boy, certain, but a fool 120
To love himself; were there not maids enough?
   Arcite. Pray, forward.
   Palamon.   Yes.
   Emilia.   Or were they all hard-hearted?
   Waiting-woman. They could not be to one so fair.
   Emilia.   Thou would'st not?
   Waiting-woman. I think I should not, madam.
   Emilia.   That's a good wench;
But take heed to your kindness though!
   Waiting-woman.   Why, madam?
   Emilia. Men are mad things.
   Arcite.   Will ye go forward, cousin?
   Emilia. Canst thou not work such flowers in silk, wench?

Waiting-woman.   Yes.
Emilia. I'll have a gown full of 'em; and of these;
This is a pretty colour: will't not do
Rarely upon a skirt, wench?
Waiting-woman.   Dainty, madam.   130
Arcite. Cousin! Cousin! How do you, sir? Why, Pala-
    mon!
Palamon. Never till now I was in prison, Arcite.
Arcite. Why, what's the matter, man?
Palamon.   Behold, and wonder!
By heaven, she is a goddess!
Arcite.   Ha!
Palamon.   Do reverence!
She is a goddess, Arcite!
Emilia.   Of all flowers
Methinks a rose is best.
Waiting-woman.   Why, gentle madam?
Emilia. It is the very emblem of a maid;
For when the west wind courts her gently,
How modestly she blows, and paints the sun
With her chaste blushes! when the north comes near her,
Rude and impatient, then, like chastity,   141
She locks her beauties in her bud again,[1]
And leaves him to base briers.
Arcite. She is wondrous fair!
Palamon.   She is all the beauty extant!
Emilia. The sun grows high; let's walk in. Keep these
    flowers;
We'll see how near art can come near their colours.
                    [*Exit with* Waiting-woman.
Palamon. What think you of this beauty?

[1] Cf. Keats's "As though a rose should shut, and be a bud again."

Arcite.   'Tis a rare one.
Palamon. Is't but a rare one?
Arcite.   Yes, a matchless beauty.
Palamon. Might not a man well lose himself, and love her?
Arcite. I cannot tell what you have done; I have,   150
Beshrew mine eyes for't! Now I feel my shackles.
Palamon. You love her then?
Arcite.   Who would not?
Palamon.   And desire her?
Arcite. Before my liberty.
Palamon.   I saw her first.
Arcite. That's nothing.
Palamon.   But it shall be.
Arcite. I saw her too.
Palamon.   Yes; but you must not love her.
Arcite. I will not, as you do, to worship her,
As she is heavenly and a blessed goddess:
I love her as a woman, to enjoy her;
So both may love.
Palamon.   You shall not love at all.
Arcite. Not love at all? who shall deny me?   160
Palamon. I that first saw her; I that took possession
First with mine eyes of all those beauties in her
Reveal'd to mankind! If thou lovest her,
Or entertain'st a hope to blast my wishes,
Thou art a traitor, Arcite, and a fellow
False as thy title to her; friendship, blood,
And all the ties between us I disclaim,
If thou once think upon her!
Arcite.   Yes, I love her;
And if the lives of all my name lay on it,

I must do so; I love her with my soul. 170
If that will lose ye, farewell, Palamon!
I say again, I love; and, in loving her, maintain
I am as worthy and as free a lover,
And have as just a title to her beauty,
As any Palamon, or any living
That is a man's son.
    Palamon.   Have I call'd thee friend?
    Arcite. Yes, and have found me so. Why are you mov'd
        thus?
Let me deal coldly with you: am not I
Part of your blood, part of your soul? you have told me
That I was Palamon, and you were Arcite. 180
    Palamon. Yes.
    Arcite.   Am not I liable to those affections,
Those joys, griefs, angers, fears, my friend shall suffer?
    Palamon. Ye may be.
    Arcite.   Why then would you deal so cunningly,
So strangely, so unlike a noble kinsman,
To love alone? Speak truly; do you think me
Unworthy of her sight?
    Palamon.   No; but unjust
If thou pursue that sight.
    Arcite.   Because another
First sees the enemy, shall I stand still,
And let mine honour down, and never charge?
    Palamon. Yes, if he be but one.
    Arcite.   But say that one 190
Had rather combat me?
    Palamon.   Let that one say so,
And use thy freedom; else, if thou pursuest her,
Be as that cursed man that hates his country,

A branded villain!
    Arcite.   You are mad.
    Palamon.   I must be,
Till thou art worthy, Arcite; it concerns me;
And, in this madness, if I hazard thee
And take thy life, I deal but truly.
    Arcite.   Fie, sir!
You play the child extremely: I will love her,
I must, I ought to do so, and I dare;
And all this justly.
    Palamon.   O, that now, that now,   200
Thy false self and thy friend had but this fortune,
To be one hour at liberty, and grasp
Our good swords in our hands! I'd quickly teach thee
What 'twere to filch affection from another!
Thou art baser in it than a cutpurse!
Put but thy head out of this window more,
And, as I have a soul, I'll nail thy life to't!
    Arcite. Thou dar'st not, fool; thou canst not; thou art
        feeble.
Put my head out! I'll throw my body out,
And leap the garden, when I see her next,   210
And pitch between her arms, to anger thee.
    Palamon. No more! the keeper's coming; I shall live
To knock thy brains out with my shackles.
    Arcite.   Do!

                Enter Gaoler.

    Gaoler. By your leave, gentlemen.
    Palamon.   Now, honest keeper?
    Gaoler. Lord Arcite, you must presently to the duke;
The cause I know not yet.

SCENE II.] THE TWO NOBLE KINSMEN. 401

Arcite. I am ready, keeper.
Gaoler. Prince Palamon, I must awhile bereave you
Of your fair cousin's company. [*Exit with* ARCITE.
Palamon. And me too,
Even when you please, of life. — Why is he sent for?
It may be, he shall marry her; he's goodly, 220
And like enough the duke hath taken notice
Both of his blood and body. But his falsehood!
Why should a friend be treacherous? If that
Get him a wife so noble and so fair,
Let honest men ne'er love again! Once more
I would but see this fair one. — Blessed garden,
And fruit and flowers more blessed, that still blossom
As her bright eyes shine on ye! Would I were,
For all the fortune of my life hereafter,
Yon little tree, yon blooming apricock![1] 230
How I would spread, and fling my wanton arms
In at her window! I would bring her fruit
Fit for the gods to feed on; youth and pleasure,
Still as she tasted, should be doubled on her;
And if she be not heavenly, I would make her
So near the gods in nature, they should fear her;
And then I am sure she would love me. —

Re-enter Gaoler.

How now, keeper!
Where's Arcite?
Gaoler. Banish'd. Prince Pirithous
Obtain'd his liberty; but never more,
Upon his oath and life, must he set foot 240
Upon this kingdom.

[1] Apricot.

Palamon. He's a blessed man!
He shall see Thebes again, and call to arms
The bold young men that, when he bids 'em charge,
Fall on like fire. Arcite shall have a fortune,
If he dare make himself a worthy lover,
Yet in the field to strike a battle for her;
And if he lose her then, he's a cold coward.
How bravely may he bear himself to win her,
If he be noble Arcite, thousand ways!
Were I at liberty, I would do things 250
Of such a virtuous greatness that this lady,
This blushing virgin, should take manhood to her,
And seek to ravish me!
   Gaoler. My lord, for you
I have this charge too —
   Palamon. To discharge my life?
   Gaoler. No; but from this place to remove your lordship;
The windows are too open.
   Palamon. Devils take 'em,
That are so envious to me! Prithee, kill me!
   Gaoler. And hang for't afterward?
   Palamon. By this good light,
Had I a sword, I'd kill thee!
   Gaoler. Why, my lord?
   Palamon. Thou bring'st such pelting[1] scurvy news continually, 260
Thou art not worthy life! I will not go.
   Gaoler. Indeed you must, my lord.
   Palamon. May I see the garden?
   Gaoler. No.

[1] Paltry, contemptible.

Palamon. Then I am resolv'd I will not go.
Gaoler. I must
Constrain you then; and, for you are dangerous,
I'll clap more irons on you.
Palamon. Do, good keeper!
I'll shake 'em so, ye shall not sleep;
I'll make ye a new morris![1] Must I go?
Gaoler. There is no remedy.
Palamon. Farewell, kind window!
May rude wind never hurt thee!—O my lady,
If ever thou hast felt what sorrow was, 270
Dream how I suffer!—Come, now bury me. [*Exeunt.*[2]

SCENE III. — *The Country near Athens.*

Enter ARCITE.

Arcite. Banish'd the kingdom? 'Tis a benefit,
A mercy I must thank 'em for; but banish'd
The free enjoying of that face I die for,
O,'twas a studied punishment, a death
Beyond imagination! such a vengeance
That, were I old and wicked, all my sins
Could never pluck upon me.—Palamon,
Thou hast the start now; thou shalt stay and see
Her bright eyes break each morning 'gainst thy window,
And let in life into thee; thou shalt feed 10
Upon the sweetness of a noble beauty,
That nature ne'er exceeded, nor ne'er shall.
Good gods, what happiness has Palamon!

[1] Morris-dance.
[2] The critics generally assign this scene and the rest of Act ii to Fletcher.

Twenty to one, he'll come to speak to her;
And, if she be as gentle as she's fair,
I know she's his; he has a tongue will tame
Tempests, and make the wild rocks wanton. Come what
    can come,
The worst is death; I will not leave the kingdom.
I know mine own is but a heap of ruins,
And no redress there; if I go, he has her.   20
I am resolv'd; another shape shall make me,[1]
Or end my fortunes; either way, I'm happy:
I'll see her, and be near her, or no more.

Enter four Countrymen; *one with a garland before them.*

1st Countryman. My masters, I'll be there, that's certain.
2d Countryman. And I'll be there.
3d Countryman.   And I.
4th Countryman. Why then, have with ye, boys, 'tis but
    a chiding;
Let the plough play to-day! I'll tickle't out
Of the jades' tails to-morrow!
    1st Countryman.   I am sure
To have my wife as jealous as a turkey:
But that's all one; I'll go through, let her mumble.   30
    3d Countryman. Do we all hold[2] against the Maying?
    4th Countryman. Hold! what should ail us?
    3d Countryman.   Arcas will be there.
    2d Countryman. And Sennois,
And Rycas; and three better lads ne'er danc'd
Under green tree; and ye know what wenches, ha!
But will the dainty domine, the schoolmaster,

---

[1] By assuming a disguise I shall succeed.
[2] Hold to an **agreement**.

Keep touch,[1] do you think? for he does all, ye know.
  3d Countryman. He'll eat a horn-book,[2] ere he fail;
    go to!
The matter's too far driven between
Him and the tanner's daughter, to let slip now; 40
And she must see the duke, and she must dance too.
  4th Countryman. Shall we be lusty?
  2d Countryman.   Here I'll be,
And there I'll be, for our town; and here again,
And there again! Ha, boys, heigh for the weavers![3]
  1st Countryman. This must be done i' the woods.
  4th Countryman.   O, pardon me!
  2d Countryman. By any means; our thing of learning
    says so;
Where he himself will edify the duke
Most parlously[4] in our behalfs: he's excellent i' the woods;
Bring him to th' plains, his learning makes no cry.
  3d Countryman. We'll see the sports; then every man
    to's tackle! 50
And, sweet companions, let's rehearse by any means,
Before the ladies see us, and do sweetly,
And God knows what may come on't.
  4th Countryman.   Content; the sports
Once ended, we'll perform. Away, boys, and hold!
  Arcite. By your leaves, honest friends; pray you, whither
    go you?

  [1] Keep his appointment; a phrase of doubtful origin. Nicholson says that it probably came from the custom of *shaking hands* on a bargain or agreement. Cf. the old word *handfast.*
  [2] The child's primer, which at first was a single leaf, containing the Lord's Prayer and alphabet, set in a frame of wood, and covered with horn to keep it from being soiled or torn.
  [3] "Hurrah for the singers!" Weavers excelled in singing.
  [4] Amazingly.

4th Countryman. Whither? why, what a question's that!
Arcite. Yes, 'tis a question
To me that know not.
3d Countryman. To the games, my friend.
2d Countryman. Where were you bred, you know it not?
Arcite. Not far, sir.
Are there such games to-day?
1st Countryman. Yes, marry, are there;
And such as you ne'er saw: the duke himself
Will be in person there.
Arcite. What pastimes are they?
2d Countryman. Wrestling and running. — 'Tis a pretty
fellow.
3d Countryman. Thou wilt not go along?
Arcite. Not yet, sir.
4th Countryman. Well, sir,
Take your own time. — Come, boys!
1st Countryman. My mind misgives me
This fellow has a vengeance trick o' the hip;[1]
Mark, how his body's made for't!
2d Countryman. I'll be hang'd though
If he dare venture; hang him, plum-porridge!
He wrestle? He roast eggs![2] Come, let's be gone, lads.
[*Exeunt* Countrymen.
Arcite. This is an offer'd opportunity
I durst not wish for. Well I could have wrestled,
The best men call'd it excellent; and run
Swifter than wind upon a field of corn,
Curling the wealthy ears, e'er flew. I'll venture,

[1] In wrestling.
[2] A contemptuous expression, intimating that the rustic thought *Arcite* good for nothing.

And in some poor disguise be there; who knows
Whether my brows may not be girt with garlands,
And happiness prefer me to a place
Where I may ever dwell in sight of her? [*Exit*

SCENE IV. — *Athens. A Room in the Prison.*

Enter Gaoler's Daughter.

Daughter. Why should I love this gentleman? 'Tis odds
He never will affect[1] me; I am base,
My father the mean keeper of his prison,
And he a prince: to marry him is hopeless,
To love him else is witless. Out upon't!
What pushes are we wenches driven to,
When fifteen once has found us! First, I saw him;
I, seeing, thought he was a goodly man;
He has as much to please a woman in him —
If he please to bestow it so — as ever   10
These eyes yet look'd on: next, I pitied him;
And so would any young wench, o' my conscience,
That ever dream'd, or vow'd her whole affection
To a young handsome man: then, I lov'd him!
Extremely lov'd him, infinitely lov'd him!
And yet he had a cousin, fair as he too;
But in my heart was Palamon, and there,
Lord, what a coil he keeps! To hear him
Sing in an evening, what a heaven it is!
And yet his songs are sad ones. Fairer spoken   20
Was never gentleman; when I come in
To bring him water in a morning, first

[1] Love.

He bows his noble body, then salutes me thus:
"Fair gentle maid, good morrow! may thy goodness
Get thee a happy husband!" Once, he kiss'd me;
I lov'd my lips the better ten days after:
Would he would do so every day! He grieves much,
And me as much to see his misery.
What should I do, to make him know I love him?
For I would fain possess him: say I ventur'd   30
To set him free? what says the law then?
Thus much for law, or kindred! I will do it,
And this night or to-morrow he shall love me.   [*Exit.*

SCENE V. — *An Open Place in Athens. A Short Flourish
of Cornets, and Shouts within.*

Enter THESEUS, HIPPOLYTA, PIRITHOUS, EMILIA; ARCITE,
disguised, wearing a garland; and Countrymen.

Theseus. You have done worthily; I have not seen,
Since Hercules, a man of tougher sinews.
Whate'er you are, you run the best and wrestle,
That these times can allow.
   Arcite.   I am proud to please you.
   Theseus. What country bred you?
   Arcite.   This; but far off, prince.
   Theseus. Are you a gentleman?
   Arcite.   My father said so,
And to those gentle uses gave me life.
   Theseus. Are you his heir?
   Arcite.   His youngest, sir.
   Theseus.   Your father,
Sure, is a happy sire, then. What proves you?

Arcite. A little of all noble qualities: 10
I could have kept a hawk, and well have halloo'd
To a deep cry of dogs; I dare not praise
My feat in horsemanship, yet they that knew me
Would say it was my best piece; last, and greatest,
I would be thought a soldier.
 Theseus.   You are perfect.
 Pirithous. Upon my soul, a proper man!
 Emilia.   He is so.
 Pirithous. How do you like him, lady?
 Hippolyta.   I admire him;
I have not seen so young a man so noble,
If he say true, of his sort.
 Emilia.   Believe,
His mother was a wondrous handsome woman; 20
His face methinks goes that way.
 Hippolyta.   But his body
And fiery mind illustrate a brave father.
 Pirithous. Mark how his virtue, like a hidden sun,
Breaks through his baser garments!
 Hippolyta.   He's well got, sure.
 Theseus. What made you seek this place, sir?
 Arcite.   Noble Theseus,
To purchase name, and do my ablest service
To such a well-found wonder as thy worth;
For only in thy court, of all the world,
Dwells fair-eyed Honour.
 Pirithous. All his words are worthy.
 Theseus. Sir, we are much indebted to your travail, 30
Nor shall you loose your wish. — Pirithous,
Dispose of this fair gentleman.
 Pirithous.   Thanks, Theseus. —

Whate'er you are, you're mine; and I shall give you
To a most noble service, — to this lady,
This bright young virgin: pray observe her goodness.
You've honour'd her fair birthday with your virtues,
And, as your due, you're hers; kiss her fair hand, sir.
    Arcite. Sir, you're a noble giver. — Dearest beauty,
Thus let me seal my vow'd faith! when your servant —
Your most unworthy creature — but offends you,   40
Command him die, he shall.
    Emilia.   That were too cruel.
If you deserve well, sir, I shall soon see't:
You're mine; and somewhat better than your rank
I'll use you.
    Pirithous. I'll see you furnish'd: and because you say
You are a horseman, I must needs entreat you
This afternoon to ride; but 'tis a rough one.
    Arcite. I like him better, prince; I shall not then
Freeze in my saddle.
    Theseus.   Sweet, you must be ready —
And you, Emilia — and you, friend — and all —   50
To-morrow, by the sun, to do observance
To flow'ry May, in Dian's wood. — Wait well, sir,
Upon your mistress! — Emily, I hope
He shall not go afoot.
    Emilia.   That were a shame, sir,
While I have horses. — Take your choice; and what
You want at any time, let me but know it.
If you serve faithfully, I dare assure you
You'll find a loving mistress.
    Arcite.   If I do not,
Let me find that my father ever hated, —
Disgrace and blows!

Theseus. Go, lead the way; you've won it; 60
It shall be so; you shall receive all dues
Fit for the honour you have won; 'twere wrong else.—
Sister, beshrew my heart, you have a servant,
That, if I were a woman, would be master;
But you are wise.
   Emilia.   I hope too wise for that, sir.
                       [*Flourish. Exeunt.*

SCENE VI.—*Before the Prison.*

Enter Gaoler's Daughter.

Daughter. Let all the dukes and all the devils roar,
He is at liberty! I've ventur'd for him;
And out I have brought him to a little wood
A mile hence. I have sent him where a cedar,
Higher than all the rest, spreads like a plane
Fast by a brook; and there he shall keep close,
Till I provide him files and food, for yet
His iron bracelets are not off. O Love,
What a stout-hearted child thou art! My father
Durst better have endur'd cold iron than done it. 10
I love him beyond love and beyond reason,
Or wit, or safety. I have made him know it:
I care not; I am desperate. If the law
Find me, and then condemn me for't, some wenches,
Some honest-hearted maids, will sing my dirge,
And tell to memory my death was noble,
Dying almost a martyr. That way he takes,
I purpose, is my way too; sure he cannot
Be so unmanly as to leave me here!

If he do, maids will not so easily   20
Trust men again : and yet he has not thank'd me
For what I have done ; no, not so much as kiss'd me ;
And that, methinks, is not so well ; nor scarcely
Could I persuade him to become a freeman,
He made such scruples of the wrong he did
To me and to my father. Yet, I hope,
When he considers more, this love of mine
Will take more root within him : let him do
What he will with me, so he use me kindly !
For use me so he shall, or I'll proclaim him,   30
And to his face, no man. I'll presently
Provide him necessaries,[1] and pack my clothes up,
And where there is a patch of ground I'll venture,
So he be with me ; by him, like a shadow,
I'll ever dwell. Within this hour the whoo-bub[2]
Will be all o'er the prison ; I am then
Kissing the man they look for. — Farewell, father !
Get many more such prisoners and such daughters,
And shortly you may keep yourself. Now to him ! [*Exit*

[1] Pronounced *nessaries*, as in *Julius Cæsar*, ii, 1, 178.
[2] Hubbub.

ACT III.

SCENE I. — *A Forest. Cornets in Sundry Places. Noise and Hallooing, as of People a-Maying.*

Enter ARCITE.

Arcite. The duke has lost Hippolyta; each took
A several laund.[1] This is a solemn rite
They owe bloom'd May, and the Athenians pay it
To the heart of ceremony. — O queen Emilia,
Fresher than May, sweeter
Than her gold buttons on the boughs, or all
Th' enamell'd knacks[2] o' the mead or garden! yea,
We challenge too the bank of any nymph,
That makes the stream seem flowers; thou, O jewel
O' the wood, o' the world, hast likewise bless'd a place   10
With thy sole presence! In thy rumination
That I, poor man, might eftsoons[3] come between,
And chop[4] on some cold thought! — Thrice blessed chance,
To drop on such a mistress, expectation
Most guiltless on't! Tell me, O lady Fortune —
Next after Emily my sovereign — how far
I may be proud. She takes strong note of me,
Hath made me near her, and this beauteous morn,

[1] Lawn, glade; *several,* separate.
[2] Ornaments.   [3] Soon after.
[4] "Exchange, make an exchange. Arcite means, Oh! that I might, whilst thou art meditating, come between, soon after some cold or sober thought, and make an exchange, by changing those cold thoughts to thoughts of love!" — *Skeat.*

The prim'st of all the year, presents me with
A brace of horses; two such steeds might well   20
Be by a pair of kings back'd, in a field
That their crowns' titles tried.   Alas, alas,
Poor cousin Palamon, poor prisoner! thou
So little dream'st upon my fortune, that
Thou think'st thyself the happier thing, to be
So near Emilia!   Me thou deem'st at Thebes,
And therein wretched, although free; but if
Thou knew'st my mistress breath'd on me, and that
I ear'd her language, liv'd in her eye, O coz,
What passion would enclose thee!

Enter PALAMON *out of a bush with his shackles; he bends his fist at* ARCITE.

  Palamon.   Traitor kinsman!   30
Thou shouldst perceive my passion, if these signs
Of prisonment were off me, and this hand
But owner of a sword!   By all oaths in one,
I, and the justice of my love, would make thee
A confess'd traitor!   O thou most perfidious
That ever gently look'd! the void'st of honour
That e'er bore gentle token! falsest cousin
That ever blood made kin! call'st thou her thine?
I'll prove it in my shackles, with these hands
Void of appointment,¹ that thou liest, and art   40
A very thief in love, a chaffy lord,
Nor worth the name of villain!   Had I a sword,
And these house-clogs away—
  Arcite.   Dear cousin Palamon—
  Palamon.   Cozener Arcite, give me language such

     ¹ Equipment for fighting.

As thou hast show'd me feat!
 Arcite.   Not finding in
The circuit of my breast any gross stuff
To form me like your blazon, holds me to
This gentleness of answer: 'tis in your passion
That thus mistakes; the which, to you being enemy,
Cannot to me be kind. Honour and honesty   50
I cherish and depend on, howsoe'er
You skip them in me, and with them, fair coz,
I'll maintain my proceedings. Pray be pleas'd
To show in generous terms your griefs, since that
Your question's with your equal, who professes
To clear his own way with the mind and sword
Of a true gentleman.
 Palamon.   That thou durst, Arcite!
 Arcite. My coz, my coz, you have been well advértis'd
How much I dare; you've seen me use my sword
Against the advice of fear. Sure, of another   60
You would not hear me doubted, but your silence
Should break out, though i' the sanctuary.
 Palamon.   Sir,
I've seen you move in such a place, which well
Might justify your manhood; you were call'd
A good knight and a bold: but the whole week's not fair,
If any day it rain. Their valiant temper
Men lose when they incline to treachery;
And then they fight like compell'd bears, would fly
Were they not tied.
 Arcite.   Kinsman, you might as well
Speak this, and act it in your glass, as to   70
His ear which now disdains you.
 Palamon.   Come up to me!

Quit me of these cold gyves,¹ give me a sword,
Though it be rusty, and the charity
Of one meal lend me ; come before me then,
A good sword in thy hand, and do but say
That Emily is thine, I will forgive
The trespass thou hast done me, yea, my life,
If then thou carry't ; and brave souls in shades,
That have died manly, which will seek of me
Some news from earth, they shall get none but this, &c
That thou art brave and noble.
  Arcite.   Be content ;
Again betake you to your hawthorn-house.
With counsel of the night, I will be here
With wholesome viands ; these impediments
Will I file off ; you shall have garments, and
Perfumes to kill the smell o' the prison ; after,
When you shall stretch yourself, and say but, "Arcite,
I am in plight !" there shall be at your choice
Both sword and armour.
  Palamon.   O you heavens, dares any
So noble bear a guilty business ? None   9c
But only Arcite ; therefore none but Arcite
In this kind is so bold.
  Arcite.   Sweet Palamon —
  Palamon. I do embrace you, and your offer : for
Your offer do't I only, sir ; your person,
Without hypocrisy, I may not wish
More than my sword's edge on't. [*Horns winded within.*
  Arcite.   You hear the horns :
Enter your musit,² lest this match between's

---

¹ Free me from these fetters.
² "The opening in a hedge through which a hare, or other beast of sport, is accustomed to pass." — *Nares.*

Be cross'd ere met. Give me your hand; farewell!
I'll bring you every needful thing; I pray you
Take comfort, and be strong.
 Palamon.   Pray hold your promise, 100
And do the deed with a bent[1] brow. Most certain
You love me not; be rough with me, and pour
This oil out of your language. By this air,
I could for each word give a cuff, my stomach
Not reconcil'd by reason!
 Arcite.   Plainly spoken!
Yet pardon me hard language: when I spur
My horse, I chide him not; content and anger
        [*Horns winded again.*
In me have but one face. — Hark, sir! they call
The scatter'd to the banquet; you must guess
I have an office there.
 Palamon.   Sir, your attendance 110
Cannot please heaven; and I know your office
Unjustly is achiev'd.
 Arcite.   I've a good title,
I am persuaded: this question, sick between's,
By bleeding must be cur'd. I am a suitor
That to your sword you will bequeath this plea,
And talk of it no more.
 Palamon.   But this one word:
You are going now to gaze upon my mistress;
For, note you, mine she is —
 Arcite.   Nay, then —
 Palamon.   Nay, pray you! —
You talk of feeding me to breed me strength:
You are going now to look upon a sun 120

[1] Angry.

That strengthens what it looks on; there you have
A vantage o'er me; but enjoy it till
I may enforce my remedy.   Farewell!   [*Exeunt.*[1]

SCENE II.— *Another Part of the Forest.*

Enter Gaoler's Daughter.

Daughter. He has mistook the brake I meant, is gone
After his fancy. 'Tis now well-nigh morning;
No matter! would it were perpetual night,
And darkness lord o' the world! — Hark! 'tis a wolf;
In me hath grief slain fear, and, but for one thing,
I care for nothing, and that's Palamon.
I reck not if the wolves would jaw me, so
He had this file. What if I halloo'd for him?
I cannot halloo; if I whoop'd, what then?
If he not answer'd, I should call a wolf,   10
And do him but that service.   I have heard
Strange howls this livelong night; why may't not be
They have made prey of him?   He has no weapons,
He cannot run; the jingling of his gyves
Might call fell things to listen, who have in them
A sense to know a man unarm'd, and can
Smell where resistance is.   I'll set it down
He's torn to pieces; they howl'd many together,
And then they fed on him: so much for that!
Be bold to ring the bell; how stand I then?   20
All's char'd[2] when he is gone.   No, no, I lie,
My father's to be hang'd for his escape;

---

[1] The critics agree in assigning this scene to Shakespeare.
[2] All is dispatched: from this stem is derived *chores.*

SCENE III.]   THE TWO NOBLE KINSMEN.   419

Myself to beg, if I priz'd life so much
As to deny my act; but that I would not,
Should I try death by dozens!— I am mop'd[1]:
Food took I none these two days —
Sipp'd some water.   I have not clos'd mine eyes,
Save when my lids scour'd off their brine.   Alas,
Dissolve, my life! let not my sense unsettle,
Lest I should drown, or stab, or hang myself!   30
O state of nature, fail together in me,
Since thy best props are warp'd!— So! which way now?
The best way is the next way to a grave;
Each errant step beside is torment.   Lo,
The moon is down, the crickets chirp, the screech-owl
Calls in the dawn! all offices are done,
Save what I fail in; but the point is this,
An end, and that is all![2]   [*Exit.*

SCENE III. — *The Same Part of the Forest as in Scene I.*

Enter ARCITE, *with meat, wine, files, etc.*

Arcite. I should be near the place. — Ho, cousin Palamon!

Enter PALAMON.

Palamon.   Arcite?
Arcite.   The same; I've brought you food and files.

---

[1] Used up.

[2] This scene is usually assigned to Shakespeare, but *Hickson* remarks: " It is to this scene that we referred by anticipation as giving an instance of Shakespeare's judgment. It can hardly be said to explain any necessary circumstance; . . . but it supplies the due gradation between a mind diseased and madness; and in connection with another scene at which we

Come forth, and fear not; here's no Theseus.
 Palamon. Nor none so honest, Arcite.
 Arcite.   That's no matter;
We'll argue that hereafter. Come, take courage;
You shall not die thus beastly;[1] here, sir, drink.
I know you're faint; then I'll talk further with you.
 Palamon. Arcite, thou might'st now poison me.
 Arcite.   I might;
But I must fear you first. Sit down; and, good now,
No more of these vain parleys! Let us not,   10
Having our ancient reputation with us,
Make talk for fools and cowards. To your health! [*Drinks.*
 Palamon. Do.
 Arcite.   Pray, sit down then; and let me entreat you,
By all the honesty and honour in you,
No mention of this woman! 'twill disturb us;
We shall have time enough.
 Palamon.   Well, sir, I'll pledge you. [*Drinks.*
 Arcite. Drink a good hearty draught; it breeds good
    blood, man.
Do not you feel it thaw you?
 Palamon.   Stay; I'll tell you
After a draught or two more.

<hr />

shall shortly arrive, it displays a depth of insight into the psychological character of this state only exceeded by Shakespeare himself, in *Lear*. Let our readers observe in particular the unselfish anxiety for Palamon's safety, and her subsequent terror at her own disordered senses. The introduction of the popular notion that wild beasts 'have a sense to know a man unarm'd' is quite a Shakespearean illustration; and we do not know an instance of finer drawing than this of her imagination painting, as absolute reality, the subject of her first fear. From this conviction (of Palamon's death) we come naturally to the concluding lines, beyond which the next step *is* madness."

 [1] Unlike a human being.

Arcite.   Spare it not;
The duke has more, coz.   Eat now.
    Palamon.   Yes.
    Arcite.   I am glad   20
You have so good a stomach.
    Palamon.   I am gladder
I have so good meat to't.
    Arcite.   Is't not mad lodging
Here in the wild woods, cousin?
    Palamon.   Yes, for them
That have wild consciences.
    Arcite.   How tastes your victuals?
Your hunger needs no sauce, I see.
    Palamon.   Not much;
But if it did, yours is too tart, sweet cousin.
What is this?
    Arcite.   Venison.
    Palamon.   'Tis a lusty meat.
Give me more wine: here, Arcite, to the wenches
We have known in our days! The lord steward's daughter;
Do you remember her?
    Arcite.   After you, coz.   30
    Palamon. She lov'd a black-hair'd man.
    Arcite.   She did so; well, sir?
    Palamon. And I have heard some call him Arcite; and --
    Arcite.   Out with it, faith!
    Palamon.   She met him in an arbour:
What did she there, coz?
    Arcite.   Well, the marshal's sister
Had her share too, as I remember, cousin,
Else there be tales abroad; you'll pledge her?
    Palamon.   Yes.

Arcite. A pretty brown wench 'tis! There was a time
When young men went a-hunting, and a wood,
And a broad beech; and thereby hangs a tale.¹—
Heign-ho!
    Palamon. For Emily, upon my life! Fool,   40
Away with this strain'd mirth! I say again,
That sigh was breath'd for Emily! Base cousin,
Dar'st thou break² first?
    Arcite.   You are wide.
    Palamon.   By heaven and earth,
There's nothing in thee honest!
    Arcite.   Then I'll leave you;
You are a beast now.
    Palamon.   As thou mak'st me, traitor.
    Arcite. There's all things needful, — files and shirts, and
        perfumes.
I'll come again some two hours hence, and bring
That that shall quiet all.
    Palamon.   A sword and armour?
    Arcite. Fear me not. You are now too foul; farewell!
Get off your trinkets! you shall want nought.
    Palamon.   Sirrah —   50
    Arcite. I'll hear no more!   [*Exit.*
    Palamon.   If he keep touch, he dies for't. [*Exit.*³

    ¹ Common Shakespearean phrase; cf. *Merry Wives*, i, 4, 159; *As You Like It*, ii, 7, 28; *Taming of the Shrew*, iv, 1, 60.
    ² Break our agreement.
    ³ "This is one of those scenes by the introduction of which Fletcher succeeded in spoiling a good play." — *Littledale*. " In most respects the scene is not very characteristic of either writer, but leans towards Fletcher; and one argument for him might be drawn from an interchange of sarcasms between the two kinsmen, in which they retort on each other former amorous adventures: such a dialogue is quite like Fletcher's men of gayety; and

SCENE IV.] THE TWO NOBLE KINSMEN. 423

SCENE IV. — *Another Part of the Forest.*

Enter Gaoler's Daughter.

Daughter. I'm very cold; and all the stars are out too,
The little stars, and all that look like aglets[1]:
The sun has seen my folly. Palamon!
Alas, no, he's in heaven! — Where am I now? —
Yonder's the sea, and there's a ship; how't tumbles!
And there's a rock lies watching under water;
Now, now, it beats upon it! now, now, now!
There's a leak sprung, a sound one; how they cry!
Run her before the wind, you'll lose all else!
Up with a course or two, and tack about, boys! 10
Good night, good night; y'are gone! — I'm very hungry:
Would I could find a fine frog! he would tell me
News from all parts of the world; then would I make
A carrack[2] of a cockle-shell, and sail
By east and north-east to the King of pygmies,[3]
For he tells fortunes rarely. Now my father,
Twenty to one is truss'd[4] up in a trice
To-morrow morning; I'll say never a word.

needless degradation of his principal characters is a fault of which Shakespeare is not guilty." — *Spalding.* " The third scene, without any doubt, is by Fletcher. Arcite brings 'food and files' to Palamon; and, after some patter of early reminiscences between them utterly out of character, they separate." — *Hickson.*

[1] Spangles.

[2] A ship of burden.

[3] " A fabulous people, said to be of the height of a *pygme* (πυγμή), or 13½ inches, mentioned by Homer (*Iliad*, iii, 5) as dwelling on the shores of Ocean, and at times subject to attacks by cranes. Dwarfs have often been credited with supernatural powers, especially in Northern mythology." — *Skeat.* Cf. *Much Ado*, ii, 1, 278.

[4] Pinioned like a fowl, hanged.

(Sings) *For I'll cut my green coat a foot above my knee;*
   And I'll clip my yellow locks an inch below mine e'e.
    Hey, nonny, nonny, nonny.   21
   He's[1] *buy me a white cut, forth for to ride,*
   And I'll go seek him through the world that is so
    wide.
    Hey, nonny, nonny, nonny.
O for a prick now, like a nightingale,[2]
To put my breast against! I shall sleep like a top else. [*Exit.*[3]

   Scene V. — *Another Part of the Forest.*

Enter Gerrold, *four* Countrymen *as morris-dancers, another as the* Bavian,[4] *five* Wenches, *and a* Taborer.

Gerrold. Fie, fie!
What tediosity and disensanity
Is here among ye! Have my rudiments
Been labour'd so long with ye, milk'd unto ye,
And, by a figure, even the very plum-broth
And marrow of my understanding laid upon ye,
And do you still cry "where," and "how," and "wherefore"?

 [1] He shall.
 [2] Poets frequently described the nightingale as leaning her breast against a thorn whilst singing. So in the *Passionate Pilgrim*, sect. 21;
    " Everything did banish moan,
     Save the nightingale alone;
     She, poor bird, as all forlorn,
     Lean'd her breast up-till a thorn,
     And there sung the dolefull'st ditty."
 [3] This scene is Fletcher's; " there is some affectation of nautical language (why, Heaven only knows), and the rest is mere incoherent nonsense." — *Hickson.*
 [4] A person dressed like a baboon, introduced into a morris-dance.

SCENE V.] THE TWO NOBLE KINSMEN. 425

You most coarse frieze capacities, ye jane[1] judgments,
Have I said "thus let be," and "there let be,"
And "then let be," and no man understand me?　　　10
Proh Deum, medius fidius,[2] ye are all dunces!
For why, here stand I; here the duke comes; there are you,
Close in the thicket; the duke appears, I meet him,
And unto him I utter learned things,
And many figures; he hears, and nods, and hums,
And then cries "rare!" and I go forward; at length
I fling my cap up; mark there! then do you,
As once did Meleager and the boar,[3]
Break comely out before him, like true lovers,
Cast yourselves in a body decently,　　　20
And sweetly, by a figure, trace[4] and turn, boys!
　　1st Countryman. And sweetly we will do it, master
　　　　Gerrold.
　　2d Countryman. Draw up the company. Where's the
　　　　taborer?
　　3d Countryman. Why, Timothy!
　　Taborer. Here, my mad boys; have at ye!
　　Gerrold. But I say, where's their women?
　　4th Countryman.　　　　Here's Friz and Maudlin.
　　2d Countryman. And little Luce with the white legs, and
　　　　bouncing Barbary.
　　1st Countryman. And freckled Nell, that never failed her
　　　　master.

[1] *Frieze* is coarse woollen cloth; *jane* is twilled cotton cloth.
[2] "An old Latin oath, apparently short for *me dius Fidius adiuvet*, may the divine Fidius help me! If *fidius* stands for *filius*, then it means, may the divine son of Jupiter help me! The reference, in that case, is most likely to the god Hercules." — *Skeat.*
[3] Meleager slew the boar infesting Calydon; see *Iliad,* ix, 527.
[4] Follow your proper track; referring to a dance.

Gerrold. Where be your ribands, maids? Swim with your bodies,
And carry it sweetly and deliverly[1];
And now and then a favour[2] and a frisk !   30
   Nell. Let us alone, sir.
   Gerrold.   Where's the rest o' the music?
   3d Countryman. Dispers'd as you commanded.
   Gerrold.   Couple, then,
And see what's wanting. Where's the Bavian? —
My friend, carry your tail without offence
Or scandal to the ladies; and be sure
You tumble with audacity and manhood;
And when you bark, you do it with judgment.
   Bavian.   Yes, sir.
   Gerrold. Quousque tandem?[3] Here is a woman wanting!
   4th Countryman. We may go whistle; all the fat's i' the fire !
   Gerrold. We have,   40
As learned authors utter, wash'd a tile;[4]
We have been fatuous, and labour'd vainly.
   2d Countryman. This is that scornful piece,[5] that scurvy hilding,[6]
That gave her promise faithfully she would
Be here, Cicely the sempster's[7] daughter !
The next gloves that I give her shall be dog-skin;
Nay, an she fail me once — You can tell, Arcas,

---

[1] Nimbly; *clever* is supposed to be derived from *deliver*.
[2] "Perhaps a love-knot made of the ribands mentioned." — *Skeat.* Cf. *favours* in the modern cotillon.
[3] How long ?
[4] A Latin proverb occurring in *Terence's Phormio*, 1, 4, 9.
[5] Contemptuously, "creature."
[6] A menial wretch; still in use in Devonshire.   [7] Old form of *sempstress.*

She swore, by wine and bread,[1] she would not break.
  Gerrold. An eel and woman,
A learned poet says, unless by the tail 50
And with thy teeth thou hold, will either fail.
In manners this was false position.
  1st Countryman. A wildfire take her! does she flinch now?
  3d Countryman. What shall we determine, sir?
  Gerrold.   Nothing;
Our business is become a nullity.
Yea, and a woeful and a piteous nullity.
  4th Countryman. Now, when the credit of our town lay on it,
Now to be frampal[2]!
Go thy ways; I'll remember thee, I'll fit thee!

Enter Gaoler's Daughter, *and sings.*

  The George alow[3] *came from the south* 60
    From the coast of Barbary-a;
  And there he met with brave gallants of war,
    By one, by two, by three-a.
  Well hail'd, well hail'd, you jolly gallants!
    And whither now are you bound-a?
  O, let me have your company
    Till I come to the Sound-a!

---

[1] The sacrament of the Eucharist.
[2] Peevish; from the Welsh *ffromi*, to fume; cf. *Merry Wives*, ii, 2.
  "She leads a very frampold life with him."
[3] "Low down; possibly referring to the appearance of a ship on the horizon." — *Skeat.*

> There was three fools fell out about an howlet;
>   The one said it was an owl,
>   The other he said nay,
> The third he said it was a hawk,
>   And her bells were cut away.

3d Countryman. There's a dainty mad woman, master,
Comes i' the nick,¹ — as mad as a March hare !
If we can get her dance, we are made again ;
I warrant her she'll do the rarest gambols !

1st Countryman. A mad woman ! We are made, boys.

Gerrold. And are you mad, good woman?

Daughter. I'd be sorry, else ;
Give me your hand.

Gerrold. Why?

Daughter. I can tell your fortune :
You are a fool. Tell ten.² I have pos'd him. Buz !
Friend, you must eat no white bread ; if you do,
Your teeth will bleed extremely. Shall we dance, ho?
I know you ; you're a tinker : sirrah tinker —

Gerrold. Dii boni ! ³
A tinker, damsel?

Daughter. Or a conjurer :
Raise me a devil now, and let him play
Qui passa ⁴ o' the bells and bones !

Gerrold. Go, take her,
And fluently persuade her to a peace.⁵

---

¹ In the nick of time.
² " It was a trial of idiocy to make a person count his fingers." — *Weber.*
³ " Good Gods ! "
⁴ Italian, " here passes." The bells are those of the morris-dancers ; the bones were used in rude music.
⁵ To be still.

Et opus exegi, quod nec Iovis ira, nec ignis — [1]
Strike up, and lead her in.

    2d Countryman.   Come, lass, let's trip it!   90
    Daughter. I'll lead.
    3d Countryman.   Do, do.   [*Wind horns*
    Gerrold. Persuasively and cunningly; away, boys!
I hear the horns; give me some meditation,
And mark your cue. —   [*Exeunt all but Gerrold.*
             Pallas inspire me!

Enter THESEUS, PIRITHOUS, HIPPOLYTA, EMILIA, ARCITE,
             and train.

    Theseus. This way the stag took.
    Gerrold.   Stay, and edify!
    Theseus. What have we here?
    Pirithous. Some country sport, upon my life, sir.
    Theseus. Well, sir, go forward; we will edify. —
Ladies, sit down! we'll stay it.
    Gerrold. Thou doughty duke, all hail! — All hail, sweet
        ladies!   100
    Theseus. This is a cold beginning.[2]
    Gerrold. If you but favour, our country pastime made is.
We are a few of those collected here,
That ruder tongues distinguish villager;
And to say verity, and not to fable,
We are a merry rout, or else a rabble,
Or company, or, by a figure, chorus,
That 'fore thy dignity will dance a morris.[3]
And I, that am the rectifier of all,

---

[1] Ovid, *Metamorph.* xv, 871.   [2] A play on the word *hail*.
[3] For an account of the morris, see Prof. F. J. Child's Introduction to *English Ballads*, vol. 5.

By title Pedagogus, that let fall 110
The birch upon the breeches of the small ones,
And humble with a ferula[1] the tall ones,
Do here present this máchine, or this frame;
And, dainty duke, whose doughty dismal fame
From Dis to Dædalus, from post to pillar,
Is blown abroad, help me, thy poor well-willer,
And with thy twinkling eyes look right and straight
Upon this mighty *morr*— of mickle weight —
— *is* now comes in, which being glued together
Makes *morris*, and the cause that we came hither, 120
The body of our sport, of no small study.
I first appear, though rude, and raw, and muddy,
To speak, before thy noble grace, this tenour;[2]
At whose great feet I offer up my penner.
The next, the Lord of May and Lady bright,
The Chambermaid and Servingman,[3] by night

[1] The schoolmaster's "instrument of punishment. It was made of wood and shaped like a battledore, but with the bat much diminished, so as to be adapted for administering a severe pat on the palm of the victim's hand." — *Skeat.*

[2] To this effect.

[3] "We have here a list of the characters in the morris-dance; namely, the Lord of May, the Lady of May (also called Queen of May, or Maid Marian), the Chambermaid, the Servingman, the Host, the Hostess, etc.; to which should be added the Bavian or Tumbler, and the Clown or Jester, who are seldom absent from such festivities. By putting together the account in this part of the scene and the preceding part, we may make out the list of the twelve principal characters, six of each sex, with the persons who took the parts: *Male.* 1. Lord of May; 2. Servingman; 3. Host; 4. Clown; 5. Bavian; 6. Taborer. *Female.* 7. Lady of May; 8. Chambermaid; 9. Hostess; 10. 11. 12. Dancers. The parts may be thus distributed among the actors: *Male.* 1. 2. 3. 4. First, Second, Third, and Fourth Countrymen; 5. A fifth Countryman; 6. A man named Timothy. *Female.* 7. Friz; 8. Gaoler's Daughter, taking the place of Cicely (for it is clearly the Second Countryman's partner who failed to appear); 9. Maudlin; 10. Luce; 11. Barbary; 12. Nell." — *Skeat.*

That seek out silent hanging; then mine host
And his fat spouse, that welcomes to their cost
The galled traveller, and with a beck'ning
Informs the tapster to inflame the reck'ning; 130
Cum multis aliis that make a dance:
Say ay, and all shall presently advance.
    Theseus. Ay, ay, by any means, dear domine!
    Pirithous. Produce.
    Gerrold. Intrate, filii! Come forth, and foot it.

Enter the four Countrymen, *the* Bavian, *the* Taborer, *the* five Wenches *and the* Gaoler's Daughter, *with others of both sexes. They dance a morris. After which* GERROLD *speaks the Epilogue.*

    Ladies, if we have been merry,
    And have pleas'd ye with a derry,
    And a derry, and a down,
    Say the schoolmaster's no clown. —
    Duke, if we have pleas'd thee too, 140
    And have done as good boys should do,
    Give us but a tree or twain
    For a Maypole, and again,
    Ere another year run out,
    We'll make thee laugh, and all this rout.

    Theseus. Take twenty, domine. — How does my sweet heart?
    Hippolyta. Never so pleas'd, sir.
    Emilia. 'Twas an excellent dance; and, for a preface, I never heard a better.
    Theseus.   Schoolmaster, I thank you. — One see 'em all rewarded.

Pirithous. And here's something 150
To paint your pole withal. [*Gives money.*
Theseus. Now to our sports again!
Gerrold. May the stag thou hunt'st stand long,
 And thy dogs be swift and strong!
Come, we are all made!— *Dii Deaeque omnes!*
 [*Wind horns.*
Ye have danc'd rarely, wenches! [*Exeunt.*[1]

SCENE VI.— *The same Part of the Forest as in Scene III.*

Enter PALAMON *from the bush.*

Palamon. About this hour my cousin gave his faith
To visit me again, and with him bring
Two swords and two good armours; if he fail,
He's neither man or soldier. When he left me,
I did not think a week could have restor'd
My lost strength to me, I was grown so low
And crest-fallen with my wants; I thank thee, **Arcite**,
Thou art yet a fair foe, and I feel myself,
With this refreshing, able once again
To out-dure danger. To delay it longer 10
Would make the world think, when it comes to hearing,
That I lay fatting like a swine, to fight,
And not a soldier. Therefore this blest morning
Shall be the last, and that sword he refuses,
If it but hold, I kill him with; 'tis justice:
So, love and fortune for me!— O, good morrow!

---

[1] "Not only imitation, but the imitation of a young and inexperienced writer."— *Hickson.* Gerrold is "a personage who has the pedantry of Shakespeare's Holofernes, without one solitary spark of his humor."— *Spalding.*

Enter ARCITE, *with armours and swords.*

Arcite. Good morrow, noble kinsman!
Palamon. I have put you
To too much pains, sir.
Arcite. That too much, fair cousin,
Is but a debt to honour, and my duty.
Palamon. Would you were so in all, sir! I could wish ye
As kind a kinsman as you force me find 21
A beneficial foe, that my embraces
Might thank ye, not my blows.
Arcite. I shall think either,
Well done, a noble recompense.
Palamon. Then I shall quit[1] you.
Arcite. Defy me in these fair terms, and you show
More than a mistress to me; no more anger,
As you love any thing that's honourable!
We were not bred to talk, man; when we are arm'd,
And both upon our guards, then let our fury,
Like meeting of two tides,[2] fly strongly from us! 30
And then to whom the birthright of this beauty
Truly pertains — without upbraidings, scorns,
Despisings of our persons, and such poutings,
Fitter for girls and schoolboys — will be seen,
And quickly, yours or mine. Will't please your arm, sir?
Or if you feel yourself not fitting yet,
And furnish'd with your old strength, I'll stay, cousin,
And every day discourse you into health,

---

[1] Requite.

[2] Spalding notes Fletcher's "want of distinctness in grasping images, and inability to see fully either their picturesque or their poetical relations"; in illustration of which he quotes this passage and below: "When I saw you charge first," etc.

As I am spar'd: your person I am friends with,
And I could wish I had not said I lov'd her, 40
Though I had died; but, loving such a lady,
And justifying my love, I must not fly from't.
 Palamon. Arcite, thou art so brave an enemy,
That no man but thy cousin's fit to kill thee.
I'm well and lusty; choose your arms.
 Arcite.   Choose you, sir.
 Palamon. Wilt thou exceed in all, or dost thou do it
To make me spare thee?
 Arcite.   If you think so, cousin,
You are deceiv'd; for, as I am a soldier,
I will not spare you!
 Palamon.   That's well said.
 Arcite.   You'll find it.
 Palamon. Then, as I am an honest man, and love 50
With all the justice of affection,
I'll pay thee soundly! This I'll take.
 Arcite.   That's mine then;
I'll arm you first.   [*Proceeds to arm* PALAMON.
 Palamon. Do. Pray thee, tell me, cousin,
Where gott'st thou this good armour?
 Arcite.   'Tis the duke's;
And, to say true, I stole it. — Do I pinch you?
 Palamon. No.
 Arcite. Is't not too heavy?
 Palamon.   I have worn a lighter;
But I shall make it serve.
 Arcite.   I'll buckle't close.
 Palamon. By any means.
 Arcite.   You care not for a grand-guard [1]?

[1] A piece of defensive armour for the breast, worn generally on horseback.

SCENE VI.]   THE TWO NOBLE KINSMEN.   435

 Palamon. No, no; we'll use no horses; I perceive 60
You'd fain be at that fight.
  Arcite.   I am indifferent.
 Palamon. Faith, so am I. Good cousin, thrust the buckle
Through far enough.
  Arcite. I warrant you.
  Palamon.   My casque now.
 Arcite. Will you fight bare-arm'd?
 Palamon.   We shall be the nimbler.
 Arcite. But use your gauntlets though: those are o' the
  least;
Prithee take mine, good cousin.
  Palamon.   Thank you, Arcite,
How do I look? am I fallen much away?
 Arcite. Faith, very little; love has us'd you kindly.
 Palamon. I'll warrant thee I'll strike home.
  Arcite.   Do, and spare not!
I'll give you cause, sweet cousin.
 Palamon (arming ARCITE*).* Now to you, sir. 70
Methinks this armour's very like that, Arcite,
Thou wor'st that day the three kings fell, but lighter.
 Arcite. That was a very good one; and that day,
I well remember, you outdid me, cousin.
I never saw such valour; when you charg'd
Upon the left wing of the enemy,
I spurr'd hard to come up, and under me
I had a right good horse.
  Palamon. You had indeed;
A bright bay, I remember.
  Arcite. Yes. But all
Was vainly labour'd in me; you outwent me, 80
Nor could my wishes reach you: yet a little

I did by imitation.
 Palamon.   More by virtue¹;
You are modest, cousin.
    Arcite.   When I saw you charge first,
Methought I heard a dreadful clap of thunder
Break from the troop.
    Palamon.   But still before that flew
The lightning of your valour. Stay a little!
Is not this piece too strait²?
    Arcite.   No, no; 'tis well.
    Palamon. I would have nothing hurt thee but my sword;
A bruise would be dishonour.
    Arcite.   Now I am perfect.
    Palamon. Stand off then!
    Arcite.   Take my sword; I hold³ it better.
    Palamon. I thank ye, no; keep it, your life lies on it. 91
Here's one, if it but hold, I ask no more
For all my hopes. My cause and honour guard me!
    Arcite. And me my love! Is there aught else to say?
         [*They bow several ways; then advance and stand.*
    Palamon. This only, and no more: thou art mine aunt's
         son,
And that blood we desire to shed is mutual;
In me thine, and in thee mine: my sword
Is in my hand, and, if thou killest me,
The gods and I forgive thee. If there be
A place prepar'd for those that sleep in honour,   100
I wish his weary soul that falls may win it.
Fight bravely, cousin; give me thy noble hand.
    Arcite. Here, Palamon; this hand shall never more
Come near thee with such friendship.

¹ Valour.   ² Tight.   ³ Esteem.

Palamon.   I commend thee.
Arcite. If I fall, curse me, and say I was a coward;
For none but such dare die in these just trials.[1]
Once more farewell, my cousin!
  Palamon.   Farewell, Arcite!
         [*They fight. Horns within; they stand.*
Arcite. Lo, cousin, lo! our folly has undone us!
Palamon. Why?
Arcite. This is the duke, a-hunting as I told you;   110
If we be found, we are wretched. O, retire,
For honour's sake and safety, presently
Into your bush again, sir! We shall find
Too many hours to die in. Gentle cousin,
If you be seen, you perish instantly,
For breaking prison; and I, if you reveal me,
For my contempt: then all the world will scorn us,
And say we had a noble difference,
But base disposers of it.
  Palamon.   No, no, cousin;
I will no more be hidden, nor put off   120
This great adventure to a second trial.
I know your cunning, and I know your cause.
He that faints now, shame take him! Put thyself
Upon thy present guard —
  Arcite.   You are not mad?
Palamon. Or I will make the advantage of this hour
Mine own; and what to come shall threaten me,
I fear less than my fortune. Know, weak cousin,

---

[1] "Our scene lies rather in the land of *knight-errantry* than of Athens; our authors follow Chaucer, and dress their heroes after the manners of his age, when trials by the sword were thought just, and the conquered always supposed guilty and held infamous." — *Seward.*

I love Emilia; and in that I'll bury
Thee, and all crosses else.
  Arcite.   Then come what can come,
Thou shalt know, Palamon, I dare as well   130
Die, as discourse or sleep; only this fears[1] me,
The law will have the honour of our ends.
Have at thy life!
  Palamon. Look to thine own well, Arcite!
         [*They fight again. Horns.*

Enter THESEUS, HIPPOLYTA, EMILIA, PIRITHOUS, *and train.*

  Theseus. What ignorant and mad-malicious traitors
Are you, that 'gainst the tenour of my laws,
Are making battle thus, like knights appointed,
Without my leave, and officers of arms?
By Castor, both shall die!
  Palamon.   Hold thy word, Theseus!
We are certainly both traitors, both despisers
Of thee and of thy goodness: I am Palamon, 140
That cannot love thee, he that broke thy prison;
Think well what that deserves! and this is Arcite;
A bolder traitor never trod thy ground,
A falser ne'er seem'd friend: this is the man
Was begg'd and banish'd; this is he contemns thee,
And what thou dar'st do; and in this disguise,
Against thine own edict, follows thy sister,
That fortunate bright star, the fair Emilia —
Whose servant, if there be a right in seeing,
And first bequeathing of the soul to, justly 150
I am — and, which is more, dares think her his!
This treachery, like a most trusty !over,

[1] Frightens.

SCENE VI.] THE TWO NOBLE KINSMEN. 439

I call'd him now to answer. If thou beest,
As thou art spoken, great and virtuous,
The true decider of all injuries,
Say, " Fight again ! " and thou shalt see me, Theseus,
Do such a justice thou thyself wilt envy ;
Then take my life ! I'll woo thee to't.
 Pirithous.   O heaven,
What more than man is this !
 Theseus.   I've sworn.
 Arcite.   We seek not
Thy breath of mercy, Theseus ! 'Tis to me   160
A thing as soon[1] to die as thee to say it,
And no more mov'd.[2] Where this man calls me traitor,
Let me say thus much : if in love be treason,
In service of so excellent a beauty —
As I love most, and in that faith will perish,
As I have brought my life here to confirm it,
As I have serv'd her truest, worthiest,
As I dare kill this cousin that denies it —
So let me be most traitor, and ye please me.
For scorning thy edict, duke, ask that lady,   170
Why she is fair, and why her eyes command me
Stay here to love her? and if she say traitor,
I am a villain fit to lie unburied.
 Palamon. Thou shalt have pity of us both, O Theseus,
If unto neither thou show mercy ; stop,
As thou art just, thy noble ear against us ;
As thou art valiant, for thy cousin's[3] soul,

---

[1] Easy.
[2] " And I am no more moved than thou wouldst be in giving the order."
— *Skeat.*
[3] Hercules.

Whose twelve strong labours crown his memory,
Let's die together, at one instant, duke!
Only a little let him fall before me, 180
That I may tell my soul he shall not have her.

Theseus. I grant your wish; for, to say true, your cousin
Has ten times more offended, for I gave him
More mercy than you found, sir, your offences
Being no more than his.—None here speak for 'em!
For ere the sun set, both shall sleep for ever.

Hippolyta. Alas, the pity! now or never, sister,
Speak, not to be denied; that face of yours
Will bear the curses else of after ages
For these lost cousins.

Emilia. In my face, dear sister, 190
I find no anger to 'em, nor no ruin;
The misadventure of their own eyes kill 'em:
Yet that I will be woman and have pity,
My knees shall grow to the ground but I'll get mercy.
Help me, dear sister! in a deed so virtuous
The powers of all women will be with us.—
Most royal brother—

Hippolyta. Sir, by our tie of marriage—

Emilia. By your own spotless honour—

Hippolyta. By that faith,
That fair hand, and that honest heart you gave me—

Emilia. By that you would have pity in another, 200
By your own virtues infinite—

Hippolyta. By valour,
By all the chaste nights I have ever pleas'd you—

Theseus. These are strange conjurings!

Pirithous. Nay, then, I'll in too!—
By all our friendship, sir, by all our dangers,

By all you love most, — wars, and this sweet lady —
    Emilia. By that you would have trembled to deny
A blushing maid —
    Hippolyta.   By your own eyes, by strength,
In which you swore I went beyond all women,
Almost all men, and yet I yielded, Theseus —
    Pirithous. To crown all this, by your most noble soul, 210
Which cannot want due mercy, I beg first!
    Hippolyta. Next hear my prayers!
    Emilia.   Last, let me entreat, sir!
    Pirithous. For mercy!
    Hippolyta.   Mercy!
    Emilia.   Mercy on these princes!
    Theseus. Ye make my faith reel; say I felt
Compassion to 'em both, how would you place it?
    Emilia. Upon their lives; but with their banishments.
    Theseus. You are a right[1] woman, sister! you have pity,
But want the understanding where to use it.
If you desire their lives, invent a way
Safer than banishment. Can these two live,   220
And have the agony of love about 'em,
And not kill one another? Every day
They'd fight about you, hourly bring your honour
In public question with their swords. Be wise then,
And here forget 'em; it concerns your credit,
And my oath equally: I have said, they die!
Better they fall by the law than one another.
Bow[2] not my honour.
    Emilia.   O my noble brother,
That oath was rashly made, and in your anger;
Your reason will not hold it: if such vows   230

    [1] Very.   [2] Abase not.

Stand for express will, all the world must perish.
Beside, I have another oath 'gainst yours,
Of more authority, I'm sure more love ;
Not made in passion neither, but good heed.
   Theseus. What is it, sister?
   Pirithous.   Urge it home, brave lady !
   Emilia. That you would ne'er deny me anything
Fit for my modest suit and your free granting.
I tie you to your word now ; if ye fail in't,
Think how you maim your honour ;
For now I am set a-begging, sir, I am deaf   240
To all but your compassion.   How their lives
Might breed the ruin of my name's opinion ! [1]
Shall any thing that loves me perish for me?
That were a cruel wisdom ; do men proin [2]
The straight young boughs that blush with thousand blos-
    soms,
Because they may be rotten? O duke Theseus,
The goodly mothers that have groan'd for these,
And all the longing maids that ever lov'd,
If your vow stand, shall curse me and my beauty,
And, in their funeral songs for these two cousins,   250
Despise my cruelty and cry woe worth me,[3]
Till I am nothing but the scorn of women.
For heaven's sake save their lives, and banish 'em !
   Theseus. On what conditions?
   Emilia.   Swear 'em never more
To make me their contention, or to know me,
To tread upon thy dukedom, and to be,
Wherever they shall travel, ever strangers
To one another.

       [1] My reputation.   [2] Prune.   [3] Woe be to me.

Palamon. I'll be cut a-pieces
Before I take this oath! Forget I love her?
O all ye gods, despise me then! Thy banishment 260
I not mislike, so we may fairly carry
Our swords and cause along; else never trifle,
But take our lives, duke! I must love, and will;
And for that love must and dare kill this cousin,
On any piece the earth has.
    Theseus.   Will you, Arcite,
Take these conditions?
    Palamon.   He's a villain, then!
    Pirithous. These are men!
    Arcite. No, never, duke; 'tis worse to me than begging,
To take my life so basely. Though I think
I never shall enjoy her, yet I'll preserve 270
The honour of affection, and die for her,
Make death a devil.[1]
    Theseus. What may be done? for now I feel compassion.
    Pirithous. Let it not fall again, sir!
    Theseus.   Say, Emilia,
If one of them were dead, as one must, are you
Content to take the other to your husband?
They cannot both enjoy you. They are princes
As goodly as your own eyes, and as noble
As ever fame yet spoke of: look upon 'em,
And if you can love, end this difference; 280
I give consent. — Are you content, too, princes?
    Both. With all our souls.
    Theseus.   He that she refuses
Must die then.
    Both.   Any death thou canst invent, duke.

[1] "Though you should make death as formidable as a devil." — *Littledale.*

Palamon. If I fall from that mouth, I fall with favour,
And lovers yet unborn shall bless my ashes.
    Arcite. If she refuse me, yet my grave will wed me,
And soldiers sing my epitaph.
    Theseus.   Make choice then.
    Emilia. I cannot, sir; they are both too excellent:
For me, a hair shall never fall of these men.
    Hippolyta. What will become of 'em?
    Theseus.   Thus I ordain it:
And, by mine honour, once again it stands,   291
Or both shall die! — You shall both to your country;
And each, within this month, accompanied
With three fair knights, appear again in this place,
In which I'll plant a pyramid: and whether,
Before us that are here, can force his cousin
By fair and knightly strength to touch the pillar,
He shall enjoy her; the other lose his head,
And all his friends;[1] nor shall he grudge to fall,
Nor think he dies with interest in this lady.   300
Will this content ye?
    Palamon.   Yes. — Here, cousin Arcite,
I am friends again till that hour.

[1] "Some readers have expressed surprise at the apparently strange doom of Theseus, in decreeing death not only to the principal, but to 'all his friends,' if worsted in the combat. Chaucer does not, it is true, go so far as this; but it was quite in accordance with the spirit of the age even in Fletcher's time. Seward's note on the subject is much to the purpose: 'As to the probability of their procuring each three seconds upon such odd terms, it may shock us to suppose any such gallant idiots; but even so low as our authors' age it was reckoned cowardice to refuse any man, even a stranger, to be a second in almost any duel whatever, of which there is a most inimitable burlesque in *The Little French Lawyer.* Mankind were mad after knight-errantry; and the reader must catch a little of the spirit himself, or he'll lose a great part of the beauties of this play; he must kindle

Arcite. I embrace ye.
Theseus. Are you content, sister?
Emilia. Yes; I must, sir,
Else both miscarry.
Theseus. Come, shake hands again then;
And take heed, as you are gentlemen, this quarrel
Sleep till the hour prefix'd, and hold your course.
Palamon. We dare not fail thee, Theseus.
Theseus. Come, I'll give ye
Now usage like to princes and to friends.
When ye return, who wins, I'll settle here;
Who loses, yet I'll weep upon his bier. [*Exeunt.*[1]

ACT IV.

SCENE I. — *Athens. A Room in the Prison.*

Enter Gaoler *and* First Friend.

Gaoler. Hear you no more? Was nothing said of me
Concerning the escape of Palamon?
Good sir, remember!
1st Friend. Nothing that I heard;

---

with the flames of military glory, think life a small stake to hazard in such a combat, and death desirable to the conquered as a refuge from shame. In Beaumont and Fletcher's play of *The Lover's Progress*, ii, 3, the seconds fight as well as the principals. Perhaps the most striking instance is afforded by the ferocious duel fought in Kensington Gardens on the 15th of November, 1712; in which not only the principals, Lord Mohun and the Duke of Hamilton, were both killed, but the seconds fought with fierce hatred, though interrupted before either of them was slain." — *Skeat.*

[1] "This scene is a spirited and excellent one; but its tone is Fletcher's, not Shakespeare's." — *Spalding.*

For I came home before the business
Was fully ended: yet I might perceive,
Ere I departed, a great likelihood
Of both their pardons; for Hippolyta
And fair-eyed Emily upon their knees
Begg'd with such handsome pity, that the duke
Methought stood staggering whether he should follow 10
His rash oath or the sweet compassion
Of those two ladies; and to second them,
That truly noble prince Pirithous,
Half his own heart, set in too, that I hope
All shall be well: neither   ard I one question
Of your name or his scape.
   Gaoler.   Pray heaven, it hold so!

            Enter Second Friend.

   2d Friend. Be of good comfort, man! I bring you news,
Good news.
   Gaoler. They're welcome.
   2d Friend.   Palamon has clear'd you
And got your pardon, and discover'd how
And by whose means he scap'd, which was your daughter's,
Whose pardon is procur'd too; and the prisoner — 21
Not to be held ungrateful to her goodness —
Has given a sum of money to her marriage,
A large one, I'll assure you.
   Gaoler.   Ye're a good man
And ever bring good news.
   1st Friend.   How was it ended?
   2d Friend. Why, as it should be; they that never begg'd
But they prevail'd had their suits fairly granted;
The prisoners have their lives.

1st Friend. I knew't would be so.
2d Friend. But there be new conditions, which you'll hear of
At better time.
Gaoler. I hope they are good.
2d Friend. They're honourable;
How good they'll prove, I know not.
1st Friend. 'Twill be known.

Enter Wooer.

Wooer. Alas, sir, where's your daughter?
Gaoler. Why do you ask?
Wooer. O, sir, when did you see her?
2d Friend. How he looks!
Gaoler. This morning.
Wooer. Was she well? was she in health, sir?
Where did she sleep?
1st Friend. These are strange questions.
Gaoler. I do not think she was very well; for, now
You make me mind her, but this very day
I ask'd her questions, and she answer'd me
So far from what she was, so childishly,
So sillily, as if she were a fool,
An innocent[1]; and I was very angry.
But what of her, sir?
Wooer. Nothing but my pity;
But you must know it, and as good by me
As by another that less loves her.
Gaoler. Well, sir?
1st Friend. Not right?
2d Friend. Not well?
Wooer. No, sir, not well;
'Tis too true, she is mad.

[1] Idiot.

1st Friend.   It cannot be.
Wooer. Believe, you'll find it so.
Gaoler.   I half suspected
What you have told me; the gods comfort her!
Either this was her love to Palamon,
Or fear of my miscarrying on his scape,   50
Or both.
  Wooer. 'Tis likely.
  Gaoler.   But why all this haste, sir?
  Wooer. I'll tell you quickly. As I late was angling
In the great lake that lies behind the palace,
From the far shore, thick-set with reeds and sedges,
As patiently I was attending sport,
I heard a voice, a shrill one, and attentive
I gave my ear; when I might well perceive
'Twas one that sung, and, by the smallness of it,
A boy or woman.[1] I then left my angle
To his own skill, came near, but yet perceiv'd not   60
Who made the sound, the rushes and the reeds
Had so encompass'd it. I laid me down
And listen'd to the words she sung; for then,
Through a small glade cut by the fishermen,
I saw it was your daughter.
  Gaoler.   Pray go on, sir!
  Wooer. She sung much, but no sense; only I heard her
Repeat this often: " Palamon is gone,
Is gone to the wood to gather mulberries;
I'll find him out to-morrow."
  1st Friend.   Pretty soul!
  Wooer. " His shackles will betray him, he'll be taken; 70
And what shall I do then? I'll bring a bevy,[2]

[1] Cf. *Hamlet*, iv, 7.   [2] Company, from the Italian, *beva*, drinking-party.

A hundred black-eyed maids that love as I do,
With chaplets on their heads of daffodillies,[1]
With cherry lips, and cheeks of damask roses,
And all we'll dance an antic 'fore the duke,
And beg his pardon." Then she talk'd of you, sir;
That you must lose your head to-morrow morning,
And she must gather flowers to bury you,
And see the house made handsome. Then she sung
Nothing but "Willow, willow, willow";[2] and between　　80
Ever was, "Palamon, fair Palamon!"
And "Palamon was a tall young man!" The place
Was knee-deep where she sat; her careless tresses
A wreath of bulrush rounded; about her stuck
Thousand fresh water-flowers of several colours;
That methought she appear'd like the fair nymph
That feeds the lake with waters, or as Iris
Newly dropt down from heaven. Rings she made
Of rushes that grew by,[3] and to 'em spoke
The prettiest posies,[4]—"Thus our true love's tied,"　　90
"This you may loose, not me," and many a one;
And then she wept, and sung again, and sigh'd,
And with the same breath smil'd and kiss'd her hand.
　2d Friend. Alas, what pity 'tis!
　Wooer.　　　　　　　　I made in to her;
She saw me, and straight sought the flood; I sav'd her,
And set her safe to land; when presently
She slipt away, and to the city made
With such a cry and swiftness that, believe me,
She left me far behind her. Three or four
I saw from far off cross her, one of 'em　　100

[1] Daffodils, corrupted from *asphodel*.　　[2] Cf. *Othello*, iv, 3.
[3] Peasants made rush rings in celebrating mock marriages.　　[4] Mottoes.

I knew to be your brother; where she stay'd,
And fell, scarce to be got away : I left them with her,
And hither came to tell you. Here they are !

 Enter Gaoler's Brother, Daughter, *and others.*

 Daughter (sings). *May you never more enjoy the light,*
  etc.
Is not this a fine song?
 Brother.   O, a very fine one !
 Daughter. I can sing twenty more.
 Brother.   I think you can.
 Daughter. Yes, truly can I ; I can sing " The Broom,"
And " Bonny Robin."[1] Are not you a tailor?
 Brother. Yes.
 Daughter. Where's my wedding-gown?
 Brother.   I'll bring it to-morrow.
 Daughter. Do, very rarely[2]; I must be abroad else, 110
To call the maids, and pay the minstrels.
   (Sings) *O fair, O sweet,* etc.
 Brother. You must even take it patiently.
 Gaoler.   'Tis true.
 Daughter. Good even, good men ! Pray did you ever
  hear
Of one young Palamon?
 Gaoler.   Yes, wench, we know him.
 Daughter. Is't not a fine young gentleman?
 Gaoler.   'Tis love !
 Brother. By no means cross her ; she is then distemper'd
Far worse than now she shows.
 1st Friend.   Yes, he's a fine man.
 Daughter. O, is he so? You have a sister?

---

  [1] Popular old songs.   [2] Early.

1st Friend. Yes.

Daughter. But she shall never have him, tell her so, 120
For a trick that I know; y' had best look to her,
For if she see him once, she's gone, she's done
And undone in an hour. All the young maids
Of our town are in love with him; but I laugh at 'em,
And let 'em all alone: is't not a wise course?

1st Friend. Yes.

Daughter. They come from all parts of the dukedom to him;
I'll warrant ye —

Gaoler. She's lost,
Past all cure!

Brother. Heaven forbid, man!

Daughter. Come hither; you're a wise man.

1st Friend. Does she know him? 130

2d Friend. No; would she did!

Daughter. You're master of a ship?

Gaoler. Yes.

Daughter. Where's your compass?

Gaoler. Here.

Daughter. Set it to the north;
And now direct your course to the wood, where Palamon
Lies longing for me; for the tackling
Let me alone: come, weigh, my hearts, cheerly![1]

All. Owgh, owgh, owgh! 'tis up, the wind is fair;
Top the bowling;[2] out with the mainsail!
Where's your whistle, master?

Brother. Let's get her in.

Gaoler. Up to the top, boy!

Brother. Where's the pilot?

---

[1] Weigh anchor cheerily.   [2] Tighten the bowline.

1st Friend. Here.
Daughter. What kenn'st[1] thou?
2d Friend. A fair wood. 140
Daughter. Bear for it, master; tack about!
(Sings) *When Cynthia with her borrowed light,* etc.
[*Exeunt.*[2]

SCENE II. — *Athens. A Room in the Palace.*

Enter EMILIA, *with two pictures.*

Emilia. Yet I may bind those wounds up, that must open
And bleed to death for my sake else. I'll choose,
And end their strife; two such young handsome men
Shall never fall for me: their weeping mothers,
Following the dead-cold ashes of their sons,
Shall never curse my cruelty. Good heaven,
What a sweet face has Arcite! If wise Nature,
With all her best endowments, all those beauties
She sows into the births of noble bodies,
Were here a mortal woman, and had in her 10
The coy denials of young maids, yet doubtless
She would run mad for this man. What an eye,
Of what a fiery sparkle and quick sweetness,

---

[1] Descry.

[2] "The fourth act may safely be pronounced wholly Fletcher's. All of it, except one scene, is taken up by the episodical adventures of the Gaoler's Daughter; and, while much of it is poetical, it wants the force and originality, and, indeed, all the prominent features of Shakespeare's manner, either of thought, illustration, or expression." — *Spalding.* "The description in this scene has a certain resemblance to the circumstances of the death of Ophelia, and was probably written with that scene in view. It has no reference whatever to the *character* of the Gaoler's Daughter, and it is the only circumstance in the whole play common to her and to Ophelia." — *Hickson.*

Has this young prince ! here Love himself sits smiling;
Just such another wanton Ganymede [1]
Set Jove afire with, and enforc'd the god
Snatch up the goodly boy, and set him by him,
A shining constellation. What a brow,
Of what a spacious majesty, he carries,
Arch'd like the great-eyed Juno's, but far sweeter,   20
Smoother than Pelops' shoulder ! [2] Fame and Honour,
Methinks, from hence, as from a promontory
Pointed in heaven, should clap their wings, and sing
To all the under-world the loves and fights
Of gods and such men near 'em. Palamon
Is but his foil; to him, a mere dull shadow;
He's swarth and meagre, of an eye as heavy
As if he had lost his mother; a still temper,
No stirring in him, no alacrity;
Of all this sprightly sharpness, not a smile. —   30
Yet these that we count errors, may become him;
Narcissus was a sad boy, but a heavenly.
O, who can find the bent of woman's fancy?
I am a fool, my reason is lost in me;
I have no choice, and I have lied so lewdly

[1] The constellation Aquarius was identified with Ganymede.

[2] " Tantalus, the favourite of the gods, once invited them to a repast, and on that occasion killed his own son Pelops, and having boiled him, set the flesh before them that they might eat it. But the immortal gods, knowing what it was, did not touch it; Demeter alone, being absorbed by grief for her lost daughter, consumed the *shoulder* of Pelops. Hereupon the gods ordered Hermes to put the limbs of Pelops into a cauldron and thereby restore him to life. When the process was over, Clotho took him out of the cauldron, and as the shoulder consumed by Demeter was wanting, the goddess supplied its place by one made of ivory; his descendants (the Pelopidæ) as a mark of their origin, were believed to have one shoulder *as white as ivory*." — *Smith's Classical Dict.*

That women ought to beat me. — On my knees
I ask thy pardon, Palamon ! Thou art alone,
And only beautiful; and these the eyes,
These the bright lamps of beauty, that command
And threaten Love, and what young maid dare cross 'em?
What a bold gravity, and yet inviting,   41
Has this brown manly face ! O Love, this only
From this hour is complexion. Lie there, Arcite !
Thou art a changeling to him, a mere gipsy,
And this the noble body. I am sotted,
Utterly lost ! my virgin's faith has fled me !
For if my brother but e'en now had ask'd me
Whether[1] I lov'd, I had run mad for Arcite ;
Now if my sister, more for Palamon. —
Stand both together ! — Now come, ask me, brother ; —   50
Alas, I know not ! — Ask me now, sweet sister ; —
I may go look ! — What a mere child is fancy,
That, having two fair gawds of equal sweetness,
Cannot distinguish, but must cry for both !—

Enter a Gentleman.

How now, sir?
   Gentleman. From the noble duke your brother,
Madam, I bring you news : the knights are come !
   Emilia. To end the quarrel?
   Gentleman.   Yes.
   Emilia.   Would I might end first !
What sins have I committed, chaste Diana,
That my unspotted youth must now be soil'd
With blood of princes? and my chastity   60
Be made the altar, where the lives of lovers —

---

[1] Which of the two.

Two greater and two better never yet
Made mothers joy — must be the sacrifice
To my unhappy beauty?

Enter THESEUS, HIPPOLYTA, PIRITHOUS, *and* Attendants.

 Theseus.   Bring 'em in
Quickly, by any means! I long to see 'em. —
Your two contending lovers are return'd,
And with them their fair knights; now, my fair sister,
You must love one of them.
 Emilia.   I had rather both,
So neither for my sake should fall untimely.
 Theseus. Who saw 'em?
 Pirithous.   I awhile.
 Gentleman.   And I.   70

    Enter Messenger.

 Theseus. From whence come you, sir?
 Messenger.   From the knights.
 Theseus.   Pray speak,
You that have seen them, what they are.
 Messenger.   I will, sir,
And truly what I think. Six braver spirits
Than these they have brought — if we judge by the outside —
I never saw nor read of. He that stands
In the first place with Arcite, by his seeming
Should be a stout man, by his face a prince, —
His very looks so say him; his complexion
Nearer a brown than black; stern, and yet noble,
Which shows him hardy, fearless, proud of dangers; 80
The circles of his eyes show fire within him,
And as a heated lion, so he looks;

His hair hangs long behind him, black and shining
Like ravens' wings; his shoulders broad and strong;
Arm'd long and round:[1] and on his thigh a sword
Hung by a curious baldrick,[2] when he frowns
To seal his will with; better, o' my conscience,
Was never soldier's friend.
    Theseus. Thou hast well describ'd him.
    Pirithous.   Yet a great deal short,
Methinks, of him that's first with Palamon.   90
    Theseus. Pray speak him, friend.
    Pirithous.   I guess he is a prince too,
And, if it may be, greater; for his show
Has all the ornament of honour in't.
He's somewhat bigger than the knight he spoke of,
But of a face far sweeter; his complexion
Is, as a ripe grape, ruddy; he has felt,
Without doubt, what he fights for, and so apter
To make this cause his own; in's face appears
All the fair hopes of what he undertakes;
And when he's angry, then a settled valour,   100
Not tainted with extremes, runs through his body,
And guides his arm to brave things; fear he cannot,
He shows no such soft temper. His head's yellow,
Hard-hair'd, and curl'd, thick twin'd, like ivy-tods,[3]
Not to undo[4] with thunder; in his face
The livery of the warlike maid appears,
Pure red and white, for yet no beard has blest him;
And in his rolling eyes sits Victory,
As if she ever meant to crown his valour;

[1] Arms long and round.   [2] A belt.
[3] Thick clusters of ivy; so Spenser, *Shepherd's Kalendar*, March, i, 67.
[4] Not to be destroyed by thunder.

His nose stands high, a character of honour;
His red lips, after fights, are fit for ladies. —
  Emilia. Must these men die too?
  Pirithous.   When he speaks, his tongue
Sounds like a trumpet; all his lineaments
Are as a man would wish 'em, strong and clean;
He wears a well steel'd axe, the staff of gold;
His age some five-and-twenty.
  Messenger.   There's another,
A little man, but of a tough soul, seeming
As great as any; fairer promises
In such a body yet I never look'd on.
  Pirithous. O, he that's freckled-fac'd?
  Messenger.   The same, my lord;
Are they not sweet ones?
  Pirithous.   Yes, they're well.
  Messenger.   Methinks,
Being so few and well dispos'd, they show
Great and fine art in nature.[1] He's white-hair'd,
Not wanton-white, but such a manly colour
Next to an auburn; tough, and nimble-set,
Which shews an active soul; his arms are brawny,
Lin'd with strong sinews; to the shoulder-piece
Gently they swell,
Which speaks him prone to labour, never fainting
Under the weight of arms; stout-hearted, still,
But, when he stirs, a tiger; he's grey-eyed,
Which yields compassion where he conquers; sharp
To spy advantages, and where he finds 'em

---

[1] The freckles were not unbecoming; women still regard a mole on the face as a mark of beauty. In the last century patches of black plaster were worn.

He's swift to make 'em his; he does no wrongs,
Nor takes none; he's round-fac'd, and when he smiles
He shows a lover, when he frowns a soldier.
About his head he wears the winner's oak,
And in it stuck the favour of his lady;
His age, some six-and-thirty. In his hand
He bears a charging-staff,[1] emboss'd with silver. 140
   Theseus. Are they all thus?
   Pirithous. They're all the sons of honour.
   Theseus. Now, as I have a soul, I long to see 'em! —
Lady, you shall see men fight now.
   Hippolyta.   I wish it,
But not the cause, my lord: they would show
Bravely about the titles of two kingdoms;
'Tis pity love should be so tyrannous. —
Oh, my soft-hearted sister, what think you?
Weep not, till they weep blood, wench! it must be.
   Theseus. You have steel'd 'em with your beauty. — Honour'd friend, 150
To you I give the field; pray order it
Fitting the persons that must use it!
   Pirithous.   Yes, sir.
   Theseus. Come, I'll go visit 'em: I cannot stay —
Their fame has fir'd me so — till they appear.
Good friend, be royal!
   Pirithous.   There shall want no bravery.[2]
   Emilia. Poor wench, go weep; for whosoever wins
Loses a noble cousin for thy sins.   [*Exeunt.*[3]

---

   [1] Lance.   [2] Rich decoration.
   [3] "Fletcher's masterpiece." — *Hickson.* "In the soliloquy of the lady, while the poetical spirit is well preserved, the alternations of feeling are given with an abruptness and a want of insight into the nicer shades of

Scene III.[1] — *Athens. A Room in the Prison.*

Enter Gaoler, Wooer, *and* Doctor.

Doctor. Her distraction is more at some time of the moon than at other some, is it not?

Gaoler. She is continually in a harmless distemper; sleeps little, altogether without appetite, save often drinking; dreaming of another world, and a better; and what broken piece of matter soe'er she's about, the name Palamon lards it; that she farces[2] every business withal, fits it to every question. — Look, where she comes! you shall perceive her behaviour.   9

Enter Daughter.

Daughter. I have forgot it quite; the burden on't was "down-a down-a;" and penned by no worse man than Giraldo, Emilia's schoolmaster: he's as fantastical, too, as ever he may go upon's legs; for in the next world will Dido see Palamon, and then will she be out of love with Æneas.

Doctor. What stuff's here! poor soul!

Gaoler. Even thus all day long.   16

Daughter. Now for this charm, that I told you of: you must bring a piece of silver on the tip of your tongue, or no ferry;[3] then if it be your chance to come where the blessed

---

association, which resemble the extravagant stage effects of the *King and No King* infinitely more than the delicate yet piercing glance with which Shakespeare looks into the human breast in the *Othello;* the language, too, is smoother and less powerful than Shakespeare's, and one or two classical allusions are a little too correct and studied for him." — *Spalding.*

[1] "The idea of this scene has some resemblance to that of *Macbeth,* v. 1." — *Skeat.*

[2] Stuffs.

[3] The ancients placed a piece of silver in the mouth of a corpse to pay Charon for passage over the Styx.

spirits are — there's a sight now! — we maids that have our livers perished, cracked to pieces with love, we shall come there, and do nothing all day long but pick flowers with Proserpine; then will I make Palamon a nosegay; then let him — mark me — then —   24

Doctor. How prettily she's amiss! note her a little further.

Daughter. Faith, I'll tell you; sometime we go to barley-break,[1] we of the blessed. Alas, 'tis a sore life they have i' the other place, such burning, hissing, howling, chattering, cursing! O, they have shrewd measure! Take heed: if one be mad, or hang or drown themselves, thither they go, Jupiter bless us! and there shall they be put in a cauldron of lead, amongst a whole million of cutpurses, and there boil like a gammon of bacon that will never be enough.   34

Doctor. How she continues this fancy! 'Tis not an engraffed[2] madness, but a most thick and profound melancholy.

Daughter. To hear there a proud lady and a proud city-wife howl together! I were a beast, an I'd call it good sport!

(Sings) *I will be true, my stars, my fate,* etc.

[*Exit* Daughter.

Gaoler. What think you of her, sir?

Doctor. I think she has a perturbed mind, which I cannot minister to.

Gaoler. Alas, what then?

---

[1] "A rural game often alluded to in the old dramatists. It was played in various ways, but generally in the South of England by six persons, three of each sex. The general idea of it was that one couple should try to catch the rest, when within certain boundaries, without letting go each other's hands." — *Rolfe.*

[2] Grafted.

Doctor. Understand you she ever affected any man ere she beheld Palamon?

Gaoler. I was once, sir, in great hope she had fixed her liking on this gentleman, my friend. 49

Wooer. I did think so too; and would account I had a great pen'worth [1] on't, to give half my state that both she and I at this present stood unfeignedly on the same terms.

Doctor. That intemperate surfeit of her eye hath distempered the other senses; they may return, and settle again to execute their preordained faculties; but they are now in a most extravagant vagary. This you must do: confine her to a place where the light may rather seem to steal in than be permitted. Take upon you, young sir, her friend, the name of Palamon; say you come to eat with her, and to commune of love; this will catch her attention, for this her mind beats upon; other objects, that are inserted 'tween her mind and eye, become the pranks and friskings of her madness. Sing to her such green [2] songs of love as she says Palamon hath sung in prison; come to her, stuck in as sweet flowers as the season is mistress of, and thereto make an addition of some other compounded odours which are grateful to the sense: all this shall become Palamon, for Palamon can sing, and Palamon is sweet, and every good thing. Desire to eat with her, carve [3] her, drink to her, and still among [4] intermingle your petition of grace and acceptance into her favour; learn what maids have been her companions and play-feres [5]; and let them repair to her with Palamon in their mouths, and appear to her with tokens, as if they suggested for him. It is a falsehood she is in, which is with falsehoods to be combated. This may bring her to

[1] A good bargain.   [2] Simple.   [3] Carve for.
[4] Thereto.   [5] Playmates; travelling companions.

eat, to sleep, and reduce what is now out of square in her into their former law and regiment.¹ I have seen it approved, how many times I know not; but to make the number more, I have great hope in this. I will, between the passages of this project, come in with my appliance. Let us put it in execution, and hasten the success, which, doubt not, will bring forth comfort. [*Exeunt.*²

ACT V.³

SCENE I.—*Athens. An Open Space before the Temples of Mars, Venus, and Diana.*

Enter THESEUS, PIRITHOUS, HIPPOLYTA, *and* Attendants.

Theseus. Now let 'em enter, and before the gods
Tender their holy prayers! Let the temples
Burn bright with sacred fires, and the altars,
In hallow'd clouds commend their swelling incense
To those above us! Let no due be wanting!
                              [*Flourish of cornets.*
They have a noble work in hand, will honour
The very powers that love 'em.

Enter PALAMON, ARCITE, *and their* Knights.

Pirithous.   Sir, they enter.

---

¹ Rule, order.

² *Spalding* assigns this scene to Fletcher; but *Hickson* thinks it is Shakespeare's "in style and language, and its freedom from all marks of imitation."

³ Most of the critics assign this act (except Scene 2) to Shakespeare; but *Skeat, Littledale,* and *Fleay* attribute the opening to Fletcher.

Theseus. You valiant and strong-hearted enemies,
You royal germane [1] foes, that this day come
To blow the nearness [2] out that flames between ye,
Lay by your anger for an hour, and dove-like
Before the holy altars of our helpers,
The all-fear'd gods, bow down your stubborn bodies.
Your ire is more than mortal; so your help be!
And as the gods regard ye, fight with justice!
I'll leave you to your prayers, and betwixt ye
I part my wishes.
   Pirithous.   Honour crown the worthiest!
                                                          [*Exeunt* THESEUS *and train.*
   Palamon. The glass is running now that cannot finish
Till one of us expire: think you but thus, —
That, were there aught in me which strove to show
Mine enemy in this business, were't one eye
Against another, arm oppress'd by arm,
I would destroy the offender; coz, I would,
Though parcel of myself: then from this gather
How I should tender you.
   Arcite.   I am in labour
To push your name, your ancient love, our kindred,
Out of my memory; and i' the self-same place
To seat something I would confound: so hoist we
The sails that must these vessels port even where
The heavenly Limiter pleases!
   Palamon.   You speak well.
Before I turn, let me embrace thee, cousin. [*They embrace.*

---

[1] Akin.

[2] Obscure: *Skeat* suggests " to extinguish that kinship that exists between you." *Rolfe* thinks that "nearness" refers to their friendship. *Ingleby* would substitute "fierceness."

This I shall never do again.
 Arcite.   One farewell!
 Palamon. Why, let it be so; farewell, coz!
 Arcite.   Farewell, sir! —
     [*Exeunt* PALAMON *and his* Knights.
Knights, kinsmen, lovers, yea, my sacrifices,
True worshippers of Mars, whose spirit in you
Expels the seeds of fear, and the apprehension
Which still is father of it, go with me
Before the god of our profession. There
Require of him the hearts of lions, and
The breath of tigers, yea, the fierceness too;   40
Yea, the speed also, — to go on, I mean,
Else wish we to be snails. You know my prize
Must be dragg'd out of blood; force and great feat
Must put my garland on, where she will stick
The queen of flowers. Our intercession, then,
Must be to him that makes the camp a cestron[1]
Brimm'd with the blood of men; give me your aid,
And bend your spirits towards him. —
   [*They advance to the altar of Mars, and fall on*
     their faces; then kneel.
Thou mighty one, that with thy power hast turn'd
Green Neptune into purple; whose approach   50
Comets prewarn; whose havoc in vast field
Unearthèd skulls proclaim; whose breath blows down
The teeming Ceres' foison[2]; who dost pluck
With hand armipotent from forth blue clouds
The mason'd turrets; that both mak'st and break'st
The stony girths of cities; me, thy pupil,
Young'st follower of thy drum, instruct this day

   [1] Cistern.   [2] Plenty.

With military skill, that to thy laud
I may advance my streamer, and by thee
Be styl'd the lord o' the day. Give me, great Mars, 60
Some token of thy pleasure.
    [*Here they fall on their faces as before, and there
      is heard clanging of armour, with a short
      thunder, as the burst of a battle, whereupon
      they all rise, and bow to the altar.*
O great corrector of enormous [1] times,
Shaker of o'er-rank states, thou grand decider
Of dusty and old titles, that heal'st with blood
The earth when it is sick, and cur'st the world
O' the plurisy [2] of people, I do take
Thy signs auspiciously, and in thy name
To my design march boldly! — Let us go. [*Exeunt.*
   Re-enter PALAMON *and his* Knights.

 Palamon. Our stars must glister with new fires, or be
To-day extinct; our argument is love,   70
Which if the goddess of it grant, she gives
Victory too: then blend your spirits with mine,
You whose free nobleness do make my cause
Your personal hazard. To the goddess Venus
Commend we our proceeding, and implore
Her power unto our party! —
    [*Here they advance to the altar of Venus, and
      fall on their faces; then kneel.*
Hail, sovereign queen of secrets! who hast power
To call the fiercest tyrant from his rage,
And weep unto a girl; that hast the might
Even with an eye-glance to choke Mars's drum, 80

---

  1 Monstrous.   2 Plethora.

And turn the alarm to whispers; that canst make
A cripple flourish with his crutch, and cure him
Before Apollo;¹ that mayst force the king
To be his subject's vassal, and induce
Stale gravity to dance; the polled² bachelor,
Whose youth, like wanton boys through bonfires,
Have skipt thy flame, at seventy thou canst catch,
And make him, to the scorn of his hoarse throat,
Abuse young lays of love. What godlike power
Hast thou not power upon? To Phœbus thou   90
Add'st flames, hotter than his; the heavenly fires
Did scorch his mortal son, thine him; the huntress,
All moist and cold, some say, began to throw
Her bow away and sigh.³ Take to thy grace
Me thy vow'd soldier, who do bear thy yoke
As 'twere a wreath of roses, yet is heavier
Than lead itself, stings more than nettles. I
Have never been foul-mouth'd against thy law,
Ne'er reveal'd secret, for I knew none, — would not,
Had I kenn'd all that were; I never practis'd   100
Upon man's wife, nor would the libels read
Of liberal wits; I never at great feasts
Sought to betray a beauty, but have blush'd
At simpering sirs that did; I have been harsh
To large⁴ confessors, and have hotly ask'd them
If they had mothers. I had one, a woman,
And women 'twere they wrong'd. I knew a man
Of eighty winters — this I told them — who

---

¹ Before Apollo can.   ² Shorn, bald-headed.
³ Compare this eulogy of Venus with Zorobabel's description of the power of woman, in the *Apocryphal Old Testament*, 1 *Esdras*, chap. 4.
⁴ Licentious boasters.

A lass of fourteen brided. 'Twas thy power
To put life into dust; the aged cramp   110
Had screw'd his square foot round,
The gout had knit his fingers into knots,
Torturing convulsions from his globy[1] eyes
Had almost drawn their spheres, that what was life
In him seem'd torture. This anatomy[2]
Had by his young fair fere a boy, and I
Believ'd it was his, for she swore it was,
And who would not believe her? Brief, I am
To those that prate, and have done, no companion;
To those that boast, and have not, a defier;   120
To those that would, and cannot, a rejoicer;
Yea, him I do not love that tells close offices
The foulest way, nor names concealments in
The boldest language: such a one I am,
And vow that lover never yet made sigh
Truer than I. O, then, most soft sweet goddess,
Give me the victory of this question, which
Is true love's merit, and bless me with a sign
Of thy great pleasure!
    [*Here music is heard, doves are seen to flutter; they
        fall again upon their faces, then on their knees.*
O thou that from eleven to ninety reign'st   130
In mortal bosoms, whose chase[3] is this world,
And we in herds thy game, I give thee thanks
For this fair token, which, being laid unto
Mine innocent true heart, arms in assurance
My body to this business! — Let us rise
And bow before the goddess; time comes on.
                [*They bow, then exeunt.*

---

[1] Bulging.   [2] Skeleton.   [3] Hunting-ground.

Still music of records. Enter EMILIA *in white, her hair about her shoulders, and wearing a wheaten wreath; one in white holding up her train, her hair stuck with flowers; one before her carrying a silver hind, in which is conveyed incense and sweet odours, which being set upon the altar of Diana, her Maids standing aloof, she sets fire to it; then they curtsy and kneel.*

Emilia. O sacred, shadowy, cold, and constant queen,
Abandoner of revels, mute, contemplative,
Sweet, solitary, white as chaste, and pure
As wind-fann'd snow, who to thy female knights   140
Allow'st no more blood than will make a blush,
Which is their order's robe, I here, thy priest,
Am humbled 'fore thine altar! O, vouchsafe,
With that thy rare green[1] eye — which never yet
Beheld thing maculate — look on thy virgin!
And, sacred silver mistress, lend thine ear —
Which ne'er heard scurril[2] term, into whose port
Ne'er entered wanton sound — to my petition,
Season'd with holy fear! This is my last
Of vestal office; I'm bride habited,   150
But maiden-hearted; a husband I have pointed,[3]
But do not know him; out of two I should
Choose one, and pray for his success, but I
Am guiltless of election; of mine eyes,
Were I to lose one — they are equal precious —

[1] Green eyes were esteemed peculiarly beautiful; so *Romeo and Juliet*, iii, 5, 221: —
  "An eagle, madam,
  Hath not so green, so quick, so fair an eye."
Dante describes Beatrice's eyes as *smeraldi*, emeralds. *Purgatorio*, xxxi, 116.
  [2] Scurrilous.   [3] Appointed.

I could doom neither; that which perish'd should
Go to't unsentenc'd: therefore, most modest queen,
He, of the two pretenders,[1] that best loves me
And has the truest title in't, let him
Take off my wheaten garland,[2] or else grant   160
The file and quality I hold I may
Continue in thy band. —
　　　　[*Here the hind vanishes under the altar, and in
　　　　the place ascends a rose-tree, having one
　　　　rose upon it.*
See what our general of ebbs and flows[3]
Out from the bowels of her holy altar
With sacred act advances! But one rose!
If well inspir'd, this battle shall confound
Both these brave knights, and I, a virgin flower,
Must grow alone, unpluck'd.
　　　　[*Here is heard a sudden twang of instruments,
　　　　and the rose falls from the tree, which van-
　　　　ishes under the altar.*
The flower is fallen, the tree descends! — O mistress,
Thou here dischargest me! I shall be gather'd,   170
I think so; but I know not thine own will:
Unclasp thy mystery! — I hope she's pleas'd;
Her signs were gracious.　　　[*They curtsy, and exeunt.*

　　　1 Suitors.　　　　　　2 Nuptial wreath.
　　　3 Refers to the moon (Diana) as ruler of the tides.

Scene II. — *A Room in the Prison.*

Enter Doctor, Gaoler, *and* Wooer *in the habit of* Palamon.

Doctor. Has this advice I told you done any good upon her?
Wooer. O, very much: the maids that kept her company
Have half persuaded her that I am Palamon;
Within this half-hour she came smiling to me,
And ask'd me what I'd eat, and when I'd kiss her:
I told her presently, and kissed her twice.
Doctor. 'Twas well done; twenty times had been far better,
For there the cure lies mainly.
Wooer. Then she told me
She would watch with me to-night, for well she knew 10
What hour my fit would take me.
Doctor. Let her do so.
Wooer. She would have me sing.
Doctor. You did so?
Wooer. No.
Doctor. 'Twas very ill done, then;
You should observe her every way.
Wooer. Alas!
I have no voice, sir, to confirm her that way.
Doctor. That's all one, if ye make a noise;
If she entreat again, do anything.
Ne'er cast your child away for honesty.
Gaoler. Thank you, doctor.
Doctor. Pray, bring her in, 20
And let's see how she is.
Gaoler. I will, and tell her

Her Palamon stays for her; but, doctor,
Methinks you are i' the wrong still. [*Exit*
  Doctor.   Go, go;
You fathers are fine fools: her honesty!
An we should give her physic till we find that —
  Wooer. Why, do you think she is not honest, sir?
  Doctor. How old is she?
  Wooer.   She's eighteen.
  Doctor.   She may be;
But that's all one, 'tis nothing to our purpose.
Whate'er her father says, if you perceive
Her mood inclining that way that I spoke of. —
  Wooer. Yes, very well, sir.   30

    Enter Gaoler, Daughter, *and* Maid.

  Gaoler. Come; your love Palamon stays for you, child;
And has done this long hour, to visit you.
  Daughter. I thank him for his gentle patience;
He's a kind gentleman, and I am much bound to him.
Did you ne'er see the horse he gave me?
  Gaoler.   Yes.
  Daughter. How do you like him?
  Gaoler.   He's a very fair one.
  Daughter. You never saw him dance?
  Gaoler.   No.
  Daughter.   I have often:
He dances very finely, very comely;
And, for a jig, come cut and long tail[1] to him!
He turns ye like a top.
  Gaoler.   That's fine indeed.   40

[1] Proverbial phrase, "Let horses of every kind compete with and beat him, if they can."

Daughter. He'll dance the morris twenty mile an hour,—
And that will founder the best hobby-horse,
If I have any skill, in all the parish, —
And gallops to the tune of " Light o' Love ";
What think you of this horse?
  Gaoler. Having these virtues,
I think he might be brought to play at tennis.
  Daughter. Alas, that's nothing!
  Gaoler. Can he write and read too?
  Daughter. A very fair hand, and casts himself the accounts
Of all his hay and provender; that hostler
Must rise betime that cozens him. You know 50
The chestnut mare the duke has?
  Gaoler. Very well.
  Daughter. She is horribly in love with him, poor beast;
But he is like his master, coy and scornful.
  Gaoler. What dowry has she?
  Daughter. Some two hundred bottles,[1]
And twenty strike[2] of oats. but he'll ne'er have her;
He lisps in's neighing, able to entice
A miller's mare;[3] he'll be the death of her.
  Doctor. What stuff she utters!
  Gaoler. Make curtsy; here your lover comes.
  Wooer. Pretty soul,
How do ye? That's a fine maid! there's a curtsy! 60
  Daughter. Yours to command, i' the way of honesty.
How far is't now to the end o' the world, my masters?
  Doctor. Why, a day's journey, wench.

---

[1] Bundles of hay. [2] Bushel; still used in provincial English.
[3] "A miller's mare, working round a beaten track (to drive the mill), was perhaps proverbial for her steady-going attention to business." — *Littledale.*

Daughter. Will you go with me?
Wooer. What shall we do there, wench?
Daughter. Why, play at stool-ball.¹
What is there else to do?
Wooer. I am content,
If we shall keep our wedding there.
Daughter. 'Tis true;
For there, I will assure you, we shall find
Some blind priest for the purpose, that will venture
To marry us, for here they are nice ² and foolish;
Besides, my father must be hang'd to-morrow,   70
And that would be a blot i' the business.
Are not you Palamon?
    Wooer. Do not you know me?
    Daughter. Yes; but you care not for me; I have nothing
But this poor petticoat and two coarse smocks.
Wooer. That's all one; I will have you.
Daughter. Will you surely?
Wooer. Yes, by this fair hand, will I. [*Kisses her.*
Daughter. O, sir, you'd fain be nibbling!
Wooer. Why do you rub my kiss off?
Daughter. 'Tis a sweet one,
And will perfume me finely against the wedding. —
Is not this your cousin Arcite?
    Doctor. Yes, sweetheart;
And I am glad my cousin Palamon   80
Has made so fair a choice.
    Daughter. Do you think he'll have me?

---

¹ A game popular among young women, played with a ball and one or two stools.

² Over-particular.

Doctor. Yes, without doubt.
Daughter. Do you think so too?
Gaoler. Yes.
Daughter. We shall have many children. — Lord, how
  y' are grown!
My Palamon I hope will grow too, finely,
Now he's at liberty; alas, poor chicken!
He was kept down with hard meat and ill lodging,
But I will kiss him up again.

Enter a Messenger.

Messenger. What do you here? you'll lose the noblest
  sight
That e'er was seen.
Gaoler. Are they i' the field?
Messenger. They are;
You bear a charge there too.
Gaoler. I'll away straight. — 90
I must even leave you here.
Doctor. Nay, we'll go with you;
I will not lose the sight.
Gaoler. How did you like her?
Doctor. I'll warrant you, within these three or four days
I'll make her right again. — You must not from her,
But still preserve her in this way.
Wooer. I will.
Doctor. Let's get her in.
Wooer. Come, sweet, we'll go to dinner;
And then we'll play at cards. [*Exeunt.*[1]

[1] This scene is "disgusting and imbecile in the extreme," and "may be dismissed with a single quotation: 'What stuff she utters!'" — *Spalding.*
"The former scene (Act iv, 3) is in prose wholly, while this is in Fletcher's

SCENE III. — *A Part of the Forest, near the Place of Combat.*

Enter THESEUS, HIPPOLYTA, EMILIA, PIRITHOUS, *and* Attendants.

Emilia. I'll no step further.
Pirithous. Will you lose this sight?
Emilia. I had rather see a wren hawk at a fly
Than this decision: every blow that falls
Threats a brave life; each stroke laments
The place whereon it falls, and sounds more like
A bell than blade. I will stay here, —
It is enough my hearing shall be punished
With what shall happen, 'gainst the which there is
No deafing but to hear, — not taint mine eye
With dread sights it may shun.
Pirithous. Sir, my good lord, 10
Your sister will no further.
Theseus. O, she must!
She shall see deeds of honour in their kind,
Which sometime show well, pencill'd; nature now
Shall make and act the story, the belief
Both seal'd with eye and ear. You must be present;
You are the victor's meed, the price and garland
To crown the question's title.
Emilia. Pardon me;
If I were there, I'd wink.
Theseus. You must be there;

verse; but, in short, the tone and moral effect of the two scenes are so different, the same characters have so altered an aspect, the language, sentiments, and allusions are so unlike, that the case of any one who can read and deliberately compare them, and still believe them to be by the same writer, we must give over as hopeless." — *Hickson.*

This trial is as 'twere i' the night, and you
The only star to shine.
    Emilia.   I am extinct;
There is but envy[1] in that light which shews
The one the other. Darkness, which ever was
The dam of Horror, who does stand accurs'd
Of many mortal millions, may even now,
By casting her black mantle over both,
That neither could find other, get herself
Some part of a good name, and many a murther
Set off[2] whereto she's guilty.
    Hippolyta.   You must go.
    Emilia. In faith, I will not.
    Theseus.   Why, the knights must kindle
Their valour at your eye; know, of this war
You are the treasure, and must needs be by
To give the service pay.
    Emilia.   Sir, pardon me;
The title of a kingdom may be tried
Out of itself.
    Theseus. Well, well, then, at your pleasure!
Those that remain with you could wish their office
To any of their enemies.
    Hippolyta.   Farewell, sister!
I am like to know your husband 'fore yourself,
By some small start of time; he whom the gods
Do of the two know best, I pray them he
Be made your lot!

    [*Exeunt all except* EMILIA *and some of the* Attendants.
    Emilia. Arcite is gently visag'd, yet his eye
Is like an engine bent,[3] or a sharp weapon

---

[1] Malice.   [2] Offset.   [3] Ready for use.

In a soft sheath; mercy and manly courage
Are bedfellows in his visage. Palamon
Has a most menacing aspect; his brow
Is grav'd, and seems to bury what it frowns on:
Yet sometimes 'tis not so, but alters to
The quality of his thoughts; long time his eye
Will dwell upon his object. Melancholy
Becomes him nobly; so does Arcite's mirth: 50
But Palamon's sadness is a kind of mirth,
So mingled as if mirth did make him sad,
And sadness merry; those darker humours that
Stick misbecomingly on others, on him
Live in fair dwelling. —
    [*Cornets. Trumpets sound as to a charge.*
Hark, how yon spurs to spirit do incite
The princes to their proof! Arcite may win me;
And yet may Palamon wound Arcite, to
The spoiling of his figure. O, what pity
Enough for such a chance ! If I were by, 60
I might do hurt; for they would glance their eyes
Toward my seat, and in that motion might
Omit a ward,[1] or forfeit an offence.[2]
Which crav'd that very time: it is much better
    [*Cornets. Cry within*, "A Palamon!"
I am not there: O, better never born
Than minister to such harm ! — What is the chance?
 Servant. The cry's "A Palamon."
 Emilia. Then he has won. 'Twas ever likely;
He look'd all grace and success, and he is
Doubtless the prim'st of men. I prithee run, 70

---

[1] Guard.   [2] Blow.

And tell me how it goes.
          [*Shout, and cornets; cry,* " A Palamon ! "
    Servant.   Still " Palamon."
    Emilia. Run and inquire. — (*Exit Servant.*) Poor ser-
       vant, thou hast lost !
Upon my right side still I wore thy picture,
Palamon's on the left : why so, I know not ;
I had no end in't else ; chance would have it so.
          [*Another cry and shout within, and cornets.*
On the sinister side the heart lies ; Palamon
Had the best-boding chance. This burst of clamour
Is, sure, the end o' the combat.
              Re-enter Servant.

    Servant. They said that Palamon had Arcite's body
Within an inch o' the pyramid, that the cry   80
Was general " A Palamon " ; but anon,
The assistants made a brave redemption,[1] and
The two bold tilters at this instant are
Hand to hand at it.
    Emilia.   Were they metamorphos'd
Both into one — O, why, there were no woman
Worth so compos'd a man ! Their single share,
Their nobleness peculiar to them, gives
The prejudice of disparity, value's shortness,
          [*Cornets. Cry within,* " Arcite, Arcite ! '
To any lady breathing. — More exulting !
" Palamon " still ?
    Servant.   Nay, now the sound is " Arcite."   90
    Emilia. I prithee lay attention to the cry ;
          [*Cornets. A great shout and cry,* " Arcite, victory ! "

            [1] Rescue.

Set both thine ears to the business.
  Servant.   The cry is
" Arcite, and victory ! " Hark " Arcite, victory ! "
The combat's consummation is proclaim'd
By the wind-instruments.
  Emilia.   Half-sights[1] saw
That Arcite was no babe ; God's lid, his richness
And costliness of spirit look'd through him ! it could
No more be hid in him than fire in flax,
Than humble banks can go to law with waters
That drift-winds force to raging. I did think
Good Palamon would miscarry ; yet I knew not
Why I did think so : our reasons are not prophets,
When oft our fancies are. They're coming off ;
Alas, poor Palamon !   [*Cornets.*

Enter THESEUS, HIPPOLYTA, PIRITHOUS, ARCITE *as victor,*
                Attendants, etc.

  Theseus. Lo, where our sister is in expectation,
Yet quaking and unsettled ! — Fairest Emily,
The gods by their divine arbitrement,
Have given you this knight ; he is a good one
As ever struck at head. — Give me your hands !
Receive you her, you him ; be plighted with
A love that grows as you decay !
  Arcite.   Emily,
To buy you I have lost what's dearest to me,
Save what is bought ; and yet I purchase cheaply,
As I do rate your value.
  Theseus.   O, lov'd sister,
He speaks now of as brave a knight as e'er

---

[1] Hasty glances.

Did spur a noble steed; surely the gods
Would have him die a bachelor, lest his race
Should show i' the world too godlike! His behaviour
So charm'd me, that methought Alcides[1] was
To him a sow[2] of lead; if I could praise 120
Each part of him to the all I've spoke, your Arcite
Did not lose by't, for he that was thus good
Encounter'd yet his better. I have heard
Two emulous Philomels[3] beat the ear o' the night,
With their contentious throats, now one the higher,
Anon the other, then again the first,
And by and by out-breasted,[4] that the sense
Could not be judge between 'em; so it fair'd
Good space between these kinsmen, till heavens did
Make hardly one the winner. — Wear the garland 130
With joy that you have won! — For the subdued,
Give them our present justice, since I know
Their lives but pinch[5] 'em; let it here be done,
The scene's not for our seeing; go we hence,
Right joyful, with some sorrow! — Arm your prize;[6]
I know you will not lose her. — Hippolyta,
I see one eye of yours conceives a tear,
The which it will deliver. [*Flourish.*

[1] Hercules.
[2] "*Sow*, like *pig*, is used to denote a mass of smelted metal." — *Rolfe.*
[3] Nightingales. [4] Out-sung.
[5] "Vex them. It was in the very spirit of chivalry that a warrior should not care to survive defeat. This doom of Palamon and his three knights would be revolting, if it were not that the spectators might be expected to know enough of Chaucer's story to make them suspect that the sentence would not really be executed. To which must be added the consideration, that the spectators of plays in the time of James I could behold, almost unmoved, many things which we now shudder even to read." — *Skeat.*
[6] Embrace.

Emilia.　　　　　　Is this winning?
O all you heavenly powers, where is your mercy?
But that your wills have said it must be so,　　　　140
And charge me live to comfort this unfriended,
This miserable prince, that cuts away
A life more worthy from him than all women,
I should and would die too.
　Hippolyta.　　　　　Infinite pity,
That four such eyes should be so fix'd on one
That two must needs be blind for't!
　Theseus.　　　　　　So it is.　[*Exeunt.*[1]

SCENE IV.—*The Same Part of the Forest as in Act III, Scene VI.*

Enter PALAMON *and his* Knights *pinioned,* Gaoler, Executioner, *and* Guard.

　Palamon. There's many a man alive that hath outliv'd
The love o' the people; yea, i' the self-same state
Stands many a father with his child.　Some comfort
We have by so considering; we expire,
And not without men's pity; to live still
Have their good wishes; we prevent
The loathsome misery of age, beguile
The gout and rheum, that in lag[2] hours attend
For grey approachers; we come towards the gods

---

[1] The details of this scene, says *Spalding*, "make it clear that Shakespeare's hand was in it. The greater part, it is true, is not of the highest excellence; but the vacillations of Emilia's feelings are well and delicately given, some individual thoughts and words mark Shakespeare; there is little of his obscure brevity, much of his thoughtfulness legitimately applied, and an instance or two of its abuse."

[2] Lingering, or late.

Young and unwapper'd,[1] not halting under crimes
Many and stale; that, sure, shall please the gods
Sooner than such, to give us nectar with 'em,
For we are more clear spirits. My dear kinsmen,
Whose lives for this poor comfort are laid down,
You've sold 'em too-too cheap.
    1st Knight.   What ending could be
Of more content? O'er us the victors have
Fortune, whose title is as momentary
As to us death is certain; a grain of honour
They not o'erweigh us.
    2d Knight.   Let us bid farewell,
And with our patience anger tottering Fortune,
Who, at her certain'st, reels.
    3d Knight.   Come; who begins?
    Palamon. Even he that led you to this banquet shall
Taste[2] to you all. — Ah ha, my friend, my friend!
Your gentle daughter gave me freedom once;
You'll see't done now for ever. Pray, how does she?
I heard she was not well; her kind of ill
Gave me some sorrow.
    Gaoler.   Sir, she's well restor'd,
And to be married shortly.
    Palamon.   By my short life,
I am most glad on't! 'Tis the latest thing
I shall be glad of; prithee, tell her so:
Commend me to her, and, to piece her portion,
Tender her this.   [*Gives a purse.*
    1st Knight.   Nay, let's be offerers all.

---

[1] Unworn.
[2] "Alluding to the ancient custom of having the king's food tasted before it was served, as a precaution against poison." — *Rolfe.*

2d Knight. Is it a maid?
Palamon.   Verily, I think so;
A right good creature, more to me deserving
Than I can quit or speak of.
   All Knights. Commend us to her.   [*Give their purses.*
   Gaoler.   The gods requite you all,
And make her thankful!
   Palamon. Adieu! and let my life be now as short
As my leave-taking.   [*Lays his head on the block.*
   1st Knight.   Lead, courageous cousin.
   2d Knight. We'll follow cheerfully.
       [*A great noise within, crying,* "Run, save, hold!"

       Enter in haste a Messenger.

Messenger. Hold, hold! O, hold, hold, hold!   40

       Enter PIRITHOUS *in haste.*

Pirithous. Hold, ho! it is a cursed haste you made,
If you have done so quickly. — Noble Palamon,
The gods will show their glory in a life
That thou art yet to lead.
   Palamon.   Can that be, when
Venus I've said is false? How do things fare?
   Pirithous. Arise, great sir, and give the tidings ear
That are most dearly sweet and bitter!
   Palamon.   What
Hath wak'd us from our dream?   [PALAMON *rises.*
   Pirithous.   List then! Your cousin,
Mounted upon a steed that Emily
Did first bestow on him, — a black one, owing[1]   50
Not a hair-worth of white, which some will say

[1] Owning.

Weakens his price, and many will not buy
His goodness with this note ; which superstition
Here finds allowance, — on this horse is Arcite,
Trotting the stones of Athens, which the calkins [1]
Did rather tell [2] than trample ; for the horse
Would make his length a mile, if't pleas'd his rider
To put pride in him : as he thus went counting
The flinty pavement, dancing as 'twere to the music
His own hoofs made — for, as they say, from iron   60
Came music's origin — what envious flint,
Cold as old Saturn, and like him possessed
With fire malevolent, darted a spark,
Or what fierce sulphur else, to this end made,
I comment not ; the hot horse, hot as fire,
Took toy [3] at this, and fell to what disorder
His power could give his will, bounds, comes on end,
Forgets school-doing, being therein trained,
And of kind manage [4] ; pig-like he whines
At the sharp rowel, which he frets at rather   70
Than any jot obeys ; seeks all foul means
Of boisterous and rough jadery,[5] to disseat
His lord that kept it bravely.   When nought serv'd,
When neither curb would crack, girth break, nor differing
    plunges
Disroot his rider whence he grew, but that
He kept him 'tween his legs, on his hind hoofs
On end he stands,
That Arcite's legs being higher than his head,

---

[1] The parts of a horseshoe which are turned up and pointed to prevent a horse from slipping.
[2] Count.
[3] Freak.
[4] Managing a horse; French *manège.*
[5] Viciousness.

Seem'd with strange art to hang; his victor's wreath
Even then fell off his head, and presently   80
Backward the jade comes o'er, and his full poise
Becomes the rider's load.   Yet is he living;
But such a vessel 'tis that floats but for
The surge that next approaches: he much desires
To have some speech with you.   Lo, he appears!

Enter THESEUS, HIPPOLYTA, EMILIA, *and* ARCITE *borne in a chair.*

Palamon. O miserable end of our alliance!
The gods are mighty!— Arcite, if thy heart,
Thy worthy manly heart, be yet unbroken,
Give me thy last words; I am Palamon;
One that yet loves thee dying.
    Arcite.   Take Emilia,   90
And with her all the world's joy.   Reach thy hand;
Farewell! I've told my last hour.   I was false,
Yet never treacherous; forgive me, cousin!—
One kiss from fair Emilia!   (*Kisses her.*) — 'Tis done:
Take her.   I die!   [*Dies.*
    Palamon.   Thy brave soul seek Elysium!
    Emilia. I'll close thine eyes, prince; blessed souls be
        with thee!
Thou art a right good man; and, while I live,
This day I give to tears.
    Palamon.   And I to honour.
    Theseus. In this place first you fought; even very here
I sunder'd you: acknowledge to the gods   100
Your thanks that you are living.
His part is play'd, and, though it were too short,
He did it well; your day is lengthen'd, and

The blissful dew of heaven does arrose[1] you.
The powerful Venus well hath grac'd her altar,
And given you your love; our master Mars
Has vouch'd his oracle, and to Arcite gave
The grace of the contention: so the deities
Have show'd due justice.—Bear this hence.
 Palamon.   O cousin,
That we should things desire which do cost us 110
The loss of our desire! that nought could buy
Dear love but loss of dear love!
 Theseus.   Never fortune
Did play a subtler game: the conquer'd triumphs,
The victor has the loss; yet in the passage
The gods have been most equal. Palamon,
Your kinsman hath confess'd the right o' the lady
Did lie in you, for you first saw her and
Even then proclaim'd your fancy; he restor'd her,
As your stolen jewel, and desir'd your spirit
To send him hence forgiven. The gods my justice 120
Take from my hand, and they themselves become
The executioners. Lead your lady off;
And call your lovers from the stage of death,
Whom I adopt my friends. A day or two
Let us look sadly, and give grace unto
The funeral of Arcite; in whose end
The visages of bridegrooms we'll put on,
And smile with Palamon, for whom an hour,
But one hour since, I was as dearly sorry
As glad of Arcite, and am now as glad 130
As for him sorry.—O you heavenly charmers,[2]
What things you make of us! For what we lack

   [1] Besprinkle.   [2] Enchanters.

We laugh, for what we have are sorry ; still
Are children in some kind. Let us be thankful
For that which is, and with you leave dispute,
That are above our question. — Let's go off,
And bear us like the time.   [*Flourish. Exeunt.*][1]

EPILOGUE.

I would now ask ye how ye like the play ;
But, as it is with school-boys, cannot say
I am cruel-fearful.   Pray, yet stay a while,
And let me look upon ye.   No man smile?
Then it goes hard, I see. — He that has

---

[1] " The manner is Shakespeare's, and some parts are little inferior to his very finest passages." — *Spalding*. " The scene is opened by Shakespeare in his most majestic vein of meditative or moral verse, pointed and coloured as usual with him alone by direct and absolute aptitude to the immediate sentiment and situation of the speaker and of no man else: then either Fletcher strikes in for a moment with a touch of somewhat more Shakespearean tone than usual, or possibly we have a survival of some lines' length, not unretouched by Fletcher, from Shakespeare's first sketch for a conclusion of the somewhat calamitous and cumbrous underplot, which in any case was ultimately left for Fletcher to expand into such a shape and bring by such means to an end as we may safely swear that Shakespeare would never have admitted ; then with the entrance and ensuing narrative of Pirithous we have none but Shakespeare before us again, though it be Shakespeare undoubtedly in the rough, and not as he might have chosen to present himself after due revision, with rejection (we may well suppose) of this point and readjustment of that ; then upon the arrival of the dying Arcite with his escort there follows a grievous little gap, a flaw but pitifully patched by Fletcher, whom we recognize at wellnigh his worst and weakest in Palamon's appeal to his kinsman for a last word, ' if his heart, *his worthy, manly heart*' (an exact and typical example of Fletcher's tragically prosaic and prosaically tragic dash of incurable commonplace), ' be yet unbroken,' and in the flaccid and futile answer which fails so signally to supply the place of the most famous and pathetic passage in all the master-

Lov'd a young handsome wench, then, show his face —
'Tis strange if none be here — and, if he will
Against his conscience, let him hiss and kill
Our market! 'Tis in vain, I see, to stay ye;
Have at the worst can come, then! Now, what say ye? 10
And yet mistake me not: I am not bold;
We've no such cause. — If the tale we have told —
For 'tis no other — any way content ye —
For to that honest purpose it was meant ye —
We have our end; and ye shall have ere long,
I dare say, many a better, to prolong
Your old loves to us. We, and all our might,
Rest at your service; gentlemen, good night!   [*Flourish.*

piece of Chaucer; a passage to which even Shakespeare could have added but some depth and grandeur of his own giving, since neither he nor Dante's very self nor any other among the divinest of men could have done more or better than match it for tender and true simplicity of words more 'dearly sweet and bitter' than the bitterest or sweetest of men's tears. Then after the duly and properly conventional engagement on the parts of Palamon and Emilia respectively to devote the anniversary 'to tears' and 'to honour,' the deeper tone returns for one grand last time, grave at once and sudden and sweet as the full choral opening of an anthem: the note which none could ever catch of Shakespeare's very voice gives out the peculiar cadence that it alone can give in the modulated instinct of a solemn change or shifting of the metrical emphasis or *ictus* from one to the other of two repeated words —

> 'that nought could buy
> Dear love but loss of dear love!'

That is a touch beyond the ear or the hand of Fletcher: a chord sounded from Apollo's own harp after a somewhat hoarse and reedy wheeze from the scrannel-pipe of a lesser player than Pan. Last of all, in words worthy to be the latest left of Shakespeare's, his great and gentle Theseus winds up the heavenly harmonies of his last beloved grand poem." —*Swinburne.*

V.

THE DUCHESS OF MALFI.

BY JOHN WEBSTER.

Probably produced in 1616; first printed in 1623. The story :s in Bandello's *Novelle*, Part I, No. 26; in Belleforest's French translation of Bandello, No. 19; in Painter's *Palace of Pleasure*, Vol. II, No. 23; in Beard's *Theatre of God's Judgments*, B. ii, chap. 22; and in Goulart's *Histoires Admirables*, Vol. I, p. 319. Lope de Vega published in 1618 *El Mayordomo de la Duquesa de Amalfi*.

DEDICATION.

To the Rt. Hon. GEORGE HARDING, *Baron Berkeley, of Berkeley Castle, and Knight of the Order of the Bath to the illustrious Prince Charles.*

My Noble Lord,

THAT I may present my excuse why, being a stranger to your lordship, I offer this poem to your patronage, I plead this warrant: — men who never saw the sea yet desire to behold that regiment of waters, choose some eminent river to guide them thither, and make that, as it were, their conduct or postilion: by the like ingenious means has your fame arrived at my knowledge, receiving it from some of worth, who both in contemplation and practice owe to your honour their clearest service. I do not altogether look up at your title; the ancientest nobility being but a relic of time past, and the truest honour indeed being for a man to confer honour on himself, which your learning strives to propagate, and shall make you arrive at the dignity of a great example. I am confident this work is not unworthy your honour's perusal; for by such poems as this poets have kissed the hands of great princes, and drawn their gentle eyes to look down upon their sheets of paper when the poets themselves were bound up in their winding-sheets. The like courtesy from your lordship shall make you live in your grave, and laurel spring out of it, when the ignorant scorners of the Muses, that like worms in libraries seem to live only to destroy learning, shall wither neglected and forgotten. This work and myself I humbly present to your approved censure, it being the utmost of my wishes to have your honourable self my weighty and perspicuous comment; which grace so done me shall ever be acknowledged

By your lordship's in all duty and observance,

JOHN WEBSTER.

THE DUCHESS OF MALFI.

DRAMATIS PERSONÆ.

FERDINAND, Duke of Calabria.
The CARDINAL, his Brother.
ANTONIO BOLOGNA, Steward of the household to the DUCHESS.
DELIO, his Friend.
DANIEL DE BOSOLA, Gentleman of the Horse to the DUCHESS.
CASTRUCCIO.
MARQUIS OF PESCARA.
COUNT MALATESTI.
RODERIGO.
SILVIO.
GRISOLAN.
Doctor.
Several Madmen, Pilgrims, Executioners, Officers, Attendants, etc.
DUCHESS OF MALFI.
CARIOLA, her Woman.
JULIA, Castruccio's Wife, and the Cardinal's Mistress.
Old Lady, Ladies, and Children.

SCENE: *Malfi, Rome, and Milan.*

ACT I.

SCENE I. — *The Presence-chamber in the* DUCHESS' *Palace at Malfi.*

Enter ANTONIO *and* DELIO.

Delio. You are welcome to your country, dear Antonio;
You have been long in France, and you return
A very formal Frenchman in your habit:
How do you like the French court?

Ant. I admire it;
In seeking to reduce both state and people
To a fixed order, their judicious king
Begins at home; quits first his royal palace
Of flattering sycophants, of dissolute
And infamous persons, — which he sweetly terms
His master's master-piece, the work of Heaven;   10
Considering duly that a prince's court
Is like a common fountain, whence should flow
Pure silver drops in general, but if't chance
Some cursed example poison 't near the head,
Death and diseases through the whole land spread.
And what is't makes this blessèd government
But a most provident council, who dare freely
Inform him the corruption of the times?
Though some o' the court hold it presumption
To instruct princes what they ought to do,   20
It is a noble duty to inform them
What they ought to foresee. — Here comes Bosola,
The only court-gall; yet I observe his railing
Is not for simple love of piety:
Indeed, he rails at those things which he wants;
Would be as lecherous, covetous, or proud,
Bloody, or envious, as any man,
If he had means to be so. — Here's the cardinal.

Enter the Cardinal *and* BOSOLA.[1]

Bos. I do haunt you still.
Card. So.

---

[1] When this play was first performed, about 1616, R. Burbadge played the part of *Ferdinand*, H. Condell that of the *Cardinal*, and J. Lowin that of *Bosola*. The *Duchess* was impersonated by the actor R. Sharpe, as female rôles were not yet taken by women.

Bos. I have done you better service than to be slighted thus. Miserable age, where only the reward of doing well is the doing of it! 32

Card. You enforce your merit too much.

Bos. I fell into the galleys in your service; where, for two years together, I wore two towels instead of a shirt, with a knot on the shoulder after the fashion of a Roman mantle. Slighted thus! I will thrive some way: black-birds fatten best in hard weather; why not I in these dog-days?

Card. Would you could become honest!

Bos. With all your divinity do but direct me the way to it. I have known many travel far for it, and yet return as arrant knaves as they went forth, because they carried themselves always along with them. (*Exit* Cardinal.) Are you gone? Some fellows, they say, are possessed with the devil, but this great fellow were able to possess the greatest devil, and make him worse. 46

Ant. He hath denied thee some suit?

Bos. He and his brother are like plum-trees that grow crooked over standing-pools; they are rich and o'er-laden with fruit, but none but crows, pies, and caterpillars feed on them. Could I be one of their flattering panders, I would hang on their ears like a horseleech, till I were full, and then drop off. I pray, leave me. Who would rely upon these miserable dependencies, in expectation to be advanced tomorrow? what creature ever fed worse than hoping Tantalus? nor ever died any man more fearfully than he that hoped for a pardon. There are rewards for hawks and dogs when they have done us service; but for a soldier that hazards his limbs in a battle, nothing but a kind of geometry is his last supportation. 60

Delio. Geometry!

Bos. Ay, to hang in a fair pair of slings, take his latter swing in the world upon an honourable pair of crutches, from hospital to hospital. Fare ye well, sir: and yet do not you scorn us; for places in the court are but like beds in the hospital, where this man's head lies at that man's foot, and so lower and lower. [*Exit.*

Delio. I knew this fellow seven years in the galleys
For a notorious murder; and 'twas thought
The cardinal suborned it: he was released   70
By the French general, Gaston de Foix,
When he recovered Naples.

Ant. 'Tis great pity
He should be thus neglected: I have heard
He's very valiant. This foul melancholy
Will poison all his goodness; for, I'll tell you,
If too immoderate sleep be truly said
To be an inward rust unto the soul,
It then doth follow want of action
Breeds all black malcontents; and their close rearing,
Like moths in cloth, do hurt for want of wearing.   80

Delio. The presence 'gins to fill: you promised me
To make me the partaker of the natures
Of some of your great courtiers.

Ant. The lord cardinal's,
And other strangers' that are now in court?
I shall. — Here comes the great Calabrian duke.

Enter FERDINAND, CASTRUCCIO, SILVIO, RODERIGO, GRISOLAN,
and Attendants.

Ferd. Who took the ring oftenest?[1]

---

[1] "The allusion is to the sport called Running at the Ring, when the tilter, riding at full speed, endeavoured to thrust the point of his lance through, and to bear away, the ring, which was suspended at a particular height." — *Dyce.*

Sil. Antonio Bologna, my lord.

Ferd. Our sister duchess' great-master of her household? give him the jewel. — When shall we leave this sportive action, and fall to action indeed? 90

Cast. Methinks, my lord, you should not desire to go to war in person.

Ferd. Now for some gravity : — why, my lord?

Cast. It is fitting a soldier arise to be a prince, but not necessary a prince descend to be a captain.

Ferd. No?

Cast. No, my lord; he were far better do it by a deputy.

Ferd. Why should he not as well sleep or eat by a deputy? this might take idle, offensive, and base office from him, whereas the other deprives him of honour. 100

Cast. Believe my experience, that realm is never long in quiet where the ruler is a soldier.

Ferd. Thou toldest me thy wife could not endure fighting.

Cast. True, my lord.

Ferd. And of a jest she broke of a captain she met full of wounds : I have forgot it.

Cast. She told him, my lord, he was a pitiful fellow, to lie, like the children of Ismael, all in tents.[1]

Ferd. Why, there's a wit were able to undo all the surgeons o' the city; for although gallants should quarrel, and had drawn their weapons, and were ready to go to it, yet her persuasions would make them put up. 112

Cast. That she would, my lord. — How do you like my Spanish gennet[2]?

[1] A play on the word *tent*, which meant also a roll of lint, or other material, used in searching a wound.
[2] A small Spanish horse (written also *jennet*). The word is of Moorish origin, there being a tribe of Zenata in Barbary noted for its cavalry.

Rod. He is all fire.

Ferd. I am of Pliny's opinion,[1] I think he was begot by the wind; he runs as if he were ballassed[2] with quicksilver.

Silvio. True, my lord, he reels from the tilt often.

Rod. Gris. Ha, ha, ha!

Ferd. Why do you laugh? methinks you that are courtiers should be my touchwood, take fire when I give fire; that is, laugh but when I laugh, were the subject never so witty. 123

Cast. True, my lord: I myself have heard a very good jest, and have scorned to seem to have so silly a wit as to understand it.

Ferd. But I can laugh at your fool, my lord.

Cast. He cannot speak, you know, but he makes faces: my lady cannot abide him.

Ferd. No?

Cast. Nor endure to be in merry company; for she says too much laughing, and too much company, fills her too full of the wrinkle. 133

Ferd. I would, then, have a mathematical instrument made for her face, that she might not laugh out of compass. — I shall shortly visit you at Milan, Lord Silvio.

Silvio. Your grace shall arrive most welcome.

Ferd. You are a good horseman, Antonio: you have excellent riders in France: what do you think of good horsemanship?

Ant. Nobly, my lord: as out of the Grecian horse issued many famous princes, so out of brave horsemanship arise

---

[1] See Pliny, *Nat. Hist.* viii, 67, where he says that in Lusitania there was a breed of fleet horses begotten by the wind Favonius; they never lived more than three years.

[2] Ballasted.

the first sparks of growing resolution, that raise the mind to noble action.

Ferd. You have bespoke it worthily.

Silvio. Your brother, the lord cardinal, and sister duchess.

Re-enter Cardinal, *with* DUCHESS, CARIOLA, *and* JULIA.

Card. Are the galleys come about?

Gris. They are, my lord. 148

Ferd. Here's the Lord Silvio is come to take his leave.

Delio. Now, Sir, your promise; what's that cardinal? I mean his temper? they say he's a brave fellow,
Will play his five thousand crowns at tennis, dance,
Court ladies, and one that hath fought single combats.

Ant. Some such flashes superficially hang on him for form; but observe his inward character: he is a melancholy churchman; the spring in his face is nothing but the engendering of toads; where he is jealous of any man, he lays worse plots for them than ever was imposed on Hercules, for he strews in his way flatterers, panders, intelligencers, atheists, and a thousand such political monsters. He should have been Pope; but instead of coming to it by the primitive decency of the church, he did bestow bribes so largely and so impudently as if he would have carried it away without Heaven's knowledge. Some good he hath done — 164

Delio. You have given too much of him. What's his brother?

Ant. The duke there? a most perverse and turbulent nature:
What appears in him mirth is merely outside;
If he laugh heartily, it is to laugh
All honesty out of fashion.

Delio. Twins?

Ant. In quality.
He speaks with others' tongues, and hears men's suits 170
With others' ears; will seem to sleep o' the bench
Only to entrap offenders in their answers;
Dooms men to death by information;
Rewards by hearsay.
   Delio. Then the law to him
Is like a foul black cobweb to a spider, —
He makes it his dwelling and a prison
To entangle those shall feed him.
   Ant. Most true:
He never pays debts unless they be shrewd turns,
And those he will confess that he doth owe.
Last, for his brother there, the cardinal, 180
They that do flatter him most say oracles
Hang at his lips; and verily I believe them,
For the devil speaks in them.
But for their sister, the right noble duchess,
You never fixed your eye on three fair medals
Cast in one figure, of so different temper.
For her discourse, it is so full of rapture,
You only will begin then to be sorry
When she doth end her speech, and wish, in wonder,
She held it less vain-glory to talk much, 190
Than your penance to hear her: whilst she speaks,
She throws upon a man so sweet a look,
That it were able to raise one to a galliard[1]
That lay in a dead palsy, and to dote
On that sweet countenance; but in that look
There speaketh so divine a continence
As cuts off all lascivious and vain hope.

   [1] A lively Spanish dance. So Shakespeare, *Twelfth Night*, i, 3.

Her days are practised in such noble virtue,
That sure her nights, nay, more, her very sleeps,
Are more in Heaven than other ladies' shrifts.   200
Let all sweet ladies break their flattering glasses,
And dress themselves in her.
　　Delio. Fie, Antonio,
You play the wire-drawer with her commendations.
　　Ant. I'll case the picture up: only thus much;
All her particular worth grows to this sum,—
She stains the time past, lights the time to come.
　　Cari. You must attend my lady in the gallery,
Some half an hour hence.
　　Ant. I shall.　　　　　　［*Exeunt* ANTONIO *and* DELIO.
　　Ferd. Sister, I have a suit to you.
　　Duch. To me, sir?
　　Ferd. A gentleman here, Daniel de Bosola,
One that was in the galleys—
　　Duch. Yes, I know him.   210
　　Ferd. A worthy fellow he is: pray, let me entreat for
The provisorship of your horse.
　　Duch. Your knowledge of him
Commends him and prefers him.
　　Ferd. Call him hither.　　　　　［*Exit* Attendant.
We are now upon parting. Good Lord Silvio,
Do us commend to all our noble friends
At the leaguer.
　　Silvio. Sir, I shall.
　　Ferd. You are for Milan?
　　Silvio. I am.
　　Duch. Bring the caroches.[1] We'll bring you down to the haven.

---

[1] Coaches (Italian *carrozza*).

[*Exeunt* DUCHESS, SILVIO, CASTRUCCIO, RODERIGO, GRISOLAN, CARIOLA, JULIA, *and* Attendants.

Card. Be sure you entertain that Bosola
For your intelligence : I would not be seen in't ;
And therefore many times I have slighted him
When he did court our furtherance, as this morning.

Ferd. Antonio, the great-master of her household,
Had been far fitter.

Card. You are deceived in him :
His nature is too honest for such business. —
He comes : I'll leave you. [*Exit.*

Re-enter BOSOLA.

Bos. I was lured to you.

Ferd. My brother, here, the cardinal could never
Abide you.

Bos. Never since he was in my debt.

Ferd. May be some oblique character in your face
Made him suspect you.

Bos. Doth he study physiognomy?
He did suspect me wrongfully.

Ferd. For that
You must give great men leave to take their times.
Distrust doth cause us seldom be deceived :
You see the oft shaking of the cedar-tree
Fastens it more at root.

Bos. Yet, take heed ;
For to suspect a friend unworthily
Instructs him the next way to suspect you,
And prompts him to deceive you.

Ferd. There's gold.

Bos. So :

What follows? never rained such showers as these
Without thunderbolts i' the tail of them : whose throat must
  I cut?
 Ferd. Your inclination to shed blood rides post
Before my occasion to use you. I gave you that
To live i' the court here, and observe the duchess ;
To note all the particulars of her haviour,
What suitors do solicit her for marriage,
And whom she best affects. She's a young widow :
I would not have her marry again.
 Bos. No, sir?
 Ferd. Do not you ask the reason ; but be satisfied
I say I would not.
 Bos. It seems you would create me
One of your familiars.
 Ferd. Familiar ! what's that?
 Bos. Why, a very quaint invisible devil in flesh,
An intelligencer.
 Ferd. Such a kind of thriving thing
I would wish thee ; and ere long thou mayest arrive
At a higher place by't.
 Bos. Take your devils,
Which hell calls angels ; these cursed gifts would make
You a corrupter, me an impudent traitor ;
And should I take these, they'd take me to hell.
 Ferd. Sir, I'll take nothing from you that I have given :
There is a place that I procured for you
This morning, the provisorship o' the horse ;
Have you heard on't?
 Bos. No.
 Ferd. 'Tis yours : is't not worth thanks?
 Bos. I would have you curse yourself now, that your bounty

(Which makes men truly noble) e'er should make me
A villain. O, that to avoid ingratitude
For the good deed you have done me, I must do
All the ill man can invent! Thus the devil
Candies all sins o'er; and what Heaven terms vile,
That names he complimental.[1]
   Ferd. Be yourself;
Keep your old garb of melancholy; 'twill express
You envy those that stand above your reach,
Yet strive not to come near 'em: this will gain   270
Access to private lodgings, where yourself
May, like a politic dormouse —
   Bos. As I have seen some
Feed in a lord's dish, half asleep, not seeming
To listen to any talk; and yet these rogues
Have cut his throat in a dream. What's my place?
The provisorship o' the horse? I am your creature.
   Ferd. Away!
   Bos. Let good men, for good deeds, covet good fame,
Since place and riches oft are bribes of shame:
Sometimes the devil doth preach.   [*Exit.*

    Re-enter DUCHESS, Cardinal, *and* CARIOLA.

   Card. We are to part from you; and your own discretion
Must now be your director.
   Ferd. You are a widow: 281
You know already what man is; and therefore
Let not youth, high promotion, eloquence —
   Card. No,
Nor any thing without the addition, honour,
Sway your high blood.

          [1] Ornamental.

Ferd. Marry! they are most luxurious [1]
Will wed twice.
　Card. O, fie!
　Ferd. Their livers are more spotted
Than Laban's sheep.
　Duch. Diamonds are of most value,
They say, that have passed through most jewellers' hands.
Will you hear me?　　　　　　　　　　　　　　290
I'll never marry.
　Card. So most widows say;
But commonly that motion lasts no longer
Than the turning of an hour-glass: the funeral sermon
And it end both together.
　Ferd. Now hear me:
You live in a rank pasture, here, i' the court;
There is a kind of honey-dew that's deadly;
'Twill poison your fame; look to't: be not cunning;
For they whose faces do belie their hearts
Are witches ere they arrive at twenty years,
Ay, and give the devil suck.　　　　　　　　　300
　Duch. This is terrible good counsel.
　Ferd. Hypocrisy is woven of a fine small thread,
Subtler than Vulcan's engine [2]: yet, believe't,
Your darkest actions, nay, your privat'st thoughts,
Will come to light.
　Card. You may flatter yourself,
And take your own choice; privately be married
Under the eaves of night —
　Ferd. Think't the best voyage
That e'er you made; like the irregular crab,

---

[1] Incontinent; query *uxorious?*
[2] The net in which he caught Mars and Venus.

Which, though't goes backward, thinks that it goes right
Because it goes its own way; but observe,
Such weddings may more properly be said 310
To be executed than celebrated.
    Card. The marriage night
Is the entrance into some prison.
    Ferd. And those joys,
Those lustful pleasures, are like heavy sleeps
Which do fore-run man's mischief.
    Card. Fare you well.
Wisdom begins at the end: remember it.   [*Exit.*
    Duch. I think this speech between you both was studied,
It came so roundly off.
    Ferd. You are my sister;
This was my father's poniard, do you see?
I'd be loth to see't look rusty, 'cause 'twas his. 320
I would have you give o'er those chargeable revels:
A visor and a mask are whispering-rooms
That were never built for goodness;—fare ye well;—
And women like variety of courtship:
What cannot a neat knave with a smooth tale
Make a woman believe? Farewell, lusty widow.   [*Exit.*
    Duch. Shall this move me? If all my royal kindred
Lay in my way unto this marriage,
I'd make them my low footsteps: and even now,
Even in this hate, as men in some great battles, 330
By apprehending danger, have achieved
Almost impossible actions (I have heard soldiers say so),
So I through frights and threatenings will assay
This dangerous venture. Let old wives report
I winked and chose a husband.—Cariola,
To thy known secrecy I have given up

More than my life — my fame.
   Cari. Both shall be safe;
For I'll conceal this secret from the world
As warily as those that trade in poison
Keep poison from their children.
   Duch. Thy protestation 340
Is ingenious [1] and hearty: I believe it.
Is Antonio come?
   Cari. He attends you.
   Duch. Good, dear soul,
Leave me; but place thyself behind the arras,
Where thou mayst overhear us. Wish me good speed;
For I am going into a wilderness
Where I shall find nor path nor friendly clue
To be my guide.   [CARIOLA *goes behind the arras.*

              Enter ANTONIO.[2]

              I sent for you: sit down;
Take pen and ink, and write: are you ready?
   Ant. Yes.
   Duch. What did I say?
   Ant. That I should write somewhat. 350
   Duch. O, I remember.
After these triumphs and this large expense,
It's fit, like thrifty husbands, we inquire
What's laid up for to-morrow.
   Ant. So please your beauteous excellence.
   Duch. Beauteous!
Indeed, I thank you: I look young for your sake;

   1 Ingenuous.
   2 "As previously Antonio has been told that he must attend the Duchess in the gallery, it would seem that here the audience were to imagine that a change of scene had taken place." — *Dyce.*

You have ta'en my cares upon you.
 Ant. I'll fetch your grace
The particulars of your revenue and expense.
 Duch. O, you are
An upright treasurer: but you 'mistook;   360
For when I said I meant to make jnquiry
What's laid up for to-morrow, I did mean
What's laid up yonder for me.
 Ant. Where?
 Duch. In Heaven.
I am making my will (as 'tis fit princes should,
In perfect memory), and, I pray, sir, tell me,
Were not one better make it smiling, thus,
Than in deep groans and terrible ghastly looks,
As if the gifts we parted with procured
That violent distraction [1]?
 Ant. O, much better.
 Duch. If I had a husband now, this care were quit: 370
But I intend to make you overseer.
What good deed shall we first remember? say.
 Ant. Begin with that first good deed began i' the world
After man's creation, the sacrament of marriage:
I'd have you first provide for a good husband;
Give him all.
 Duch. All!
 Ant. Yes, your excellent self.
 Duch. In a winding-sheet?
 Ant. In a couple.
 Duch. Saint Winifred,[2] that were a strange will!

---

[1] The Quarto of 1640 has *destruction*.
[2] A noble British maiden of the seventh century. Prince Cradocus fell in love with her; but as she would not accept his suit, he cut off her head,

Ant. 'Twere stranger if there were no will in you
To marry again.
  Duch. What do you think of marriage? 380
  Ant. I take't, as those that deny purgatory,
It locally contains or Heaven or hell;
There's no third place in't.
  Duch. How do you affect it?
  Ant. My banishment, feeding my melancholy,
Would often reason thus.
  Duch. Pray, let's hear it.
  Ant. Say a man never marry, nor have children,
What takes that from him? only the bare name
Of being a father, or the weak delight
To see the little wanton ride a-cock-horse
Upon a painted stick, or hear him chatter 390
Like a taught starling.
  Duch. Fie, fie, what's all this?
One of your eyes is blood-shot; use my ring to't,
They say 'tis very sovereign: 'twas my wedding-ring,
And I did vow never to part with it
But to my second husband.
  Ant. You have parted with it now.
  Duch. Yes, to help your eye-sight.
  Ant. You have made me stark blind.
  Duch. How?

which rolled to the foot of a hill: stopping there, a spring gushed up. St. Bueno picked up the head, put it back on her shoulders: Winifred came to life, and lived fifteen years thereafter. The fame of her holiness spread: a shrine was built at the spring, and during many centuries that shrine, Holywell, in Flintshire, was the resort of pilgrims. Her day in the Saints' Calendar is November 3. Her violent lover Cradocus was swallowed up by the earth's opening immediately after he severed her head from its trunk. See *Chambers's Book of Days*, ii, 6.

Ant. There is a saucy and ambitious devil
Is dancing in this circle.
   Duch. Remove him.
   Ant. How? 400
   Duch. There needs small conjuration, when your finger
May do it: thus; is it fit?
              [*She puts the ring upon his finger: he kneels.*
   Ant. What said you?
   Duch. Sir,
This goodly roof of yours is too low built;
I cannot stand upright in't nor discourse,
Without I raise it higher: raise yourself;
Or, if you please, my hand to help you: so. [*Raises him.*
   Ant. Ambition, madam, is a great man's madness,
That is not kept in chains and close-pent rooms,
But in fair lightsome lodgings, and is girt
With the wild noise of prattling visitants, 410
Which makes it lunatic beyond all cure.
Conceive not I am so stupid but I aim
Whereto your favours tend: but he's a fool
That, being a-cold, would thrust his hands i' the fire
To warm them.
   Duch. So, now the ground's broke,
You may discover what a wealthy mine
I make you lord of.
   Ant. O my unworthiness!
   Duch. You were ill to sell yourself:
This darkening of your worth is not like that
Which tradesmen use i' the city; their false lights 420
Are to rid bad wares of: and I must tell you,
If you will know where breathes a complete man
(I speak it without flattery), turn your eyes,

And progress through yourself.
  Ant. Were there nor Heaven nor hell,
I should be honest : I have long served virtue,
And ne'er ta'en wages of her.
  Duch. Now she pays it.
The misery of us that are born great !
We are forced to woo, because none dare woo us ;
And as a tyrant doubles with his words,   430
And fearfully equivocates, so we
Are forced to express our violent passions
In riddles and in dreams, and leave the path
Of simple virtue, which was never made
To seem the thing it is not. Go, go brag
You have left me heartless ; mine is in your bosom :
I hope 'twill multiply love there. You do tremble :
Make not your heart so dead a piece of flesh,
To fear more than to love me. Sir, be confident :
What is't distracts you ? This is flesh and blood, sir ;   440
'Tis not the figure cut in alabaster
Kneels at my husband's tomb. Awake, awake, man !
I do here put off all vain ceremony,
And only do appear to you a young widow
That claims you for her husband, and, like a widow,
I use but half a blush in't.[1]
  Ant. Truth speak for me ;
I will remain the constant sanctuary
Of your good name.

---

[1] "The passion of the *Duchess* for *Antonio*, a subject most difficult to treat, is managed with infinite delicacy : in a situation of great peril for the author, she condescends without being degraded, declares to her dependant that he is the husband of her choice without losing anything of dignity and respect, and seems only to exercise the privilege of rank in raising merit

Duch. I thank you, gentle love :
And 'cause you shall not come to me in debt,
Being now my steward, here upon your lips   450
I sign your *Quietus est.* This you should have begged now :
I have seen children oft eat sweetmeats thus,
As fearful to devour them too soon.
   Ant. But for your brothers?
   Duch. Do not think of them :
All discord without this circumference
Is only to be pitied, and not feared :
Yet, should they know it, time will easily
Scatter the tempest.
   Ant. These words should be mine,
And all the parts you have spoke, if some part of it
Would not have savoured flattery.
   Duch. Kneel.   [CARIOLA *comes from behind the arras.*
   Ant. Ha !   460
   Duch. Be not amazed ; this woman's of my counsel :
I have heard lawyers say, a contract in a chamber
Per verba presenti is absolute marriage.
                         [*She and* ANTONIO *kneel.*
Bless, Heaven, this sacred gordian, which let violence
Never untwine !
   Ant. And may our sweet affections, like the spheres,
Be still in motion !
   Duch. Quickening, and make
The like soft music !

---

from obscurity." — *Dyce.* It may be added that neither in the English Drama nor in English Fiction shall we find a scene in which womanly dignity and womanly love are exhibited more naturally than in this. A noble woman, as Webster here depicts her, is neither the unreal, ethereal creature of the Age of Chivalry, nor is she the toy or servant of man.

Ant. That we may imitate the loving palms,[1]
Best emblem of a peaceful marriage, 470
That never bore fruit, divided !
　Duch. What can the church force more?
　Ant. That fortune may not know an accident,
Either of joy or sorrow, to divide
Our fixèd wishes !
　Duch. How can the church build faster?
We now are man and wife, and 'tis the church
That must but echo this. — Maid, stand apart :
I now am blind.
　Ant. What's your conceit in this?
　Duch. I would have you lead your fortune by the hand
Unto your marriage bed : 480
(You speak in me this, for we now are one :)
We'll only lie, and talk together, and plot
To appease my humourous kindred ; and if you please,
Like the old tale in Alexander and Lodowick,[2]
Lay a naked sword between us, keep us chaste.
O, let me shrowd my blushes in your bosom,
Since 'tis the treasury of all my secrets !
　　　　　　　[*Exeunt* DUCHESS *and* ANTONIO.

[1] Cf. *T. Campbell*, in his poem " The Dead Eagle."

"The village planted near the Maraboot's
Round roof has aye its feathery palm trees
Pair'd, for in solitude they bear no fruits."

[2] " *The Two Faithful Friends, the pleasant History of Alexander and Lodwicke, who were so like one another, that none could know them asunder ; wherein is declared how Lodwicke married the Princesse of Hungaria, in Alexander's name, and how each night he layd a naked sword betweene him and the Princesse, because he would not wrong his friend*, is reprinted from the Pepys collection in Evans's *Old Ballads*. There was also a play written by Martin Slaughter, called *Alexander and Lodowick*, the acting of which is several times mentioned in Henslowe's *Diary;* but it was never published."
—*Dyce.*

Cari. Whether the spirit of greatness or of woman
Reign most in her, I know not; but it shows
A fearful madness: I owe her much of pity.   [*Exit.* 490

ACT II.

SCENE I. — *An Apartment in the Palace of the* DUCHESS.

Enter BOSOLA *and* CASTRUCCIO.

Bos. You say you would fain be taken for an eminent courtier?

Cast. 'Tis the very main of my ambition.

Bos. Let me see: you have a reasonable good face for't already, and your night-cap expresses your ears sufficient largely. I would have you learn to twirl the strings of your band with a good grace, and in a set speech, at the end of every sentence, to hum three or four times, or blow your nose till it smart again, to recover your memory. When you come to be a president in criminal causes, if you smile upon a prisoner, hang him; but if you frown upon him and threaten him, let him be sure to scape the gallows.   12

Cast. I would be a very merry president.

Bos. Do not sup o' nights; 'twill beget you an admirable wit.

Cast. Rather it would make me have a good stomach to quarrel; for they say, your roaring boys[1] eat meat seldom, and that makes them so valiant. But how shall I know whether the people take me for an eminent fellow?

Bos. I will teach you a trick to know it: give out you lie

---

[1] Cant term for insolent bullies and vaporers of the time.

a-dying, and if you hear the common people curse you, be sure you are taken for one of the prime night-caps.¹ 22

Enter an Old Lady.

You come from painting now.

Old Lady. From what?

Bos. Why, from your scurvy face-physic. To behold thee not painted inclines somewhat near a miracle; these in thy face here were deep ruts and foul sloughs the last progress.² There was a lady in France that, having had the small-pox, flayed the skin off her face to make it more level; and whereas before she looked like a nutmeg-grater, after she resembled an abortive hedgehog. 31

Old Lady. Do you call this painting?

Bos. No, no, but you call it careening³ of an old morphewed⁴ lady to make her disembogue⁵ again: there's rough-cast phrase to your plastic.⁶

Old Lady. It seems you are well acquainted with my closet.

Bos. One would suspect it for a shop of witchcraft, to find in it the fat of serpents, spawn of snakes, Jews' spittle, and their young children's ordure; and all these for the face. I would sooner eat a dead pigeon taken from the soles of the feet of one sick of the plague than kiss one of you fasting. Here are two of you, whose sin of your youth

---

¹ Another cant term, used by Webster in *The Devil's Law Case*, ii, 1:—

"Among a shoal or swarm of reeking night-caps."

² State journey of the English sovereign into the provinces.

³ To lay a ship on its side, in order to calk and clean the hull.

⁴ Morphew: a scurf or cutaneous disease on the face.

⁵ Literally, flow into the sea (as a river). The meaning of the speech is: You old women paint your face and hide your wrinkles in order that you may launch out for new conquests. ⁶ Moulding.

is the very patrimony of the physician; makes him renew
his foot-cloth[1] with the spring, and change his high-priced
courtezan with the fall of the leaf. I do wonder you do
not loathe yourselves. Observe my meditation now.   47
What thing is in this outward form of man
To be beloved? We account it ominous,
If nature do produce a colt, or lamb,
A fawn or goat, in any limb resembling
A man, and fly from't as a prodigy:
Man stands amazed to see his deformity
In any other creature but himself.
But in our own flesh, though we bear diseases
Which have their true names only ta'en from beasts, —
As the most ulcerous wolf and swinish measle, —
Though we are eaten up of lice and worms,
And though continually we bear about us
A rotten and dead body, we delight   60
To hide it in rich tissue: all our fear,
Nay, all our terror, is lest our physician
Should put us in the ground to be made sweet. —
Your wife's gone to Rome: you two couple, and get you to
the wells at Lucca to recover your aches. I have other
work on foot.   [*Exeunt* CASTRUCCIO *and* Old Lady.
I observe our duchess
Is sick a-days, she pukes, her stomach seethes,
The fins of her eye-lids look most teeming blue,
She wanes i' the cheek, and waxes fat i' the flank,   70
And, contrary to our Italian fashion,
Wears a loose-bodied gown: there's somewhat in't.
I have a trick may chance discover it,
A pretty one; I have bought some apricocks,[2]

---

[1] Enables him to buy new housings for his horse.   [2] Apricots.

The first our spring yields.

Enter ANTONIO *and* DELIO.

Delio. And so long since married!
You amaze me.
  Ant. Let me seal your lips for ever:
For, did I think that any thing but the air
Could carry these words from you, I should wish
You had no breath at all. — Now, sir, in your contemplation?
You are studying to become a great wise fellow.   80
  Bos. O, sir, the opinion of wisdom is a foul tetter that runs all over a man's body:[1] if simplicity direct us to have no evil, it directs us to a happy being; for the subtlest folly proceeds from the subtlest wisdom: let me be simply honest.
  Ant. I do understand your inside.
  Bos. Do you so?
  Ant. Because you would not seem to appear to the world
Puffed up with your preferment, you continue
This out-of-fashion melancholy: leave it, leave it.   90
  Bos. Give me leave to be honest in any phrase, in any compliment whatsoever. Shall I confess myself to you? I look no higher than I can reach: they are the gods that must ride on winged horses. A lawyer's mule of a slow pace will both suit my disposition and business; for, mark me, when a man's mind rides faster than his horse can gallop, they quickly both tire.
  Ant. You would look up to Heaven, but I think
The devil, that rules i' the air, stands in your light.   99
  Bos. O, sir, you are lord of the ascendant, chief man with the duchess; a duke was your cousin-german removed.

---

[1] Observe throughout how *Bosola's* images harmonize with his character.

Say you are lineally descended from King Pepin, or he himself, what of this? search the heads of the greatest rivers in the world, you shall find them but bubbles of water. Some would think the souls of princes were brought forth by some more weighty cause than those of meaner persons: they are deceived, there's the same hand to them; the like passions sway them; the same reason that makes a vicar to go to law for a tithe-pig, and undo his neighbours, makes them spoil a whole province, and batter down goodly cities with the cannon. 111

Enter DUCHESS *and* Ladies.

Duch. Your arm, Antonio: do I not grow **fat?**
I am exceeding short-winded. — Bosola,
I would have you, sir, provide for me a litter;
Such a one as the Duchess of Florence rode in.

Bos. The duchess used one when she was great with child.

Duch. I think she did. — Come hither, mend my ruff;
Here, when [1]? thou art such a tedious lady; and
Thy breath smells of lemon-pills; would thou hadst done!
Shall I swoon under thy fingers! I am 120
So troubled with the mother [2]!

Bos. (*aside*). I fear too much.

Duch. I have heard you say that the French courtiers
Wear their hats on 'fore the king.

Ant. I have seen it.

Duch. In the presence?

Ant. Yes.

[1] *When*, an exclamation of impatience.
[2] Hysterical passion; so *Lear*, ii, 4: —

" O, how this mother swells up toward my heart!
Hysterica passio, — down, thou climbing sorrow,
Thy element's below!"

Duch. Why should not we bring up that fashion?
'Tis ceremony more than duty that consists
In the removing of a piece of felt:
Be you the example to the rest o' the court;
Put on your hat first.
   Ant. You must pardon me:
I have seen, in colder countries than in France,   130
Nobles stand bare to the prince; and the distinction
Methought showed reverently.
   Bos. I have a present for your grace.
   Duch. For me, sir?
   Bos. Apricocks, madam.
   Duch. O, sir, where are they?
I have heard of none to-year.[1]
   Bos. (*aside*). Good; her colour rises.
   Duch. Indeed, I thank you: they are wondrous fair ones.
What an unskilful fellow is our gardener!
We shall have none this month.
   Bos. Will not your grace pare them?   140
   Duch. No: they taste of musk, methinks; indeed they do.
   Bos. I know not: yet I wish your grace had pared 'em.
   Duch. Why?
   Bos. I forgot to tell you, the knave gardener,
Only to raise his profit by them the sooner,
Did ripen them in horse-dung.
   Duch. O, you jest.—
You shall judge: pray taste one.
   Ant. Indeed, madam,
I do not love the fruit.
   Duch. Sir, you are loth
To rob us of our dainties: 'tis a delicate fruit;

[1] This year.

They say they are restorative.

Bos. 'Tis a pretty art, 150
This grafting.

Duch. 'Tis so; bettering of nature.

Bos. To make a pippin grow upon a crab,
A damson on a blackthorn — (*Aside*) How greedily she eats
    them!

Duch. I thank you, Bosola: they are right good ones.
If they do not make me sick.

Ant. How now, madam!

Duch. This green fruit and my stomach are not friends:
How they swell me!
O, I am in an extreme cold sweat!

Bos. I am very sorry.

Duch. Lights to my chamber! — O good Antonio, 160
I fear I am undone!

Delio. Lights there, lights!

      [*Exeunt* DUCHESS *and* Ladies. — *Exit, on the
      other side,* BOSOLA.

Ant. O my most trusty Delio, we are lost!

Delio. Have you prepared
Those ladies to attend her? and procured
That politic safe conveyance for the midwife
Your duchess plotted?

Ant. I have.

Delio. Make use, then, of this forced occasion:
Give out that Bosola hath poisoned her
With these apricocks; that will give some colour
For her keeping close.

Ant. Fie, fie, the physicians 170
Will then flock to her.

Delio. For that you may pretend

She'll use some prepared antidote of her own,
Lest the physicians should re-poison her.
 Ant. I am lost in amazement: I know not what to think on't. [*Exeunt.*

SCENE II. — *A Hall in the same Palace.*

Enter BOSOLA.

Bos. So, so, there's no question but her techiness[1] and most vulturous eating of the apricocks are apparent signs of breeding. — Now?

Enter an Old Lady.

Old Lady. I am in haste, sir.

Bos. There was a young waiting-woman had a monstrous desire to see the glass-house —

Old Lady. I will hear no more of the glass-house. You are still abusing women? 8

Bos. Who, I? no; only, by the way now and then, mention your frailties. The orange-tree bears ripe and green fruit and blossoms all together; and some of you give entertainment for pure love, but more for more precious reward. The lusty spring smells well; but drooping autumn tastes well. If we have the same golden showers that rained in the time of Jupiter the thunderer, you have the same Danaës still, to hold up their laps to receive them. Didst thou never study the mathematics?

Old Lady. What's that, sir? 18

Bos. Why to know the trick how to make a many lines

---

[1] Fretfulness, peevishness; from the Middle English *tecche, tache,* a habit; hence a bad habit, vice, freak. Cf. French *tache.*

meet in one centre. Go, go, give your foster-daughters good counsel: tell them, that the devil takes delight to hang at a woman's girdle, like a false rusty watch, that she cannot discern how the time passes. [*Exit* Old Lady.

Enter ANTONIO, RODERIGO, *and* GRISOLAN.

Ant. Shut up the court-gates.
Rod. Why, sir? what's the danger?
Ant. Shut up the posterns presently, and call all the officers o' the court.
Gris. I shall instantly. [*Exit.*
Ant. Who keeps the key o' the park-gate?
Rod. Forobosco.
Ant. Let him bring't presently.

Re-enter GRISOLAN *with* Servants.

1st Serv. O, gentlemen o' the court, the foulest treason!
Bos. (*aside*). If that these apricocks should be poisoned now,
Without my knowledge!
1st Serv. There was taken even now a Switzer in the duchess' bed chamber —
2d Serv. A Switzer!
1st Serv. With a pistol.
Bos. Ha, ha, ha!
2d Serv. There was a cunning traitor!
1st Serv. And all the moulds of his buttons were leaden bullets.
2d Serv. O wicked cannibal!
1st Serv. 'Twas a French plot, upon my life.
2d Serv. To see what the devil can do!
Ant. Are all the officers here?

Servants. We are.

Ant. Gentlemen,
We have lost much plate you know; and but this evening
Jewels, to the value of four thousand ducats,
Are missing in the duchess' cabinet. 50
Are the gates shut?

Serv. Yes.

Ant. 'Tis the duchess' pleasure
Each officer be locked into his chamber
Till the sun-rising; and to send the keys
Of all their chests and of their outward doors
Into her bed-chamber.   She is very sick.

Rod. At her pleasure.

Ant. She entreats you to tak't not ill: the innocent
Shall be the more approved by it. 60

Bos. Gentlemen o' the wood-yard, where's your Switzer
  now?

1st Serv. By this hand, 'twas credibly reported by one o'
the black guard.[1]   [*Exeunt all except* ANTONIO *and* DELIO.

Delio. How fares it with the duchess?

Ant. She's exposed
Unto the worst of torture, pain and fear.

Delio. Speak to her all happy comfort.

Ant. How I do play the fool with mine own **danger**!
You are this night, dear friend, to post to Rome:
My life lies in your service.

Delio. Do not doubt me. 70

Ant. O, 'tis far from me: and yet fear presents me
Somewhat that looks like danger.

---

[1] "The meanest drudges in royal residences and great houses, who **rode** in the vehicles which carried the furniture and domestic utensils from mansion to mansion." — *Dyce.*

Delio. Believe it,
'Tis but the shadow of your fear, no more :
How superstitiously we mind our evils !
The throwing down salt, or crossing of a hare,
Bleeding at nose, the stumbling of a horse,
Or singing of a cricket, are of power
To daunt [the] whole man in us. Sir, fare you well :
I wish you all the joys of a blessed father :
And, for my faith, lay this unto your breast, — 80
Old friends, like old swords, still are trusted best. [*Exit.*

Enter CARIOLA.

Cari. Sir, you are the happy father of a son :
Your wife commends him to you.
    Ant. Blessèd comfort ! —
For Heaven's sake tend her well : I'll presently
Go set a figure for's nativity.[1] [*Exeunt.*

SCENE III. — *The Court of the same Palace.*

Enter BOSOLA, *with a dark lantern.*

Bos. Sure I did hear a woman shriek : list, ha !
And the sound came, if I received it right,
From the duchess' lodgings. There's some stratagem
In the confining all our courtiers
To their several wards : I must have part of it ;
My intelligence will freeze else. List, again !
It may be 'twas the melancholy bird,
Best friend of silence and of solitariness,
The owl, that screamed so. — Ha ! Antonio !

[1] Make out his horoscope.

Enter ANTONIO.

Ant. I heard some noise.—Who's there? What art thou? speak. 10

Bos. Antonio, put not your face nor body
To such a forced expression of fear:
I am Bosola, your friend.

Ant. Bosola!—
(*Aside*) This mole does undermine me.—Heard you not
A noise even now?

Bos. From whence?

Ant. From the duchess' lodging.

Bos. Not I: did you?

Ant. I did, or else I dreamed.

Bos. Let's walk towards it.

Ant. No: it may be 'twas
But the rising of the wind.

Bos. Very likely.
Methinks 'tis very cold, and yet you sweat:
You look wildly.

Ant. I have been setting a figure
For the duchess' jewels. 20

Bos. Ah, and how falls your question?
Do you find it radical?

Ant. What's that to you?
'Tis rather to be questioned what design,
When all men were commanded to their lodgings,
Makes you a night-walker.

Bos. In sooth, I'll tell you:
Now all the court's asleep, I thought the devil
Had least to do here; I came to say my prayers;
And if it do offend you I do so,

You are a fine courtier.
 Ant. (*aside*). This fellow will undo me. —
You gave the duchess apricocks to-day :
Pray Heaven they were not poisoned !
 Bos. Poisoned ! A Spanish fig
For the imputation.
 Ant. Traitors are ever confident
Till they are discovered. There were jewels stol'n too :
In my conceit none are to be suspected
More than yourself.
 Bos. You are a false steward.
 Ant. Saucy slave, I'll pull thee up by the roots.
 Bos. Maybe the ruin will crush you to pieces.
 Ant. You are an impudent snake indeed, sir :
Are you scarce warm, and do you show your sting ?
You libel well, sir.
 Bos. No, sir : copy it out,
And I will set my hand to't.
 Ant. (*aside*). My nose bleeds.
One that were superstitious would count
This ominous, when it merely comes by chance :
Two letters that are wrote here for my name,
Are drowned in blood !
Mere accident. — For you, sir, I'll take order
I' the morn you shall be safe : — (*aside*) 'tis that must
    colour
Her lying-in : — sir, this door you pass not :
I do not hold it fit that you come near
The duchess' lodgings, till you have quit yourself. —
(*Aside*) The great are like the base, nay, they are the same,
When they seek shameful ways to avoid shame. [*Exit.*
 Bos. Antonio hereabouts did drop a paper : —

Some of your help, false friend : — O, here it is.
What's here? a child's nativity calculated ! [*Reads.*
"The duchess was delivered of a son, 'tween the hours twelve and one in the night, *Anno Dom.* 1504," — that's this year — "*decimo nono Decembris,*" — that's this night, — "taken according to the meridian of Malfi," — that's our duchess : happy discovery ! — "The lord of the first house being combust[1] in the ascendant, signifies short life ; and Mars being in a human sign, joined to the tail of the Dragon, in the eighth house, doth threaten a violent death. *Cætera non scrutantur.*" 65
Why, now 'tis most apparent : this precise fellow
Is the duchess' bawd : — I have it to my wish !
This is a parcel of intelligency
Our courtiers were cased up for : it needs must follow
That I must be committed on pretence
Of poisoning her ; which I'll endure, and laugh at.
If one could find the father now ! but that
Time will discover. Old Castruccio
I' the morning posts to Rome : by him I'll send
A letter that shall make her brothers' galls 75
O'erflow their livers. This was a thrifty way.
Though lust do mask in ne'er so strange disguise,
She's oft found witty, but is never wise. [*Exit.*

[1] Astrological term, used of a heavenly body not above eight and one-half degrees distant from the sun.

SCENE IV. — *An Apartment in the Palace of the* Cardinal *at Rome.*

Enter Cardinal *and* JULIA.

Card. Sit: thou art my best of wishes. Prithee, tell me
What trick didst thou invent to come to Rome
Without thy husband.

Julia. Why, my lord, I told him
I came to visit an old anchorite
Here for devotion.

Card. Thou art a witty false one, —
I mean, to him.

Julia. You have prevailed with me
Beyond my strongest thoughts: I would **not now**
Find you inconstant.

Card. Do not put thyself
To such a voluntary torture, which proceeds
Out of your own guilt.

Julia. How, my lord!

Card. You fear
My constancy, because you have approved
Those giddy and wild turnings in yourself.

Julia. Did you e'er find them?

Card. Sooth, generally for women,
A man might strive to make glass malleable,
Ere he should make them fixèd.

Julia. So, my lord.

Card. We had need go borrow that fantastic glass[1]
Invented by Galileo the Florentine
To view another spacious world i' the moon,

---

[1] Another anachronism; the telescope was not invented until about 1608.

And look to find a constant woman there. 20
 Julia. This is very well, my lord.
 Card. Why do you weep?
Are tears your justification? the self-same tears
Will fall into your husband's bosom, lady,
With a loud protestation that you love him
Above the world. Come, I'll love you wisely,
That's jealously.
 Julia. I'll go home
To my husband.
 Card. You may thank me, lady,
I have taken you off your melancholy perch,
Bore you upon my fist, and showed you game,
And let you fly at it. — I pray thee, kiss me. — 30
When thou wast with thy husband, thou wast watched
Like a tame elephant : — still you are to thank me : —
Thou hadst only kisses from him and high feeding ;
But what delight was that? 'twas just like one
That hath a little fingering on the lute,
Yet cannot tune it : — still you are to thank me.
 Julia. You told me of a piteous wound i' the heart
And a sick liver, when you wooed me first,
And spake like one in physic.
 Card. Who's that? —

Enter Servant.

Rest firm, for my affection to thee, 40
Lightning moves slow to't.
 Serv. Madam, a gentleman,
That's come post from Malfi, desires to see you.
 Card. Let him enter : I'll withdraw. [*Exit.*
 Serv. He says

Your husband, old Castruccio, is come to Rome,
Most pitifully tired with riding post. [*Exit*.

Enter DELIO.

Julia (*aside*). Signior Delio! 'tis one of my old suitors.
Delio. I was bold to come and see you.
Julia. Sir, you are welcome.
Delio. Do you lie here?
Julia. Sure, your own experience   50
Will satisfy you no: our Roman prelates
Do not keep lodging for ladies.
Delio. Very well:
I have brought you no commendations from your husband,
For I know none by him.¹
Julia. I hear he's come to Rome.
Delio. I never knew man and beast, of a horse and a
    knight
So weary of each other: if he had had a good back,
He would have undertook to have borne his horse,
His breech was so pitifully sore.
Julia. Your laughter
Is my pity.
Delio. Lady, I know not whether
You want money, but I have brought you some.   60
Julia. From my husband?
Delio. No, from mine own allowance.
Julia. I must hear the condition, ere I be bound to take it.
Delio. Look on't, 'tis gold: hath it not a fine colour?
Julia. I have a bird more beautiful.

---

¹ Following the old quartos, here and later in this scene, the lines are printed metrically, although, as *Dyce* remarks, "some of these speeches hardly read like verse."

Delio. Try the sound on't.
Julia. A lute string far exceeds it:
It hath no smell, like cassia or civet;
Nor is it physical, though some fond doctors
Persuade us seethe't in cullises[1]; I'll tell you, 70
This is a creature bred by —

Re-enter Servant.

Serv. Your husband's come,
Hath delivered a letter to the Duke of Calabria
That, to my thinking, hath put him out of his wits. [*Exit.*
Julia. Sir, you hear:
Pray, let me know your business and your suit
As briefly as can be.
Delio. With good speed: I would wish you,
At such time as you are non-rèsident
With your husband, my mistress.
Julia. Sir, I'll go ask my husband if I shall,
And straight return your answer. [*Exit.*
Delio. Very fine!
Is this her wit, or honesty, that speaks thus?
I heard one say the duke was highly moved
With a letter sent from Malfi. I do fear
Antonio is betrayed: how fearfully
Shows his ambition now! unfortunate fortune!
They pass through whirlpools, and deep woes do shun,
Who the event weigh ere the action's done. [*Exit.*

---

[1] "A cullis was a strong and savory broth of boiled meat strained, for debilitated persons: the old receipt-books recommend 'pieces of gold among its ingredients." — *Dyce.*

SCENE V. — *Another Apartment in the same Palace.*

Enter Cardinal, *and* FERDINAND *with a letter.*

Ferd. I have this night digged up a mandrake.
Card. Say you?
Ferd. And I am grown mad with't.[1]
Card. What's the prodigy?
Ferd. Read there, — a sister dammed: she's loose i' the
   hilts;
Grown a notorious strumpet.
Card. Speak lower.
Ferd. Lower!
Rogues do not whisper't now, but seek to publish't
(As servants do the bounty of their lords)
Aloud; and with a covetous searching eye,
To mark who note them. O, confusion seize her!
She hath had most cunning bawds to serve her turn,
And more secure conveyances for lust   10
Than towns of garrison for service.
   Card. Is't possible?
Can this be certain?
   Ferd. Rhubarb, O, for rhubarb
To purge this choler! here's the cursèd day
To prompt my memory; and here't shall stick
Till of her bleeding heart I make a sponge
To wipe it out.
   Card. Why do you make yourself
So wild a tempest?

---

[1] Cf. *Romeo and Juliet*, iv, 3: —

   " And shrieks like mandrakes torn out of the earth,
   That living mortals hearing them run mad."

Ferd. Would I could be one,
That I might toss her palace 'bout her ears,
Root up her goodly forests, blast her meads,
And lay her general territory as waste
As she hath done her honours.
 Card. Shall our blood,
The royal blood of Arragon and Castile,
Be thus attainted?
 Ferd. Apply desperate physic:
We must not now use balsamum, but fire,
The smarting cupping-glass, for that's the mean
To purge infected blood, such blood as hers.
There is a kind of pity in mine eye,—
I'll give it to my handkercher; and now 'tis here,
I'll bequeath this to her bastard.
 Card. What to do?
 Ferd. Why, to make soft lint for his mother's wounds,
When I have hewed her to pieces.
 Card. Cursèd creature!
Unequal nature, to place women's hearts
So far upon the left side!
 Ferd. Foolish men,
That e'er will trust their honour in a bark
Made of so slight weak bulrush as is woman,
Apt every minute to sink it!
 Card. Thus
Ignorance, when it hath purchased honour,
It cannot wield it.
 Ferd. Methinks I see her laughing—
Excellent hyena! Talk to me somewhat quickly,
Or my imagination will carry me
To see her in the shameful act of sin.

Card. How idly shows this rage, which carries you,
As men conveyed by witches through the air,
On violent whirlwinds! this intemperate noise
Fitly resembles deaf men's shrill discourse,
Who talk aloud, thinking all other men
To have their imperfection.
    Ferd. Have not you
My palsy?
    Card. Yes, but I can be angry
Without this rupture[1] : there is not in nature
A thing that makes man so deformed, so beastly,
As doth intemperate anger. Chide yourself.   50
You have divers men who never yet expressed
Their strong desire of rest but by unrest,
By vexing of themselves. Come, put yourself
In tune.
    Ferd. So I will only study to seem
The thing I am not. I could kill her now,
In you, or in myself; for I do think
It is some sin in us Heaven doth revenge
By her.
    Card. Are you stark mad?
    Ferd. I would have their bodies
Burnt in a coal-pit with the ventage stopped,
That their cursed smoke might not ascend to Heaven;   60
Or dip the sheets they lie in in pitch or sulphur,
Wrap them in't, and then light them like a match!
    Card. I'll leave you.
    Ferd. Nay, I have done.
I am confident, had I been damned in hell,
And should have heard of this, it would have put me

---

[1] Dyce suggests *rapture*.

Into a cold sweat. In, in; I'll go sleep.
Till I know who wrongs my sister, I'll not stir:
That known, I'll find scorpions to string my whips,
And fix her in a general eclipse. [*Exeunt.*

ACT III.

SCENE I. — *An Apartment in the Palace of the* DUCHESS.

Enter ANTONIO *and* DELIO.

Ant. Our noble friend, my most belovèd Delio!
O, you have been a stranger long at court;
Came you along with the Lord Ferdinand?
  Delio. I did, sir: and how fares your noble duchess?
  Ant. Right fortunately well: she's an excellent
Feeder of pedigrees; since you last saw her,
She hath had two children more, a son and daughter.
  Delio. Methinks 'twas yesterday: let me but wink,
And not behold your face, which to mine eye
Is somewhat leaner, verily I should dream   10
It were within this half hour.
  Ant. You have not been in law, friend Delio,
Nor in prison, nor a suitor at the court,
Nor begged the reversion of some great man's place,
Nor troubled with an old wife, which doth make
Your time so insensibly hasten.
  Delio. Pray, sir, tell me,
Hath not this news arrived yet to the ear
Of the lord cardinal?

Ant. I fear it hath :
The Lord Ferdinand, that's newly come to court,
Doth bear himself right dangerously.
 Delio. Pray, why?
 Ant. He is so quiet that he seems to sleep
The tempest out, as dormice do in winter :
Those houses that are haunted are most still
Till the devil be up.
 Delio. What say the common people?
 Ant. The common rabble do directly say
She is a strumpet.
 Delio. And your graver heads
Which would be politic, what censure they?
 Ant. They do observe I grow to infinite purchase,[1]
The left hand way, and all suppose the duchess
Would amend it, if she could ; for, say they,
Great princes, though they grudge their officers
Should have such large and unconfinèd means
To get wealth under them, will not complain,
Lest thereby they should make them odious
Unto the people ; for other obligation
Of love or marriage between her and me
They never dream of.
 Delio. The Lord Ferdinand
Is going to bed.

   Enter Duchess, Ferdinand, *and* Attendants.

 Ferd. I'll instantly to bed,
For I am weary. — I am to bespeak
A husband for you.
 Duch. For me, sir ! pray, who is't?

---

[1] **Cant term** for stolen goods; here means riches, property.

Ferd. The great Count Malatesti.

Duch. Fie upon him!
A count! he's a mere stick of sugar-candy;
You may look quite through him. When I choose
A husband, I will marry for your honour.

Ferd. You shall do well in't. — How is't, worthy Antonio?

Duch. But, sir, I am to have private conference with you
About a scandalous report is spread
Touching mine honour.

Ferd. Let me be ever deaf to't: 50
One of Pasquil's[1] paper bullets, court-calumny,
A pestilent air, which princes' palaces
Are seldom purged of. Yet say that it were true,
I pour it in your bosom, my fixed love
Would strongly excuse, extenuate, nay, deny
Faults, were they apparent in you. Go, be safe
In your own innocency.

Duch. (*aside*). O blessed comfort!
This deadly air is purged.

      [*Exeunt* DUCHESS, ANTONIO, DELIO, *and* Attendants.

Ferd. Her guilt treads on
Hot-burning coulters.

         Enter BOSOLA.

         Now, Bosola,

---

[1] "A Roman cobbler of the latter half of the fifteenth century, whose shop stood near the Braschi palace, near the Piazza Navona. He was notorious for caustic remarks, and gradually every bitter saying became attributed to him or his workmen. After his death, a mutilated statue was dug out and set up near his shop, upon which the populace declared that Pasquin has come to life again. Then the custom arose of attaching to the torso stinging epigrams or satirical verses (*pasquinades*) often directed against the Pope and cardinals, and no prohibition nor penalty could put a stop to the practice." — *Wheeler*, *Noted Names of Fiction.*

How thrives our intelligence?

Bos. Sir, uncertainly: 60
'Tis rumoured she hath had three bastards, but
By whom we may go read i' the stars.

Ferd. Why, some
Hold opinion all things are written there.

Bos. Yes, if we could find spectacles to read them.
I do suspect there hath been some sorcery
Used on the duchess.

Ferd. Sorcery! to what purpose?

Bos. To make her dote on some desertless fellow
She shames to acknowledge.

Ferd. Can your faith give way
To think there's power in potions or in charms,
To make us love whether we will or no? 70

Bos. Most certainly.

Ferd. Away! these are mere gulleries,[1] horrid things,
Invented by some cheating mountebanks
To abuse us. Do you think that herbs or charms
Can force the will? Some trials have been made
In this foolish practice, but the ingredients
Were lenitive poisons, such as are of force
To make the patient mad; and straight the witch
Swears by equivocation they are in love.
The witchcraft lies in her rank blood. This night 80
I will force confession from her. You told me
You had got, within these two days, a false key
Into her bed-chamber.

Bos. I have.

Ferd. As I would wish.

Bos. What do you intend to do?

[1] Impostures.

Ferd. Can you guess?

Bos. No.

Ferd. Do not ask, then:
He that can compass me, and know my drifts,
May say he hath put a girdle 'bout the world,[1]
And sounded all her quicksands.

Bos. I do not
Think so. 90

Ferd. What do you think, then, pray?

Bos. That you are
Your own chronicle too much, and grossly
Flatter yourself.

Ferd. Give me thy hand; I thank thee:
I never gave pension but to flatterers,
Till I entertainèd thee.   Farewell.
That friend a great man's ruin strongly checks,
Who rails into his belief all his defects. [*Exeunt.*

SCENE II. — *The Bed-chamber of the* DUCHESS.

Enter DUCHESS, ANTONIO, *and* CARIOLA.

Duch. (*to Cari.*). Bring me the casket hither, and the glass. —
You get no lodging here to-night, my lord.

Ant. Indeed, I must persuade one.

Duch. I'll stop your mouth. [*Kisses him.*

Ant. Nay, that's but one; Venus had two soft doves
To draw her chariot; I must have another —
[*She kisses him again.*

---

[1] Cf. *Midsummer-Night's Dream*, ii, 2: —

"I'll put a girdle round about the earth
In forty minutes."

When wilt thou marry, Cariola?

Cari. Never, my lord.

Ant. O, fie upon this single life ! forego it.
We read how Daphne, for her peevish[1] flight,
Became a fruitless bay-tree ; Syrinx[2] turned
To the pale empty reed ; Anaxarete[3]
Was frozen into marble : whereas those
Which married, or proved kind unto their friends,
Were by a gracious influence transhaped
Into the olive, pomegranate, mulberry,
Became flowers, precious stones, or eminent stars.

Cari. This is a vain poetry : but I pray you tell me,
If there were proposed me, wisdom, riches, and beauty,
In three several young men, which should I choose.

Ant. 'Tis a hard question : this was Paris' case,
And he was blind in't, and there was great cause ;
For how was't possible he could judge right,
Having three amorous goddesses in view,
And they stark naked? 'twas a motion
Were able to benight the apprehension
Of the severest counsellor of Europe.
Now I look on both your faces so well formed,
It puts me in mind of a question I would ask.

Cari. What is't?

Ant. I do wonder why hard-favoured ladies,
For the most part, keep worse-favoured waiting-women
To attend them, and cannot endure fair ones.

---

[1] Foolish.

[2] "An Arcadian nymph, who being pursued by Pan, fled into the river Ladon, and at her own prayer was metamorphosed into a reed, of which Pan then made his flute." — *Smith's Classical Dict.*

[3] A Cyprian maid, whose lover, Iphis, hung himself in despair at her door. Venus turned her into a statue.

Duch. O, that's soon answered.
Did you ever in your life know an ill painter
Desire to have his dwelling next door to the shop
Of an excellent picture-maker? 'twould disgrace
His face-making, and undo him.   I prithee,
When were we so merry? — My hair tangles.
   Ant. (*aside to Cari.*). Pray thee, Cariola, let's steal forth
      the room,
And let her talk to herself: I have divers times
Served her the like, when she hath chafed extremely.   40
I love to see her angry.   Softly, Cariola.
                  [*Exeunt* ANTONIO *and* CARIOLA.
   Duch. Doth not the colour of my hair 'gin to change?
When I wax gray, I shall have all the court
Powder their hair with orris to be like me.
You have cause to love me; I entered you into my heart
Before you would vouchsafe to call for the keys.

         Enter FERDINAND *behind.*

We shall one day have my brothers take you napping;
Methinks his presence, being now in court,
Should make you keep your own bed; but you'll say
Love mixed with fear is sweetest.   50
Have you lost your tongue?   'Tis welcome:
For know, whether I am doomed to live or die,
I can do both like a prince.
   Ferd. Die, then, quickly!   [*Giving her a poniard.*
Virtue, where art thou hid? what hideous thing
Is it that doth eclipse thee?
   Duch. Pray, sir, hear me.
   Ferd. Or is it true thou art but a bare name,
And no essential thing?

Duch. Sir,—
Ferd. Do not speak.
Duch. No, sir:
I will plant my soul in mine ears, to hear you.
    Ferd. O most imperfect light of human reason,
That mak'st us so unhappy to foresee
What we can least prevent! Pursue thy wishes,
And glory in them: there's in shame no comfort
But to be past all bounds and sense of shame.
    Duch. I pray, sir, hear me: I am married.
    Ferd. So!
    Duch. Happily, not to your liking: but for that,
Alas, your shears do come untimely now
To clip the bird's wing that's already flown!
Will you see my husband?
    Ferd. Yes, if I could change
Eyes with a basilisk.
    Duch. Sure, you came hither
By his confederacy.
    Ferd. The howling of a wolf
Is music to thee, screech-owl: prithee, peace.—
Whate'er thou art that hast enjoyed my sister,
For I am sure thou hear'st me, for thine own sake
Let me not know thee. I came hither prepared
To work thy discovery; yet am now persuaded
It would beget such violent effects
As would damn us both. I would not for ten millions
I had beheld thee: therefore use all means
I never may have knowledge of thy name;
Enjoy thy lust still, and a wretched life,
On that condition.— And for thee, vile woman,
I would have thee build

Such a room for him as our anchorites
To holier use inhabit. Let not the sun
Shine on him till he's dead; let dogs and monkeys
Only converse with him, and such dumb things
To whom nature denies use to sound his name;
Do not keep a paraquito, lest she learn it;
If thou do love him, cut out thine own tongue,
Lest it bewray him.
 Duch. Why might not I marry?
I have not gone about in this to create   90
Any new world or custom.
 Ferd. Thou art undone:
And thou hast ta'en that massy sheet of lead
That hid thy husband's bones, and folded it
About my heart.
 Duch. Mine bleeds for't.
 Ferd. Thine! thy heart!
What should I name't unless a hollow bullet
Filled with unquenchable wild-fire?
 Duch. You are in this
Too strict; and were you not my princely brother,
I would say, too wilful: my reputation
Is safe.
 Ferd. Dost thou know what reputation is?
I'll tell thee, — to small purpose, since the instruction   100
Comes now too late.
Upon a time Reputation, Love, and Death,
Would travel o'er the world; and it was concluded
That they should part, and take three several ways.
Death told them, they should find him in great battles,
Or cities plagued with plagues: Love gives them counsel
To inquire for him 'mongst unambitious shepherds,

Where dowries were not talked of, and sometimes
'Mongst quiet kindred that had nothing left
By their dead parents: "Stay," quoth Reputation,
" Do not forsake me; for it is my nature,
If once I part from any man I meet,
I am never found again." And so for you:
You have shook hands with Reputation,
And made him invisible. So, fare you well:
I will never see you more.
 Duch. Why should only I,
Of all the other princes of the world,
Be cased up, like a holy relic? I have youth
And a little beauty.
 Ferd. So you have some virgins
That are witches. I will never see thee more. [*Exit.*
   Re-enter ANTONIO *with a pistol, and* CARIOLA.

 Duch. You saw this apparition?
 Ant. Yes: we are
Betrayed. How came he hither? I should turn
This to thee, for that.
 Cari. Pray, sir, do; and when
That you have cleft my heart, you shall read there
Mine innocence.
 Duch. That gallery gave him entrance.
 Ant. I would this terrible thing would come again,
That, standing on my guard, I might relate
My warrantable love. —   [*She shows the poniard.*
   Ha! what means this?
 Duch. He left this with me.
 Ant. And it seems did wish
You would use it on yourself.

Duch. His action
Seemed to intend so much.
　Ant. This hath a handle to't,
As well as a point: turn it towards him,
And so fasten the keen edge in his rank gall.
　　　　　　　　　　　　　　[*Knocking within.*
How now! who knocks? more earthquakes?
　Duch. I stand
As if a mine beneath my feet were ready
To be blown up.
　Cari. 'Tis Bosola.
　Duch. Away!
O misery! methinks unjust actions
Should wear these masks and curtains, and not we.　139
You must instantly part hence: I have fashioned it already.
　　　　　　　　　　　　　　[*Exit* ANTONIO.

　　　　　　Enter BOSOLA.

　Bos. The duke your brother is ta'en up in a whirlwind,
Hath took horse, and's rid post to Rome.
　Duch. So late?
　Bos. He told me, as he mounted into the saddle,
You were undone.
　Duch. Indeed, I am very near it.
　Bos. What's the matter?
　Duch. Antonio, the master of our household,
Hath dealt so falsely with me in's accounts:
My brother stood engaged with me for money
Ta'en up of certain Neapolitan Jews,
And Antonio lets the bonds be forfeit.　　　　　150
　Bos. Strange!— (*Aside*) This is cunning.
　Duch. And hereupon

My brother's bills at Naples are protested
Against. — Call up our officers.
　Bos. I shall.　　　　　　　　　　　　　　　　*[Exit.*
　　　　　　Re-enter ANTONIO.

　Duch. The place that you must fly to is Ancona:
Hire a house there; I'll send after you
My treasure and my jewels.　Our weak safety
Runs upon enginous[1] wheels: short syllables
Must stand for periods.　I must now accuse you
Of such a feignèd crime as Tasso calls
Magnanima menzogna,[2] a noble lie,　　　　　　160
'Cause it must shield our honours. — Hark! they are coming.
　　　　Re-enter BOSOLA *and* Officers.

　Ant. Will your grace hear me?
　Duch. I have got well by you; you have yielded me
A million of loss: I am like to inherit
The people's curses for your stewardship.
You had the trick in audit-time to be sick,
Till I had signed your quietus; and that cured you
Without help of a doctor. — Gentlemen,
I would have this man be an example to you all;
So shall you hold my favour; I pray, let him;　　17
For h'as done that, alas, you would not think of,
And, because I intend to be rid of him,
I mean not to publish. — Use your fortune elsewhere.
　Ant. I am strongly armed to brook my overthrow,
As commonly men bear with a hard year:
I will not blame the cause on't; but do think

---

[1] The Quarto of 1640 has *ingenious.*

[2] See Tasso, *Gerusalemme Liberata,* ii, 22.　Horace uses the expression *splendide mendax.*

The necessity of my malevolent star
Procures this, not her humour. O, the inconstant
And rotten ground of service! you may see,
'Tis even like him, that in a winter night, 180
Takes a long slumber o'er a dying fire,
A-loth to part from't; yet parts thence as cold
As when he first sat down.

Duch. We do confiscate,
Towards the satisfying of your accounts,
All that you have.

Ant. I am all yours; and 'tis very fit
All mine should be so.

Duch. So, sir, you have your pass.

Ant. You may see, gentlemen, what 'tis to serve
A prince with body and soul. [*Exit.*

Bos. Here's an example for extortion: what moisture is drawn out of the sea, when foul weather comes, pours down, and runs into the sea again. 191

Duch. I would know what are your opinions
Of this Antonio.

2d Off. He could not abide to see a pig's head gaping: I thought your grace would find him a Jew.[1]

3d Off. I would you had been his officer, for your own sake.

4th Off. You would have had more money.

1st Off. He stopped his ears with black wool, and to those came to him for money said he was thick of hearing.

4th Off. How scurvy proud he would look when the treasury was full! Well, let him go. 201

1st Off. Yes, and the chippings of the buttery fly after him, to scour his gold chain.[2]

---

[1] Cf. *Merchant of Venice*, iv, 1.
[2] Stewards wore a gold chain as a symbol of their office.

Duch. Leave us.   [*Exeunt* Officers.
What do you think of these?
  Bos. That these are rogues that in's prosperity,
But to have waited on his fortune, could have wished
His dirty stirrup riveted through their noses,
And followed after's mule, like a bear in a ring;
Made their first-born intelligencers[1]; thought none happy
But such as were born under his blest planet,   210
And wore his livery: and do these lice drop off now?
Well, never look to have the like again:
He hath left a sort of flattering rogues behind him;
Their doom must follow. Princes pay flatterers
In their own money: flatterers dissemble their vices,
And they dissemble their lies; that's justice.
Alas, poor gentleman!
  Duch. Poor! he hath amply filled his coffers.
  Bos. Sure, he was too honest. Pluto,[2] the god of riches,
When he's sent by Jupiter to any man,   220
He goes limping, to signify that wealth
That comes on God's name comes slowly; but when he's sent
On the devil's errand, he rides post and comes in by scuttles.
Let me show you what a most unvalued jewel
You have in a wanton humour thrown away,
To bless the man shall find him. He was an excellent
Courtier and most faithful; a soldier that thought it
As beastly to know his own value too little
As devilish to acknowledge it too much.
Both his virtue and form deserved a far better fortune;   230
His discourse rather delighted to judge itself than show
    itself:

[1] Tale-bearers.
[2] Plutus. Cf. this passage with Bacon's Essay *Of Riches*.

His breast was filled with all perfection,
And yet it seemed a private whispering-room,
It made so little noise of't.
  Duch. But he was basely descended.
  Bos. Will you make yourself a mercenary herald,
Rather to examine men's pedigrees than virtues?
You shall want him:
For know an honest statesman to a prince
Is like a cedar planted by a spring; 240
The spring bathes the tree's root, the grateful tree
Rewards it with his shadow: you have not done so.
I would sooner swim to the Bermoothes[1] on
Two politicians' rotten bladders, tied
Together with an intelligencer's heart-string,
Than depend on so changeable a prince's favour.
Fare thee well, Antonio! since the malice of the world
Would needs down with thee, it cannot be said yet
That any ill happened unto thee, considering thy fall
Was accompanied with virtue.[2] 250
  Duch. O, you render me excellent music!
  Bos. Say you?
  Duch. This good one that you speak of is my husband.
  Bos. Do I not dream! can this ambitious age
Have so much goodness in't as to prefer
A man merely for worth, without these shadows
Of wealth and painted honours? possible?
  Duch. I have had three children by him.

---

[1] The Bermudas; so Shakespeare in *The Tempest*, i, 2:—
"The still vex'd Bermoothes."

[2] "This and the two preceding speeches of *Bosola* consist partly of lines which it would be difficult to read as prose, and partly of sentences which will not admit of any satisfactory metrical arrangement." — *Dyce.*

Bos. Fortunate lady!
For you have made your private nuptial bed
The humble and fair seminary of peace. 260
No question but many an unbeneficed scholar
Shall pray for you for this deed, and rejoice
That some preferment in the world can yet
Arise from merit. The virgins of your land
That have no dowries shall hope your example
Will raise them to rich husbands. Should you want
Soldiers, 'twould make the very Turks and Moors
Turn Christians, and serve you for this act.
Last, the neglected poets of your time,
In honour of this trophy of a man, 270
Raised by that curious engine, your white hand,
Shall thank you, in your grave, for't; and make that
More reverend than all the cabinets
Of living princes. For Antonio,
His fame shall likewise flow from many a pen,
When heralds shall want coats[1] to sell to men.
    Duch. As I taste comfort in this friendly speech,
So would I find concealment.
    Bos. O, the secret of my prince,
Which I will wear on the inside of my heart! 280
    Duch. You shall take charge of all my coin and jewels,
And follow him; for he retires himself
To Ancona.
    Bos. So.
    Duch. Whither, within few days,
I mean to follow thee.
    Bos. Let me think:
I would wish your grace to feign a pilgrimage

---

[1] Coats-of-arms.

To our Lady of Loretto, scarce seven leagues
From fair Ancona; so may you depart
Your country with more honour, and your flight
Will seem a princely progress, retaining
Your usual train about you.
 Duch. Sir, your direction 290
Shall lead me by the hand.
 Cari. In my opinion,
She were better progress to the baths at Lucca,
Or go visit the Spa
In Germany; for, if you will believe me,
I do not like this jesting with religion,
This feignèd pilgrimage.
 Duch. Thou art a superstitious fool:
Prepare us instantly for our departure.
Past sorrows, let us moderately lament them;
For those to come, seek wisely to prevent them. 300
     [*Exeunt* DUCHESS *and* CARIOLA.
 Bos. A politician is the devil's quilted anvil;
He fashions all sins on him, and the blows
Are never heard: he may work in a lady's chamber,
As here for proof. What rests but I reveal
All to my lord? O, this base quality
Of intelligencer! why, every quality i' the world
Prefers but gain or commendation:
Now for this act I am certain to be raised,
And men that paint weeds to the life are praised. [*Exit.*

SCENE III.[1]—*An Apartment in the* Cardinal's *Palace at Rome.*

Enter Cardinal, FERDINAND, MALATESTI, PESCARA, DELIO, *and* SILVIO.

Card. Must we turn soldier, then?
Mal. The emperor,
Hearing your worth that way, ere you attained
This reverend garment, joins you in commission
With the right fortunate soldier the Marquis of Pescara,
And the famous Lannoy.
Card. He that had the honour
Of taking the French king prisoner?[2]
Mal. The same.
Here's a plot drawn for a new fortification
At Naples.
Ferd. This great count Malatesti, I perceive,
Hath got employment?
Delio. No employment, my lord;
A marginal note in the muster-book, that he is   10
A voluntary lord.
Ferd. He's no soldier.
Delio. He has worn gunpowder in's hollow tooth for the toothache.
Sil. He comes to the leaguer[3] with a full intent
To eat fresh beef and garlic, means to stay
Till the scent be gone, and straight return to court.

---

[1] " Another scene that hovers between prose and verse." — *Dyce.*
[2] In 1525, Francis I was defeated at Pavia, by the generals of Charles V,— Pescara, Bourbon, and Lannoy, viceroy of Naples,— and surrendered to the last-mentioned.
[3] Camp.

Delio. He hath read all the late service
As the city chronicle relates it;
And keeps two pewterers going, only to express
Battles in model.
   Sil. Then he'll fight by the book.
   Delio. By the almanac, I think,   20
To choose good days and shun the critical;
That's his mistress' scarf.
   Sil. Yes, he protests
He would do much for that taffeta.
   Delio. I think he would run away from a battle,
To save it from taking prisoner.
   Sil. He is horribly afraid
Gunpowder will spoil the perfume on't.
   Delio. I saw a Dutchman break his pate once
For calling him pot-gun; he made his head   30
Have a bore in't like a musket.
   Sil. I would he had made a touchhole to't.
He is indeed a guarded[1] sumpter-cloth,
Only for the remove of the court.

Enter BOSOLA.

   Pes. Bosola arrived! what should be the business?
Some falling out amongst the cardinals.
These factions amongst great men, they are like
Foxes, when their heads are divided,
They carry fire in their tails, and all the country
About them goes to wreck for't.
   Sil. What's that Bosola?   40
   Delio. I knew him in Padua — a fantastical scholar, like such who study to know how many knots was in Hercules'

---

[1] With facings, trimmings.

club, of what colour Achilles' beard was, or whether Hector were not troubled with the toothache. He hath studied himself half blear-eyed to know the true symmetry of Cæsar's nose by a shoeing-horn; and this he did to gain the name of a speculative man.

Pes. Mark Prince Ferdinand:
A very salamander lives in's eye,
To mock the eager violence of fire. 50

Sil. That cardinal hath made more bad faces with his oppression than ever Michael Angelo made good ones: he lifts up's nose, like a foul porpoise before a storm.

Pes. The Lord Ferdinand laughs.

Delio. Like a deadly cannon
That lightens ere it smokes.

Pes. These are your true pangs of death,
The pangs of life that struggle with great statesmen.

Delio. In such a deformed silence witches whisper their charms.

Card. Doth she make religion her riding-hood 60
To keep her from the sun and tempest?

Ferd. That,
That damns her. Methinks her fault and beauty,
Blended together, show like leprosy,
The whiter, the fouler. I make it a question
Whether her beggarly brats were ever christened.

Card. I will instantly solicit the state of Ancona
To have them banished.

Ferd. You are for Loretto:
I shall not be at your ceremony; fare you well.—
Write to the Duke of Malfi, my young nephew
She had by her first husband, and acquaint him 70
With's mother's honesty.

Bos. I will.

Ferd. Antonio!
A slave that only smelled of ink and counters,
And never in's life looked like a gentleman,
But in the audit-time. — Go, go presently,
Draw me out an hundred and fifty of our horse,
And meet me at the fort-bridge. [*Exeunt.*

SCENE IV. — *The Shrine of our Lady of Loretto.*

Enter Two Pilgrims.

1st Pil. I have not seen a goodlier shrine than this;
Yet I have visited many.

2d Pil. The Cardinal of Arragon
Is this day to resign his cardinal's hat:
His sister duchess likewise is arrived
To pay her vow of pilgrimage. I expect
A noble ceremony.

1st Pil. No question. — They come.

Here the ceremony of the Cardinal's *instalment, in the habit of a soldier, is performed by his delivering up his cross, hat, robes, and ring, at the shrine, and the investing of him with sword, helmet, shield, and spurs; then* ANTONIO, *the* DUCHESS, *and their children, having presented themselves at the shrine, are, by a form of banishment in dumb-show expressed towards them by the* Cardinal *and the state of Ancona, banished: during all which ceremony, this ditty is sung, to very solemn music, by divers churchmen.*

Arms and honours deck thy story,
To thy fame's eternal glory!

Adverse fortune ever fly thee ;   10
No disastrous fate come nigh thee !
I alone will sing thy praises,
Whom to honour virtue raises ;
And thy study, that divine is,
Bent to martial discipline is.
Lay aside all those robes lie by thee ;
Crown thy arts with arms, they'll beautify thee.
O worthy of worthiest name, adorned in this manner,
Lead bravely thy forces on under war's warlike banner !
O, mayst thou prove fortunate in all martial courses !   20
Guide thou still by skill in arts and forces !
Victory attend thee nigh, whilst fame sings loud thy powers ;
Triumphant conquest crown thy head, and blessings pour
        down showers ![1]

                          [*Exeunt all except the* Two Pilgrims.

   1st Pil. Here's a strange turn of state ! who would have
       thought
So great a lady would have matched herself
Unto so mean a person? yet the cardinal
Bears himself much too cruel.

   2d Pil. They are banished.

   1st Pil. But I would ask what power hath this state
Of Ancona to determine of a free prince?

   2d Pil. They are a free state, sir, and her brother showed
How that the Pope, forehearing of her looseness,   31
Hath seized into the protection of the church
The dukedom which she held as dowager.

   1st Pil. But by what justice?

   2d Pil. Sure, I think by none,

     [1] The Quarto of 1623 has the following marginal note : " The Author disclaimes this Ditty to be his."

Only her brother's instigation.
　　1st Pil. What was it with such violence he took
Off from her finger?
　　2d Pil. 'Twas her wedding-ring;
Which he vowed shortly he would sacrifice
To his revenge.
　　1st Pil. Alas, Antonio!
If that a man be thrust into a well,　　　　　　　　　40
No matter who sets hand to't, his own weight
Will bring him sooner to the bottom. Come, let's hence.
Fortune makes this conclusion general,
All things do help the unhappy man to fall.　　[*Exeunt.*

Scene V. — *Near Loretto.*

Enter Duchess, Antonio, Children, Cariola, *and* Servants.

　　Duch. Banished Ancona!
　　Ant. Yes, you see what power
Lightens in great men's breath.
　　Duch. Is all our train
Shrunk to this poor remainder?
　　Ant. These poor men,
Which have got little in your service, vow
To take your fortune: but your wiser buntings,[1]
Now they are fledged, are gone.
　　Duch. They have done wisely.
This puts me in mind of death: physicians thus,[2]
With their hands full of money, use to give o'er
Their patients.
　　Ant. Right the fashion of the world:
From decayed fortunes every flatterer shrinks;　　　　10

---

[1] Birds of the sparrow family.　　　　[2] Cf. *Timon of Athens*, iii, 3.

Men cease to build where the foundation sinks.
 Duch. I had a very strange dream to-night.
 Ant. What was't?
 Duch. Methought I wore my coronet of state,
And on a sudden all the diamonds
Were changed to pearls.
 Ant. My interpretation
Is, you'll weep shortly; for to me the pearls
Do signify your tears.
 Duch. The birds that live i' the field
On the wild benefit of nature live
Happier than we; for they may choose their mates, 20
And carol their sweet pleasures to the spring.

Enter BOSOLA *with a letter.*

 Bos. You are happily o'erta'en.
 Duch. From my brother?
 Bos. Yes, from the Lord Ferdinand your brother
All love and safety.
 Duch. Thou dost blanch mischief,
Wouldst make it white. See, see, like to calm weather
At sea before a tempest, false hearts speak fair
To those they intend most mischief.   [*Reads.*
"Send Antonio to me; I want his head in a business."
A politic equivocation!
He doth not want your counsel, but your head; 30
That is, he cannot sleep till you be dead.
And here's another pitfall that's strewed o'er
With roses; mark it, 'tis a cunning one: [*Reads.*
"I stand engaged for your husband for several debts at Naples: let not that trouble him; I had rather have his heart than his money:"—

And I believe so too.

Bos. What do you believe?

Duch. That he so much distrusts my husband's love
He will by no means believe his heart is with him
Until he sees it: the devil is not cunning enough
To circumvent us in riddles.

Bos. Will you reject that noble and free league
Of amity and love which I present you?

Duch. Their league is like that of some politic kings,
Only to make themselves of strength and power
To be our after-ruin: tell them so.

Bos. And what from you?

Ant. Thus tell him; I will not come.

Bos. And what of this?

Ant. My brothers have dispersed
Blood-hounds abroad; which till I hear are muzzled,
No truce, though hatched with ne'er such politic skill,
Is safe, that hangs upon our enemies' will.
I'll not come at them.

Bos. This proclaims your breeding:
Every small thing draws a base mind to fear,
As the adamant draws iron.   Fare you well, sir:
You shall shortly hear from's.   [*Exit.*

Duch. I suspect some ambush:
Therefore by all my love I do conjure you
To take your eldest son, and fly towards Milan.
Let us not venture all this poor remainder
In one unlucky bottom.

Ant. You counsel safely.
Best of my life, farewell, since we must part:
Heaven hath a hand in't; but no otherwise
Than as some curious artist takes in sunder

A clock or watch, when it is out of frame,
To bring't in better order.
   Duch. I know not which is best,
To see you dead, or part with you. — Farewell, boy:
Thou art happy that thou hast not understanding
To know thy misery; for all our wit
And reading brings us to a truer sense   70
Of sorrow. — In the eternal church, sir,
I do hope we shall not part thus.
   Ant. O, be of comfort!
Make patience a noble fortitude,
And think not how unkindly we are used:
Man, like to cassia, is proved best being bruised.
   Duch. Must I, like a slave-born Russian,
Account it praise to suffer tyranny?
And yet, O Heaven, thy heavy hand is in't!
I have seen my little boy oft scourge his top,
And compared myself to't: naught made me e'er   80
Go right but Heaven's scourge-stick.
   Ant. Do not weep:
Heaven fashioned us of nothing, and we strive
To bring ourselves to nothing. — Farewell, Cariola,
And thy sweet armful. — If I do never see thee more,
Be a good mother to your little ones,
And save them from the tiger: fare you well.
   Duch. Let me look upon you once more, for that speech
Came from a dying father: your kiss is colder
Than that I have seen an holy anchorite
Give to a dead man's skull.   90
   Ant. My heart is turned to a heavy lump of lead,
With which I sound my danger: fare you well.
          [*Exeunt* ANTONIO *and his* Son.

Duch. My laurel is all withered.
Cari. Look, madam, what a troop of armèd men
Make towards us.
Duch. O, they are very welcome:
When fortune's wheel is over-charged with princes,
The weight makes it move swift: I would have my ruin
Be sudden.

Re-enter BOSOLA *visarded, with a* Guard.

I am your adventure, am I not?
Bos. You are: you must see your husband no more.
Duch. What devil art thou that counterfeit'st Heaven's
    thunder?
Bos. Is that terrible? I would have you tell me whether
Is that note worse that frights the silly birds 101
Out of the corn, or that which doth allure them
To the nets? you have hearkened to the last too much.
Duch. O misery! like to a rusty o'er-charged cannon,
Shall I never fly in pieces? — Come, to what prison?
Bos. To none.
Duch. Whither, then?
Bos. To your palace.
Duch. I have heard
That Charon's boat serves to convey all o'er
The dismal lake, but brings none back again.
Bos. Your brothers mean you safety and pity.
Duch. Pity! 110
With such a pity men preserve alive
Pheasants and quails, when they are not fat enough
To be eaten.
Bos. These are your children?
Duch. Yes.

Bos. Can they prattle?
Duch. No;
But I intend, since they were born accursed,
Curses shall be their first language.
Bos. Fie, madam!
Forget this base, low fellow,—
Duch. Were I a man,
I'd beat that counterfeit face into thy other.
Bos. One of no birth.
Duch. Say that he was born mean,   120
Man is most happy when's own actions
Be arguments and examples of his virtue.
Bos. A barren, beggarly virtue.
Duch. I prithee, who is greatest? can you tell?
Sad tales befit my woe: I'll tell you one.
A salmon, as she swam unto the sea,
Met with a dog-fish, who encounters her
With this rough language: "Why art thou so bold
To mix thyself with our high state of floods,[1]
Being no eminent courtier, but one   130
That for the calmest and fresh time o' the year
Dost live in shallow rivers, rank'st thyself
With silly smelts and shrimps? and darest thou
Pass by our dog-ship without reverence?"
"O!" quoth the salmon, "sister, be at peace:
Thank Jupiter we both have passed the net!
Our value never can be truly known,
Till in the fisher's basket we be shown:
I' the market then my price may be the higher,
Even when I am nearest to the cook and fire."   140
So to great men the moral may be stretched;

[1] Cf. *II Henry IV*, v, 2.

Men oft are valued high, when they're most wretched. —
But come, whither you please. I am armed 'gainst misery;
Bent to all sways of the oppressor's will:
There's no deep valley but near some great hill. [*Exeunt.*

ACT IV.

SCENE I. — *An Apartment in the* DUCHESS' *Palace at Malfi.*

Enter FERDINAND *and* BOSOLA.

Ferd. How doth our sister duchess bear herself
In her imprisonment?
  Bos. Nobly: I'll describe her.
She's sad as one long used to't, and she seems
Rather to welcome the end of misery
Than shun it; a behaviour so noble
As gives a majesty to adversity:
You may discern the shape of loveliness
More perfect in her tears than in her smiles:
She will muse four hours together; and her silence,
Methinks, expresseth more than if she spake.   10
  Ferd. Her melancholy seems to be fortified
With a strange disdain.
  Bos. 'Tis so; and this restraint,
Like English mastiffs that grow fierce with tying,
Makes her too passionately apprehend
Those pleasures she's kept from.
  Ferd. Curse upon her!
I will no longer study in the book
Of another's heart. Inform her what I told you.   [*Exit.*

Enter DUCCHESS.[1]

Bos. All comfort to your grace!

Duch. I will have none.
Pray thee, why dost thou wrap thy poisoned pills
In gold and sugar? 20

Bos. Your elder brother, the Lord Ferdinand,
Is come to visit you, and sends you word,
'Cause once he rashly made a solemn vow
Never to see you more, he comes i' the night;
And prays you gently neither torch nor taper
Shine in your chamber: he will kiss your hand,
And reconcile himself; but for his vow
He dares not see you.

Duch. At his pleasure. —
Take hence the lights. — He's come.

Enter FERDINAND.

Ferd. Where are you? 30
Duch. Here, sir.
Ferd. This darkness suits you well.
Duch. I would ask your pardon.
Ferd. You have it;
For I account it the honourabl'st revenge,
Where I may kill, to pardon. — Where are your cubs?
Duch. Whom?
Ferd. Call them your children;
For though our national law distinguish bastards
From true legitimate issue, compassionate nature
Makes them all equal.

[1] Dyce suggests that here the audience had to imagine a change of scene to the lodging of the Duchess.

Duch. Do you visit me for this?
You violate a sacrament o' the church
Shall make you howl in hell for't.
  Ferd. It had been well,   40
Could you have lived thus always; for, indeed,
You were too much i' the light: — but no more;
I come to seal my peace with you.   Here's a hand
      [*Gives her a dead man's hand.*
To which you have vowed much love; the ring upon't
You gave.
  Duch. I affectionately kiss it.
  Ferd. Pray, do, and bury the print of it in your heart.
I will leave this ring with you for a love-token;
And the hand as sure as the ring; and do not doubt
But you shall have the heart too: when you need a friend,
Send it to him that owned it; you shall see   50
Whether he can aid you.
  Duch. You are very cold:
I fear you are not well after your travel. —
Ha! lights! —— O, horrible!
  Ferd. Let her have lights enough.   [*Exit.*
  Duch. What witchcraft does he practise, that he hath left
A dead man's hand here?

  [*Here is discovered, behind a traverse,*[1] *the artificial
    figures of* ANTONIO *and his* Children, *appearing
    as if they were dead.*

  Bos. Look you, here's the piece from which 'twas ta'en.
He doth present you this sad spectacle,
That, now you know directly they are dead,
Hereafter you may wisely cease to grieve   60
For that which cannot be recoverèd.

[1] Curtain.

Duch. There is not between Heaven and earth one wish
I stay for after this: it wastes me more
Than were't my picture, fashioned out of wax,
Stuck with a magical needle, and then buried
In some foul dunghill; and yond's an excellent property
For a tyrant, which I would account mercy.
　Bos. What's that?
　Duch. If they would bind me to that lifeless trunk,
And let me freeze to death.
　Bos. Come, you must live.
　Duch. That's the greatest torture souls feel in hell, 70
In hell, that they must live, and cannot die.[1]
Portia, I'll new kindle thy coals again,
And revive the rare and almost dead example
Of a loving wife.
　Bos. O, fie! despair? remember
You are a Christian.
　Duch. The church enjoins fasting:
I'll starve myself to death.
　Bos. Leave this vain sorrow.
Things being at the worst begin to mend: the bee
When he hath shot his sting into your hand,
May then play with your eyelid. 80
　Duch. Good comfortable fellow,
Persuade a wretch that's broke upon the wheel
To have all his bones new set; entreat him live
To be executed again. Who must despatch me?
I account this world a tedious theatre,
For I do play a part in't 'gainst my will.
　Bos. Come, be of comfort; I will save your life.
　Duch. Indeed, I have not leisure to tend

---

[1] Cf. Dante, *Inferno*, iii, 46.

So small abusiness.
    Bos. Now, by my life, I pity you.
    Duch. Thou art a fool, then,   90
To waste thy pity on a thing so wretched
As cannot pity itself. I am full of daggers.
Puff, let me blow these vipers from me.

                Enter Servant.

What are you?
    Serv. One that wishes you long life.
    Duch. I would thou wert hanged for the horrible curse
Thou hast given me: I shall shortly grow one
Of the miracles of pity. I'll go pray;—
No, I'll go curse.
    Bos. O, fie!
    Duch. I could curse the stars.
    Bos. O, fearful.
    Duch. And those three smiling seasons of the year   100
Into a Russian winter: nay, the world
To its first chaos.
    Bos. Look you, the stars shine still.
    Duch. O, but you must
Remember, my curse hath a great way to go.—
Plagues, that make lanes through largest families,
Consume them!—
    Bos. Fie, lady!
    Duch. Let them, like tyrants,
Never be remembered but for the ill they have done;
Let all the zealous prayers of mortified
Churchmen forget them!—
    Bos. O, uncharitable!   110
    Duch. Let Heaven a little while cease crowning martyrs,

To punish them!—
Go, howl them this, and say, I long to bleed:
It is some mercy when men kill with speed. *[Exit.*

Re-enter FERDINAND.

Ferd. Excellent, as I would wish; she's plagued in art:
These presentations are but framed in wax
By the curious master in that quality,
Vincentio Lauriola, and she takes them
For true substantial bodies.
   Bos. Why do you do this? 120
   Ferd. To bring her to despair.
   Bos. Faith, end here,
And go no farther in your cruelty:
Send her a penitential garment to put on
Next to her delicate skin, and furnish her
With beads and prayer-books.
   Ferd. Damn her! that body of hers,
While that my blood ran pure in't, was more worth
Than that which thou wouldst comfort, called a soul.
I will send her masks of common courtezans,
Have her meat served up by bawds and ruffians, 130
And, 'cause she'll needs be mad, I am resolved
To remove forth the common hospital
All the mad-folk, and place them near her lodging;
There let them practise together, sing and dance,
And act their gambols to the full o' the moon:
If she can sleep the better for it, let her.
Your work is almost ended.
   Bos. Must I see her again?
   Ferd. Yes.
   Bos. Never.

Ferd. You must.

Bos. Never in mine own shape;
That's forfeited by my intelligence 140
And this last cruel lie: when you send me next,
The business shall be comfort.

Ferd. Very likely;
Thy pity is nothing of kin to thee. Antonio
Lurks about Milan: thou shalt shortly thither,
To feed a fire as great as my revenge,
Which never will slack till it have spent his fuel:
Intemperate agues make physicians cruel. [*Exeunt.*

SCENE II. — *Another Room in the* DUCHESS' *Lodging.*

Enter DUCHESS *and* CARIOLA.

Duch. What hideous noise was that?

Cari. 'Tis the wild consort[1]
Of madmen, lady, which your tyrant brother
Hath placed about your lodging: this tyranny,
I think, was never practised till this hour.

Duch. Indeed, I thank him: nothing but noise and folly
Can keep me in my right wits; whereas reason
And silence make me stark mad. Sit down;
Discourse to me some dismal tragedy.

Cari. O, 'twill increase your melancholy.

Duch. Thou art deceived: 10
To hear of greater grief would lessen mine.
This is a prison?

Cari. Yes, but you shall live
To shake this durance off.

Duch. Thou art a fool:

[1] Company.

The robin-redbreast and the nightingale
Never live long in cages.
　Cari. Pray, dry your eyes.
What think you of, madam?
　Duch. Of nothing;
When I muse thus, I sleep.
　Cari. Like a madman, with your eyes open?
　Duch. Dost thou think we shall know one another
In the other world?
　Cari. Yes, out of question.
　Duch. O, that it were possible we might
But hold some two days' conference with the dead!
From them I should learn somewhat, I am sure,
I never shall know here. I'll tell thee a miracle;
I am not mad yet, to my cause of sorrow:
The Heaven o'er my head seems made of molten brass,
The earth of flaming sulphur, yet I am not mad.
I am acquainted with sad misery
As the tanned galley-slave is with his oar;
Necessity makes me suffer constantly,
And custom makes it easy. Who do I look like now?
　Cari. Like to your picture in the gallery,
A deal of life in show, but none in practice;
Or rather like some reverend monument
Whose ruins are even pitied.
　Duch. Very proper;
And Fortune seems only to have her eyesight
To behold my tragedy. — How now!
What noise is that?

　　　　　　　Enter Servant.

　Serv. I am come to tell you

Your brother hath intended you some sport.
A great physician, when the Pope was sick   40
Of a deep melancholy, presented him
With several sorts of madmen, which wild object
Being full of change and sport, forced him to laugh,
And so the imposthume broke : the self-same cure
The duke intends on you.
    Duch. Let them come in.
    Serv. There's a mad lawyer ; and a secular priest ;
A doctor that hath forfeited his wits
By jealousy ; an astrologian
That in his works said such a day o' the month
Should be the day of doom, and, failing of't,   50
Ran mad ; an English tailor crazed i' the brain
With the study of new fashions ; a gentleman-usher
Quite beside himself with care to keep in mind
The number of his lady's salutations,
Or " How do you," she employed him in each morning ;
A farmer, too, an excellent knave in grain,
Mad 'cause he was hindered transportation :
And let one broker that's mad loose to these,
You'd think the devil were among them.
    Duch. Sit, Cariola. — Let them loose when you please, 60
For I am chained to endure all your tyranny.

Enter Madmen.

Here this Song is sung to a dismal kind of music by a
                        Madman.

      O, let us howl some heavy note,
        Some deadly doggèd howl,
      Sounding as from the threatening throat
        Of beasts and fatal fowl !

       As ravens, screech-owls, bulls, and bears,
         We'll bell,[1] and bawl our parts,
       Till irksome noise have cloyed your ears
         And còrrosived your hearts.
       At last, whenas our quire wants breath,   70
         Our bodies being blest,
       We'll sing, like swans, to welcome death,
         And die in love and rest.

    1st Madman. Doom's-day not come yet! I'll draw it nearer by a perspective, or make a glass that shall set all the world on fire upon an instant. I cannot sleep; my pillow is stuffed with a litter of porcupines.

    2d Madman. Hell is a mere glass-house, where the devils are continually blowing up women's souls on hollow irons, and the fire never goes out.   80

    1st Madman. I have skill in heraldry.

    2d Madman. Hast?

    1st Madman. You do give for your crest a wood-cock's head with the brains picked out on't; you are a very ancient gentleman.

    3d Madman. Greek is turned Turk: we are only to be saved by the Helvetian translation.

    1st Madman. Come on, sir, I will lay the law to you.

    2d Madman. O, rather lay a corrosive: the law will eat to the bone.   90

    3d Madman. He that drinks but to satisfy nature is damned.

    4th Madman. If I had my glass here, I would show a sight should make all the women here call me mad doctor.

---

[1] Bellow; so Chaucer, "As loud as *belleth* wind in helle." — *House of Fame*, iii, 713.

1st Madman. What's he? a rope-maker?

2d Madman. No, no, no, a snuffling knave that, while he shows the tombs, will have his hand in a wench's placket.[1]

3d Madman. Woe to the caroche[2] that brought home my wife from the masque at three o'clock in the morning! it had a large feather-bed in it. 100

4th Madman. I have pared the devil's nails forty times, roasted them in raven's eggs, and cured agues with them.

3d Madman. Get me three hundred milchbats, to make possets to procure sleep.

4th Madman. All the college may throw their caps at me: I have made a soap-boiler costive; it was my masterpiece.

[*Here a dance of* Eight Madmen, *with music answerable thereto; after which,* BOSOLA, *like an* Old Man, *enters.*

Duch. Is he mad too?

Serv. Pray, question him. I'll leave you.

[*Exeunt* Servant *and* Madmen.

Bos. I am come to make thy tomb.

Duch. Ha! my tomb! 110
Thou speak'st as if I lay upon my deathbed,
Gasping for breath: dost thou perceive me sick?

Bos. Yes, and the more dangerously, since thy sickness is insensible.

Duch. Thou art not mad, sure: dost thou know me?

Bos. Yes.

Duch. Who am I?

Bos. Thou art a box of worm-seed, at best but a salvatory[3] of green mummy.[4] What's this flesh? a little crudded

---

[1] Petticoat. [2] Coach. [3] A place where anything is preserved.
[4] Mummies were used for medicinal purposes. "The Egyptian mummies, which Cambyses or time hath spared, avarice now consumeth.

milk, fantastical puff-paste. Our bodies are weaker than those paper-prisons boys use to keep flies in; more contemptible, since ours is to preserve earth-worms. Didst thou ever see a lark in a cage? Such is the soul in the body: this world is like her little turf of grass, and the Heaven o'er our heads, like her looking-glass, only gives us a miserable knowledge of the small compass of our prison.

Duch. Am not I thy duchess? 127

Bos. Thou art some great woman, sure, for riot begins to sit on thy forehead (clad in grey hairs) twenty years sooner than on a merry milkmaid's. Thou sleepest worse than if a mouse should be forced to take up her lodging in a cat's ear: a little infant that breeds its teeth, should it lie with thee, would cry out, as if thou wert the more unquiet bedfellow.

Duch. I am Duchess of Malfi still.

Bos. That makes thy sleep so broken:
Glories like glow-worms, afar off shine bright,
But looked to near, have neither heat nor light.[1]

Duch. Thou art very plain. 139

Bos. My trade is to flatter the dead, not the living; I am a tomb-maker.

Duch. And thou comest to make my tomb?

Bos. Yes.

Duch. Let me be a little merry: — of what stuff wilt thou make it?

Bos. Nay resolve me first, of what fashion?

Duch. Why do we grow fantastical in our deathbed? do we affect fashion in the grave? 148

Mummy is become merchandize. Mizraim cures wounds, and Pharaoh is sold for balsams." — *Sir Th. Browne, Urn Burial.*

[1] This fine couplet is found also in Webster's *White Devil.*

Bos. Most ambitiously. Princes' images on their tombs
do not lie, as they were wont, seeming to pray up to Heaven ;
but with their hands under their cheeks, as if they died of
the toothache : they are not carved with their eyes fixed
upon the stars ; but as their minds were wholly bent upon
the world, the self-same way they seem to turn their faces.[1]
    Duch. Let me know fully therefore the effect
Of this thy dismal preparation,
This talk, fit for a charnel.
    Bos. Now I shall : —

    Enter Executioners, *with a coffin, cords, and a bell.*

Here is a present from your princely brothers ;
And may it arrive welcome, for it brings
Last benefit, last sorrow.
    Duch. Let me see it :   160
I have so much obedience in my blood,
I wish it in their veins to do them good.
    Bos. This is your last presence-chamber.
    Cari. O my sweet lady !
    Duch. Peace ; it affrights not me.
    Bos. I am the common bellman,
That usually is sent to condemned persons
The night before they suffer.
    Duch. Even now thou said'st
Thou wast a tomb-maker.
    Bos. 'Twas to bring you
By degrees to mortification. Listen.   170

---

[1] This apt criticism might have been the text from which Ruskin wrote his chapter on the funeral monuments of Venice, as illustrating the worldly spirit of the Renaissance. See *Stones of Venice*, Vol. II, chap. 3, edition of 1885.

Hark, now everything is still
The screech-owl and the whistler shrill[1]
Call upon our dame aloud,
And bid her quickly don her shroud!
Much you had of land and rent;
Your length in clay's now competent:
A long war disturbed your mind;
Here your perfect peace is signed.
Of what is't fools make such vain keeping?
Sin their conception, their birth weeping, 180
Their life a general mist of error,
Their death a hideous storm of terror.
Strew your hair with powders sweet.
Don clean linen, bathe your feet,
And (the foul fiend more to check)
A crucifix let bless your neck:
'Tis now full tide 'tween night and day;
End your groan, and come away.

Cari. Hence, villains, tyrants, murderers! alas!
What will you do with my lady?— Call for help. 190

Duch. To whom? to our next neighbours? they are mad folks.

Bos. Remove that noise.

Duch. Farewell, Cariola.
In my last will I have not much to give:
A many hungry guests have fed upon me;
Thine will be a poor reversion.

Cari. I will die with her.

Duch. I pray thee, look thou giv'st my little boy
Some syrup for his cold, and let the girl

---

[1] Cf. Spenser, *Faerie Queene*, Bk. II, chap. xii, st. 36:—
"The whistler shrill, that whoso heares doth dy."

Say her prayers ere she sleep.
 [CARIOLA *is forced out by the* Executioners.
 Now what you please :
What death?
 Bos. Strangling; here are your executioners.
 Duch. I forgive them :
The apoplexy, catarrh, or cough o' the lungs,
Would do as much as they do.
 Bos. Doth not death fright you?
 Duch. Who would be afraid on't,
Knowing to meet such excellent company
In the other world?
 Bos. Yet, methinks,
The manner of your death should much afflict you :
This cord should terrify you.
 Duch. Not a whit :
What would it pleasure me to have my throat cut
With diamonds? or to be smotherèd
With cassia? or to be shot to death with pearls?
I know death hath ten thousand several doors
For men to take their exits ; and 'tis found
They go on such strange geometrical hinges,
You may open them both ways ; any way, for Heaven's sake,
So I were out of your whispering. Tell my brothers
That I perceive death, now I am well awake,
Best gift is they can give or I can take.
I would fain put off my last woman's fault,
I'd not be tedious to you.
 1st Execut. We are ready.
 Duch. Dispose my breath how please you ; but my body
Bestow upon my women, will you?
 1st Execut. Yes.

Duch. Pull, and pull strongly, for your able strength
Must pull down Heaven upon me : —
Yet stay ; Heaven-gates are not so highly arched
As princes' palaces ; they that enter there
Must go upon their keees (*kneels*).—Come, violent death,
Serve for mandragora to make me sleep ! —
Go tell my brothers, when I am laid out,
They then may feed in quiet.
     [*The* Executioners *strangle the* DUCHESS.[1]
Bos. Where's the waiting woman?
Fetch her : some other strangle the children.
   [CARIOLA *and* Children *are brought in by the* Executioners ; *who presently strangle the* Children.
Look you, there sleeps your mistress.
 Cari. O, you are damned
Perpetually for this ! My turn is next,
Is't not so ordered?

---

[1] " All the several parts of the dreadful apparatus with which the Duchess's death is ushered in, are not more remote from the conceptions of ordinary vengeance, than the strange character of suffering which they seem to bring upon their victim, is beyond the imagination of ordinary poets. As they are not like inflictions *of this life,* so her language seems *not of this world.* She has lived among horrors till she is become ' native and endowed unto that element.' She speaks the dialect of despair, her tongue has a smatch of Tartarus and the souls in bale. What are ' Luke's iron crown,' the brazen bull of Perillus, Procrustes's bed, to the waxen images which counterfeit death, to the wild masque of madmen, the tomb-maker, the bell-man, the living person's dirge, the mortification by degrees ! To move a horror skilfully, to touch a soul to the quick, to lay upon fear as much as it can bear, to wean and weary a life till it is ready to drop, and then step in with mortal instruments to take its last forfeit ; this only a Webster can do. Writers of an inferior genius may ' upon horror's head horrors accumulate,' but they cannot do this. They mistake quantity for quality, they ' terrify babes with painted devils,' but they know not how a soul is capable of being moved ; their terrors want dignity, their affrightments are without decorum." — *C. Lamb.*

Bos. Yes, and I am glad
You are so well prepared for't
    Cari. You are deceived, sir,
I am not prepared for't, I will not die;
I will first come to my answer, and know
How I have offended.
    Bos. Come, despatch her. —
You kept her counsel; now you shall keep ours.
    Cari. I will not die, I must not; I am contracted
To a young gentleman.
    1st Execut. Here's your wedding-ring. 240
    Cari. Let me but speak with the duke; I'll discover
Treason to his person.
    Bos. Delays: — throttle her.
    1st Execut. She bites and scratches.
    Cari. If you kill me now,
I am damned; I have not been at confession
This two years.
    Bos. (*to* Executioners). When?
            [*The* Executioners *strangle* CARIOLA.
            Bear her into the next room;
Let these lie still.
        [*Exeunt the* Executioners *with the body of* CARIOLA.
            Enter FERDINAND.
Ferd. Is she dead?
Bos. She is what
You'd have her. But here begins your pity:
            [*Shows the* Children *strangled.*
Alas, how have these offended?
    Ferd. The death
Of young wolves is never to be pitied.

Bos. Fix your eye here.
Ferd. Constantly.
Bos. Do you not weep?
Other sins only speak; murder shrieks out:
The element of water moistens the earth,
But blood flies upwards and bedews the heavens.
Ferd. Cover her face; mine eyes dazzle: she died young.[1]
Bos. I think not; her infelicity
Seemed to have years too many.
Ferd. She and I were twins;
And should I die this instant, I had lived
Her time to a minute.
Bos. It seems she was born first:
You have bloodily approved the ancient truth,
That kindred commonly do worse agree
Than remote strangers.
Ferd. Let me see her face
Again. Why didst not thou pity her? what
An excellent honest man mightst thou have been,
If thou hadst borne her to some sanctuary!
Or, bold in a good cause, opposed thyself,
With thy advancèd sword above thy head,
Between her innocence and my revenge!
I bade thee, when I was distracted of my wits,
Go kill my dearest friend, and thou hast done't.
For let me but examine well the cause:
What was the meanness of her match to me?
Only I must confess I had a hope,
Had she continued widow, to have gained
An infinite mass of treasure by her death:

[1] This is one of those lines, peculiar to Webster, in which a character is revealed in half-a-dozen words.

And what was the main cause? her marriage,
That drew a stream of gall quite through my heart.
For thee, as we observe in tragedies
That a good actor many times is cursed
For playing a villain's part, I hate thee for't,
And, for my sake, say, thou hast done much ill well.

   Bos. Let me quicken your memory, for I perceive
You are falling into ingratitude: I challenge
The reward due to my service.

   Ferd. I'll tell thee
What I'll give thee.

   Bos. Do.

   Ferd. I'll give thee a pardon
For this murder.

   Bos. Ha!

   Ferd. Yes, and 'tis
The largest bounty I can study to do thee.
By what authority didst thou execute
This bloody sentence?

   Bos. By yours.

   Ferd. Mine! was I her judge?
Did any ceremonial form of law
Doom her to not-being? did a complete jury
Deliver her conviction up i' the court?
Where shalt thou find this judgment registered,
Unless in hell? See, like a bloody fool,
Thou'st forfeited thy life, and thou shalt die for't.

   Bos. The office of justice is perverted quite
When one thief hangs another. Who shall dare
To reveal this?

   Ferd. O, I'll tell thee;
The wolf shall find her grave, and scrape it up,

Not to devour the corpse, but to discover 300
The horrid murder.¹
   Bos. You, not I, shall quake for't.
   Ferd. Leave me.
   Bos. I will first receive my pension.
   Ferd. You are a villain.
   Bos. When your ingratitude
Is judge, I am so.
   Ferd. O horror,
That not the fear of him which binds the devils
Can prescribe man obedience ! —
Never look upon me more.
   Bos. Why, fare thee well.
Your brother and yourself are worthy men :
You have a pair of hearts are hollow graves, 310
Rotten, and rotting others ; and your vengeance,
Like two chained bullets, still goes arm in arm :²
You may be brothers ; for treason, like the plague,
Doth take much in a blood. I stand like one
That long hath ta'en a sweet and golden dream :
I am angry with myself, now that I wake.
   Ferd. Get thee into some unknown part o' the world,
That I may never see thee.³
   Bos. Let me know
Wherefore I should be thus neglected. Sir,
I served your tyranny, and rather strove 320
To satisfy yourself than all the world :

---

[1] A common superstition.
[2] Cf. Heywood's *A Challenge for Beautie :*
        " My friend and I
      Like two chain-bullets, side by side, will fly
      Thorow the jawes of death."
[3] Cf. *King John,* iv, 2.

And though I loathed the evil, yet I loved
You that did counsel it; and rather sought
To appear a true servant than an honest man.
   Fera. I'll go hunt the badger by owl-light:
'Tis a deed of darkness.   [*Exit.*
   Bos. He's much distracted. Off, my painted honour!
While with vain hopes our faculties we tire,
We seem to sweat in ice and freeze in fire.
What would I do, were this to do again?   330
I would not change my peace of conscience
For all the wealth of Europe. — She stirs; here's life: —
Return, fair soul, from darkness, and lead mine
Out of this sensible hell: — She's warm, she breathes: —
Upon thy pale lips I will melt my heart,
To store them with fresh colour. — Who's there?
Some cordial drink! — Alas, I dare not call:
So pity would destroy pity. — Her eye opes,
And Heaven in it seems to ope, that late was shut,
To take me up to mercy.
   Duch. Antonio![1]   340
   Bos. Yes, madam, he is living;
The dead bodies you saw were but feigned statues:
He's reconciled to your brothers; the Pope hath wrought
The atonement.[2]
   Duch. Mercy!   [*Dies.*
   Bos. O, she's gone again! there the cords of life broke.
O sacred innocence, that sweetly sleeps
On turtles' feathers, whilst a guilty conscience

---

[1] "The idea of making the Duchess speak after she has been strangled, was doubtless taken from the death of Desdemona in *Othello*, v, last scene." — *Dyce.*

[2] Reconciliation.

Is a black register wherein is writ
All our good deeds and bad, a perspective
That shows us hell ! That we cannot be suffered
To do good when we have a mind to it !
This is manly sorrow ;
These tears, I am very certain, never grew
In my mother's milk : my estate is sunk
Below the degree of fear : where were
These penitent fountains while she was living?
O, they were frozen up ! Here is a sight
As direful to my soul as is the sword
Unto a wretch hath slain his father. Come,
I'll bear thee hence,
And execute thy last will ; that's deliver
Thy body to the reverend dispose
Of some good women : that the cruel tyrant
Shall not deny me. Then I'll post to Milan,
Where somewhat I will speedily enact
Worth my dejection. [*Exit.*

ACT V.

SCENE I. — *A Public Place in Milan.*

Enter ANTONIO *and* DELIO.

Ant. What think you of my hope of reconcilement
To the Arragonian brethren?
Delio. I misdoubt it ;
For though they have sent their letters of safe-conduct
For your repair to Milan, they appear

But nets to entrap you. The Marquis of Pescara,
Under whom you hold certain lands in cheat,
Much 'gainst his noble nature hath been moved
To seize those lands; and some of his dependants
Are at this instant making it their suit
To be invested in your revenues.   10
I cannot think they mean well to your life
That do deprive you of your means of life,
Your living.
 Ant. You are still an heretic
To any safety I can shape myself.
 Delio. Here comes the marquis: I will make myself
Petitioner for some part of your land,
To know whither it is flying.
 Ant. I pray do.

Enter PESCARA.

 Delio. Sir, I have a suit to you.
 Pes. To me?
 Delio. An easy one:
There is the Citadel of Saint Bennet,
With some demesnes, of late in the possession   20
Of Antonio Bologna, — please you bestow them on me.
 Pes. You are my friend; but this is such a suit,
Not fit for me to give, nor you to take.
 Delio. No, sir?
 Pes. I will give you ample reason for't
Soon in private: — here's the cardinal's mistress.

Enter JULIA.

 Julia. My lord, I am grown your poor petitioner,
And should be an ill beggar, had I not

A great man's letter here, the cardinal's,
To court you in my favour.   [*Gives a letter.*
  Pes. He entreats for you
The Citadel of Saint Bennet, that belonged   30
To the banished Bologna.
  Julia. Yes.
  Pes. I could not have thought of a friend I could rather
Pleasure with it : 'tis yours.
  Julia. Sir, I thank you ;
And he shall know how doubly I am engaged
Both in your gift, and speediness of giving
Which makes your grant the greater.   [*Exit.*
  Ant. How they fortify
Themselves with my ruin !
  Delio. Sir, I am
Little bound to you.
  Pes. Why?
  Delio. Because you denied this suit to me, and gave't
To such a creature.
  Pes. Do you know what it was?   40
It was Antonio's land ; not forfeited
By course of law, but ravished from his throat
By the cardinal's entreaty : it were not fit
I should bestow so main [1] a piece of wrong
Upon my friend ; 'tis a gratification
Only due to a strumpet, for it is injustice.
Shall I sprinkle the pure blood of innocents
To make those followers I call my friends
Look ruddier upon me? I am glad
This land, ta'en from the owner by such wrong,   50
Returns again unto so foul an use

[1] Mighty, important; (Latin *magnus*).

As salary for his lust.   Learn, good Delio,
To ask noble things of me, and you shall find
I'll be a noble giver.
   Delio. You instruct me well.
   Ant. Why, here's a man now would fright impudence,
From sauciest beggars.
   Pes. Prince Ferdinand's come to Milan,
Sick, as they give out, of an apoplexy;
But some say 'tis a frenzy: I am going
To visit him.   [*Exit.*
   Ant. 'Tis a noble old fellow.
   Delio. What course do you mean to take, Antonio?   60
   Ant. This night I mean to venture all my fortune,
Which is no more than a poor lingering life,
To the cardinal's worst of malice: I have got
Private access to his chamber; and intend
To visit him about the mid of night,
As once his brother did our noble duchess.
It may be that the sudden apprehension
Of danger, — for I'll go in mine own shape, —
When he shall see it fraight [1] with love and duty,
May draw the poison out of him, and work   70
A friendly reconcilement: if it fail,
Yet it shall rid me of this infamous calling;
For better fall once than be ever falling.
   Delio. I'll second you in all danger; and, howe'er,
My life keeps rank with yours.
   Ant. You are still my loved and best friend.   [*Exeunt.*

                 [1] Fraught.

SCENE II. — *A Gallery in the* Cardinal's *Palace at Milan.*

Enter PESCARA *and* Doctor.

Pes. Now, doctor, may I visit your patient?
Doc. If't please your lordship : but he's instantly
To take the air here in the gallery
By my direction.
Pes. Pray thee, what's his disease?
Doc. A very pestilent disease, my lord,
They call lycanthropia.[1]
Pes. What's that?
I need a dictionary to't.
Doc. I'll tell you.
In those that are possessed with't there o'erflows
Such melancholy humour they imagine
Themselves to be transformed into wolves ;   10
Steal forth to churchyards in the dead of night,
And dig dead bodies up : as two nights since
One met the duke 'bout midnight in a lane
Behind Saint Mark's church, with the leg of a man
Upon his shoulder ; and he howled fearfully ;
Said he was a wolf, only the difference

---

[1] " A kind of melancholy, but strangely black and vehement. For those attacked by it quit their houses in the month of February, imitate wolves in almost every respect, and each night do but frequent cemeteries and graveyards. One of these melancholic lycanthropes, whom we call *loups garoux*, carried on his shoulders the whole thigh and leg of a corpse. There was also, as Job Fincel relates, a villager near Pavia in 1541 who believed that he was a wolf, and assailed several men in the fields, and killed some of them. At last, having been captured, but not without great difficulty, he firmly asserted that he was a wolf, and that there was no other difference except that wolves ordinarily were hairy outside, whereas he was hairy between his skin and flesh." — From the French of Goulart, *Histoires admirables et memorables de nostre temps*, 1620.

Was, a wolf's skin was hairy on the outside,
His on the inside; bade them take their swords,
Rip up his flesh, and try: straight I was sent for,
And, having ministered to him, found his grace 20
Very well recovered.
  Pes. I am glad on't.
  Doc. Yet not without some fear
Of a relapse. If he grow to his fit again,
I'll go a nearer way to work with him
Than ever Paracelsus dreamed of;[1] if
They'll give me leave, I'll buffet his madness out of him.
Stand aside; he comes.

  Enter FERDINAND, Cardinal, MALATESTI, *and* BOSOLA.

  Ferd. Leave me.
  Mal. Why doth your lordship love this solitariness?
  Ferd. Eagles commonly fly alone: they are crows, daws, and starlings that flock together. Look, what's that follows me? 31
  Mal. Nothing, my lord.
  Ferd. Yes.
  Mal. 'Tis your shadow.
  Ferd. Stay it: let it not haunt me.
  Mal. Impossible, if you move, and the sun shine.
  Ferd. I will throttle it.
          [*Throws himself down on his shadow.*
  Mal. O, my lord, you are angry with nothing.
  Ferd. You are a fool: how is't possible I should catch my shadow, unless I fall upon't? When I go to hell, I mean to carry a bribe; for, look you, good gifts evermore make way for the worst persons. 42

---

[1] Paracelsus was born in 1493, died 1541.

Pes. Rise, good my lord.

Ferd. I am studying the art of patience.

Pes. 'Tis a noble virtue.

Ferd. To drive six snails before me from this town to Moscow; neither use goad nor whip to them, but let them take their own time; — the patient'st man i' the world match me for an experiment; — and I'll crawl after like a sheep-biter.

Card. Force him up.   [*They raise him.* 50

Ferd. Use me well, you were best. What I have done, I have done: I'll confess nothing.[1]

Doc. Now let me come to him. — Are you mad, my lord? are you out of your princely wits?

Ferd. What's he?

Pes. Your doctor.

Ferd. Let me have his beard sawed off, and his eyebrows filed more civil.

Doc. I must do mad tricks with him, for that's the only way on't. — I have brought your grace a salamander's skin to keep you from sun-burning.   61

Ferd. I have cruel sore eyes.

Doc. The white of a cockatrix's egg is present remedy.

Ferd. Let it be a new laid one, you were best. — Hide me from him: physicians are like kings, — They brook no contradiction.

Doc. Now he begins to fear me: now let me alone with him.

Card. How now! put off your gown![2]

---

[1] Cf. *Othello,* v, last scene, where Iago says:

"Demand me nothing: what you know, you know:
From this time forth I never will speak word."

[2] "A piece of buffoonery. The stage direction (edition of 1708) is, 'puts off his four cloaks, one after another.' The Gravedigger in *Hamlet* used to do the same as late as 1830." — *Dyce.*

Doc. Now he begins to fear me. — Can you fetch a frisk, sir? — Let him go, let him go, upon my peril : I find by his eye he stands in awe of me; I'll make him as tame as a dormouse. 73

Ferd. Can you fetch your frisks, sir ! — I will stamp him into a cullis, flay off his skin, to cover one of the anatomies[1] this rogue hath set i' the cold yonder in Barber-Surgeon's-hall. — Hence, hence ! you are all of you like beasts for sacrifice : there's nothing left of you but tongue and belly.
[*Exit.*

Pes. Doctor, he did not fear you throughly.

Doc. True ; I was somewhat too forward. 80

Bos. Mercy upon me, what a fatal judgment
Hath fall'n upon this Ferdinand !

Pes. Knows your grace
What accident hath brought unto the prince
This strange distraction?

Card. (*aside*). I must feign somewhat. — Thus they say it grew.
You have heard it rumoured, for these many years
None of our family dies but there is seen
The shape of an old woman, which is given
By tradition to us to have been murdered
By her nephews for her riches. Such a figure 90
One night, as the prince sat up late at's book,
Appeared to him ; when crying out for help,
The gentleman of's chamber found his grace
All on a cold sweat, altered much in face
And language : since which apparition,
He hath grown worse and worse, and I much fear
He cannot live.

[1] Skeletons.

Bos. Sir, I would speak with you.
Pes. We'll leave your grace,
Wishing to the sick prince, our noble lord,
All health of mind and body.
    Card. You are most welcome. 100
            [*Exeunt* PESCARA, MALATESTI, *and* Doctor.
Are you come? so. — (*Aside*) This fellow must not know
By any means I had intelligence
In our duchess' death; for, though I counselled it,
The full of all the engagement seemed to grow
From Ferdinand. — Now, sir, how fares our sister?
I do not think but sorrow makes her look
Like to an oft-dyed garment: she shall now
Taste comfort from me. Why do you look so wildly?
O, the fortune of your master here the prince
Dejects you; but be you of happy comfort: 110
If you'll do one thing for me I'll entreat,
Though he had a cold tombstone o'er his bones,
I'd make you what you would be.
    Bos. Any thing;
Give it me in a breath, and let me fly to't:
They that think long small expedition win,
For musing much o' the end cannot begin.

           Enter JULIA.

    Julia. Sir, will you come in to supper?
    Card. I am busy; leave me.
    Julia (*aside*). What an excellent shape hath that fellow!
                                        [*Exit.*
    Card. 'Tis thus. Antonio lurks here in Milan: 120
Inquire him out, and kill him. While he lives,
Our sister cannot marry; and I have thought

Of an excellent match for her. Do this, and style me
Thy advancement.
  Bos. But by what means shall I find him out?
  Card. There is a gentleman called Delio
Here in the camp, that hath been long approved
His loyal friend. Set eye upon that fellow;
Follow him to mass; may be Antonio,
Although he do account religion   130
But a school-name, for fashion of the world
May accompany him; or else go inquire out
Delio's confessor, and see if you can bribe
Him to reveal it. There are a thousand ways
A man might find to trace him; as to know
What fellows haunt the Jews for taking up
Great sums of money, for sure he's in want;
Or else to go to the picture-makers, and learn
Who bought her picture lately: some of these
Happily may take.
  Bos. Well, I'll not freeze i' the business: 140
I would see that wretched thing, Antonio,
Above all sights i' the world.
  Card. Do, and be happy.   [*Exit.*
  Bos. This fellow doth breed basilisks in's eyes,
He's nothing else but murder; yet he seems
Not to have notice of the duchess' death.
'Tis his cunning: I must follow his example;
There cannot be a surer way to trace
Than that of an old fox.

      Re-enter JULIA.

  Julia. So, sir, you are well met.
  Bos. How now!

Julia. Nay, the doors are fast enough :
Now, sir, I will make you confess your treachery.   150
   Bos. Treachery !
   Julia. Yes, confess to me
Which of my women 'twas you hired to put
Love-powder into my drink?
   Bos. Love-powder !
   Julia. Yes, when I was at Malfi.
Why should I fall in love with such a face else?
I have already suffered for thee so much pain,
The only remedy to do me good
Is to kill my longing.
   Bos. Sure, your pistol holds
Nothing but perfumes or kissing-comfits.[1]
Excellent lady !   160
You have a pretty way on't to discover
Your longing. Come, come, I'll disarm you,
And arm you thus : yet this is wondrous strange.
   Julia. Compare thy form and my eyes together,
You'll find my love no such great miracle.
Now you'll say
I am wanton : this nice modesty in ladies
Is but a troublesome familiar
That haunts them.
   Bos. Know you me, I am a blunt soldier.   170
   Julia. The better :
Sure, there wants fire where there are no lively sparks
Of roughness.
   Bos. And I want compliment.
   Julia. Why, ignorance
In courtship cannot make you do amiss,

---

[1] Perfumed sugar-plums for the breath.

If you have a heart to do well.
 Bos. You are very fair.
 Julia. Nay, if you lay beauty to my charge,
I must plead unguilty.
 Bos. Your bright eyes
Carry a quiver of darts in them sharper   180
Than sunbeams.
 Julia. You will mar me with commendation,
Put yourself to the charge of courting me,
Whereas now I woo you.
 Bos. (*aside*). I have it, I will work upon this creature. —
Let us grow most amorously familiar:
If the great cardinal now should see me thus,
Would he not count me a villain?
 Julia. No; he might count me a wanton,
Not lay a scruple of offence on you;
For if I see and steal a diamond,   190
The fault is not i' the stone, but in me the thief
That purloins it. I am sudden with you:
We that are great women of pleasure use to cut off
These uncertain wishes and unquiet longings,
And in an instant join the sweet delight
And the pretty excuse together. Had you been i' the street,
Under my chamber-window, even there
I should have courted you.
 Bos. O, you are an excellent lady!
 Julia. Bid me do somewhat for you presently   200
To express I love you.
 Bos. I will; and if you love me,
Fail not to effect it.
The cardinal is grown wondrous melancholy;
Demand the cause, let him not put you off

With feigned excuse ; discover the main ground on't.
  Julia. Why would you know this?
  Bos. I have depended on him,
And I hear that he is fall'n in some disgrace
With the emperor : if he be, like the mice
That forsake falling houses, I would shift
To other dependance.
  Julia. You shall not need   210
Follow the wars : I'll be your maintenance.
  Bos. And I your loyal servant : but I cannot
Leave my calling.
  Julia. Not leave an ungrateful
General for the love of a sweet lady !
You are like some cannot sleep in feather-beds,
But must have blocks for their pillows.
  Bos. Will you do this?
  Julia. Cunningly.
  Bos. To-morrow I'll expect the intelligence.
  Julia. To-morrow ! get you into my cabinet ;
You shall have it with you. Do not delay me,   220
No more than I do you : I am like one
That is condemned ; I have my pardon promised,
But I would see it sealed. Go, get you in :
You shall see me wind my tongue about his heart
Like a skein of silk.   [*Exit* BOSOLA.

          Re-enter Cardinal.

  Card. Where are you?

          Enter Servants.

  Servants. Here.
  Card. Let none, upon your lives, have conference
With the Prince Ferdinand, unless I know it. —

(*Aside*) In this distraction he may reveal
The murder.   [*Exeunt* Servants.
            Yond's my lingering consumption :
I am weary of her, and by any means
Would be quit of.
    Julia. How now, my lord ! what ails you?
    Card. Nothing.
    Julia. O, you are much altered :
Come, I must be your secretary, and remove
This lead from off your bosom : what's the matter?
    Card. I may not tell you.
    Julia. Are you so far in love with sorrow
You cannot part with part of it? or think you
I cannot love your grace when you are sad
As well as merry? or do you suspect
I, that have been a secret to your heart
These many winters, cannot be the same[1]
Unto your tongue?
    Card. Satisfy thy longing, —
The only way to make thee keep my counsel
Is, not to tell thee.
    Julia. Tell your echo this,
Or flatterers, that like echoes still report
What they hear though most imperfect, and not me ;
For if that you be true unto yourself,
I'll know.
    Card. Will you rack me?
    Julia. No, judgment shall
Draw it from you : it is an equal fault,
To tell one's secrets unto all or none.
    Card. The first argues folly.

---

[1] Cf. this passage with *1 Henry IV*, ii, 3.

Julia. But the last tyranny.

Card. Very well: why, imagine I have committed
Some secret deed which I desire the world
May never hear of.

Julia. Therefore may not I know it?
You have concealed for me as great a sin
As adultery. Sir, never was occasion
For perfect trial of my constancy
Till now: sir, I beseech you —

Card. You'll repent it.

Julia. Never.

Card. It hurries thee to ruin: I'll not tell thee.
Be well advised, and think what danger 'tis   260
To receive a prince's secrets: they that do,
Had need have their breasts hooped with adamant
To contain them. I pray thee, yet be satisfied;
Examine thine own frailty; 'tis more easy
To tie knots than unloose them: 'tis a secret
That, like a lingering poison, may chance lie
Spread in thy veins, and kill thee seven year hence.

Julia. Now you dally with me.

Card. No more; thou shalt know it.
By my appointment the great Duchess of Malfi
And two of her young children, four nights since,   270
Were strangled.

Julia. O Heaven! sir, what have you done?

Card. How now? how settles this? think you your bosom
Will be a grave dark and obscure enough
For such a secret?

Julia. You have undone yourself, sir.

Card. Why?

Julia. It lies not in me to conceal it.

Card. No?
Come, I will swear you to't upon this book.
Julia. Most religiously.
  Card. Kiss it. [*She kisses the book.*
Now you shall never utter it; thy curiosity
Hath undone thee: thou'rt poisoned with that book;
Because I knew thou couldst not keep my counsel, 280
I have bound thee to't by death.

         Re-enter BOSOLA.

Bos. For pity-sake, hold!
Card. Ha, Bosola!
Julia. I forgive you
This equal piece of justice you have done;
For I betrayed your counsel to that fellow:
He overheard it; that was the cause I said
It lay not in me to conceal it.
  Bos. O foolish woman,
Couldst not thou have poisoned him?
  Julia. 'Tis weakness,
Too much to think what should have been done. I go,
I know not whither.   [*Dies.*
  Card. Wherefore com'st thou thither? 290
  Bos. That I might find a great man like yourself,
Not out of his wits as the Lord Ferdinand,
To remember my service.
  Card. I'll have thee hewed in pieces.
  Bos. Make not yourself such a promise of that life
Which is not yours to dispose of.
  Card. Who placed thee here?
  Bos. Her lust, as she intended.
  Card. Very well:

Now you know me for your fellow-murderer.

Bos. And wherefore should you lay fair marble colours
Upon your rotten purposes to me?
Unless you imitate some that do plot great treasons, 300
And when they have done, go hide themselves i' the graves
Of those were actors in't?

Card. No more; there is
A fortune attends thee.

Bos. Shall I go sue to Fortune any longer?
'Tis the fool's pilgrimage.

Card. I have honours in store for thee.

Bos. There are many ways that conduct to seeming
honour,
And some of them very dirty ones.

Card. Throw to the devil
Thy melancholy. The fire burns well;
What need we keep a stirring of't, and make
A greater smother? Thou wilt kill Antonio? 310

Bos. Yes.

Card. Take up that body.

Bos. I think I shall
Shortly grow the common bier for churchyards.

Card. I will allow thee some dozen of attendants
To aid thee in the murder.

Bos. O, by no means. Physicians that apply horse-leeches to any rank swelling used to cut off their tails, that the blood may run through them the faster; let me have no train when I go to shed blood, lest it make me have a greater when I ride to the gallows.

Card. Come to me after midnight, to help to remove 320
That body to her own lodging: I'll give out
She died o' the plague; 'twill breed the less inquiry

After her death.
  Bos. Where's Castruccio her husband?
  Card. He's rode to Naples, to take possession
Of Antonio's citadel.
  Bos. Believe me, you have done a very happy turn.
  Card. Fail not to come: there is the master-key
Of our lodgings; and by that you may conceive
What trust I plant in you.
  Bos. You shall find me ready.   [*Exit* Cardinal.
O poor Antonio, though nothing be so needful   330
To thy estate as pity, yet I find
Nothing so dangerous; I must look to my footing:
In such slippery ice-pavements men had need
To be frost-nailed well, they may break their necks else;
The precedent's here afore me. How this man
Bears up in blood! seems fearless! Why, 'tis well:
Security some men call the suburbs of hell,
Only a dead wall between. Well, good Antonio,
I'll seek thee out; and all my care shall be
To put thee into safety from the reach   340
Of these most cruel biters that have got
Some of thy blood already. It may be,
I'll join with thee in a most just revenge:
The weakest arm is strong enough that strikes
With the sword of justice. Still methinks the duchess
Haunts me: there, there! 'Tis nothing but my melancholy.
O Penitence, let me truly taste thy cup,
That throws men down only to raise them up!   [*Exit.*[1]

---

[1] The numbering of the lines in this scene, and in other parts of this volume, is only approximately exact: for in the Elizabethan plays many passages are printed as blank verse that cannot possibly be scanned.

SCENE III. — *A Fortification at Milan.*

Enter ANTONIO *and* DELIO.

Delio. Yond's the cardinal's window. This fortification
Grew from the ruins of an ancient abbey;
And to yond side o' the river lies a wall,
Piece of a cloister, which in my opinion
Gives the best echo that you ever heard,
So hollow and so dismal, and withal
So plain in the distinction of our words,
That many have supposed it is a spirit
That answers.
 Ant. I do love these ancient ruins.
We never tread upon them but we set   10
Our foot upon some reverend history:
And, questionless, here in this open court,
Which now lies naked to the injuries
Of stormy weather, some men lie interred
Loved the church so well, and gave so largely to't,
They thought it should have canopied their bones
Till doomsday; but all things have their end:
Churches and cities, which have diseases like to men,
Must have like death that we have.
 Echo. "Like death that we have."   20
 Delio. Now the echo hath caught you.
 Ant. It groaned, methought, and gave
A very deadly accent.
 Echo. "Deadly accent."
 Delio. I told you 'twas a pretty one: you may make it
A huntsman, or a falconer, a musician,
Or a thing of sorrow.

Echo. " A thing of sorrow."
Ant. Ay, sure, that suits it best.
Echo. " That suits it best."
Ant. 'Tis very like my wife's voice.
Echo. " Ay, wife's voice."
Delio. Come, let us walk further from't.
I would not have you go to the cardinal's to-night :
Do not.
Echo. " Do not." 30
Delio. Wisdom doth not more moderate wasting sorrow
Than time : take time for't ; be mindful of thy safety.
Echo. " Be mindful of thy safety."
Ant. Necessity compels me :
Make scrutiny throughout the passages
Of your own life, you'll find it impossible
To fly your fate.
Echo. " O, fly your fate."
Delio. Hark ! the dead stones seem to have pity on you,
And give you good counsel.
Ant. Echo, I will not talk with thee, 40
For thou art a dead thing.
Echo. " Thou art a dead thing."
Ant. My duchess is asleep now,
And her little ones, I hope sweetly : O Heaven,
Shall I never see her more ?
Echo. " Never see her more."
Ant. I marked not one repetition of the echo
But that ; and on the sudden a clear light
Presented me a face folded in sorrow.
Delio. Your fancy merely.
Ant. Come, I'll be out of this ague,
For to live thus is not indeed to live ; 50

It is a mockery and abuse of life:
I will not henceforth save myself by halves;
Lose all, or nothing.
  Delio. Your own virtue save you!
I'll fetch your eldest son, and second you:
It may be that the sight of his own blood
Spread in so sweet a figure may beget
The more compassion. However, fare you well,
Though in our miseries Fortune have a part,
Yet in our noble sufferings she hath none:
Contempt of pain, that we may call our own. [*Exeunt.* 60

SCENE IV.—*An Apartment in the* Cardinal's *Palace.*

Enter Cardinal, PESCARA, MALATESTI, RODERIGO, *and* GRISOLAN.

  Card. You shall not watch to-night by the sick prince;
His grace is very well recovered.
  Mal. Good my lord, suffer us.
  Card. O, by no means;
The noise, and change of object in his eye,
Doth more distract him: I pray, all to bed;
And though you hear him in his violent fit,
Do not rise, I entreat you.
  Pes. So, sir; we shall not.
  Card. Nay, I must have you promise
Upon your honours, for I was enjoined to't
By himself; and he seemed to urge it sensibly.   10
  Pes. Let our honours bind this trifle.
  Card. Nor any of your followers.
  Mal. Neither.

Card. It may be, to make trial of your promise,
When he's asleep, myself will rise and feign
Some of his mad tricks, and cry out for help,
And feign myself in danger.
　Mal. If your throat were cutting,
I'd not come at you, now I have protested against it.
　Card. Why, I thank you.
　Gris. 'Twas a foul storm to-night.
　Rod. The Lord Ferdinand's chamber shook like an osier.
　Mal. 'Twas nothing but pure kindness in the devil,
To rock his own child.　[*Exeunt all except the* Cardinal.
　Card. The reason why I would not suffer these
About my brother, is, because at midnight
I may with better privacy convey
Julia's body to her own lodging. O, my conscience!
I would pray now; but the devil takes away my heart
For having any confidence in prayer.
About this hour I appointed Bosola
To fetch the body : when he hath served my turn,
He dies.　　　　　　　　　　　　　　　　[*Exit.*
　　　　　　　Enter BOSOLA.

　Bos. Ha! 'twas the cardinal's voice; I heard him name
Bosola and my death. Listen; I hear one's footing.

　　　　　　　Enter FERDINAND.

　Ferd. Strangling is a very quiet death.
　Bos. (*aside*). Nay, then, I see I must stand upon my guard.
　Ferd. What say you to that? whisper softly; do you agree to't? So; it must be done i' the dark : the cardinal would not for a thousand pounds the doctor should see it.
　　　　　　　　　　　　　　　　　　　　　[*Exit.*

Bos. My death is plotted; here's the consequence of
    murder.
We value not desert nor Christian breath,
When we know black deeds must be cured with death.

        Enter ANTONIO *and* Servant.

Serv. Here stay, sir, and be confident, I pray:
I'll fetch you a dark lantern.   [*Exit.*
  Ant. Could I take him at his prayers,[1]
There were hope of pardon.
  Bos. Fall right, my sword!—   [*Stabs him.*
I'll not give thee so much leisure as to pray.
  Ant. O, I am gone! Thou hast ended a long suit
In a minute.
  Bos. What art thou?
  Ant. A most wretched thing,
That only have thy benefit in death,
To appear myself.

       Re-enter Servant *with a lantern.*

  Serv. Where are you, sir?
  Ant. Very near my home.—Bosola!
  Serv. O, misfortune!
  Bos. Smother thy pity, thou art dead else.—Antonio!
The man I would have saved 'bove mine own life!
We are merely the stars' tennis-balls, struck and bandied
Which way please them.—O good Antonio,
I'll whisper one thing in thy dying ear
Shall make thy heart break quickly! thy fair duchess
And two sweet children—
  Ant. Their very names
Kindle a little life in me.

[1] Cf. *Hamlet*, iii. 3.

Bos. Are murdered.

Ant. Some men have wished to die   60
At the hearing of sad things; I am glad
That I shall do't in sadness[1]: I would not now
Wish my wounds balmed nor healed, for I have no use
To put my life to. In all our quest of greatness,
Like wanton boys, whose pastime is their care,
We follow after bubbles blown in the air.
Pleasure of life, what is't? only the good hours
Of an ague; merely a preparative to rest,
To endure vexation. I do not ask
The process of my death; only commend me   70
To Delio.
   Bos. Break, heart!
   Ant. And let my son fly the courts of princes.   [*Dies.*
   Bos. Thou seem'st to have loved Antonio?
   Serv. I brought him hither,
To have reconciled him to the cardinal.
   Bos. I do not ask thee that.
Take him up, if thou tender thine own life,
And bear him where the lady Julia
Was wont to lodge. — O, my fate moves swift;
I have this cardinal in the forge already;
Now I'll bring him to the hammer. O direful misprision[2]!
I will not imitate things glorious,   81
No more than base; I'll be mine own example. —
On, on, and look thou represent, for silence,
The thing thou bear'st.   [*Exeunt*

[1] Seriousness.   [2] Neglect, oversight; hence, mistake.

SCENE V. — *Another Apartment in the Same.*

Enter Cardinal, *with a book.*

Card. I am puzzled in a question about hell:
He says, in hell there's one material fire,
And yet it shall not burn all men alike.
Lay him by. How tedious is a guilty conscience!
When I look into the fish-ponds in my garden,
Methinks I see a thing armed with a rake,
That seems to strike at me.

Enter BOSOLA, *and* Servant *bearing* ANTONIO'S *body.*

Now, art thou come?
Thou look'st ghastly:
There sits in thy face some great determination
Mixed with some fear.
 Bos. Thus it lightens into action: 10
I am come to kill thee.
 Card. Ha! — Help! our guard!
 Bos. Thou art deceived;
They are out of thy howling.
 Card. Hold; and I will faithfully divide
Revenues with thee.
 Bos. Thy prayers and proffers
Are both unreasonable.
 Card. Raise the watch! we are betrayed!
 Bos. I have confined your flight:
I'll suffer your retreat to Julia's chamber,
But no further.
 Card. Help! we are betrayed!

Enter, above,[1] PESCARA, MALATESTI, RODERIGO, *and*
                    GRISOLAN.
Mal. Listen.
Card. My dukedom for rescue!
Rod. Fie upon his counterfeiting! 20
Mal. Why, 'tis not the cardinal.
Rod. Yes, yes, 'tis he:
But I'll see him hanged ere I'll go down to him.
  Card. Here's a plot upon me; I am assaulted! I am lost,
Unless some rescue.
  Gris. He doth this pretty well;
But it will not serve to laugh me out of mine honour.
  Card. The sword's at my throat!
  Rod. You would not bawl so loud then.
  Mal. Come, come, let's go
To bed: he told us thus much aforehand.
  Pes. He wished you should not come at him; but,
      believe't,
The accent of the voice sounds not in jest: 30
I'll down to him, howsoever, and with engines
Force ope the doors. [*Exit above.*
  Rod. Let's follow him aloof,
And note how the cardinal will laugh at him.
    [*Exeunt, above,* MALATESTI, RODERIGO, *and* GRISOLAN.
  Bos. There's for you first,
'Cause you shall not unbarricade the door
To let in rescue. [*Kills the* Servant.
  Card. What cause hast thou to pursue my life?
  Bos. Look there.
  Card. Antonio!
  Bos. Slain by my hand unwittingly.

---

[1] The raised platform towards the back of the stage.

Pray, and be sudden: when thou killed'st thy sister,
Thou took'st from Justice her most equal balance,
And left her naught but her sword.

   Card. O, mercy! 40

   Bos. Now it seems thy greatness was only outward;
For thou fall'st faster of thyself than calamity
Can drive thee. I'll not waste longer time; there!
                                      [*Stabs him.*

   Card. Thou hast hurt me.

   Bos. Again!   [*Stabs him again.*

   Card. Shall I die like a leveret,
Without any resistance? — Help, help, help!
I am slain!

                 Enter FERDINAND.

   Ferd. The alarum! give me a fresh horse;
Rally the vaunt-guard, or the day is lost.
Yield, yield! I give you the honour of arms,
Shake my sword over you; will you yield?

   Card. Help me; I am your brother!

   Ferd. The devil!
My brother fight upon the adverse party! 50
      [*He wounds the* Cardinal, *and, in the scuffle, gives*
         BOSOLA *his death-wound.*
There flies your ransom.

   Card. O justice!
I suffer now for what hath former bin:
Sorrow is held the eldest child of sin.[1]

   Ferd. Now you're brave fellows. Cæsar's fortune was
harder than Pompey's; Cæsar died in the arms of pros-

---

[1] Cf. Webster's *White Devil*, p. 44 (Dyce's edit.):

    "'Twere fit you'd think on what hath former bin;
    I heard grief nam'd the eldest child of sin."

perity, Pompey at the feet of disgrace. You both died in
the field. The pain's nothing : pain many times is taken
away with the apprehension of greater, as the toothache with
the sight of the barber that comes to pull it out : there's
philosophy for you. 60
 Bos. Now my revenge is perfect. — Sink, thou main
  cause   [*Kills* FERDINAND.
Of my undoing ! — The last part of my life
Hath done me best service.
 Ferd. Give me some wet hay ; I am broken-winded.
I do account this world but a dog kennel :
I will vault credit and affect high pleasures
Beyond death.
 Bos. He seems to come to himself,
Now he's so near the bottom.
 Ferd. My sister, O my sister ! there's the cause on't.
Whether we fall by ambition, blood, or lust,   70
Like diamonds we are cut with our own dust. [*Dies.*
 Card. Thou hast thy payment too.
 Bos. Yes, I hold my weary soul in my teeth ;
'Tis ready to part from me. I do glory
That thou, which stood'st like a huge pyramid
Begun upon a large and ample base,
Shalt end in a little point, a kind of nothing.

 Enter below, PESCARA, MALATESTI, RODERIGO, *and* GRISOLAN.

 Pes. How now, my lord !
 Mal. O sad disaster !
 Rod. How comes this?
 Bos. Revenge for the Duchess of Malfi murdered
By the Arragonian brethren ; for Antonio   80
Slain by this hand ; for lustful Julia

Poisoned by this man; and lastly for myself,
That was an actor in the main of all
Much 'gainst mine own good nature, yet i' the end
Neglected.
 Pes. How now, my lord!
 Card. Look to my brother:
He gave us these large wounds, as we were struggling
Here i' the rushes.¹ And now, I pray, let me
Be laid by and never thought of. [*Dies.*
 Pes. How fatally, it seems, he did withstand
His own rescue!
 Mal. Thou wretched thing of blood² 90
How came Antonio by his death?
 Bos. In a mist; I know not how:
Such a mistake as I have often seen
In a play. O, I am gone!
We are only like dead walls or vaulted graves,
That, ruined, yield no echo. Fare you well.
It may be pain, but no harm, to me to die
In so good a quarrel. O, this gloomy world!
In what a shadow, or deep pit of darkness,
Doth womanish and fearful mankind live! 100
Let worthy minds ne'er stagger in distrust
To suffer death or shame for what is just:
Mine is another voyage. [*Dies.*
 Pes. The noble Delio, as I came to the palace,
Told me of Antonio's being here, and showed me
A pretty gentleman, his son and heir.

Enter DELIO *and* ANTONIO'S Son.

 Mal. O sir, you come too late!

¹ Floors were commonly strewn with rushes.
² Cf. *Coriolanus*, ii, 2: " He was a thing of blood."

Delio. I heard so, and
Was armed for't, ere I came. Let us make noble use
Of this great ruin; and join all our force
To establish this young hopeful gentleman 110
In's mother's right. These wretched eminent things
Leave no more fame behind 'em, than should one
Fall in a frost, and leave his print in snow;
As soon as the sun shines, it ever melts,
Both form and matter. I have ever thought
Nature doth nothing so great for great men
As when she's pleased to make them lords of truth:
Integrity of life is fame's best friend,
Which nobly, beyond death, shall crown the end.
[*Exeunt*

AUG 1 7 1970